ESSENTIALS OF PERFORMANCE ANALYSIS IN SPORT

Now in a fully revised and updated second edition, *Essentials of Performance Analysis in Sport* is a comprehensive and authoritative guide to this core discipline of contemporary sport science. It introduces the fundamental theory of match and performance analysis, using real–world illustrative examples and data throughout, and explores the applied contexts in which analysis can have a significant influence on performance.

This second edition includes three completely new chapters covering the key emerging topics of dynamic systems, momentum and performance profiling, as well as updated coverage of core topics in the performance analysis curriculum such as:

- designing notation systems
- analysing performance data
- qualitative analysis of technique
- time–motion analysis
- probability
- using feedback technologies
- performance analysis and coaching.

With extended coverage of contemporary issues in performance analysis and contributions from leading performance analysis researchers and practitioners, *Essentials of Performance Analysis in Sport* is a complete textbook for any performance analysis course, as well as an invaluable reference for sport science or sport coaching students and researchers, and any coach, analyst or athlete looking to develop their professional insight.

Mike Hughes is Emeritus Professor of Performance Analysis at Cardiff Metropolitan University, UK, and a visiting professor at the Institute of Technology, Carlow, Ireland; Nottingham Trent University, UK; Otto von Guericke University, Germany; Edith Cowan University, Australia; University of Putra, Malaysia; and the University of California, Berkeley, USA. He is an accredited level 5 performance analyst (ISPAS), a BOA-registered performance analyst, and a Fellow of the Royal Statistical Society. His professional consultancy has included work in squash, rugby, football and hockey, and his publications include the seminal performance analysis textbooks, *Essentials of Performance Analysis* and *Notational Analysis of Sport* (both with Ian Franks and published by Routledge).

Ian M. Franks is a Professor in the School of Kinesiology, University of British Columbia, Canada. His research is primarily concerned with the control and acquisition of human motor skills, and he is a leading authority in sport performance analysis and the analysis of coaching behaviour. Ian is a Fellow of the Canadian Society for Psychomotor Learning and Sport Psychology (SCAPPS) and a Fellow of the American Academy for Kinesiology and Physical Education (AAKPE). As well as numerous publications in peer-reviewed journals, Ian is the co-editor and co-author (with Mike Hughes) of the seminal performance analysis textbooks, *Essentials of Performance Analysis* and *Notational Analysis of Sport* (both published by Routledge).

ESSENTIALS OF PERFORMANCE ANALYSIS IN SPORT

Second edition

Edited by Mike Hughes and Ian M. Franks

Routledge
Taylor & Francis Group

LONDON AND NEW YORK

First published 2007
By Routledge

This edition published 2015
by Routledge
2 Park Square, Milton Park, Abingdon, Oxon OX14 4RN

and by Routledge
711 Third Avenue, New York, NY 10017

Routledge is an imprint of the Taylor & Francis Group, an informa business

© 2015 M. Hughes & I. Franks

British Library Cataloguing-in-Publication Data
A catalogue record for this book is available from the British Library

Library of Congress Cataloging in Publication Data
Essentials of performance analysis in sport/edited by Mike Hughes and Ian M. Franks. – Second edition.
pages cm
Includes bibliographical references and index.
1. Sports sciences. 2. Physical education and training. 3. Performance.
I. Hughes, M. (Mike) editor of compilation. II. Franks, Ian M., editor of compilation.
GV558.E87 2015
613.7'1 – dc23
2014034258

ISBN: 978-1-138-02298-0 (hbk)
ISBN: 978-1-138-02299-7 (pbk)
ISBN: 978-1-315-77674-3 (ebk)

Typeset in Bembo
by Florence Production Limited, Stoodleigh, Devon, UK

Printed and bound in Great Britain by
TJ International Ltd, Padstow, Cornwall

CONTENTS

14   Dynamic systems and 'perturbations'   **239**
Matthew Robins and Mike Hughes

15   Momentum and 'hot hands'   **270**
Mike Hughes, Nic James, Michael T. Hughes, Stafford Murray,
Ed Burt and Luke Heath

16   Performance profiling   **292**
Mike Hughes, Michael T. Hughes, Nic James, Julia Wells and
Stafford Murray

17   Rule changes in sport and the role of notation   **334**
Jason Williams

FIGURES

TABLES

CONTRIBUTORS

Roger Bartlett was employed in higher education for 41 years before retiring in August 2014. In a university career that ran from 1992 to 2013, Roger was a full Professor at Manchester Metropolitan University, Staffordshire University, Sheffield Hallam University, all in the UK, and the University of Otago in New Zealand.

Ed Burt is a freelance performance analyst, lecturer and coach. He has held the posts of Programme Leader for the MSc Sport Performance Analysis at Middlesex University, as well as module leader in sport coaching at Buckinghamshire New University. He graduated in 1994 with a BSc(Hons) from Brunel University, before embarking on a 13-year career in various dotcom businesses. He then returned to academia, and has since completed an FdA, an MSc, a PgCert Higher Education and is due to complete his PgCert in Education in 2015. He is also working towards a PhD. Ed is a Fellow of the Royal Statistical Society; Fellow of the Higher Education Academy and is an ISPAS accredited performance analyst for both Scientific and Applied pathways.

Ewan Cameron has a BSc in Computing Science and an MBA, followed by several years of industrial experience. He is currently a Director of Elite Sports Analysis, working as a consultant in a wide range of professional, Olympic and Commonwealth sports, with his main focus on national teams in Badminton, Swimming and Cross Country Skiing. Ewan is also a consultant to the ECB, implementing the use of specific technologies in Cricket. He also has ISPAS Level 5 Accreditation.

Jo Clubb graduated from Loughborough University with a First Class Honours Degree in Sport and Exercise Science in 2009, after which she landed an internship at Chelsea Football Club. At the end of the Double-winning 2009/10 season

Jo was offered a full-time Sport Scientist role at the Club. Other professional experiences include England and Wales Cricket Board, England RFU, Australian Institute of Sport, Leicester City FC, Adidas High Performance Centre and McLaren Applied Technologies. Alongside her job, Jo is undertaking a part-time distance learning Master's Degree in High Performance Sport with Australian Catholic University (ACU).

Ian M. Franks attended St Luke's College, Exeter (Cert. Ed., 1968); McGill University (BEd in Physical Education, 1975); and University of Alberta (MSc, 1975 and PhD in Motor Learning and Control, 1980). He now specialises in the neural control of skilful movement in his Motor Learning and Control Laboratory at the School of Kinesiology, University of British Columbia, Canada.

Luke Heath completed his MSc at Brunel University and his undergraduate studies at Middlesex University. His interests lie in developing methodologies in notational analysis. He has collaborated actively with researchers in several other disciplines of sport science, particularly sport rehabilitation.

Nicola J. Hodges works in the area of motor behaviour and studies the mechanisms of motor skill learning, with a particular focus on the roles of instructions and demonstrations on the performance and retention of motor skills. She studies both novices and more skilled individuals, predominantly using sports-based tasks and athletes to allow conclusions about motor learning processes. Her work also extends beyond sports to special populations (e.g. people post-stroke and with Down's syndrome) and to more basic motor control questions.

Michael T. Hughes has worked in elite level sport for the last ten years, working with some outstanding teams, including the British and Irish Lions, England Rugby, British Cycling and England Squash. Since starting with the RFU in 2008, Michael has been responsible for designing and implementing all data collection and processing protocols from the senior team, throughout the Performance Pathway, to the Academy teams. He was a Senior Performance Analyst on the British Lions Tour in 2013 when the Lions won a test series for the first time in 16 years and for the first time in Australia in 24 years, and was a part of the England management team at the 2011 Rugby World Cup.

Mike Hughes is Emeritus Professor of Sport and Exercise Science at Cardiff Metropolitan University, UK, and a Visiting Professor at Nottingham Trent University, UK; OvG, Magdeburg, Germany; Zagreb, Croatia; WHU, Hungary; University of California, Berkeley, USA; UPM, Malaysia; Edith Cowan University, Perth, Australia; and the Institute of Technology Carlow, Eire. He is founder and now President of ISPAS (International Society of Performance Analysis of Sport); President of the International Society of Performance Analysis of Sport Asia; Member of the Coordination Council, and Chair of the Performance Analysis Group for the International Network of Sport and Health Science.

Nic James is Professor of Sport and Exercise Science at Middlesex University, UK. He has been invited to be a Visiting Professor at the University of Zagreb, Croatia, sits as Chair of the International Society of Performance Analysis of Sport, is a Member of the Coordination Council for the International Network of Sport and Health Science and a Fellow of the Higher Education Academy.

Adrian Lees received a BSc degree in Physics (1972), and a PhD in Biomechanics (1977) from the University of Leeds. He joined the Centre for Sport and Exercise Sciences at Liverpool John Moores University in 1980 as a biomechanist, retired in 2011 and is currently Emeritus Professor of Biomechanics. In 2003 he was awarded Doktor Honoris Causa from the Academy of Physical Education, Warsaw. His research interests cover both sport and rehabilitation biomechanics.

Dario G. Liebermann has been the Chair of the Physical Therapy Department, Sackler Faculty of Medicine, Tel Aviv University since 2010. He assumed a faculty appointment in 2000 after spending two years of post-doctoral training at the University of Calgary and previously completing a PhD (Applied Mathematics and Computer Science) at the Weizmann Institute of Science with an emphasis on kinematic simulations of upper limb motion based on theoretical models of joint control.

Keith R. Lohse has recently taken up a faculty position as Assistant Professor at the University of Auburn. Prior to this he was working as a post-doctoral research fellow in the Motor Skills Lab at the University of British Columbia, Canada. He received a joint PhD in Psychology, Cognitive Science and Neuroscience in 2012 from the University of Colorado and his present research focuses on understanding the psychological and physiological processes that underlie the (re)acquisition of motor skills.

Dana Maslovat is a faculty member and Department Chair of Kinesiology at Langara College in Vancouver as well as being a Research Associate in the School of Kinesiology, University of British Columbia, Canada. He has also served as a Course Conductor for the National Coaching Certification Program. Dr Maslovat completed a BSc degree at Simon Fraser University followed by a Master's and PhD degree at UBC. His area of expertise is motor learning and control, with research focusing on the preparation of movements and the effects of practice on skill acquisition.

Tim McGarry completed his undergraduate studies at Liverpool John Moore University, UK, under the guidance of Professor Mike Hughes, and graduate studies at the University of British Columbia, Canada, under the guidance of Professor Ian Franks. His teaching and research interests include motor control (brain, behaviour, muscle, excitatory-inhibitory control) and sports performance (system analysis, dynamics, pattern detection, decision making, strategies and tactics).

Kenny More has a BEd (Jordanhill) and MA (UBC Vancouver) where he conducted applied research into the systematic observation and analysis of coaching behaviour. He is currently a Director of Elite Sports Analysis, working as a consultant in a wide range of Professional, Olympic and Commonwealth sports, with his main focus on national teams in Association Football, Curling and Field Hockey. Kenny has BASES 'High Performance Accreditation' as a Sport and Exercise Scientist, and teaches in the Master of Performance Coaching at the University of Sterling.

Stafford Murray is Head of Performance Analysis at EIS, delivering performance solutions and expert consultancy to teams such as McLaren and GB Sailing.

Ben Pollard is a Sport Scientist with the England Rugby Union team, responsible for all monitoring data collection and feedback to the performance and coaching team. This included the 2012 and 2013 Six Nations, 2012 South Africa Summer Tour, 2012 August Training Camp and 2012 Autumn Series.

Athalie Redwood-Brown has worked in academia for the past 12 years with appointments at Reading University, UK (2002–2006); Oxford Brookes University, UK (2006–2009); and currently at Nottingham Trent University, UK. For the past six years Athalie has also worked within the football industry, most recently as Pro Market Manager for an automated tracking company bringing together academic research and cutting-edge technology to the applied field.

Matthew Robins completed the BSc (2002) and MSc (2003) in Sport and Exercise Science at Cardiff Metropolitan University (formally UWIC), and a PhD in Sports Biomechanics (2013) at Sheffield Hallam University. Matt worked as Senior Lecturer at Nottingham Trent University from 2007–2011, and was programme coordinator for the MSc International Performance Analysis of Sport (IMPAS) course (2009–2011) and coordinator for the Performance Analysis pathway for the MRes Sport Science degree (2008–2011). He joined the University of Chichester in 2012 as Senior Lecturer in Biomechanics and Performance Analysis. He is the programme coordinator for the MSc Sports Performance Analysis programme. Matt is also a Fellow of the Higher Education Academy and Associate Editor for the Journal of Applied Case Studies in Sport and Exercise Science (JACSSES) (Performance Analysis Section). Matt has published in the fields of both sports biomechanics and performance analysis, and is a reviewer for numerous international periodicals. Matt's research interests include variability of sports performance, dynamical systems theory and its application for study of individual and team behaviour, performance profiling, and biomechanical analysis of basketball shooting.

Mark Robinson is an early career academic at Liverpool John Moores University. He teaches performance analysis, biomechanics and statistics on the Sport and

Exercise Science, Science and Football undergraduate degree courses and the MSc course in Sport and Clinical Biomechanics. He completed his PhD in 2012 and has published 15 peer-reviewed journal articles since 2010 in topics including lower-limb musculoskeletal injury, biomechanical modelling techniques and statistical analysis of biomechanical data.

Julia Wells is Senior Performance Analyst at the English Institute of Sport, having started out providing performance analysis consultancy with Cardiff Metropolitan's Centre for Performance Analysis team and with GB Canoeing's Canoe Slalom Olympic Programme for the Beijing 2008 and London 2012 Olympic Games.

Jason Williams has worked in academia for over 15 years in the areas of Performance Analysis and Computing, with a particular focus on rugby union. He has worked as an analyst for the International Rugby Board and the BBC, and as Treasurer of the International Society of Performance Analysis of Sport.

PREFACE

Welcome to the *Essentials of Performance Analysis of Sport, 2nd edition.*

The main function of this book is to act as an introductory manual for the sports scientist, coach, athlete or any interested reader. It is probably impossible to write sections of a book such as this that would be readable and appealing to all this cross-section of intended clientele. Consequently, the various chapters in the book should be regarded as the different sections of a manual – many can be used as stand-alone units without reference to others; some, on the other hand, have recommended prior reading. Notational analysis is a developing subject area, attractive to many sports scientists and coaches because of the applied nature of any material developed or data gathered. For anyone who wishes to understand their own sport, and thereby the structure and tactics of most other sports, there is no better way of understanding the real logic behind the structure of the game. The more coaches and players that come to understand that notation systems are going to improve the players' performance, their team's performance and especially the coaches' performance, then the better for sport in general.

ACKNOWLEDGEMENTS

Ian M. Franks would like to acknowledge funding support from the Social Sciences and Humanities Research Council of Canada.

ABBREVIATIONS

AAKPE	American Academy for Kinesiology and Physical Education
AI	artificial intelligence
ANN	artifical neural network
AR	action reaction
ASUOI	Arizona State University Observation Instrument
BOA	British Olympic Committee
CAI	Coach Analysis Instrument
CAIS	Coach Analysis and Intervention System
CBAS	Coaching Behaviour Assessment System
CI	confidence interval
CL	confidence limit
CNS	central nervous system
CV	coefficient of variation
ECB	English Cricket Board
eIJCSS	International Journal of Computers in Sport Science (electronic)
eIJPAS	International Journal of Performance Analysis in Sport (electronic)
EMG	electromyographic
EPS	end point speed
FIAS	Flanders Interaction Analysis System
GIR	greens in regulation
GPS	global positioning system
IPPAS	Intensive Programme in Performance Analysis of Sport
IRB	International Rugby Board
ISPAS	International Society of Performance Analysis of Sport
IT	Information Technology
KFM	Kohonen Feature Map
KP	knowledge of performance

KPI	key performance indicator
KR	knowledge of results
lbw	leg before wicket
MLR	multivariate linear regression
MNS	mirror neuron system
MVC	maximum voluntary contraction
NCF	National Coaching Foundation
ODI	One Day International
PA	performance analysis
PDS	proximal-to-distal sequence
PGA	Professional Golfers' Association of America
PI	performance indicator
ROM	range of motion
SCAPPS	Canadian Society for Psychomotor Learning and Sport Psychology
SHM	simple harmonic motion
SRA	Squash Rackets Association
SSC	stretch–shorten cycle
SWEAT	squash winner and error analysis technology
VB	virtual best

INTRODUCTION

The aim of this book is to deliver a 'Level One' textbook to fill the gap in the market. The theme of the book will be to provide a ready manual for beginners in performance analysis.

The book is written for the sports scientist, the coach, the athlete, or for anyone who wishes to apply analysis to any aspect of a performance operation, but in the simplest way. Although this book is applied directly to sport, performance analysis is a procedure that can be used in any discipline that requires assessment and analysis of performance, e.g. nursing, surgical operations, skilled manufacturing processes, unskilled manufacturing processes, haute cuisine, and so on.

To cater for the anticipated spectrum of readership, the book is written to balance the needs for a practical approach, with plenty of examples, and yet provide a sound basis for the scientific analysis of the subject area. In this way it is hoped that both the practitioners of sport, the athletes and coaches, and sports scientists will find the book useful.

About this book

Like most texts the information within this book is presented in an order that is considered logical and progressive. It is not totally necessary, however, to use the book in this way. It is anticipated that at times certain sections will be needed to be used for immediate practical requirements. At the start of each chapter is advice on how to use that chapter and also which chapters, if any, require reading and understanding beforehand. All the references for the book, including all those in each chapter, are collated at the end of the book.

Organisation of this book

Chapter 1 The importance of feedback to performance

Dana Maslovat and Ian M. Franks

One of the most important variables in the learning process is feedback, especially that offered by an external source such as a coach. Historically, coaching intervention has been based on subjective observations, which have been shown to be problematic. Bias, highlighting, limitations of memory and observational difficulties are just a few of the pitfalls associated with a subjective evaluation. Thus, successful coaching hinges on the collection and analysis of unbiased, objective data. Technological advances have allowed coaches greater access to video-based feedback; however, the increased volume of information provided by such a tool requires careful consideration in terms of what aspect of the performance should be focused on by coach and athlete alike. While visual demonstrations can be effective, either through video feedback or the use of a model, it is important the display match the performance level of the observer to ensure 'motor resonance' with the observed movement pattern. Additionally, coaches should carefully consider the many other factors associated with feedback presentation, such as content, amount and timing as these also significantly impact the learning process.

Chapter 2 What is performance analysis?

Mike Hughes and Roger Bartlett

Based on the essays of Mike Hughes and Roger Bartlett, written for the UKSI website, on 'What is Performance Analysis', the aim of this chapter is to provide a full and complete understanding of the breadth of performance analysis and its possible applications. It will summarise the similarities of approach of biomechanics and notational analysis, and how through the application of motor control theories these different types of objective feedback can help the performer and their coaches or managers.

Chapter 3 Providing information for teaching skills in sport

Keith R. Lohse and Nicola J. Hodges

This chapter introduces new literature and ideas that impact how information might effectively be delivered during practice to aid learning. Consideration is given to the information processing stages that surround a single action (i.e. planning, execution, evaluation) and these individual actions combine to form multiple trials during physical practice of a skill. These multiple skills can then be grouped together into a single practice session where we need to consider what sort of information is available to learners in the intervening periods. Furthermore, motor control processes are seen as dynamic and as an athlete becomes more proficient with a skill over the course of a season (or longer) the structure of information in the practice environment needs to change as well. Also general principles of skill acquisition are discussed in relation to the learner's use of augmented feedback.

Chapter 4 Video-feedback and information technologies

Dario G. Liebermann and Ian M. Franks

The concept that information technologies that are based on video are not only meant to enhance feedback but also facilitate its delivery by reducing the video information to its essential components are discussed in detail. This chapter explores how feedback information can be made manageable, efficient and specifically adjusted for each individual's needs. Certain video-based technologies are recommended in this chapter because they are relatively inexpensive and popular. The gains of such technologies are many and varied but the main advantages are visualisation power, image comparisons, blending features, and primarily the ease by which these new technologies allow administering multimodal feedback to athletes and coaches.

Chapter 5 An overview of the development of notation analysis

Mike Hughes

The chapter is written in the form of a selective and applied literature review of the research work already published in this field. Great strides have been made in the last 15 years with seven world conferences in performance analysis providing a platform for the development of ideas and further research. These new research initiatives will enhance this chapter for the analyst. Although this is written for, and by, sports scientists, it is hoped that anyone with an interest in this rapidly growing area of practice and research will find it equally interesting and rewarding.

The review is aimed at being as practical as possible and it is structured to follow the main developments in notational analysis. After tracing a historical perspective of the roots of notation, the application of these systems to sport is then developed. These early systems were all hand notation systems, their emerging sophistication is followed until the advent of computerised notation. Although the emphasis is given to the main research developments in both hand and computerised notational systems, where possible the innovations of new systems and any significant data outputs within specific sports are also assessed. These applications will be examined for the main team, racket and individual sports only.

Chapter 6 Analysis of notation data: performance indicators

Mike Hughes and Roger Bartlett

Performance indicators are variables, or more likely, combinations of variables by which we determine a performance has been successful or otherwise. The aims of this chapter are to examine the application of performance indicators in different sports from both a performance analysis perspective and, using the different structural definitions of games, to make general recommendations about the use and application of these indicators. Formal games are classified into three categories: net and wall games, invasion games, and striking and fielding games. The different types of sports are also sub-categorised by the rules of scoring and ending the respective matches. These classes are analysed further, to enable definition of useful performance indicators and to examine similarities and differences in the analysis of the different categories of game. The indices of performance are sub-categorised into general match indicators, tactical indicators, technical indicators and biomechanical indicators. Different examples and the accuracy of their presentation are discussed. It is very easy to use simple data analyses in sports that are too complex to justify that utilisation; more care needs to be taken in presenting performance indicators in isolation.

Chapter 7 Sports analysis

Mike Hughes

The aim of this chapter is to provide an insight into how different sports can be broken down into a series of decisions represented by a limited number of actions and their possible outcomes. These logical progressions provide the inherent structure within each sport. The construction of flowcharts of different sports is examined, together with the definition of key events in these respective sports. The next step is to design a data collection and data processing system, so anyone interested in designing a notation system should read this chapter first.

Chapter 8 How do we design simple systems? How to develop a notation system

Mike Hughes

This chapter will enable the reader to be able to develop their own hand notation system for any sport; no matter how simple or complicated you wish to make it, the underlying principles apply. If the reader is hoping to develop a computerised system, the same logical process must be followed, so this section is a vital part of that developmental process too.

Chapter 9 Examples of notation systems

Mike Hughes

The best way to appreciate the intricacies of notational analysis is to examine systems for the sport(s) in which you are interested, or sports that are similar. Presented here are a number of examples of different systems for different sports. They have been devised by students of notational analysis and are therefore of differing levels of complexity and sophistication – but there are always lessons to be learned even from the simplest of systems. Some of the explanations and analyses are completed by beginners at notational analysis; coaches of these sports should not therefore be irritated at the simplistic levels of analysis of the respective sports. The encouraging aspect about these examples is the amount of information that the systems provide – even the simplest of these.

Chapter 10 Analysis of notation data: reliability

Mike Hughes

It is vital that the reliability of a data gathering system is demonstrated clearly and in a way that is compatible with the intended analyses of the data. The data must be tested in the same way and to the same depth in which it will be processed in the subsequent analyses. In general, the work of Bland and Altman (1986) has transformed the attitude of sport scientists to testing reliability; can similar techniques be applied to the non-parametric data that most notational analysis studies generate? There are also a number of questions that inherently reoccur in these forms of data-gathering – this chapter aims to demonstrate practical answers to some of these questions. These ideas have been developed over the last couple of years and represent a big step forward in our understanding the reliability of systems in this area of sports science.

The most common form of data analysis in notation studies is to record frequencies of actions and their respective positions on the performance area; these are then presented as sums or totals in each respective area. What are the effects of cumulative errors nullifying each other, so that the overall totals appear less incorrect than they actually are?

The application of parametric statistical techniques is often misused in notational analysis – how does this affect the confidence of the conclusions to say something about the data, with respect to more appropriate non-parametric tests? By using practical examples from recent studies, this chapter investigates these issues associated with reliability studies and subsequent analyses in performance analysis.

Chapter 11 Qualitative biomechanical analysis of technique

Adrian Lees and Mark Robinson

Qualitative analysis is descriptive, usually based on video but with no measurements. In teaching or coaching, it can provide the learner with detailed feedback to improve performance. This has two stages: first, observation to identify and diagnose the causes of any discrepancies between the desired and observed movement patterns; second, instruction to try to eradicate these discrepancies. In performance analysis, it can be used to differentiate between individuals when judging performance, in gymnastics for example. It can also be used in descriptive comparisons of performance. The recommended approach uses hierarchical models to identify the basic mechanical principles underlying the specific sports movement. Qualitative analysts need a good grasp of the techniques involved, experience of specific sport and exercise activities, and the ability to relate to coaches and athletes.

Chapter 12 Applied motion analysis

a) Systems of measurement in time-motion analysis – a case study of soccer

Athalie Redwood-Brown

b) Some practical notes on GPS systems

Michael T. Hughes, Jo Clubb and Ben Pollard

a) Performance analysis involves the investigation of actual sports performance or training. Performance analysis can be undertaken as part of academic investigations into sports performance or as part of applied activities in coaching, media or judging contexts. There is considerable overlap between performance analysis and other disciplines as most performance analysis exercises are concerned with investigating aspects of performance such as technique, energy systems or tactical aspects. What distinguishes performance analysis from other disciplines is that it is concerned with actual sports performance rather than activity undertaken in laboratory settings or data gathered from self-reports such as questionnaires or interviews. There are a variety of methods that can be used to gather data for performance analysis, including highly quantitative biomechanical analysis, motion analysis and notational analysis. This chapter reviews a range of motion analysis methods and their application in the performance environment, with a particular emphasis on soccer and commercially available motion analysis systems.

b) GPS technology has been available and used in elite professional rugby for around 8 years. Throughout this period hardware, software, popularity and understanding of its capabilities have increased considerably.

Uses

Each rugby team, like many other sports technologies out there, will use GPS differently whether due to budget, the user, the previous user, the head strength and conditioning coach or the head coach. In general, the uses of GPS in order of direct relevant use are:

a)   rehab running;
b)   monitoring training volume and intensity;
c)   assessing training performance;
d)   assessing match performance and match 'load'.

GPS can provide objective data to solve answers to rugby players and staff in certain situations. In others they will support the answer to what you are trying to solve, and in some they may even side track you from what the answer is. There will be questions posed from a physical performance standpoint, whether from head coaches, strength and conditioning coaches or medical teams, where thought is required into how best to answer them. The user can pick the outputs available to them to answer these.

Chapter 13 Probability analysis of notated events in sport contests: skill and chance

Tim McGarry

This chapter furthers our understanding of the restrictions and applications of probability analysis for describing sports behaviour and informing subsequent decision making that affords competitive advantage to the knowledgeable sports coach and/or support staff. Various aspects of sports contests are considered on the basis of chance as described in formal terms using probability analysis. Behaviours in sports contests are good candidates for this form of analysis and examples are provided using game strategies based on future expectations derived from percentage play approaches.

Chapter 14 Dynamic systems and 'perturbations'

Matthew Robins and Mike Hughes

The physics of open (complex) systems seeks to explain how regularity emerges from within a system that consists of many degrees of freedom in constant flux. There are common ideas in the related theories for complex systems (e.g. Thom, 1975; Soodak and Iberall, 1978; Haken, 1983; Iberall and Soodak, 1987; Glass and Mackey, 1988) and it is the inherent property of self-(re)organisation in response to changes in the elements that comprise the system, or to changes in the constraints that surround the system. In essence, small changes *to* the system can prompt large (nonlinear) changes *in* the system as it reorganises. Kelso, Turvey and colleagues have been instrumental in applying these types of theories to the experimental analysis of perception and action (see Kelso, 1995).

Match play sports exhibit rhythms when competitors perform at equal levels. A perturbation exists where the usual stable rhythm of play is disturbed by extreme elements of high or low skill. In soccer, should the resulting instabilities in playing patterns lead to a shot on goal, then the outcome is termed a critical incident.

Research confirming the existence of perturbations by McGarry and Franks (1995) in squash identified particularly weak or strong shots that place one player at a recognised disadvantage to another.

Squash however is regimented in structure, requiring alternate shots and definitive passages of play ending in points; conversely team sports contain unlimited periods of possessions with irregular scoring patterns. We examine the application of these theories and ideas to different sports and evaluate their merits.

Chapter 15 Momentum and 'hot hands'

Mike Hughes, Nic James, Michael T. Hughes, Stafford Murray, Ed Burt and Luke Heath

Calculating the momentum of a performance by a team or individual, by arbitrarily assigning positive and negative values to the actions, might indicate unexpected turning points in defeat or success. This concept of gathering momentum, or the reverse in a performance, can give the coaches, athletes and sports scientists further insights into winning and losing performances.

Momentum investigations also indicate dependencies between performances, or question whether future performances are reliant upon past streaks. Squash and volleyball share the characteristic of being played up to a certain amount of points. Squash was examined according to the momentum of players by Hughes *et al.* (2006a). The initial aim was to expand normative profiles of elite squash players using momentum graphs of winners and errors to explore 'turning points' in a performance.

Together with the analysis of one's own performance, it is essential to have an understanding of your opposition's tactical strengths and weaknesses. By modelling the opposition's performance it is possible to predict certain outcomes and patterns, and therefore intervene or change tactics before the critical incident occurs. The modelling of competitive sport is an informative analytic technique as it directs the attention of the modeller to the critical aspects of data that delineate successful performance (Franks and McGarry, 1996). Using tactical performance profiles to pull out and visualise these critical aspects of performance, players can build justified and sophisticated tactical plans. The area is discussed and reviewed, critically appraising the research completed in this element of performance analysis.

Chapter 16 Performance profiling

Mike Hughes, Michael T. Hughes, Nic James, Julia Wells and Stafford Murray

Both individual and team performance in sport has typically been assessed through the comparison of performance indicators of winning and losing teams or players; however, the distinction between winning and losing was used as the sole independent variable. Thus potential confounding variables that may affect performance such as match venue, weather conditions and the strength of the opposition were not considered in this profile. Insufficient data currently exist regarding the development and measurement of performance indicators in most sports. In particular, there is little research concerning position-specific performance indicators in team sports and their subsequent performance profiles. Research has also yet to establish the confidence to which these performance profiles are representative of an individual's performance. The aim of this chapter was to explore the examples of data taken from previous studies, in an attempt to identify a more focused direction for the analysis of individual and team sports.

Chapter 17 Rule changes in sport and the role of notation

Jason Williams

Any sporting event is defined and played within a predetermined framework of rules and the number and complexity of these rules may differ significantly. The processes for changing them occur within the environment of a governing body or administrators, but little is known about why they occur. Traditional sport that is played today is the product of many years of evolution and development, but little is known as to why these rules change. This chapter will review literature regarding rule changes in sport and will identify and categorise why rules change in sport and will investigate the use of notation in tracking the changes.

Chapter 18 Notational analysis of coaching behaviour

Kenny More and Ewan Cameron

Effective coaching is crucial to the pursuit of optimal sporting performance, yet current literature suggests that coaching behaviour continues to be guided by the traditions of the sport, the coaches' intuition and the emulation of other coaches. However, building on its initial teacher effectiveness framework, research into coaching effectiveness continues in its attempts to analyse, describe and modify a variety of coaching behaviours.

The large majority of published literature reviewed by the authors for this chapter states that this is an area requiring further systematic research and analysis. Coaching science continues to develop, and by nature, requires descriptive studies for basic understanding and accumulation of knowledge (Gilbert and Trudel 2004). This chapter stresses the need for more research to add to our understanding of coaching behaviours.

Chapter 19 Performance analysis in the media

Nic James

Performance analysis is usually thought of in terms of providing feedback for players and coaches to enable improvement in sports performance. This is not necessarily so, as media coverage of sport often adds statistical detail to their reporting of events for the purpose of informing the sports fan. Consequently, two separate explanations for carrying out performance analysis can be seen to exist, i.e. by those involved in a sport for performance improvement and by media groups for the enlightenment of sports fans. Identifying this distinction also raises the interesting question as to what extent these two performance analysis tasks differ or indeed are similar. This chapter will focus on presenting performance analysis as commonly depicted in the media. Some reference will be made to academic and professional sports teams' use of similar information, although this will not be exhaustive since other publications offer more of this type of information. For example, students of sport have been well served by previous books edited by Hughes and Franks (1997, 2004) as well as original research published in scientific journals, e.g. *electronic International Journal of Performance Analysis in Sport*. Soccer players and coaches have also had a book written for them (Carling *et al.* 2005) detailing the types of analysis performed at elite clubs. There have also been books aimed at the general public; one, which achieved bestseller status in the USA (Lewis, 2003), told the account of how Billy Beane, a highly talented but low-achieving baseball player became general manager of the Oakland Athletics and transformed the team's fortunes by picking new players solely on the analysis of their playing statistics rather than trusting his scouts' reports and recommendations.

Newspaper, television and internet coverage of sporting events usually presents performance analysis in the form of summary statistics or 'performance indicators' to use the terminology of Hughes and Bartlett (2002). These statistical insights are often debated over in the television studio by the assembled pundits or form the basis of in-depth analysis in the newspapers. However, they may also be used as the basis of the topic of conversation in school playgrounds, university cafeterias and business meeting rooms all over the world. Indeed, these statistics are now so common that it would be surprising if anyone with an interest in sport was not familiar with this form of performance analysis, although they might not recognise it as such.

This chapter will review the type of information portrayed in the various forms of media and discuss the extent to which they achieve their aim of describing the events of the sport in question. Potential limitations of these methods are also discussed with suggestions given for how performance analysts working for sports teams or undertaking research might amend or apply these methods.

A bibliography, and references for the book

Editors: Mike Hughes and Ian M. Franks

1

THE IMPORTANCE OF FEEDBACK TO PERFORMANCE

Dana Maslovat and Ian M. Franks

1.1 Introduction

Participation in sport is typically undertaken with the intent to improve performance. One of the most important variables affecting learning and subsequent performance of a skill is feedback (see Schmidt and Lee, 2014, pp. 255–285, for an overview). Feedback involves sensory information resulting from a particular movement and one source of feedback is from the athlete's own sensory channels (i.e. sight, hearing, touch, etc.), known as intrinsic or inherent feedback. Although some information from these sources provides a clear indication of performance (i.e. the ball missed the goal), the more detailed information (i.e. coordination of joint activity, amount of force produced) often requires experience in order for the performer to evaluate what they have just achieved. A second source of feedback usually comes from an outside source, typically a coach, and is meant to complement the intrinsic feedback. This information is known as extrinsic feedback and helps the athlete compare what was done to what was intended. This is usually achieved by drawing the attention of the performer to some key element of performance error.

For most complex skills, it is thought that extrinsic information accelerates the learning process and may be necessary to assist the athlete in reaching optimal performance levels (see Magill, 2001a, 2001b, for a review). Presumably, the experience and background of the coach allows him or her to provide useful information about a given movement to aid in the development of that skill along with error detection and correction mechanisms. Thus extrinsic feedback can be thought of as a complement to intrinsic feedback. Extrinsic feedback can be delivered in two main forms; knowledge of results (KR) and knowledge of performance (KP). KR involves information pertaining to the *outcome* of the action, while KP involves information pertaining to the *movement pattern* that caused the result.

The majority of feedback from the coach involves KP, as often KR is inherently obvious from the athlete's own feedback sources.

1.2 The need for valid and reliable feedback

In order to provide meaningful and reliable feedback, the coach must first observe and evaluate performance. Traditional coaching intervention has often involved subjective observations and conclusions based on the coach's perceptions, biases and previous experiences. However, a number of earlier studies revealed that subjective observations are potentially both unreliable and inaccurate. Human memory systems have limitations, and it is almost impossible to remember accurately all the meaningful events that take place during an extended period of time (e.g. competition). These studies have shown, for example, that international level soccer coaches could only recollect 30 percent of the key factors that determined successful soccer performance and were less than 45 percent correct in the post-game assessment of what occurred during a game (Franks and Miller, 1986, 1991). Furthermore even when experienced coaches are allowed to take notes while watching a game the probability of recalling critical events accurately was still only 59 percent (Laird and Waters, 2008).

If we consider how humans process information, the above results are not particularly surprising. Committing data to memory and then retrieving it at a later time is a complex process with many opportunities for interference. Distinctive portions of a competition (i.e. controversial decisions, exceptional technical performances, actions following stoppages in play, etc.) are often easily remembered by coaches and spectators alike, while non-critical events are more likely to be forgotten. This form of *highlighting*, when combined with emotions and personal bias of the observer, may cause a distorted perception of the game in total (for a review of episodic memory and its processes, see Gronlund *et al.*, 2007). Furthermore, our processing system has limitations that make it near impossible to view, assimilate and store all actions that take place within the playing area. These limitations result in the coach focusing attention on a specific area of play (usually what is considered to be the most critical area) with the peripheral action largely ignored.

Interestingly, the inaccuracies of subjective coaching observations are very similar to eyewitness reports during criminal situations, which are also typically considered to be unreliable and often incorrect (see Wright and Davies, 2007). In his paper on Eyewitness Testimony in Ulrich Neisser's book *Memory Observed*, Robert Buckhout (1982) explains succinctly the problem facing both eyewitnesses and coaches alike.

> The observer is an active rather than a passive perceiver and recorder; they reach conclusions on what they have seen by evaluating fragments of information and reconstructing them. They are motivated by a desire to be accurate

as they impose meaning on the overabundance of information that impinges on their senses, but also by a desire to live up to the expectations of other people and to stay in their good graces.

(p. 117)

Errors in eyewitness reports have been attributed to such things as increased arousal level (Clifford and Hollin, 1980), improper focus of attention (Wells and Leippe, 1981) or bias of the observer (Malpass and Devine, 1981). These factors are also present in a coaching environment. While accurate eyewitness testimony is of critical importance during a criminal investigation, the same can also be said of coaching observations during competition situations, as this information forms the basis of the feedback presented by the coach.

The coaching process can be thought of as an ongoing cycle of performance and practice (see Franks *et al.*, 1983a). During and following athletic performance, it is the responsibility of the coach to observe and analyze the performance and combine this information with previous results and observances. This information provides the basis for planning and implementation of upcoming practices to improve performance. Thus a successful coaching process hinges on the accuracy of collection and analysis of performance. Clearly, given the previous discussion, personal subjective observations are not sufficient and different observation tools are necessary for coaches to effectively instigate observable changes in athlete performance.

Surprisingly, given the importance of observation and analysis in the coaching process, there does not seem to be a standard or predefined system to monitor and evaluate performance. If reliance on the human information processing system is problematic, we should find other ways to collect information during athletic performances. It should be apparent from the arguments presented earlier in this chapter that this information be objective, unbiased and as comprehensive as possible. This can be achieved by creating a sport evaluation system, through the use of notational analysis. The purpose of this book is to provide the reader with information pertaining to the development and implementation of such systems to improve coaching and performance in sport.

1.3 Video feedback

Advances in technology have made the development of a notational analysis system a much less onerous task. Computerized recording allows for almost limitless storage, retrieval and analysis of data from a sporting competition in real-time. Although these technologies will be further discussed in upcoming chapters, we introduce them now to highlight the importance of collecting objective information that can be used as feedback for athletes. Obvious benefits of interactive computer video analysis systems are that they can collect and store information that can be replayed to the athlete and reviewed numerous times. This reduces observer bias and enables a visual image of the event to be collected. It has been suggested that a potential drawback of using video is that too much information may be presented and the learner may not be able to concentrate on the important details of the skill. Thus, effective presentation of video feedback likely involves *cuing* from a coach to highlight salient features during the viewing period (Kernodle and Carlton, 1992). Other alternatives include editing the videotape before showing it to an athlete or using slow motion to reduce the attention demands of the viewer. Use of video feedback also may change with skill level of the learner. As opposed to experts, athletes at an early stage of learning will likely need considerable instruction from a coach to ensure they pay attention to the critical skill features and not be overwhelmed by the volume of information presented.

A further consideration is that analytical requirements differ greatly from sport to sport, thus resulting in a potentially very different video analysis system. For example, the coaching intervention for a team sport may differ far more than for an individual sport. Also, individual *closed* skills (in which events or the environment are predictable) may differ in their analysis when compared to individual *open* skills (in which events or the environment are unpredictable) (Del Rey, 1972). For individual sports involving closed skills (e.g. diving, gymnastics, golf), the focus of the evaluation typically revolves around how the pattern of movement is performed, as this is what primarily determines success in the sport. This is often achieved by comparing the movement pattern to a set criterion performance in order to determine where differences (errors) occur. To ensure this comparison is effective, clear criteria of expected performance must be established and understood by the athlete. Therefore, it is expected that the athlete should be involved in the analysis, such that they can improve their error detection and correction mechanisms to assist them with future attempts of the skill. When examining individual sports involving open skills (e.g. tennis, boxing, squash) a greater emphasis should be placed on the analysis of decision making and tactics. Tactics play a much larger role in team sports; therefore the evaluation of performance should reflect this fact. For example, if we consider the involvement of the 22 players during a 90 minute soccer game, it becomes apparent that each player spends a majority of the time not in contact with the ball. It is critical therefore that visual information related to "off the ball" behaviour be taken into consideration.

1.4 Presenting visual feedback to athletes

Even when reliable and valid information is collected about a performance the coach still has a number of decisions regarding how and when this feedback is to be presented (see Wulf and Shea, 2004, for a review). One consideration is the mode of presentation. Historically, most coaches have tended to provide feedback verbally to their athletes; however, coaches are now realizing the benefits of presenting visual information in their instruction (a picture is really worth a thousand words (Weiss and Kimberley, 1987)). One method of presenting this information to learners is via a model of performance. This model can either be the coach or peer demonstrating, or a video image (see Maslovat *et al.*, 2010a, for a review). This particular method of instruction has been shown to be more effective than simply allowing the performer to learn through practice alone (Ashford *et al.*, 2006). The process of observing an image of correct performance has been extensively examined, due to the recent discovery of what is now known as the mirror neuron system (MNS): a network of neurons in the brain that activate during both physical performance and passive observation of a given movement (see Rizzolatti and Sinigaglia, 2010, for a recent review). This discovery provides neurophysiological evidence that during observation of a skill the body is experiencing similar neural activity in our motor system as if performing the skill, and may help explain why visual images of skilled performance are useful in accelerating the learning process. Watching a skill can be considered as a form of practice in which the brain performs all the same neurological actions required to perform the skill, yet the motor commands are inhibited from reaching the muscles and thus no movement occurs.

Interestingly, research has shown that the MNS is only active for movements with which the observer has had physical experience, or is part of the performer's "motor repertoire." For example, female ballet dancers show MNS activation while watching movements that are performed only by female dancers but do not show activation when observing movements that are performed only by male dancers (and vice versa for male ballet dancers), even though the dancers have watched movements of the opposite sex for many years (Calvo-Merino *et al.*, 2006). In addition, watching a new dance routine did not produce MNS activation in observers, yet after five weeks of practicing the routine, MNS activation occurred during observation confirming that motor experience with the task is necessary for this system to be active (Cross *et al.*, 2006). The practical application of this research is that demonstrations should show the to-be-learned movement pattern at a skill level and manner similar to that being performed by the learner. For example, same-sex models have been shown to be more beneficial than opposite-sex models for observational learning (e.g., Griffin and Meaney, 2000). Similarly, a model that is learning the to-be-performed task can be a more effective demonstration than an expert model, especially if feedback is given pertaining to the errors made by the learning model (McCullagh and Caird, 1990). In both examples, it is likely that the disparity between the motor repertoire of the observer and modeled movement pattern did not allow for MNS activation and thus reduced the effectiveness of the demonstration.

If familiarity with the model is an important factor in determining the usefulness of a demonstration, then it would be logical to assume that viewing oneself perform the action would be a most effective form of modeling. Indeed, self-observation has been considered to be superior to viewing another individual due to greater similarity in neural activation between observation and execution (Holmes and Calmels, 2008). Self-observation can be used as a *feedback* method, in which the observer watches the best attempt of the skill he or she just performed, or in a *feedforward* method, in which a video of past performances is artificially manipulated to show the individual performing movements at a higher level than he or she can actually perform (known as self-modeling, see Dowrick, 1999, for a review). While both types of self-observation can be effective, feedforward self-modeling has been shown to significantly improve an athlete's performance (Ste-Marie *et al.*, 2011a, 2011b; see also Maile, 1985, as cited in Franks & Maile, 1991); however, it is important to realize that this method requires substantial time and effort by the coach to edit and assemble the appropriate videos.

1.5 Precision and timing of feedback

In addition to the mode of feedback presentation, the coach must also consider the precision and timing of this feedback. More precise feedback seems to be of more benefit; however, this does seem to be dependent on the skill level of the athlete. As the athlete's skill level increases, so too must the precision of the feedback. Also dependent on skill level appears to be the amount of feedback. Although large amounts of feedback may be beneficial early on in the learning process, too much feedback later in learning may actually impair performance. It is thought that high frequency feedback may result in a dependence on that feedback by the athlete, and therefore not allow him or her to perform correctly when the extrinsic feedback is no longer present (i.e. a competition situation) (Schmidt *et al.*, 1989). Thus, error detection and correction mechanisms may develop faster with reduced feedback or feedback that guides the athlete to the correction rather than simply changing behavior.

In terms of timing of feedback presentation, feedback during a skill will often interfere with performance as the athlete's attention is divided between the feedback source and the skill itself (Maslovat *et al.*, 2009). It also appears that feedback immediately following performance may not be optimal. Once an athlete performs a skill he or she should be encouraged to evaluate the performance and then compare the intrinsic feedback to the desired (even predicted) result. Providing feedback during this "self-reflection" time frame can interfere with this process and in some cases may retard skill development, again by disrupting internal error detection and correction mechanisms (see Salmoni *et al.*, 1984, for a review of KR timing). Thus although presentation of feedback is a critical role of the coach, there are many considerations to ensure this feedback is given correctly to maximize learning for the athlete. More on the topic of feedback presentation is outlined in later chapters of this text.

1.6 Summary

Extrinsic feedback provided by a coach has the potential to greatly affect performance by the athlete. Historically, coaching intervention has been based on subjective observations, which have been shown to be problematic. Bias, highlighting, limitations of memory and observational difficulties are just a few of the pitfalls associated with a subjective evaluation. Thus, successful coaching hinges on the collection and analysis of unbiased, objective data. Coaches should also carefully consider the many factors associated with feedback presentation, such as content, amount and timing. Of prime consideration is the mode of feedback, with the use of appropriate visual demonstrations being one of the most useful methods to employ.

2

WHAT IS PERFORMANCE ANALYSIS?

Mike Hughes and Roger Bartlett

This chapter will seek to provide a comprehensive description of performance analysis, its purpose and its broad possible applications.

The chapter will summarise the similarities of approach of biomechanics and notational analysis, and will show how, through the application of motor control theories, these two different approaches to objective feedback can combine to help the sports performer, coach and manager.

2.1 Introduction

This presentation will consider what performance analysis is, what biomechanical and notational analysis have in common and how they differ. The main focus will be how they have helped, and can better help, coaches and athletes to analyse and improve sports performance.

Biomechanics and notational analysis both involve the analysis and improvement of sport performance. They make extensive use of video analysis and technology. They require careful information management for good feedback to coaches and performers and systematic techniques of observation. They have theoretical models – based on performance indicators – amenable to AI developments and strong theoretical links with other sport science and Information Technology (IT) disciplines. They differ in that biomechanists analyse, in fine-detail, individual sports techniques and their science is grounded in mechanics and anatomy. Notational analysis studies gross movements or movement patterns in team sports, is primarily concerned with strategy and tactics and has a history in dance and music notation.

The practical value of performance analysis is that well-chosen performance indicators highlight good and bad techniques or team performances. They help coaches to identify good and bad performances of an individual or a team member and facilitate comparative analysis of individuals, teams and players. In addition, biomechanics helps to identify injurious techniques while notational analysis helps to assess physiological and psychological demands of sports.

Drawing on a range of sports examples, we will argue that performance analysts require a unified approach, examining interactions between players and their individual skill elements. Of fundamental importance is the need for us to pay far greater attention to the principles of providing feedback – technique points that a coach can observe from video and simple counts of events are unlikely to enhance individual or team performance. We should also address the role of variability in sports skills and its implications for coaching. We must pay more attention to the role of 'normalisation' of performance indicators to aid coaches. Finally, further development of IT- and AI-based coaching tools by performance analysts is a high priority.

2.2 Notational analysis

2.2.1 Introduction

Notational analysis is an objective way of recording performance, so that critical events in that performance can be quantified in a consistent and reliable manner. This enables quantitative and qualitative feedback that is accurate and objective. No change in performance of any kind will take place without feedback. The role of feedback is central in the performance improvement process, and by inference, so is the need for accuracy and precision of such feedback. The provision of this accurate and precise feedback can only be facilitated if performance and practice are subjected to a vigorous process of analysis.

Augmented feedback has traditionally been provided by subjective observations, made during performance by the coaches, in the belief that they can accurately report on the critical elements of performance without any observation aids. Several studies not only contradict this belief, but also suggest that the recall abilities of experienced coaches are little better than those of novices, and that even with observational training, coaches' recall abilities improved only slightly. Furthermore, research in applied psychology has suggested that these recall abilities are also influenced by factors that include the observer's motives and beliefs. The coach is not a passive perceiver of information, and as such his or her perception of events is selective and constructive, not simply a copying process. This importance of feedback to performance improvement, and the limitations of coaches' recall abilities alluded to above, implies a requirement for objective data upon which to base augmented feedback, and the main methods of 'objectifying' these data involve the use of video/notational analysis (Hughes and Franks, 1997, p.11).

Coaches have been aware, consciously or unconsciously, of these needs for accuracy of feedback and have been using simple data gathering systems for decades. More recently, sports scientists have been using notational analysis systems to answer fundamental questions about game play and performance in sport. An early work, over some decades, on analysis of soccer was picked up by the then

Director of Coaching at the Football Association, and this had a profound effect on the patterns of play in British football – the adoption of the 'long ball' game. Generally, the first publications in Britain of the research process by notational analysis of sport were in the mid 1970s, so as a discipline it is one of the more recent to be embraced by sports science. The publication of a number of notation systems in racket sports provided a fund of ideas used by other analysts. Because of the growth and development of sports science as an academic discipline, a number of scientists began using and extending the simple hand notation techniques that had served for decades. This also coincided with the introduction of personal computers, which transformed all aspects of data gathering in sports science. Currently, hand and computerised notation systems are both used to equal extents by working analysts, although the use of computer databases to collate hand notated data post–event makes the analyses much more powerful.

The applications of notation have been defined as:

1   tactical evaluation;
2   technical evaluation;
3   analysis of movement;
4   development of a database and modelling; and
5   for educational use with both coaches and players.

Most pieces of research using notation, or indeed any practical applications working directly with coaches and athletes, will span more than one of these purposes.

2.2.2 The applications of notation

2.2.2.1 Tactical evaluation

The definition of tactical patterns of play in sports has been a profitable source of work for a number of researchers. The maturation of tactics can be analysed at different levels of development of a specific sport, usually by means of a cross-sectional design. The different tactics used at each level of development within a sport will inevitably depend upon technical development, physical maturation and other variables. The 'maturation models' have very important implications for coaching methods and directions at the different stages of development in each of the racket sports. These tactical 'norms' or 'models', based upon both technique and tactics, demonstrate how the different applications, defined above, can overlap.

Sanderson and Way (1979) used symbols to notate 17 different strokes, as well as incorporating court plans for recording accurate positional information. The system took an estimated 5–8 hours of use and practice before an operator was sufficiently skilful to record a full match actually during the game. In an average squash match there are about 1,000 shots, an analyst using this system will gather over 30 pages of data per match. Not only were the patterns of rally-ending shots (the Nth shot of the rally) examined in detail, but also those shots that preceded the end shot, (N–1) to a winner or error, and the shots that preceded those, (N–2) to a winner or error. In this way the rally ending patterns of play were analysed. Not surprisingly, processing the data for just one match could take as long as 40 hours of further work. The major emphasis of this system was on the gathering of information concerning 'play patterns' as well as the comprehensive collection of descriptive match data. Sanderson felt that 'suggestive' symbols were better than codes, being easier for the operator to learn and remember. The main disadvantages of this system, as with all longhand systems, was the time taken to learn the system and the large amounts of data generated, which in turn needed so much time to process.

The 1980s and 1990s saw researchers struggling to harness the developing technology to ease the problems inherent in gathering and interpreting large amounts of complex data. Hughes (1985) modified the method of Sanderson and Way so that the hand-notated data could be processed on a mainframe computer. Eventually, the manual method was modified so that a match could be notated in-match at courtside directly into a microcomputer. This work was then extended to examine the patterns of play of male squash players at recreational, county and elite levels, thus creating empirical models of performance, although the principles of data stabilisation were not thoroughly understood at the time. This form of empirical modelling of tactical profiles is fundamental to a large amount of the published work in notational analysis. Comparing the patterns of play of successful and unsuccessful teams or players in elite competitions, world cup competitions, for example, enables the definition of those performance indicators that differentiate between the two groups. This research template has been used in a number of sports to highlight the tactical parameters that determine success, and it has been extended in tennis to compare the patterns of play that are successful on the different surfaces on which the major tournaments are played.

Most of the examples for tactical applications of notation could appear in the other sections of direct applications of notational analysis, but their initial aims were linked with analysis of tactics. The interesting theme that is emerging, from some of the recent research, is that the tactical models that are defined are changing with time, as players become fitter, stronger, faster, bigger (think of the changes in rugby union since professionalisation in 1996), and the equipment changes – for example, the rackets in all the sports have become lighter and more powerful. Over a period of less than 15 years the length of rallies in squash, for elite players, has decreased from about 20 shots, to about 12 shots per rally. Reviews (Croucher, 1996; Hughes *et al.*, 2007b; Nevill *et al.*, 2008) of the application of strategies using notational analysis of different sports outline the problems, advantages and disadvantages associated with this function.

2.2.2.2 Technical evaluation

To define quantitatively where technique fails or excels has very practical uses for coaches, in particular, and also for sports scientists aiming to analyse performance at different levels of development of athletes.

Winners and errors are powerful indicators of technical competence in racket sports and have often been used in research in notational analysis of net–wall games. It has been found that, for all standards of play in squash, if the winner:error ratio for a particular player in a match was greater than one, then that player usually won. (This was achieved with English scoring and a 19-inch tin.) Although this ratio is a good index of technique, it would be better used with data for both players, and the ratios should not be simplified nor decimalised. Rally end distributions, winners and errors in the different position cells across the court, have often been used to define technical strengths and weaknesses. This use of these distributions as indicators is valid as long as the overall distribution of shots across the court is evenly balanced. This even distribution of shots rarely occurs in any net or wall game. Dispersions of winners and errors should be normalised with respect to the totals of shots from those cells. It would be more accurate to represent the winner, or error, frequency, from particular position cells, as a ratio to the total number of shots from those cells.

Similarly, performance indicators such as shots are insufficient and need to be expressed with more detail, for example shot to goal ratios (soccer). Even these, powerful as they are, need to be viewed with caution and perhaps integrated with some measure of shooting opportunities. In rugby union, simple numbers of rucks and mauls won by teams may not give a clear impression of the match: the ratio of 'rucks won' to 'rucks initiated' is a more powerful measure of performance. This too could be improved by some measure of how quickly the ball was won in critical areas of the pitch.

Many coaches seek the template of tactical play at the highest level for preparation and training of both elite players and/or teams, and also for those developing players who aspire to reach the highest position. Particular databases, aimed at specific individuals or teams, can also be used to prepare in anticipation of potential opponents for match play. This modelling of technical attainment has been replicated in many sports and forms the basis of preparation at the highest levels by the sports science support teams.

2.2.2.3 Movement analysis

Reilly and Thomas (1976) recorded and analysed the intensity and extent of discrete activities during match play in field soccer. With a combination of hand notation and the use of an audio tape recorder, they analysed in detail the movements of English first division soccer players. They were able to specify work-rates of the different positions, distances covered in a game and the percentage time of each position in each of the different ambulatory classifications. Reilly continually added to this database enabling him to clearly define the specific physiological demands in not just soccer, but later all the football codes. This piece of work by Reilly and Thomas has become a standard against which other similar research projects can compare their results and procedures, and it has been replicated by many other researchers in many different sports.

Modern tracking systems have taken the chore out of gathering movement data, which was the most time-consuming application of notational analysis, and advanced computer graphics make the data presentation very simple to understand. Modelling movement has created a better understanding of the respective sports and has enabled specific training programmes to be developed to improve the movement patterns, and fitness, of the respective athletes.

2.2.2.4 Development of a database and modelling

Teams and performers often demonstrate a stereotypical way of playing and these are idiosyncratic models that include positive and negative aspects of performance. Patterns of play will begin to establish over a period of time but the greater the database then the more accurate the model. An established model provides for the opportunity to compare single performances against it.

The modelling of competitive sport is an informative analytic technique because it directs the attention of the modeller to the critical aspects of data that delineate successful performance. The modeller searches for an underlying signature of sport performance, which is a reliable predictor of future sport behaviour. Stochastic models have not yet, to our knowledge, been used further to investigate sport at the behavioural level of analysis. However, the modelling procedure is readily applicable to other sports and could lead to useful and interesting results.

Once notational analysis systems are used to collect amounts of data that are sufficiently large to define 'norms' of behaviour, then all the ensuing outcomes of the work are based upon the principles of modelling. It is an implicit assumption in notational analysis that in presenting a performance profile of a team or an individual that a 'normative profile' has been achieved. Inherently, this implies that all the variables that are to be analysed and compared have stabilised. Most researchers assume that this will have happened if they analyse enough performances. But how many is enough? In the literature there are large differences in sample sizes.

These problems have very serious direct outcomes for the analyst working with coaches and athletes, both in practical and theoretical applications. It is vital that when analysts are presenting profiles of performance that some measure of the stability of these data is known (Hughes *et al.*, 2001; O'Donoghue, 2005; James *et al.*, 2005), otherwise any statement about that performance is spurious. The whole process of analysis and feedback of performance has many practical difficulties. The performance analyst working in this applied environment will experience strict deadlines and acute time pressures defined by the date of the next tournament, the schedule and the draw. The need then is to provide coaches with accurate information on as many of the likely opposition players, or teams, as possible in the amount of time available. This may be achieved by the instigation of a library of team and/or player analysis files that can be extended over time and receive frequent updating. Player files must be regularly updated by adding analyses from recent matches to the database held on each player.

Finally, some scientists have considered the use of a number of sophisticated techniques, such as neural networks, chaos theory, fuzzy logic and catastrophe theory, for recognising structures, or processes, within sports contests. Each of these system descriptions, while incomplete, may assist in our understanding of the behaviours that form sports contests. Furthermore, these descriptions for sports contests need not be exclusive of each other, and a hybrid type of description (or model) may be appropriate in the future, a suggestion that remains only a point of conjecture at this time.

2.2.2.5 Educational applications

It is accepted that feedback, if presented at the correct time and in the correct quantity, plays a great part in the learning of new skills and the enhancement of performance. Recent research, however, has shown that the more objective or quantitative the feedback, the greater effect it has on performance. However, in order to gauge the exact effect of feedback alone, complete control conditions would be needed in order to minimise the effect of other external variables, which is by definition impossible in real competitive environments. This experimental design is also made more difficult because working with elite athletes precludes large numbers of subjects.

Hughes and Robertson (1998) were using notation systems as an adjunct to a spectrum of tactical models that they have created for squash. The hand notation systems were used by the Welsh national youth squads, the actual notation being completed by the players, for the players. It is believed that in this way the tactical awareness of the players, doing the notation, was heightened by their administration of these systems. This type of practical educational use of notation systems has been used in a number of team sports – soccer, rugby union, rugby league, basketball, cricket and so on – by players in the squads, substitutes and injured players, as a way of enhancing their understanding of their sport, as well as providing statistics on their team.

2.3 Biomechanics – what is the biomechanical view of performance analysis?

When the British Olympic Committee (BOA) set up the Performance Analysis Steering Group, bringing together biomechanists and notational analysts, there was some scepticism as to whether these two groups of sport scientists had enough in common to make the group meaningful. After all, sports biomechanics is concerned with fine detail about individual sports techniques while notational analysts are more concerned with gross movements or movement patterns in games or teams. Furthermore, notational analysts are more concerned with strategic and tactical issues in sport than with technique analysis and the two disciplines do not share a common historical background.

However, the similarities between the two groups of analysts are far more marked than the differences. A crucial similarity is evident when we look at the other sport science disciplines: sports psychology and physiology (including nutrition) essentially focus on preparing the athlete for competition. Performance analysts, in contrast, focus on the performance in competition to draw lessons for improving performance and this is true of both notational and biomechanical analysis. Both are fundamentally concerned with the analysis and improvement of performance. Both are rooted in the analysis of human movement. Both make extensive use of video analysis and video-based technology. Although both evolved from manual systems, they now rely heavily on computerised analysis systems. Both have a strong focus on data collection and processing. Both produce vast amounts of information – this is sometimes claimed to be a strength of both sports biomechanics and notational analysis; however, it often requires careful attention in providing feedback to athletes and coaches. Many of these important topics were covered in a special issue of the *Journal of Sports Sciences* on performance analysis that appeared in the latter half of 2002.

In addition, biomechanists and notational analysts both emphasise the development of systematic techniques of observation. This is more obvious in notational analysis and, perhaps, in the somewhat neglected 'qualitative' analysis approach of biomechanics than in fully quantitative 'computerised biomechanical analysis', which seems somewhat out of fashion with coaches at present – for reasons that we will explore in a later chapter. Both have a strong focus on the provision of feedback to the coach and performer to improve performance and each group is now learning and adopting best practice from the other.

Biomechanics and notational analysis are, somewhat mischievously if with some justification, accused by other sports scientists of lacking theoretical foundations and being over-concerned with methodology: this might explain the attraction of notational analysis and qualitative biomechanical analysis to coaches as they are immediately seen as being of practical relevance. However, theoretical models do exist in both biomechanics and notational analysis. These can also be effectively represented graphically – by flowcharts for notational analysis and hierarchical technique models for biomechanics (Hughes and Franks, 1997; Bartlett, 1999). Both disciplines have 'key events' as important features of their theoretical foundations. This again helps to present information clearly and simply to coaches and sports performers, as evidenced by the current popularity of 'coach-friendly' biomechanical analysis packages, such as Dartfish (www.dartfish.com/en/), Silicon COACH (www.silicon coach.com) and Quintic (www.quintic.com). These theoretical models can, at least in principle, be mapped onto the sophisticated approaches of artificial intelligence, such as expert systems and neural net processing, hopefully offering exciting developments in performance enhancement by the middle of this decade. The theoretical models are highly sport, or technique, specific but with general principles, particularly across groups of similar sports or techniques. Both have strong theoretical and conceptual links with other areas of sport science and information technology, for example the dynamical systems approach of motor control.

Many practical issues that impinge strongly on performance improvement are common to biomechanics and notational analysis. These include optimising feedback to coaches and athletes, the management of information complexity, reliability and validity of data and future exploitation of the methods of artificial intelligence. Sharing of approaches and ideas has already begun to have mutual benefits as was evident in the very successful National Coaching Foundation (NCF)/BOA High-performance Coaches workshop held in Cardiff at Easter 1999, which was highly acclaimed by many of the coaches attending. But since then many biomechanists have clung to their more traditional roles and have shied away from direct involvement in performance analysis, Fortunately, recent research into dynamic systems has opened common ground for notational analysts (perturbations and critical incident theories), biomechanists (variance in performance) and motor control analysts (skillacquisition theory) – see Kelso (1995); Franks and McGarry (1996); Glazier *et al.* (2003); Hughes (2005).

But, you might ask, is performance analysis really helpful in improving performance? Perhaps your sport uses sports psychologists, nutritionists, physiologists and conditioning consultants but no performance analyst of any 'hue'. Well, biomechanics are employed in the Sports Science Support teams for athletics, gymnastics, swimming and speed skating. Notational analysts are employed, for example, for netball, badminton, hockey, squash, sailing, cycling, canoeing, badminton, Tae Kwando and disability basketball. Cricket, from the English Cricket Board (ECB) to county cricket clubs, uses the services of biomechanists and notational analysts, as do many other sports, such as golf and tennis (biomechanics) and rugby and soccer (notational analysis).

As to their value for the coach, biomechanics identifies the features of performance that relate to good and bad techniques, thereby helping to identify how techniques can be improved. It also facilitates comparative analysis of individual performers and helps to identify injurious techniques. The latter is well exemplified by the contribution made by biomechanists in establishing the link between low back injury and the mixed technique in cricket fast bowling (for a brief review, see Elliott *et al.*, 1996). Notational analysis identifies the performance indicators that relate to good and bad team performance and identifies good and bad performances of team members. It, therefore, facilitates comparative analysis of teams and players. In addition, it helps to assess the physiological and psychological demands of various games (for examples, see Bartlett, 2001).

Of all the sports sciences, performance analysis is the one most influenced by technological changes. Digital video and improvements in computer processing speeds and capacities have transformed biomechanical and notational analysis almost beyond recognition in the last 10 years, enabling faster turn-around times for feedback (another topic for a later article) and a far more realistic response to coaches and performers. The latter is evident, for example, by comparing crude 'stick-figure' displays (Figure 2.1) of earlier biomechanical analyses (often only produced weeks after filming) with the models available in real-time from modern optoelectronic systems such as SIMM (Figure 2.2) (from the Motion Analysis

FIGURE 2.1 Stick figure.

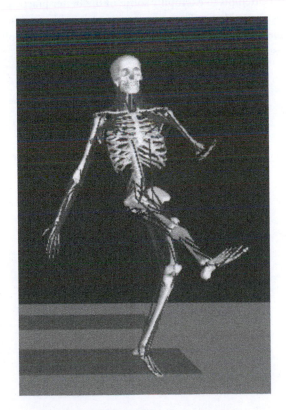

FIGURE 2.2 SIMM Skeleton and muscles.

Corporation of Santa Rosa, CA: www.motionanalysis.com) and Vicon (from Oxford Dynamics: www.vicon.com). These systems are not yet routinely used by coaches and performers, but this is changing rapidly: the Squash Rackets Association (SRA) is looking to install such a system for training and feedback in the squash centre in Manchester, where the English Institute of Sport Regional Centres have a staff of 29 analysts who use both notation and biomechanical software with a variety of sports, but mainly squash and cycling.

2.4 Conclusions

The use of systematic observation instruments provides researchers with a method of collecting behavioural data on both the coach and the athlete. These data can be analysed and processed in a variety of ways to provide a descriptive profile that can be used for giving both the athlete and the coach feedback about their actions. Advances in both computer and video technology can make this observation process more efficient and also provide the coach with audio-visual feedback about their interactions with athletes. The next phase of solving these problems in their entirety is translating the use of these objective observation systems into practice. The presentation here attempts to exemplify some of the better practical uses of analysis by elite coaches and athletes. The next step is to be able to describe in generic terms the whole process of performance analyses and their applications to the coaching process, so that it can be applied to any type of sport.

3

PROVIDING INFORMATION FOR TEACHING SKILLS IN SPORT

Keith R. Lohse and Nicola J. Hodges

3.1 Introduction

The goal of this chapter is to provide a discussion of general motor learning principles that relate to coaching and instruction. The coach has a critical role to play in the learning process. However, there are important and non-intuitive research findings to suggest that coaches often need to provide athletes with 'space' to explore movements and make errors during practice, avoiding the seductive tendency to provide frequent and detailed information or continually cue athletes to the mechanics of their movement. In this chapter, we review how information provided before, during and after motor performance affects the quality of learning. We consider these different periods when information can be imparted on a short/immediate timescale (i.e. from trial to trial), across a practice session as well as across a season and the longer term development of an athlete.

In Chapter 1, the sources of information that are available to the learner during performance were discussed. It should be clear from this discussion that information feedback, whether it is available intrinsically, via the senses, or provided extrinsically, such as by the coach, alerts the performer to errors. Information thus plays an important *error-alerting* role. There is, of course, also a critical need for information about how to correct errors or become more accurate. Information, and often extrinsic information, can thus play an important *error-correcting* role. Missing a set-shot in basketball, for instance, often contains little information about how the movement needs to be corrected. If the shot was too long, the shooter might realize the need to change their release angle, release velocity, or some combination of the two. Even recognizing the need to change these parameters, however, does not inform the shooter about how to control the ball through a complex interaction of leg, trunk and arm movements in order to effect the appropriate change in the outcome. A person develops their own intrinsic error-detection and correction

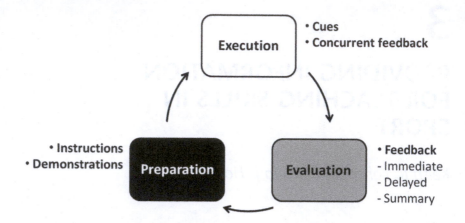

FIGURE 3.1 Different mechanisms for information transfer are available to the coach at different points during practice. Typically instructions and demonstrations are provided in the preparation phase, cues (and sometimes concurrent feedback) during the movement execution phase, and different types of feedback after the movement in the evaluation phase.

mechanisms with practice, but often these self-directed processes benefit from supplemental extrinsic information provided by a coach, trainer, or by observing one's peers. In this chapter, we explore how practitioners might best provide this sort of extrinsic information based on four types of information transfer: instructions, cues, demonstrations and feedback. These four mechanisms of information transfer can be given at different times throughout performance of a skill and during practice. At the most basic level, we refer to three periods: preparation, execution and evaluation; as illustrated in Figure 3.1, instructions are often given before a performance attempt, during the preparation phase of the skill and often early in learning. Cues are typically provided during the execution of the movement. Demonstrations are given before the movement, often early in learning as the movement is being assembled or prepared. Feedback, as the name implies, is provided during and after a movement has been performed, most frequently early in practice, to allow evaluation, reflection and either change or maintenance.

These 'phases' of an actual movement (preparation, execution, evaluation) are terms we use to delineate cut-off points to help frame our discussion of information transfer with respect to various findings, theories and principles. While this model fits more discrete skills well (that are defined by clear start and end points, such as kicking, throwing or hitting a ball), there are certainly more continuous-type skills that occur over longer timescales where evaluation could be happening as the movement takes place (such as swimming). Moreover, the preparation of a subsequent movement or the next phase of movement can certainly occur during the execution of a prior movement. Thus, although we use these three phases as a guide for discussing motor learning effects, they are not necessarily distinct, but can overlap and run in parallel.

Building on these three phases for a single action, we consider how information should be provided from trial to trial, what we call the *micro-cycle*, over the course of a longer practice session, what we call the *meso-cycle*, or over even longer time scales such as a calendar year or competitive season when progressions in skill learning are more obvious, what we call the *macro-cycle*. In the sections that follow we use these three cycles to section our discussion of how various sources of information are used and might impact performance and learning. Our aim in doing this is to point out how coaching from trial to trial might be different to coaching within a practice session or within a season, with respect to various considerations for information provision. Yet we also wish to highlight how information provided over a short time-scale can have long-lasting, positive and negative influences.

3.2 The micro-cycle: coaching from trial to trial

Information is available to a learner immediately before, during, and immediately after a movement. This immediacy of information represents the lowest level of our discussion of various time courses of learning, what we refer to as the micro-cycle (see Figure 3.2). In this context, coaches and learners often develop short verbal cues to help maintain focus on task relevant aspects of performance. These cues are often born out of the instructions and feedback that an athlete might receive from a coach between practice trials that serve to direct attention during execution. The potentially harmful feature of these cues is that they can become active or what has been termed 'reinvested' during competition when attention away from the movement is more beneficial (e.g. Porter *et al.*, 2010). Thus, coaches need to be mindful of the content of cues, instructions and feedback, in order to avoid disrupting performance during competition at the expense of potentially faster/more efficient performance during practice.

There is considerable research in the field of motor learning to suggest that instructions, feedback and verbal cues should be framed externally whenever possible (Wulf, 2013) and that coaches should try to reduce the amount of explicit instruction they give to athletes (Masters and Maxwell, 2008). Detailed instructions about movement form during practice promotes reinvestment of these instructions and explicit strategies during competition, disrupting performance. In general, when athletes are encouraged to focus *internally* on their own mechanics this disrupts performance relative to getting athletes to focus *externally* on the effects

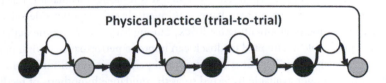

FIGURE 3.2 A schematic for a micro-cycle of practice. Black, white and grey circles correspond to preparation, execution and evaluation, respectively, for a single action.

of their actions in the environment (see Wulf, 2013, for a review). An internal focus of attention disrupts the coordination of the movement, creating movement patterns that are not only ineffective, but also inefficient (Kal *et al.*, 2013; Lohse *et al.*, 2014a). The reason for this disruption appears to be that adopting an internal focus of attention takes motor control processes that are normally implicit (i.e. performed without attention and conscious control) and makes them explicit (Ehrlenspiel, 2001; Snyder and Logan, 2012). Explicitly monitoring movement details can slow down processing of other more relevant information, leading to the inappropriate selection and/or sequencing of movements, with the ultimate effect of disrupting performance.

This can be a difficult proposition, as coaches want to share their domain-knowledge with their athletes and an error in movement form can be very directly and verbally explained. However, research suggests that a preferable method for correcting errors is to frame instructions and feedback in an external way. For example, asking learners to reflect on an aspect of the outcome after a trial, rather than asking learners to reflect on an aspect of their movement, helps to prevent any disruptions in performance (Sherwood *et al.*, 2014). An external focus could also be achieved by instructions that encourage athletes to focus their attention on the motion of the club in golf rather than on the trunk or shoulders. In situations where the correct movement is the outcome (e.g. gymnastics or diving), there is evidence to suggest that using analogies is an effective means of conveying the correct movement form to athletes, without encouraging them to focus internally on their own mechanics.

In addition to the importance of framing the message carefully when providing feedback (i.e. focusing externally), there are other important considerations with respect to trial-to-trial movement evaluation. In general, there are positive effects for learning when performers are provided with outcome-based feedback (Magill and Anderson, 2012). This is feedback about success in relation to achieving a goal (e.g. giving people performance times or accuracy feedback). It has been shown that the effects of outcome feedback are so powerful that even when this feedback is not very reliable and seemingly contradicts valid, intrinsic feedback from the senses (i.e. what is seen or felt), learners heavily weight this extrinsic information and potentially erroneously correct performance (Bueckers *et al.*, 1992).

Repeated extrinsic feedback from trial to trial can guide the learner to the correct response, enabling the athlete to calibrate their own intrinsic feedback with an external referent of what is correct or desired. Yet trial-to-trial provision of feedback can lead to later dependencies (when it is no longer available). For many years, motor learning researchers have cautioned about potential side-effects of regularly presenting or augmenting feedback, causing learners to become dependent upon it. Thus, while augmented feedback can improve performance during practice when it is available, this benefit is transitory and performance will suffer when the feedback is no longer available (referred to as the guidance hypothesis of feedback; Salmoni *et al.*, 1984; Winstein and Schmidt, 1990). One theoretical explanation for this dependency is that providing extrinsic feedback after every trial (or even just a majority of trials) extinguishes the learner's need to evaluate their own intrinsic feedback and hence intrinsic error-detection/-correction mechanisms are not adequately tuned. If learners do not engage in a form of self-generated error detection, they are unable to judge the accuracy of their movements when extrinsic feedback is no longer available.

The amount of feedback and when it is delivered could have a significant impact on how dependent the performer will be on this information for accurate performance. Very generally, feedback provided during execution, referred to as *concurrent feedback*, has been found to be more guiding and promote greater dependency than feedback about task success provided after the movement has been completed, referred to as *terminal feedback*. Vander-Linden *et al.* (1993) showed that concurrent feedback about the amount of force expended during an elbow extension task was more helpful at reducing error in acquisition when compared to terminal feedback. However, when performance was assessed in retention, the concurrent feedback group performed with the most error. Concurrent feedback guides the performer to the correct response such that they do not learn to reduce error based on other sources of intrinsic information. There is no incentive to engage in error-detection and actively work out why an error occurred and what changes in the movement led to the correction of this error.

Although we have discussed potential negative consequences associated with providing too much feedback, there are instances when frequent feedback in practice is desirable for learning (and hence retention). Generally it has been shown that more frequent feedback is beneficial for acquiring features of a movement that change across different skills of a similar class of action. For example, in shooting a basketball, the overall force of a throw will change across similar shots from different distances outside the key. Hence feedback about this aspect of performance can be provided frequently without negative consequences in retention when it is removed. However, a reduction in feedback benefits the learning of the more stable or relative features of the shot (i.e. the throwing action which might be indexed by the consistent relative timing of the knee bend, body straightening, and release of the ball). There is also evidence that the effects of feedback are dependent on the complexity of the skill. When skills are rich in intrinsic information about how the movement feels, frequent extrinsic feedback has been shown to help learners relate their own intrinsic feedback to outcome success (see Wulf and Shea, 2004). Knowing that a shot cleared the top goal post by 1 metre in soccer does not guide the learner to the correct solution for reducing this error. There are many features of the movement that can be changed to reduce the height of the ball (such as the positioning of the head and trunk when the ball is struck, the follow through of the kicking leg, the force imparted on the ball). In contrast, if the movement is constrained to one limb moving in one dimension (i.e. horizontally as is typical in many simple target aiming experiments), then feedback about the error in displacement guides the performer in terms of what to change on the next trial (i.e. the extent of the contraction). Therefore, when feedback provides more of a descriptive role (specifying what was done), rather than a prescriptive role (as a guide to what should be done), performers are less likely to become dependent on it.

Thus, in the micro-cycle (or 'in the moment', as it were) data support the suggestion that coaches should provide instructions and augmented feedback to help athletes develop a reference for the correct movement that can supplement intrinsic error-detection and correction mechanisms. However, these instructions and feedback should be low in complexity, focused on the most success-relevant features of the skill and should be framed with respect to the outcome of the task, focused externally on the effects that movements have on the environment. Complex and internally focused instructions/feedback can lead to conscious control of the movement during practice, but this can also lead athletes to use internally focused cues during competition, disrupting performance when it matters most. Moreover, the feedback should not be provided immediately after the movement, as immediate presentation reduces self-evaluation and creates later reliance on the feedback such that performance suffers in its absence.

Although we talk more extensively about demonstration effectiveness in the section that follows, demonstrations have been provided as guiding templates or as feedback over a trial-to-trial basis. Yet showing people what to do before each attempt of an action (i.e., in the preparation stage) can also be to the detriment of retention of that skill. On a trial-to-trial basis, there is considerable evidence that people retain skills better if the action is demonstrated after the learner has tried the action first (i.e. in the evaluation, rather than preparation stage). One reason for this is that demonstrations provided before an action potentially inhibit the planning and problem-solving processes that lead to better memory. Merely withholding this information until after an attempt (such that it functions more like feedback) encourages the cognitive processes that aid subsequent recall (e.g. Richardson and Lee, 1999; Patterson and Lee, 2013). For example, if a dancer is learning a choreographed sequence of dance steps, then getting the dancer to practice through active recall followed by a demonstration as feedback would be preferable to demonstrating before the attempt.

In summary, on a trial-to-trial basis, both the content and the frequency of information provision are important considerations for a coach. Generally the content should be externally focused away from the movement wherever possible. Instructions and feedback should also be provided sparingly, not before each attempt or immediately following each attempt. The athlete should develop their own sense of 'correctness' and use this to adapt or maintain behaviours when performing in the competitive environment.

3.3 The meso-cycle: considerations for planning a practice session

In the micro-cycle, we were concerned with types of information that coaches might provide during physical performance. There are, of course, plenty of opportunities to share information with athletes in a context that is removed from the immediate physical practice. For instance, a coach might sit down with their athlete before the warm-up begins and discuss what the goals are for that training session and maybe watch a video demonstration to see what kind of skill they will focus on that day ('pre-practice'). Similarly, a coach might sit down with their athlete after practice to watch a film of their performance from that day and discuss positive and negative aspects of that training session ('post-practice'). These phases are similar to the preparation and evaluation phases for a single movement discussed above, but for our purposes pre- and post-practice are different because they are removed from physical performance by longer periods of time. We have illustrated the concept of meso-practice in Figure 3.3, showing how this timescale of practice encompasses the stages outlined in the micro-practice cycle. Pre- and post-practice might of course refer to physical practice for a particular skill, such that within a practice session there may be a number of opportunities for the delivery of pre- and post-practice information. For instance, Athlete A could spend several minutes training with a coach, while Athlete B watches and Athlete A receives instructions and feedback about their physical practice. At a certain point, it is Athlete B's turn to physically practice while Athlete A observes. Athlete A thus moves into a post-practice phase and becomes an observer, even though Athlete A might physically practice again in a few minutes. Importantly, learning does not stop in the pre- or post-practice phase and these observational learning periods can be useful in correcting errors.

In order to acquire a movement pattern, some knowledge of the movement is necessary. The same applies to updating/refining an existing movement; some knowledge of what change is required is necessary. Effective instructions and demonstrations will convey a reference for what the correct movement should be. Feedback, as either intrinsic feedback (information available from the senses) or extrinsic feedback (information that is augmented in some fashion, potentially by a coach or some technical device), will then alert the athlete to errors or the degree of success.

Movement goals can be conveyed through instructions and demonstrations to provide what has been referred to in the literature as a reference-of-correctness,

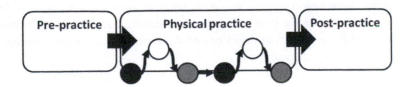

FIGURE 3.3 A schematic for a meso-cycle of practice. The micro-cycle ('Physical practice') is retained with black, white and grey circles representing preparation, execution and evaluation for single movements, but we have added pre- and post-practice phases. Typically, no physical practice occurs in these phases, but they do provide the opportunity for coaching and the provision of information in the form of demonstrations, instructions and feedback.

improving the ability of the learner to judge how well their movements match the movements that are deemed appropriate, necessary or strategically optimal for outcome success. This is not an easy process, however, and the complexity of the problem can be better understood by considering all of the different translations that the information has to go through. The 'ideal' movement might be seen (visual) and perhaps explained (verbal), conveying a general strategy and some elements of movement form to the learner who then tries to execute the skill (motor). Errors in the movement outcome will often be seen (visual), but errors in the movement itself will usually be felt (proprioceptive). If detected, the person (and their motor system) still has the arduous task of mapping an error in the movement outcome to the part(s) of the movement that went wrong (the 'credit assignment' problem in control systems). Comparisons between these various information sources are important and necessary steps in learning, but clearly translating from one modality to another is a complex proposition.

We should also consider that there are types of actions that have no immediate 'outcome' as their movement goal, but rather have as their goal a specific technique or movement pattern. For example, a pike jump on the trampoline, a cartwheel in gymnastics or a choreographed dance sequence. For these and similar skills some sort of reference information is potentially more important as the means define the goal of the task, rather than the means being merely a potential solution to goal attainment. Usually a demonstration is used in these situations to convey movement requirements. Although feedback will still be important, it potentially has decreased value in terms of bringing about an appropriate change in the movement, as feedback alone cannot be adequately evaluated against a standard. For example, Kernodle et al. (2001) showed that verbal information that alerted participants to errors (i.e. what a desired throw should look like) and how to correct them was more beneficial for acquiring a desired throwing pattern than only providing video feedback. The authors concluded that because no reference information was provided to the video feedback group, they were unable to perform comparisons and thus detect errors in performance over and above their existing knowledge concerning the correct throwing motion. Similarly, video feedback can be used more effectively to aid learning when it is coupled with demonstrations, allowing for important comparative information about what should be done and what was done (Hodges et al., 2003). Moreover, the potential benefits of video feedback and demonstrations are improved if the coach can direct or cue the learner to the specific aspects of performance that need correcting.

Some of the most convincing research showing that demonstrations help to convey important features of a movement, which are then translated into effective motor execution, comes from Carroll and Bandura (1982, 1985, 1990). These researchers showed how repeated exposure to visual demonstrations improved the retention of a motor skill and how supplementary verbal instructions (which highlighted salient features of the demonstration) enhanced retention further. Verbal information was only beneficial, however, when learners had multiple opportunities to view demonstrations. Most critically, performance on a subsequent motor test could be explained by learners' accuracy in recognizing the correct movement. This close correspondence between execution and recognition suggests that demonstrations and verbal instructions can aid the development of a cognitive representation of the skill that can positively impact motor performance. However, there do appear to be some limitations on the transfer between what is viewed and what is later performed. Repeated demonstrations in the absence of physical practice, especially for more complex skills that require the coordination between components, seem to positively aid these discrimination processes but not necessarily skill execution (Maslovat *et al.*, 2010b).

The idea that action and perception show a close correspondence (or a common representation), at least for relatively simple skills, or skills that can be performed by the observer, fits with neurophysiological models of action–observation. Motor areas of the cortex have been shown to be active during both performance of an action and observation of an action (as well as perceptual and associative areas of the cortex). Importantly, action observation is more likely to activate cortical, motor-related areas of the brain if the observer has had experience performing the action (e.g. Calvo-Merino *et al.*, 2005; Cross *et al.*, 2006). This makes sense in as much as what we can do impacts our understanding of what we see and that our perceptions of the same scene can change and become more nuanced as we develop movement skill. Thus, having increased motor experience allows a learner to perceive a demonstration in a fundamentally different way. Prior physical experience might allow learners to get more out of a demonstration (either more information, or more relevant information) compared to learners who do not have physical experience with the movement, which might partially explain the benefits of blending physical and observational practice (see Ong and Hodges, 2012). Of course, this means that the initial skill acquisition stages and the potential benefits of demonstrations will be limited until physical experience is gained. There have been a number of recent studies showing that demonstrations potentially function differently depending on when they are given in practice. Before physical experience with an action, they may serve a more strategic role, whereas later in practice and after physical experience, they may aid learning through a low-level activation (or resonance) with the observed action helping to refine or strengthen an under-developed skill (Ong *et al.*, 2012).

Perhaps not surprisingly, physical practice is generally shown to be more effective than purely observational practice on later tests of retention (Blandin *et al.*, 1994; Buchanan *et al.*, 2008; Maslovat *et al.*, 2010b). However, for skills with greater perceptual-cognitive requirements (e.g. highly sequential tasks such as dance or gymnastics routines), there is some evidence that observational practice can be as effective as or more effective than physical practice in retention tests (e.g. Black *et al.*, 2005; Badets *et al.*, 2006). Certainly, there are numerous studies showing that mixed physical and observational practice leads to comparable or better learning than physical practice alone (for a review see Ong and Hodges, 2012).

Even when physical and mixed practice groups are matched on the total amount of practice, thus mixed practice groups are actually doing less physical practice, there is evidence for comparable learning benefits. There is also evidence that demonstrations serve to aid and restore confidence in one's ability to perform a skill, even in the face of physical failure. When watching with the intention of acquiring a juggling action, observers showed a general tendency to linearly increase their confidence in their ability to perform over repeated observations and that when they were actually allowed an attempt and did not succeed, confidence was restored quite quickly by watching further demonstrations (Hodges and Coppola, in press). Bandura (1986) has also written on the potential benefits of demonstrations in aiding perceptions of success, which relate to later success (so termed self-efficacy).

In considering the meso-time cycle of practice it is important to also talk about feedback methods that have been adopted in the post-practice phase to aid learning and evaluation. For example, there is a considerable amount of research showing that summary feedback based on performance over a number of trials, rather than every trial, is better for learning of relatively simple skills. Also, feedback provided only when a person is within or outside a particular criterion has been shown to positively affect retention performance when that feedback is no longer available (see Swinnen, 1996; Wulf and Shea, 2004). When people get to choose when to receive feedback or demonstrations, they also show a preference to not get feedback on every trial, showing some evidence that people are quite good at judging when and how much information they need to aid performance yet without being detrimental to learning (see Sanli et al., 2012). There is also evidence that learners prefer to receive feedback following a perceived successful trial rather than one where they thought they made an error (or a relatively larger error). It is thought that this success-affirming role of feedback (rather than merely an information-giving role) is important for learning, serving to reinforce good behaviours and enhance motivation during practice, positively impacting later retention (Lewthwaite and Wulf, 2012).

In summary, at the meso-cycle level, where pre- and post-practice are more likely to be separated from actual physical performance, there is considerable evidence that building a reference or template that helps to convey the primary goals of a skill, and somewhat how to achieve them, is important for skill acquisition. Whether to use demonstrations or instructions will depend somewhat on the skill, but there is evidence that some combination will work best, as long as the instructions do not encourage a primary focus onto the movement itself. Combining demonstrations with physical practice appears to be the best method for learning, allowing the learner opportunities to calibrate what they have seen with their capabilities. In the post-practice phase, feedback also helps to convey what was done in relation to what was desired (i.e. the reference), and hence combining demonstrations with feedback about how the movement looked appears to be a good practice principle.

3.4 The macro-cycle: coaching for long-term development

At the longest timescale, we want to consider how information can be provided over months (or perhaps even years) to help athletes continue to improve and refine their skills. We have provided an illustration of this macro-cycle in Figure 3.4. As with the other figures, this macro timescale of practice encompasses the other timescales, with information provision considered at various timescales of the performer's development. Hence, the most important consideration at this level is that the provision of information should be seen as dynamic. The amount and type of information provided is going to change as learners become better at the task, freeing up cognitive resources to attend to additional information as the skill is increasingly proceduralized (i.e. performed in a seemingly automatic manner, requiring little cognitive attention). Thus, as learners become more proficient with a skill, they can successfully deal with complexities and difficulties during execution that would have been overwhelming before. In a very general sense, this can be achieved by *adding* task-relevant *difficulty* to the training environment (e.g. more choices, faster pace, opponents) or by *removing* the artificial *supports* that were present early in practice to more accurately reflect the competitive environment (e.g. gradually fading out the use of extrinsic feedback and demonstrations).

Behaviourally, we know that experts and novices perform complex skills in very different ways. Experts are generally faster, more accurate, more efficient, and more fluent in their movements than novices (Newell, 1991; Vereijken *et al.*, 1992; Sparrow and Newell, 1998; Wilson *et al.*, 2008). Psychologically, there is also evidence to suggest that learners progress from a cognitively demanding stage early

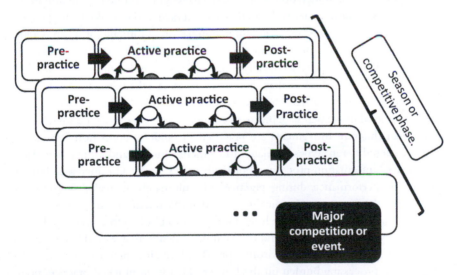

FIGURE 3.4 A schematic representation of a macro-cycle of practice. Composed of meso- and micro-cycles, the macro-cycle could represent a competitive season (leading to a major competition) or a longer period of time in which the athlete will be acquiring and refining their motor skills.

in practice (Newell, 1991) to more 'automatic' stages later in practice when skills have been proceduralized. This proceduralization leads to reduced cognitive control of the movement, so much so that when explicit cognitive control is reinvested (e.g. through instructions to focus on specific aspects of the skill, or as a result of pressure and anxiety), speed and accuracy suffer (Beilock and Carr, 2001; Beilock et al., 2002) and the coordination of the movement is disrupted (Gray, 2004; Beilock and Gray, 2012). Part of the reason reinvesting cognitive control might be disruptive is that brain areas supporting motor control and the functional connectivity of those areas changes with learning (Willingham, 1998; Coynel et al., 2010; Lohse et al., 2014b). This shift in neural control of movement is supported by physiological signals recorded from the brain showing that the coherence between verbal processing and motor planning regions (i.e. left temporal cortex and frontal midline regions) decreases as people become more skilled or when expert athletes are compared to novices (e.g. Deeny et al., 2003; Janelle and Hatfield, 2008). Additionally, increased coherence in these areas is correlated with increased (and unwelcome) movement variability in expert rifle shooters (Deeny et al., 2009), consistent with the idea that explicitly trying to control movement disrupts skilled performance (Masters and Maxwell, 2008).

In sum, learning leads to changes in performance at the behavioural, psychological and neurophysiological levels. These changes lead to some important considerations for how information should be provided to learners over the long term. First, as skill level increases, more information and different types of information can be provided to keep practice challenging (see Guadagnoli and Lee, 2004). A key consideration is that these challenges must be meaningful in the competitive setting in order to be beneficial in practice (i.e. making the practice environment faster is only a meaningful manipulation of difficulty if speed is a key component of the competitive environment). One method of introducing difficulty during practice that appears to reliably improve long-term learning is to *randomize* the practice schedule rather than *blocking* a practice schedule (see Kantak and Winstein, 2012; Lee, 2012). In this context, a blocked schedule means that similar/identical movements are practised contiguously, whereas a random schedule means that different movements are practised in random alternation. Having to shift between different types of related movements during random practice places an increased information processing burden on the learner. This increased burden can impair performance during practice, but ultimately increases retention of the skill in the long term (as measured by delayed retention and transfer tests). Over the macro-cycle, we can see how shifting from a blocked to a random schedule of practice would provide the kind of dynamic difficulty that would keep learners challenged by the practice environment. Randomizing practice increases the information processing burden on the learner. That is, in blocked practice, preparation, execution and evaluation processes are roughly the same from one movement to the next. In random practice, however, evaluation occurs and then preparations are made for a new movement.

A second way to adjust difficulty over the macro-cycle is to remove the supports that were in place early in the practice session to be more commensurate with the competition environment. For example, a long-jumper who is provided with extrinsic feedback about foot contact errors in relation to the take-off board during practice will not typically have this information available under competitive conditions. In contrast, outcome information concerning the length of the jump is present in practice and competition, so the assessment of the skill with this information is a valid and realistic measure of learning. While it might be beneficial to present augmented feedback about take-off early in practice, the coach wants to prevent the learner from being dependent on this additional information and be able to rely on their own internal feedback sources (see Salmoni et al., 1984). Of course, this information provision needs also to be weighed up against the need for information and the stage of learning. Although more feedback might be helpful early in learning, if the feedback or instruction is at a level of control that the performer does not have, then at best it will not be useful and at worst, disruptive. For example, there are many potential types of process feedback that can be provided to an athlete during practice, such as heart rate data or accelerations of the arm or club/bat in striking sports. While this information might be useful to an experienced performer, such as an expert archer or golfer respectively, it may be too sophisticated or complex for a less seasoned athlete. Empirical data do suggest, however, that coaches should be careful that feedback not be internally focused, which induces explicit monitoring and disrupts execution, when working with novice or expert athletes.

Similarly, precise, quantitative information about performance and frequent feedback might be unusable by a more novice performer and could lead to an over-correction of performance. If the level of feedback is too specific for the level of control that the performer is able to exert over the skill (such as errors in timing that are at the millisecond level or errors in aiming or distance that are within one millimetre or one degree), then this feedback could prevent a stable level of performance from forming, leading to high trial-to-trial variability. The level of feedback provided should therefore be appropriate for the skill level of the individual and appropriate to the level of control they have over their performance.

Thus, over the macro-cycle, it seems reasonable to decrease the amount of extrinsic feedback being provided to learners in order to make the practice environment more commensurate with the competition environment. By gradually fading out the use of video feedback, for instance, a coach allows the learner to reap some of the benefits of this extrinsic information early in practice when intrinsic processes are not well tuned for detecting and correcting errors. As learning continues and extrinsic feedback is reduced, the learner builds up their own intrinsic error-detection and error-correction processes, which are important because the learner will usually only be able to rely on these intrinsic information sources in competition. Although there is not a good experimental demonstration to show the efficacy of this method in sport, this method of fading the amount and frequency of video feedback has been detailed as part of a successful intervention in elite archery and marksmanship (Williams *et al.*, 2012).

3.5 Summary

Since the first edition of this book, the basic tenets and principles concerning augmented information provision have remained largely the same. In the first edition, the chapter on augmented feedback was more of a historical overview of the literature on this topic. Although we have revisited many of these topics in this new chapter, we see this current version as complementary, bringing in new literature and ideas that impact how information might effectively be delivered during practice to aid learning. Therefore, we would still direct the reader to the first edition for a broader overview of this topic with respect to positive and negative aspects of feedback and instructions.

The idea to section the current chapter with respect to timescales of practice is new and we think important in framing how to think about information delivery. Although the principles are relatively consistent across the timescales, it should be clear from the above that information delivery should be viewed as an evolving process. Unfortunately, there is not much empirical research on information provision among skilled performers, most likely because it is challenging to isolate single variables and get performance changes over relatively manageable time periods. Most of our data on skilled performers and practice comes from the study of relatively simple skills where it is possible to train people to a relatively high level of skill on a relatively simple task. Despite this limit in research, the challenge-point framework outlined above (Guadagnoli and Lee, 2004) helps to underline some important practice principles concerning information provision that are likely to generalize beyond the typical period of skill development considered in the empirical literature.

In summary, we think that information provision should be considered across multiple timescales. We start this chapter by considering the information processing stages that surround a single action (i.e. planning, execution, evaluation). These individual actions combine to form multiple trials during physical practice of a skill. Multiple skills can then be grouped together into a single practice session where we need to consider what sort of information is available to learners in the intervening periods: when they are observing, receiving instructions in advance of physical practice, or receiving feedback after physical practice is over. Furthermore, we need to consider that motor control processes are dynamic, and as an athlete becomes more proficient with a skill over the course of a season (or longer) the structure of information in the practice environment needs to change as well.

With respect to general principles, it has been shown repeatedly that augmented information pertaining to how to perform a skill should be delivered in such a way that the learner does not overly think about the characteristics of the movement, but more about the outcome goal and the effects of the movement on the environment. This type of external cueing or instructing, even with respect to feedback and movement evaluation, seems to define optimal performance across a range of skills and across timescales of skill development. Indeed, highly skilled performers seem to suffer more than beginners from instructions that direct their attention internally, towards the mechanics of the movement. Moreover, because performance effects can be separated from retention and later recall of the skill, it is important to provide augmented information only when needed and in ways that performers do not become dependent upon it. Too much information can lead to over-correction of movements or passive learning where the expectation of feedback about what was done wrong and how to correct it prevents self-evaluation and thus hinders development of the athlete's own error-detecting and error-correcting mechanisms.

4

VIDEO-BASED TECHNOLOGIES, SUBSTITUTION OF REALITY AND PERFORMANCE FEEDBACK

Dario G. Liebermann and Ian M. Franks

4.1 Introduction

Information Technologies in general, and those that are based on video in particular, are today strongly associated with motor skill acquisition. They can be subdivided in those that enable the provision of feedback for improving performance and those that enable notational analysis of performance. The former ITs are based on the assumption that augmented feedback enhances the learning process, while the latter ones are intended mainly for coaches to improve the management of movement-related or game information that affects the chances of success. Although healthy individuals (Crossman 1959) may spontaneously improve a motor skill even without external feedback (simply by practicing), augmented feedback affects learning depending on the quantity and the quality of the feedback provided to the performer during the motor training.

In the following paragraphs, we re-evaluate the use of feedback-based technologies in enhancement of sport performance, and focus on different ITs that evolved from video applications adapted for the purpose of measuring, analyzing, facilitating and manipulating information that coaches used in making their decisions.

4.2 Augmented feedback in elite sports: true "need" or "fashion"?

In general, IT may act as a "feedback facilitator" expected to bring improvements in the quality of performance and reductions in the acquisition time (i.e., to influence the rate of learning). At least at the initial stage of performance, such effects are well documented (Schmidt and Lee 2011) and need no further attention within the current chapter. As the individual gains expertise, externally mediated (visual or auditory) feedback often becomes less important because reliance on intrinsic (kinesthetic) sources replace it. Most likely, elite athletes do not need any further skill acquisition, i.e., their learning curve reaches an asymptote. Common augmented sensory feedback may not be enough for this purpose, and subtle measures of error can make the difference between winning and losing an event. The "winning edge" can only be achieved by improving minor details in the performance and by improving strategies, and more importantly by decreasing the variance. High-resolution IT can help in this respect. At high competitive level, learning may manifest in terms of increase in consistency rather than in terms of absolute performance measures (Shmuelof *et al.* 2012). At advanced stages of learning, a skill should become consolidated into memory (Ungerleider *et al.* 2002; Krakauer 2009). A sign of such consolidation process is the reduction in variance.

In daily training conditions, technologies aid not only in enhancing the feedback provided by the coach but also its administration. Diverse feedback modes are integrated today in IT, allowing for richer and more intense training experiences. They are developed to provide terminal feedback information (at the end of the performance) as well as concurrent feedback (during the ongoing performance). For example, Kinect™ and Wii™ platforms, initially developed for gaming purposes, are more and more adapted to collect data, and to provide kinematic information aside success/failure rates. Summary feedback at the end of the performance or the game is also provided by such technologies. They may be combined with "substitute environments" where performers are immersed in realistic virtual settings that blend force and sound feedbacks. People in sports are becoming more and more aware of haptic stimulation and sonification of movement. For example, auditory information about motor performances in sports has been suggested as an effective means to provide concurrent feedback about modeled temporal structures of movement (Liebermann *et al.* 2002).

Not only do athletes benefit from new technologies, coaches are also main beneficiaries of using video-based IT to make decisions about training protocols, particularly in team sports. However, this depends on applying and administering them correctly. The current chapter is concerned with the question of whether or not improvements in motor performance are a consequence of using IT, and in what circumstances it may be used.

4.3 Extrinsic and intrinsic feedback in sports

Most athletes are able to translate feedback information to motor performance almost immediately, while others are unable. Why are some individuals better able to correct performance more efficiently and more effectively than others? The time it takes to adapt and master a skill may be regarded as a criterion for discriminating between different potential athletes. Naturally, with so much technology at hand enabling performance feedbacks, athletes are expected to achieve better results regardless of their individual potential. Google glasses™ or similar "wearable technologies" (e.g., helmet cameras) of late may collect information in real-time while training, and also enable performance feedback with integrated audio technology. Similarly, smartphones today are equipped with enough sensing technology (GPS, accelerometers, gyros and video) to enable motion capture, large "cloud" storage (i.e., in an external nonspecific internet repository) and immediate analyses. But are these enough to enhance performance of every athlete or does it depend on individual characteristics and experience?

Differences among individuals may be found in the capability to use the information available through new technologies and the capability to associate the information provided with the actual movement performance. Information about "how we actually performed" together and in parallel with information about "how we feel about our motor performance" arrives at the central nervous system (CNS) via different neural paths. Cues about the outcomes of one's performance may arrive from outside via exteroceptive senses (vision, audition). On the other hand, cues about how one feels about a performance arrive from within the system, in particular, via proprioception. A traditional view proposes that modifications in a movement are done by comparison between what we do (i.e., the actual motor act) and what we should do (i.e., a forward model or a virtual plan of how to perform). Specifically, such comparisons may be carried out by cerebellar structures (Miall *et al.*, 1993).

Matching motor plans with actual movements implies a correlation process. Lack of correlation between expected and actual performance is perceived as a motor error, and thus, the performance should be corrected. In parallel, the plan should be updated via an internal close-loop process (feedback-dependent). Such a learning mode is supported by early neurobiological and neuroanatomical evidence (von Holst and Mittelstaedt 1950). Sperry's experiments (see Trevarthen 1990, for an overview of his work) were among the first to show functional correlates between neuro-anatomy and performance. The behavioral studies of Held (1965) showed adaptation processes that may involve the previously hypothesized neural structures. In those adaptation experiments, passive performers received distorted visual input and this was enough to induce motor adaptations. Nevertheless, the greatest and sometimes irreversible sensorimotor changes were produced when the performers were active. Such processes happen because the CNS is endowed with neuroplasticity, a feature (e.g., in the primary motor cortex) that expresses initially as a widespread increase in the volume of active cells followed by a decrease in volume (Shmuelof *et al.* 2012). This paradoxical change suggests that once the system has learned a skill, it adapts and consolidates such that the learned skill can be used in the long term. This is a process whereby unnecessary synapses are omitted and eventually disappear, whereas new specific interconnections (deemed essential for the acquired task) are reinforced. While vision captures external events (including the outcomes of our own motor actions), proprioception relates to our internal motor experience. The former allows for a posteriori corrections of motor errors while the latter enables online corrections during a motor performance. Reliance on vision may induce a dependence on external information, while reliance on proprioception enhances autonomic learning (i.e., independent of external sources of information). It should be mentioned that proprioception is a main sensory channel facilitating feedback. Proprioceptive sensors are suited to capture changes in muscle length (displacement), the rate of change of length (velocity), muscle stiffness (the change in muscle tension as a function of the change in muscle length), and/or postures (static joint configurations of one segment relative to another or relative to the gravity force vector) conveyed to the CNS through the interplay between agonist–antagonist muscles' stiffness. In brief, proprioception allows for sensing posture and movement (i.e., kinesthetic sense). However, special attention is dedicated lately to haptic sensing which conveys information about pressure and force, both static and dynamic.

It should be mentioned that IT may be used to strengthen the link between movements and our internal experience about them. That is, feedback-based technologies play a role in facilitating the shift from dependence on extrinsic information (e.g., augmented feedback provided by a coach) to an independent performance that relies mainly on intrinsic sources (i.e., an autonomous performance).

4.4 Feedback, video and motor learning

Visual information is massive and complex, and thus, it requires higher-order CNS involvement for processing and interpretation, i.e., visual perception involves higher-order cognitive processes. Vision enables the brain to recognize environmental features, faces and objects, but seeing is more than just sensing.

Learning via video observation may, therefore, result in a complex and slow process that requires expert guidance to focus attention on those aspects of movement that should be imitated. Yet, imitation of movement is a natural and common form of learning that activates specific brain cells called mirror neurons (see Chapter 1 in this text) found in primates (Rizzolatti and Craighero 2004) and in humans (Mukamel et al. 2010).

Video technology has significantly developed to enhance learning by observation and imitation. In its latest form, it has become popular in cellphone applications that are equal or superior in quality to the video technologies used a decade ago. In all cases, video is a rich source of visual and auditory information that has significantly influenced movement evaluation and movement training methods. With such technologies in hand, coaches can pinpoint the relevant information and athletes can focus on specific motor events recorded on video, watch replays as many times as required and attempt to correct the errors. Such is common routine in analysis of combat sports. In judo, for example, video-based technologies benefit all parties. Referees base their decisions on video recordings during the fights, judokas watch their fights shortly after their performance, and coaches analyze and manage training routines based on errors and successes they identify on video. A similar but more advanced application of video in sports has been developed in rhythmic gymnastics for algorithmic identification of errors in performance that promises to benefit gymnasts as well as judges (Pino Díaz-Pereira et al. 2014).

However, how should video feedback be provided to make its application more efficient in sport situations? This is still a concern regardless of the improvements in the technologies.

Trainers often use video replays of previous performances as training aids, but for the inexperienced athlete the information provided by such a medium should always be redirected to general performance parameters (e.g., general posture, timing errors). For the more experienced athletes, video feedback and guidance should be specific and as close as possible to the real event (e.g., errors in implementation of a tactic, errors in specific postural configurations during a skill, information about kinematic features).

Coaches may use video as a tool for the provision of elaborated feedback. For instance, coaches observe team performance and then analyze and quantify individual and group performances. While some athletes may find it difficult to associate the expected movement pattern with the previous errors, video technologies today enable immediate replays. Such immediacy is essential to associate what the athlete has recently perceived with what they see as video images. Yet, athletes have to gain experience in order to use video information appropriately to correct motor skills in competitive situations.

In some instances, video-based IT may even benefit coaches more than their own athletes because coaches are able to elaborate more on strategies. From video-based IT, coaches also extract information about the qualitative aspects of performance and quantitative information if they can access suitable software. The athlete then only receives the pre-processed information and is not usually involved in the analyses.

As discussed in detail in this text, technologies used for notational analyses in sports enable the integration of several applications (database, digital video coding and data storage) into a single system that allows an efficient shift from a data collection process to a data analysis stage and a synthesis of the performance. Some questions that still remain to be answered are whether athletes should participate in notational analyses as part of their skill training process? Is it beneficial for the athlete to get involved in biomechanical analyses of their own performances? Should the athlete become a coach of his/her own given that notational analysis software and video technologies are available and simple to use? These questions need to be investigated further.

4.5 Qualitative feedback and quantification of performance using video-based technologies

Demonstration and imitation may be fundamental to motor development and to motor learning because most movement features are expressed as extrinsic (external) features that are usually perceived. Imitation of an observed movement might actually reduce complexity of the motor learning process by allowing a performer to bypass the dynamic aspects of a motor plan (i.e., the muscle moments and joint torques required to move; Wolpert *et al.* 1995), particularly when the sensory information constrains the number of possible solutions to maximize a performance.

Software developed for implementing motor imitation is readily available in sport. Basic hardware technology coupled with appropriate software enables users to split a computer screen in two halves. In one half, the actual performance is observed and in the other half a model performance is presented. The same technology enables a user to superimpose two synchronized video footages.

In recent years, improvements in the interface between video cameras and PCs facilitated the process. Video feedback for example can be provided at the training site for immediate comparisons. The number of such video-based technologies in sport has grown significantly, and consequently, learning by visual comparison is now very popular. Given the wide range of options, it is recommended to focus on those technologies that allow a fast digital blending of images (i.e., a superposition of two appropriately scaled, translated and rotated video sequences). Such software tools also enable performers to compare their own movements and, eventually, to match themselves to another elite athlete simply by retrieving performances from a "video repository." This may prove to be a powerful skill learning tool, as essential differences between two observed performances are exposed.

Consistency is a feature of well-learned motor skill. Athletes should aim at maintaining the same correct motor performance repeatedly. Nevertheless, no two performances are identical and certainly no two athletes are equal. Therefore, what is optimal for one athlete is not for another (Bartlett and Bussey 2011). Qualitative comparison of sport performances has not yet been validated as a general learning strategy at all levels because, as mentioned earlier, visual feedback provided via video technologies may be too complex. Beginners, rather than improving a complex motor act by using video replays and other multimedia means, may learn basic movement drills (e.g., in tennis; Zheng and Zu 2009). However, it is likely that competitive athletes and experienced coaches could take advantage of such technologies to improve performance at the top level.

One should remember that video images are two-dimensional (2D) representations of a three-dimensional (3D) reality. However, experienced people may be able to reconstruct a 3D movement sequence in their mind and imagine the performance after receiving only a series of 2D views kept in memory. However, with complexity comes an increase in processing time (Shepard and Metzler 1971; Cooper and Shepard 1973). One advantage of today's technologies is that they enable a fairly fast and accurate reconstruction of 3D based on stereovision where the two eyes receive slightly rotated views of the same images facilitating the process of mentally reconstructing 3D environments. In fact, this is quite useful in training, for example, new cycling circuits (Sörös *et al.* 2013).

Quantitative information provided to novice performers via video raises similar concerns regarding qualitative movement information. The major concern is the complexity of the quantitative information. There are many video-based systems today that enable biomechanical analyses of sport performances. Such systems synthesize movement to its essential mechanical characteristics. For example, they may provide information about the direction and magnitude of the center of mass of the performer or about the motion of single, most relevant segments. However, one may wonder what the meaning of such information is for the inexperienced athlete. The level of abstraction of such feedback is high. We should assume that the more complex and abstract the information, the less efficient such feedback would be. Only simple and specific kinematic variables may be appropriate for most individuals. Although video analysis technology makes such feedback readily available, the coach should be selective about what information to provide to the athlete since many new ITs in sports may be redundant.

4.6 Modeling and learning from simulation: feedback about differences between simulated and observed performance

Models and simulations based on optimization or maximization criteria are used to understand motor performance in general, and sport techniques in particular. Computer models can predict the effects of combining, increasing or decreasing performance parameters. Simulations are often run to visualize a model's outcomes, which in turn allow coaches to see and become aware of potentially unnoticed weaknesses. Modeling and simulation based on video-based recorded performances enable optimized movements to be created (e.g., What would a swim stroke look like when optimizing energy expenditure?) or maximized performances (e.g., What would a maximal-distance hammer throw look like with a minor change in the angle of release?). Optimal models are based on equations of constraint that limit the endless number of solutions to a limit set that is said to be optimal in some sense.

The information retrieved from models may not be directly applicable for an athlete. Only the experienced coach could use such feedback once it is understood, interpreted and translated into subtle skill modifications. In fact, coaches may act only as the conduit to transmit and explain complex information to the performer. Computerized technologies (from personal computers to cellphones) are only a means for fast calculation and visualization of the simulated performance. Computer graphic power, as well as storage capabilities, is important in the process of implementation of modeling and simulation in real-time performance because visual comparisons between real and optimized performances are part of learning by imitation, provided that visualizations can be provided immediately. Hubbard and Alaways (1989) were among the first to report an implementation of such an approach. They measured simple kinematic variables at release during a javelin throw and optimized the flight path by instructing the performers to change the angle of release, the angle of attack and the pitch rate, and provided feedback about actual and expected results after each throw. Yeadon (1997; and earlier) used mathematical models to predict the results of several gymnastics exercises. More recently, Yeadon and Knight (2012) combined modeling, simulation and virtual reality (VR). They immerse non-elite performers in a scene where the simulation is carried out for achieving better learning. However, it is not known yet to what extent such a multi-modal approach is beneficial for elite athletes. In fact, it appears that such high complexity in the quantification of sport motor performance may not always be justified. Most coaches and athletes would simply rely on their hands-on experience and their intuition rather than on information provided by biomechanical models. However, this does not imply that such an approach should not be used.

4.7 Watching versus performing movements in virtual and real environments

A common assumption of learning by imitation movements shown on video is that athletes are able to translate the observed images into action. The generation of virtual environments where the subject perceives a 3D world has evolved over the past several years. Yet the principle remains simple. Each eye receives a slightly different perspective of the same 2D images while fusion of the two planar views (one for each eye of the same object) takes place in higher brain centers. This augmented virtual reality is used for training movements in different sporting and non-sporting scenarios (Feiner, 2002). A potential advantage of using virtual environments is that a coach may manipulate feedback to enhance motor learning by allowing training in unknown conditions or using exaggerated feedbacks that cause motor compensation. The latter is more common in motor rehabilitation (e.g., Patton *et al.* 2013) where error feedback is manipulated to create compensatory movements and torques that benefit the training of the patient.

In healthy individuals, research suggests that feedback during virtual reality training may accelerate the learning process compared to standard coaching techniques (Todorov *et al.* 1997). However, for precise actions (as opposed to the gross movements cited above) this is not recommended because of the discrepancies between real and virtual environments.

To summarize, training in virtual reality may enhance motivation to learn, at least while the conditions challenge the performer. Sometimes the mere practice in a novel setting is just enough to captivate some individuals (e.g., children and young athletes). In spite of the widespread use of virtual reality training, the information about its effectiveness in sports is limited. In clinical conditions, in some industry applications and in the military, results are positive. However, further research is required to support the use of virtual settings in sports.

4.8 Video technology and temporal feedback

It has been suggested previously that video technology enables encoding temporal information. Such information can be useful for the improvement of motor skill under the assumption that timing and rhythm constrain the spatial aspects of a movement. The duration of the movement, for example, seems to be perceived and learned better than other aspects even when the performer does not pay attention (Liebermann *et al.* 1988). Intuitively, coaches whistle or clap their hands to convey information about how to perform. Such temporal information about one's performance may be extracted from simple time codes inherent in the video frames and this information can be reduced to a rhythmical structure of the movement in its simplest form.

The fact that humans are able to extrapolate from temporal information the spatial configuration of a movement became evident in the early experiments of Johansson (1975). This researcher showed that visual perception may be used to reconstruct a complete movement pattern from limited inputs. Johansson showed that a body in the dark, as defined by visual markers attached to the joints of the performer, may be easily used to identify a type of movement (e.g., dancing or walking). The same information may even be used to discriminate among people of different identities or gender, by simply looking at the moving markers (Johansson 1975).

Using a reverse engineering approach, a mechanically optimal movement pattern may be characterized by a specific inter-joint timing that can be transformed into identifiable and harmonic auditory cues (i.e., a motor melody). That is, rhythmical structures that correspond to idealized mechanical systems could lead to the use of the appropriate inter-segmental coordination; for example, during actions that resemble catapult or whip-like motions (Chapman and Sanderson 1990; Wilson and Watson 2003). Liebermann (1997) implemented such an approach for improving the tennis serve of elite athletes.

More advanced methods of the same principles have been investigated and developed later because the advantages of such rhythmical structure feedback became obvious as a natural source of movement information, either auditory or visual (Höner *et al.* 2011). Results seem encouraging particularly in a multimodal feedback provision. Sigrist and colleagues investigated the effect of visual and auditory feedback in conjunction with haptic feedback particularly to trained expert rowers (Sigrist *et al.* 2013a, 2013b). They reported positive effects at elite levels. Their results suggest further research is needed to assess the real impact and benefit of diverse forms of multimodal feedback in sports.

4.9 Immediacy as a prerequisite for the effective use of feedback during skill acquisition

Coaches may often assume that immediate feedback is a prerequisite to improve skill. Thus, it is also assumed that technologies providing immediate feedback are beneficial for learning. However, this may not always be the case. Sometimes it may be just as effective to give feedback information after some long delay, in a specific and limited manner. This is because too much information interferes with performance and sometimes athletes need time to assimilate the information (Salmoni *et al.* 1984). Augmented feedback that is provided after each trial is counterproductive in the sense that the athlete becomes dependent on such external information instead of becoming independent. Recall that in order to learn movement based on intrinsic feedback the individual must learn the relationship between the movement produced and the proprioceptive information it provides. This is a process whereby movement outcomes are associated with the afferent information. Feedbacks of different kinds become only indispensable at the beginning of the learning process. As skill acquisition progresses and performers gain experience, augmented feedback is not essential (Winstein and Schmidt 1989; Hodges and Franks 2002). That is, as skill improves, feedback allowance should be reduced progressively until only specialized and elaborated summary feedback is relevant (Schmidt et al. 1990). Sigrist and colleagues (2013b) investigated multimodal sensory cues provided as concurrent feedback during learning, and reported that experienced athletes benefit from such a mode of training by making their performance more stable (i.e., reducing variance) but more significant improvements were seen in self-controlled terminal feedback.

4.10 Summary

Video technology has been and will continue to be used to augment feedback concurrently with motor performance. Information technologies based on video are meant to not only enhance feedback but also facilitate its delivery by reducing the video information to its essential components (e.g., through video compression, classification and feature detection algorithms; Zhang et al. 2012). IT oriented to sport has converged into efficient and easy-to-use software that allows for feedback regulation and immediacy of its provision. Feedback information therefore becomes manageable, efficient and specifically adjusted for each individual need, including those of judges, coaches and media workers. Some of the new software technologies are relatively inexpensive, including downloadable applications for cellular phones. However, the laboratory-designed hardware that may be used to convey objective, accurate information may still involve high costs and, for the time being, may be limited to research purposes. Video-based technologies are recommended in this chapter because they are relatively inexpensive and popular. The gains of such technologies are many and varied but a main advantage is visualization power, image comparisons, blending features, and primarily the ease by which these new technologies allow administering multimodal feedback to athletes and coaches.

5

AN OVERVIEW OF THE DEVELOPMENT OF NOTATION ANALYSIS

Mike Hughes

5.1 Introduction

The aim of this section is to offer as much information about notation systems as possible. The chapter is written in the form of a literature review of the research work already published in this field. Although this is written for, and by, sports scientists, it is hoped that anyone with an interest in this rapidly growing area of practice and research will find it interesting and rewarding.

It is not possible to trace the work of all those coaches and sports scientists who have contributed in one way or another to notational analysis. A large number of these innovative people did not see the point of publishing the work that they did, regarding it as merely part of their job, and consequently cannot receive the just acclaim that they deserve here in this compilation. There is no doubt that all the published workers mentioned within the following chapter could cite five or six other 'unsung' innovators who either introduced them into the field or gave them help and advice along the way.

Literature in notational analysis has been difficult to find until recently. Researchers have had to find different types of journals that would accept their papers, and so they are spread throughout many different disciplines. This chapter should help initiate a search for information on a specific sport or technique.

There are a number of texts that contain sections devoted to research in notational analysis; the best of these were, until recently, copies of the proceedings of four conferences on football (Reilly *et al.*, 1988; Reilly *et al.*, 1991; 1997; Spinks *et al.*, 2002) and racket sports respectively (Reilly *et al.*, 1995; Lees *et al.*, 1998). There is also a book *Science and Soccer*, again edited by Reilly (2003), which is a compendium of contributions by different sports scientists on the application of their own specialisms to soccer. There are three chapters in this book that are based on notational analysis and review current developments and ideas in the field.

A big step forward, to enable notational analysts to share their research and ideas, has been the introduction of world conferences on notational analysis of sport.

The proceedings of these conferences offer an invaluable compilation of notational analysis. The presentations of the first two conferences, that were in Liverpool and Cardiff respectively, are compiled in one book, *Notational Analysis of Sport I & II* (Hughes, 1998a) and the first section has a number of keynote speakers who present a varied but enlightened overview of different aspects of notational analysis. The third conference was in Turkey; Hughes (2000a) edited the proceedings, *Notational Analysis of Sport III*. The fourth was in Porto, Portugal and the book *Notational Analysis of Sport IV* was produced by Hughes and Tavares (2001). *Pass.com* are the proceedings of the Fifth World Conference of Performance Analysis of Sport which was combined with the Third International Symposium of Computers in Sports Science (Hughes and Franks, 2001). Over the 18 months preceding this conference, biomechanists and notational analysts had come together, at the request of the British Olympic Association, to explore common areas of interest and had agreed on a generic title of 'performance analysis' – hence the change in the title of the world conference. Each of these books of proceedings is sectionalised: first the keynote presentations and then into different sports or equipment development, for ease of access for the reader. The keynote speakers at *pass.com* presented their papers and they were reviewed and edited into the first edition of the International Journal of Performance Analysis of Sport (eIJPAS) (http://ramiro.catchword.com/). This is organised and managed by the Centre for Performance Analysis in Cardiff Metropolitan University. So that now we have, at last, a research journal that is for performance analysis; at this moment in time not many biomechanists are using it, so it is principally concerned with notational analysis. Since then the number of editions per year has increased to three, so there is a growing number of publications each year. The two most recent world conferences, in Belfast, 2004, Hungary, 2006, Magdeburg, 2008, Worcestor, 2012 and Opatija, 2014, also increased proportionately in size and this is reflected in the breadth and quality of the proceedings (O'Donoghue and Hughes, 2004; Dancs *et al.*, 2006; and so on).

This review is not aimed at being as comprehensive as possible, there are many reviews in the literature (Hughes and Franks, 2004; O'Donoghue, 2004; Hughes and Hughes, 2005; James, 2006), but is structured to follow the main developments in notational analysis. After tracing a historical perspective of the roots of notation, the applications of these systems to sport are then developed. These early systems were all hand notation systems, their emerging sophistication is followed until the advent of computerised notation. Although the emphasis is given to the main research developments in both hand and computerised notational systems, where possible the innovations of new systems and any significant data outputs within specific sports are also assessed.

5.2 The development of sport-specific notation systems (hand notation)

The earliest publication in notation of sport is that by Fullerton (1912) which explored the combinations of players batting, pitching and fielding and the probabilities of success. But probably the first attempt to devise a notation system specifically for sport analysis was that by Messersmith and Corey (1931), who attempted to notate distance covered by specific basketball players during a match. Messersmith led a research group at Indiana State University that initially explored movement in basketball, but went on to analyse American football and field hockey. Lyons (1996) presented a fascinating history of Messersmith's life for those interested in understanding the man behind the work.

The first publication of a comprehensive racket sport notation was not until 1973, when Downey developed a detailed system that allowed the comprehensive notation of lawn tennis matches. Detail in this particular system was so intricate that not only did it permit notation of such variables as shots used, positions, etc., but it catered for type of spin used in a particular shot. The Downey notation system has served as a useful base for the development of systems for use in other racket sports, specifically badminton and squash.

An alternative approach towards match analysis was exemplified by Reep and Benjamin (1968), who collected data from 3,213 matches between 1953 and 1968. They were concerned with actions such as passing and shooting rather than work-rates of individual players. They reported that 80 per cent of goals resulted from a sequence of three passes or less. Fifty per cent of all goals came from possession gained in the final attacking quarter of the pitch.

Bate (1988) found that 94 per cent of goals scored at all levels of international soccer were scored from movements involving four or fewer passes, and that 50–60 per cent of all movements leading to shots on goal originated in the attacking third of the field. Bate explored aspects of chance in soccer and its relation to tactics and strategy in the light of the results presented by Reep and Benjamin (1968). It was claimed that goals are not scored unless the attacking team gets the ball and one, or more, attacker(s) into the attacking third of the field. The greater the number of possessions a team has, the greater chance it has of entering the attacking third of the field, therefore creating more opportunities to score. The higher the number of passes per possession, the lower the total number of match possessions, the total number of entries into the attacking third, and the total chances of shooting at goal. Thus Bate rejected the concept of possession football and favoured a more direct strategy. He concluded that to increase the number of scoring opportunities a team should play the ball forward as often as possible; reduce square and back passes to a minimum; increase the number of long passes forward and forward runs with the ball and play the ball into space as often as possible.

These recommendations are in line with what is known as the 'direct method' or 'long-ball game'. The approach has proved successful with some teams in the lower divisions of the English league. It is questionable whether it provides a recipe for success at higher levels of play, but these data have fuelled a debate that continued through several decades. Hughes and Franks (2005) tried to demonstrate that perhaps these analyses of the data were too simplistic and that broader non-dimensional analyses give a different answer.

The definitive motion analysis of soccer, using hand notation, was by Reilly and Thomas (1976), who recorded and analysed the intensity and extent of discrete activities during match play. They combined hand notation with the use of an audio tape recorder to analyse in detail the movements of English First Division soccer players. They were able to specify work-rates of the players in different positions, distances covered in a game and the percentage time of each position in each of the different ambulatory classifications. They also found that typically a player carries the ball for less than 2 per cent of the game. Reilly *et al.* (1997) has continually added to this database, enabling him to define clearly the specific physiological demands in soccer, as well as all the football codes. The work by Reilly and Thomas has become a standard against which other similar research projects can compare their results and procedures.

Several systems have been developed for the notation of squash, the most prominent being that by Sanderson and Way (1979). Most of the different squash notation systems possess many basic similarities. The Sanderson and Way method made use of illustrative symbols to notate 17 different strokes, as well as incorporating court plans for recording accurate positional information. The major emphasis of this system was on the gathering of information concerning 'play patterns' as well as the comprehensive collection of descriptive match data. Sanderson felt that 'suggestive' symbols were better than codes, being easier for the operator to learn and remember, and devised the code system shown in Figure 5.1. These were used on a series of court representations, one court per activity, so that the player, action and position of the action were all notated (see Figure 5.2). In addition, outcomes of rallies were also recorded, together with the score and the initials of the server. The position was specified using an acetate overlay with the courts divided into 28 cells. The system took an estimated 5–8 hours of use and practice before an operator was sufficiently skilful to record a full match actually during the game. Processing the data could take as long as 40 hours of further work. Sanderson (1983) used this system to gather a database and show that squash players play in the same patterns, winning or losing, despite the supposed coaching standard of 'if you are losing change your tactics'. It would seem that the majority of players are unable to change the patterns in which they play.

Most of the data that Sanderson and Way (1979) presented was in the form of frequency distributions of shots with respect to position on the court. This was then a problem of presenting data in three dimensions – two for the court and one for the value of the frequency of the shots. Three-dimensional graphics at that time were very difficult to present in such a way that no data were lost, or that was easily visualised by those viewing the data. Sanderson overcame this problem by using longitudinal and lateral summations, Figure 5.3. Not only were the patterns of rally-ending shots examined in detail, but also those shots, ($N-1$), that preceded the end shot, and the shots that preceded those, ($N-2$). In this way the rally ending patterns of play were analysed. The major pitfall inherent in this

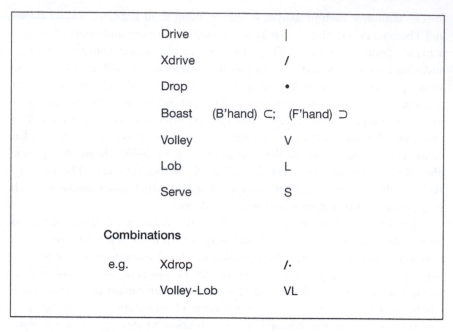

Drive |

Xdrive   /

Drop   •

Boast   (B'hand) ⊂;   (F'hand) ⊃

Volley   V

Lob   L

Serve   S

Combinations

e.g.   Xdrop   /•

       Volley-Lob   VL

FIGURE 5.1 The shot codes, or suggestive symbols, used by Sanderson (1983) for his data gathering system for squash.

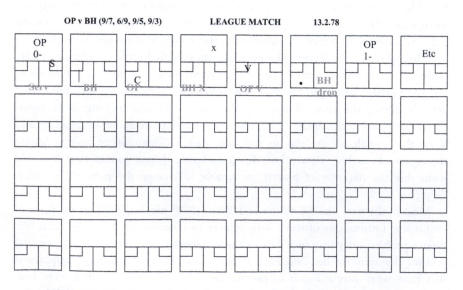

FIGURE 5.2 The data gathering sheets and example data of the shot codes, or suggestive symbols, used by Sanderson (1983) for his data gathering system for squash.

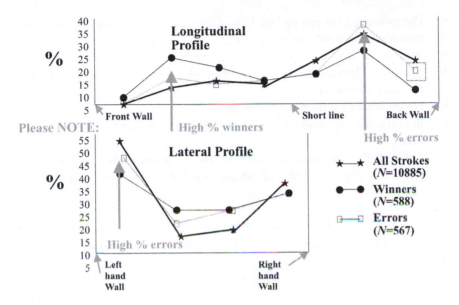

FIGURE 5.3 Example from some of Sanderson's data showing frequency distributions of all shots, winners and errors.

system, as with all long–hand systems, was the time taken to learn the system and the sheer volume of raw data generated, requiring so much time to process it.

Penalties are now a subject of myth, romance, excitement, dread, fear and pressure – depending upon whether you are watching or taking them. They have either helped careers of footballers or destroyed them. Yet little research has been completed on penalty kicks. Using a hand notation system, Hughes and Wells (2002) notated and analysed 129 penalties with an intention to examine:

- the time in preparing the shot;
- the number of paces taken to approach the ball;
- the speed of approach;
- the pace of the shot; and
- its placement and the outcome.

In addition, the actions of the goalkeeper were notated – position, body shape, movements as the player approached, his first movements and the subsequent direction, the outcome. Not all video recordings enabled all of these data to be notated, so in the subsequent analyses some of the totals are 128 and 127.

A summary of their findings is presented below:

- One in five penalties was saved (20%; 3/15), one in 15 missed (7%; 1/15) and three in four resulted in a goal (73%; 11/15).

- Players using a fast run up had 25% of their efforts saved, because the player then tried either 50% or 75% power.
- Best success ratios are from an even run up of 4, 5 and 6 paces.
- There is no laterality in the success ratios – left footers and right footers have the same success %s.
- No shots above waist height were saved.
- In every case, the goalkeeper moved forward off the line before the ball was struck.
- Although there is only a small data set, the goalkeepers who did not dive to either side while the striker approached the ball, had the best save and miss ratios.

This is a good example of hand notation providing accurate data in this age of computers, in fact the data were then entered into Access, and analysed through this database, a method used more and more. In addition, because of the nature of these data, and a performance analysis of what is virtually a closed skill situation, the data analysis provides a clear picture of the most efficient ways of penalty taking and saving.

5.3 Introduction to computerised notational analysis

Using computers does introduce extra problems of which the system-users and programmers must be aware. Increases in error possibilities are enhanced by either operator errors, or hardware and software errors. The former type of error is when the system-user unintentionally enters incorrect data, e.g. presses the wrong key on the keyboard. Any system is subject to perception-error where the observer misunderstands an event, or incorrectly fixes a position but the computer-operator interface can result in the operator thinking the correct data is being entered when it is not. This is particularly so in real-time analysis when the data must be entered quickly.

Hardware and software errors are introduced by the machinery itself, or the programs of instructions controlling the operation of the computer. Careful programming can eradicate this latter problem. To minimise both of these types of problems, careful validation of computerised notation systems must be carried out. Results from both the computerised system and a hand system should be compared and the accuracy of the computerised system quantitatively assessed.

Computers have been used by notational analysts as soon as PCs became available – and even before then Hughes (1985) was executing post-event analysis of hand notation data gathered on squash. Notation analysis readily embraced the advantages that computers brought and, as a discipline, has strived to keep abreast of the technological advances in the electronic industries, utilising the new developments in video and computing to ease data collection and enhance the interpretation of data analyses. Franks *et al.* (1983a) maintained that these forms of technology are likely to enhance manipulation and presentation due to improved efficiency. This postulation is supported by the work of Hughes (1985).

Four major purposes of notation have been delineated – they are:

1   analysis of movement
2   tactical evaluation
3   technical evaluation
4   statistical compilation.

Many of the traditional systems outlined above are concerned with the statistical analysis of events which previously had to be recorded by hand. The advent of online computer facilities overcame this problem, since the game could then be digitally represented first, via data collection directly onto the computer, and then later documented via the response to queries pertaining to the game (Franks *et al.* 1983a). The major advantage of this method of data collection is that the game is represented in its entirety and stored in read-only memory (ROM) or on disk. A database is therefore initiated and is a powerful tool once manipulated.

Team sports have the potential to benefit immensely from the development of computerised notation. The sophistication of data manipulation procedures available can aid the coach in their efforts to ameliorate performance. Many of the traditional systems outlined above are concerned with the statistical analysis of events that previously had to be recorded by hand. The advent of online computer facilities overcame this problem, since the game could then be digitally represented first, via data collection directly onto the computer, and then later documented via the response to queries pertaining to the game.

The information derived from this type of computerised system can be used for several purposes as suggested by Franks *et al.* (1983a):

(i)   immediate feedback;
(ii)   development of a database;
(iii) indication of areas requiring improvement;
(iv)   evaluation;
(v)   as a mechanism for selective searching through a video recording of the game.

All of the above functions are of paramount importance to the coaching process, the initial *raison d'être* of notational analysis. The development of a database is a crucial element, since it is sometimes possible, if the database is large enough, to formulate predictive models as an aid to the analysis of different sports, subsequently enhancing future training and performance.

5.4 Some research using computer systems

One of the first developments in computerised notation has been the development of a mini system devised by Franks *et al.* (1983a). Franks configured a keyboard on a mini-computer to resemble the layout of a soccer field and designed a program that yielded frequency tallies of various features of play. The path of the ball during the game was followed, so off-ball incidents were considered extraneous. A video was time-locked into the system so that relevant sections of the match could be replayed visually alongside the computer analysis.

An essential prerequisite of evaluation is that it must be carried out as objectively as possible; Franks *et al.* (1983b) maintained that "'if it can be measured – it is fact, if it cannot be measured – it remains opinion", also applies to the coaching arena' (p. 77). It was suggested as a result of the analysis, that it would be extremely beneficial to performance if coaches could advise players to keep the number of passes in sequence down to three or fewer. This application of the research could be improved and a more thorough analysis of the parameters required to enhance the result. Minimal consideration was given to the number of games to be notated prior to the establishment of a recognised system of play. This is an important point, since any fluctuation in the patterns and profile will affect the deduced consequences, particularly with reference to the match outcome. Teams may also vary their system and pattern of play according to opponents, although these factors are not considered. Furthermore, the existence of patterns of play peculiar to individual players was not illustrated. It is in this area that the study by Church and Hughes (1986) concentrated, in an attempt to investigate the presence of patterns of play in a soccer team and whether any reasons can be found to explain the results.

Church and Hughes developed a computerised notation system for analysing soccer matches using an alternative type of keyboard, called a concept keyboard. This is a touch sensitive pad that can be programmed to accept input to the computer. This permitted pitch representation to be graphically accurate and action and player keys to be specific and labelled. This considerably reduced the learning time of the system, and made the data input quicker and more accurate. The system enabled an analysis of patterns of play on a team and player level, and with respect to match outcome. An analysis of six matches played by Liverpool during the 1985/6 season resulted in a number of conclusions, the most important of which were:

1   a greater number of passes were attempted when losing than when winning;
2   possession was lost more often when losing;
3   a greater number of shots were taken when losing than when winning.

Hughes, Robertson and Nicholson (1988) used the same concept keyboard and hardware system developed by Church and Hughes (1986), but with modified software, to analyse the 1986 World Cup finals. Patterns of play of successful teams, those teams that reached the semi-finals, were compared with those of unsuccessful teams, i.e. teams that were eliminated at the end of the first rounds. A summary of the main observations is as follows:

1   Successful teams played significantly more touches of the ball per possession than unsuccessful teams.

2   The unsuccessful teams ran with the ball and dribbled the ball in their own defensive area in different patterns to the successful teams. The latter played up the middle in their own half, the former used the wings more.

3   This pattern was also reflected in the passing of the ball. The successful teams approached the final sixth of the pitch by playing predominantly in the central areas while the unsuccessful teams played significantly more to the wings.

4   Unsuccessful teams lost possession of the ball significantly more in the final one sixth of the playing area both in attack and defence.

Hughes (1985) modified the method of Sanderson and Way so that the hand-notated data could be processed on a mainframe computer. The manual method was modified so that a match could be notated live at courtside using a microcomputer. Because of difficulties with the speed of the game and the storage capacity only one player was notated. Hughes established a considerable database on different standards of squash players and reviewed his work in squash in 1986. He examined and compared the differences in patterns of play between recreational players, country players and nationally ranked players, using the computerised notational analysis system he had developed. The method involved the digitisation of all the shots and court positions, and there were entered via the QWERTY keyboard.

A detailed analysis of the frequency distribution of shots showed that the recreational players were not accurate enough to sustain a tactical plan, being erratic with both their straight drives and their cross-court drives. They played more short shots, and although they hit more winners they also hit more errors.

The county players played a simple tactical game generally, keeping the ball deep and predominantly on the backhand, the weaker side of most players. They hit significantly more winners with straight drives. Their short game, consisting of boasts, drops and rally-drops, although significantly less accurate than the nationally ranked players, was significantly more accurate than the recreational players.

The nationally ranked players, because of their far greater fitness, covering ability and better technique, employed the more complex tactics, using an 'all-court' game. Finally, the serves of the county players and the recreational players, because of shorter rallies, assumed greater importance than the serves of the ranked players.

Hughes, Franks and Nagelkerke (1989) were interested in analysing the motions of athletes of any sport, without having to resort to the long and arduous job of cinematographic analysis, nor the semi–qualitative methods associated with notational methods, used live or from video. They attempted to combine the best of both systems without the faults of either. They designed a tracking system that enabled the use of the immediacy of video, and, by using mixed images on the same VDU screen, accurate measurements of the velocities and accelerations of the players, usually associated with film analysis. A 'Power Pad ' was used to gather positional data along with the time base. The playing area representation on the Power Pad was videotaped and its image mixed with that of the subject tape. Careful alignment of the images of the two 'playing areas' enabled the subject and the tracking stylus on the bit pad to be both viewed at the same time, and an accurate tracing of the movements of the player onto the simulated playing area in real-time. A careful validation of the system showed its accuracy and the short learning time required by operators.

Hughes and Franks (1991) utilised this system and applied it to squash, comparing the motions of players of differing standards. They presented comparative profiles for four different standards of players, spanning from club players to the world elite. The profiles consisted of analyses of distance travelled, velocities and accelerations during rallies. The work provides reference data against which physiological studies of squash play can be compared. In addition the distance travelled during rallies by both recreational and regular club players was surprisingly short, the mean distance being approximately 12 metres for both top club players and recreational players. Hughes and Franks were able to present suggestions about specific training drills for the sport. Their system could also compare the individual profile of a player to those of his peer group, so giving a direct expression of his relative fitness; as an example they chose to analyse some of the reasons why Jahangir Khan had dominated squash for so long. This profile was of the 1989, and seven times, World Champion Jahangir Khan, compared to the top six in the world (which data included his own profile). The data clearly showed the vast physical advantage that he had over the best athletes in the world at this sport.

A more recent innovation in attempting to solve the problems of data entry was the utilisation of a new language, visual basic, that enables a graphical user interface, that is, the operator, to enter data by moving an arrow round the screen using the 'mouse' and clicking to enter a selected item. All IBM-compatible systems can run these software packages. This language was used to write a system for squash, which was used by Brown and Hughes (1995) to examine the effectiveness of quantitative feedback to squash players. While this system of data entry will not be as quick as the concept keyboard, when used by a fully trained and experienced operator, it is again very easy to use, attractive to the eye and the extra hardware requirements are nil. It was used by Hughes and Knight (1995) to examine the differences in the game of squash when played under 'point-per-rally' scoring as opposed to the more traditional English scoring. The former had been introduced to most senior international tournaments because it was believed to promote more 'attacking' play, shorter rallies and hence make the game more attractive. It was found that the rallies were slightly longer on average, not significantly so, that there were more winners and the same errors – this being attributed to the lower height of the 'tin' under these new rules.

A similar system was used by Hughes and Clarke (1995) to analyse the differences in the playing patterns of players at Wimbledon, on grass, to those of players at the Australian Open, on a synthetic surface. They found very significant differences between the two surfaces, particularly with the ball in play time. This averaged about 10 per cent for the synthetic surface (14 mins in an average match of just over two hours) while it was as low as 5 per cent on grass (7 mins in an average match of just over two hours). This work, that of Hughes and Knight (1995) and some analyses of squash tournaments using tennis scoring, prompted Hughes (1995a) to analyse and recommend a new scoring system in squash to try to make the game more attractive. Hughes recognised the need to shorten the cycles of play leading to 'critical' points in squash – currently it takes about 15–20 minutes to reach a game-ball. By having more, shorter games, more critical points will arise and this will raise the levels of excitement and crowd interest. Badminton has the same problems with its scoring systems and the ensuing activity cycles.

McGarry and Franks (1994) created a stochastic model of championship squash match-play that inferred prospective patterns of play from previous performance through forecasting shot response and associated outcome from the preceding shot. The results were restricted because it was found that players produced the same patterns of responses against the same opponent ($p > 0.25$) but an inconsistent response was found when competing against different opponents ($p < 0.25$). This contradicts earlier work by Sanderson (1983) who found that squash players played in the same patterns against different opponents, whether winning or losing, but this may well be a function of the finer degree to which McGarry and Franks were measuring the responses of the players. However, these results led to further analysis by these authors (1995) of behavioural response to a preceding athletic event and they again found the same results. They confirmed that sport analysis can reliably assume a prescriptive application in preparing for future athletic competition, but only if consistent behavioural data can be established. The traditional planning of match strategies from a priori sport information (scouting) against the same opponent would otherwise seem to be an expedient and necessary constraint. A review of work completed in the computerised analysis of racket sports (Hughes, 1995b), together with a number of papers in match analysis of racket sports, is included in *Science and Racket Sports* (Reilly et al., 1995).

Murray, Maylor and Hughes (1998) researched into the effect of computerised notational analysis as feedback on improving squash performance. This study used a similar method to that of Brown and Hughes (1995) on the effectiveness of quantitative and qualitative feedback in squash. It was concluded that both groups reacted positively to the feedback provided and the feedback from notation analysis accounted for an increase in the number of winners and a decrease in the number of errors. From this evidence it is clear that notation analysis has its uses as an effective practical tool during the coaching of performance.

5.5 Modelling

The modelling of competitive sport is an informative analytic technique because it directs the attention of the modeller to the critical aspects of data which delineate successful performance. The modeller searches for an underlying signature of sport performance which is a reliable predictor of future sport behaviour. Stochastic models have not yet, to our knowledge, been used further to investigate sport at the behavioural level of analysis.

However, the modelling procedure is readily applicable to other sports and could lead to useful and interesting results.

(Franks and McGarry, 1996, p. 282)

Some exciting trends are to be found in modelling performances and match play, using a variety of techniques; many examples can be found in the Journals now available in these disciplines, the *International Journal of Performance Analysis of Sport* (electronic – eIJPAS) and the *International Journal of Computers in Sport Science* (electronic – eIJCSS). The simplest, and traditional, form is using empirical methods of producing enough performance data to define a performance profile at that particular level. Some researchers are extending the use of these forms of databases to attempt to predict performances; stochastic probabilities, neural networks and fuzzy logic have been used, singly or in combinations, to produce the outputs. McGarry and Perl (2004) presented a good overview of models in sports contest which embraces most of these techniques. So far results have been a little disappointing in practical terms. It does seem to have potential – perhaps if we added a dash of feng shui?

Early research of modelling in sport includes Mosteller (1979), who set out guidelines when he developed a predictive model, and these ideas are eminently practical and many researchers in the area use these, or modifications of these to delimit their models.

Other attempts to model team games (Ladany and Machol, 1977) theoretically have tended to founder upon the complexity of the numbers of variables involved and, at that time, did not base their predictions upon sound databases. The advent of computer notation systems has enabled the creation of large databases of sports performances in different sports; these in turn have helped the development of a number of different techniques in modelling performance in sport. These will be discussed under the following generic headings:

- Empirical modelling
- Stochastic modelling
- Dynamic systems
- Statistical techniques
- Artificial intelligence
- Expert systems
- Neural networks.

5.5.1 Empirical models

Hughes (1985) pioneered using databases to create empirical models of tactics and technique – he used a PC to gather data and established a considerable database on different standards of squash players. He examined and compared the differences in patterns of play between recreational players, country players and nationally ranked players, using the computerised notational analysis system he had developed.

The method involved the digitisation of all the shots and court positions, and these were entered via the QWERTY keyboard. Hughes (1986) was able then to define models of tactical patterns of play, and inherently technical ability, at different playing levels in squash. Although racket developments have affected the lengths of the rallies, and there have been a number of rule changes in the scoring systems in squash, these tactical models still apply to the game today. This study was replicated, with a far more thorough methodology, for the women's game by Hughes *et al.* (2000d).

Fuller (1990) developed and designed a Netball Analysis System and focused on game modelling from a database of 28 matches in the 1987 World Netball Championships. There were three main components to the research – to develop a notation and analysis system, to record performance, and to investigate the prescience of performance patterns that would distinguish winners from losers. The system could record how each tactical entry started; the player involved and the court area through which the ball travelled; the reason for each ending; and an optional comment. The software produced the data according to shooting analysis; centre pass analysis; loss of possession; player profiles; and circle feeding. Fuller's (1990) intention of modelling play was to determine the routes that winning, drawing and losing teams took and to identify significantly different patterns. From the results Fuller was able to differentiate between the performances of winning and losing teams. The differences were both technical and tactical.

The research was an attempt to model winning performance in elite netball and more research needed in terms of the qualitative aspects, i.e. how are more shooting opportunities created. The model should be used to monitor performance over a series of matches not on one-off performances.

Empirical models enable both the academic and consultant sports scientist to make conclusions about patterns of play of sample populations of athletes within their sport. This, in turn, gives the academic the potential to examine the development and structures of different sports with respect to different levels of play, rule changes, introduction of professionalism, etc. The consultant analyst can utilise these models to compare performances of peer athletes or teams to the performances of those with whom the analyst is working.

5.5.2 Dynamic systems

Modelling human behaviour is implicitly a very complex mathematical exercise; it is multidimensional, and these dimensions will depend upon two or three spatial dimensions together with time. But the outcomes of successful analyses offer huge rewards, as Kelso (1995) pointed out:

- If we study a system only in the linear range of its operation where change is smooth, it's difficult if not impossible to determine which variables are essential and which are not.
- Most scientists know about nonlinearity and usually try to avoid it.

• Here we exploit qualitative change, a nonlinear instability, to identify collective variables, the implication being that because these variables change abruptly, it is likely that they are also the key variables when the system operates in the linear range.

Recent research exploring mathematical models of human behaviour led to populist theories categorised by 'Catastrophe Theory' and 'Chaos Theory'.

5.5.2.1 Critical incident technique

At the First World Congress of Notational Analysis of Sport (1992), Downey talked of rhythms in badminton rackets, athletes in 'cooperation' playing rhythmic rallies, until there was a dislocation of the rhythm (a good shot or conversely a poor shot) – a 'perturbation' – sometimes resulting in a rally end situation (a 'critical incident'), sometimes not. A good defensive recovery can result in the re-establishment of the rhythm. This was the first time that most of us had considered different sports as an example of a multidimensional, periodic dynamic system.

The term 'critical incident' was first coined by Flanagan (1954) in a study designed to identify why student pilots were exhausted at flight school. 'The critical incident technique outlines procedures for collecting observed incidents having special significance and meeting systematically defined criteria' (p. 30). The critical incident technique is a powerful research tool but as with other forms of notating behaviour there are limitations inherent in the technique. Flanagan (1954) admitted that 'Critical incidents represent only raw data and do not automatically provide solutions to problems' (p. 30). But Flanagan also pointed to the advantages of such a technique: 'The critical incident technique, rather than collecting opinions, hunches and estimates, obtains a record of specific behaviours from those in the best position to make the necessary observations and evaluations.'

These opinions sound very much like the debates that have surrounded notational analysis within the halls of sports science over the last decade.

Research in sport has addressed some of these issues and notation and movement analysis systems have been developed that can overcome some of these disadvantages. Since Downey's suggestions in 1992, some researchers have investigated the possibilities that analysing 'perturbations' and 'critical incidents' offer. McGarry and Franks (1996a, b and d) applied further research to tennis and squash. They derived that every sporting situation contains unique rhythmical patterns of play. This behavioural characteristic is said to be the stable state or dynamic equilibrium. The research suggested that there are moments of play where the cycle is broken and a change in flow occurs. Such a moment of play is called a 'perturbation'. It occurs when either a poorly executed skill or a touch of excellence forces a disturbance in the stability of the game. For example, in a game of rugby this could be a bad pass or immediate change of pace. From this situation the game could unfold one of two ways; either the flow of play could be re-established through defensive excellence or an attacking error, or it could result in loss of possession or a try that would end the flow. When the perturbation results in a loss of possession or a try, it was then defined as a 'critical incident'; sometimes the perturbation may be 'smoothed out' by good defensive play or poor attacking play and not lead to a critical incident. A more in–depth approach is essential in order to derive a system for analysing the existence of perturbations. In order to do so, entire phases of play must be analysed and notated accordingly.

Applying McGarry and Franks' (1995) work on perturbations in squash, Hughes et al. (2000a) attempted to confirm and define the existence of perturbations in soccer. Using 20 English league matches, the study found that perturbations could be consistently classified and identified, but also that it was possible to generate specific profiles of variables that identify winning and losing traits. After further analyses of the 1996 European Championship matches ($N=31$), Hughes et al. (2000c) attempted to create a profile for nations that had played more than five matches. Although supporting English league traits for successful and unsuccessful teams, there was insufficient data for the development of a comprehensive normative profile. Consequently, although failing to accurately predict perform-ance it introduced the method of using perturbations to construct a prediction model. By identifying 12 common attacking and defending perturbations that exist in English football leading to scoring opportunities, Hughes et al. (2000c) had obtained variables that could underpin many studies involving perturbations. These 12 causes were shown to occur consistently, covering all possible eventualities and had a high reliability. Although Hughes et al. (2000a and b) had classified per-turbations, the method prevented the generation of a stable and accurate performance profile. In match play, teams may alter tactics and style according to the game state; for instance a team falling behind may revert to a certain style of play to create goal-scoring chances and therefore skew any data away from an overall profile.

In some instances, a perturbation may not result in a shot, owing to high defensive skill or a lack of attacking skill. Developing earlier work on British league football, Hughes et al. (2000b) analysed how the international teams stabilise or 'smooth out' the disruption. Analysing the European Championships in 1996, attempts were made to identify perturbations that did not lead to a shot on goal. Hughes et al. (2000b) refined the classifications to three types of causes: actions by the player in possession, actions by the receiver and interceptions. Inaccuracy of pass accounted for 62 per cent of the player in possession variables and interception by the defence accounted for the vast majority of defensive actions (68 per cent). Actions of the receiver (12 per cent) were dominated by a loss of control; however, these posses-sions have great importance because of the increased proximity to the shot (critical incident). Conclusions therefore focussed on improvements in technical skill of players; however, with patterns varying from team to team, combining data provides little benefit for coaches and highlights the need for analysing an individual team's 'signature'.

Squash is potentially an ideal sport for analysing perturbations, and as such has received considerable attention from researchers. It is of a very intense nature and is confined to a small space. The rhythms of the game are easy to see, and the rallies are of a length (mean number of shots at elite level = 14; Hughes and Robertson, 1998) that enables these rhythms and their disruption, i.e. perturbations and critical incidents. In defining perturbations, it may help to understand the reasons for this occurrence: consider the simplest model of a dynamic oscillating system. What are the main parameters and do the equivalent variables in sports contests conform to the same behaviour?

Squash coaches often talk about players imposing their own rhythms on the game – can this be measured by identifying specific values of ω, the frequency of play, for specific players and how does this vary against different opponents? This could be repeated in different individual and team sports.

Critical incident and/or perturbation analysis seems to offer a way of making sense of all the masses of data that is available from an analysis of a team sport such as soccer – even a 'simple' sport such as squash will have 4000–6000 bits of data per match. The resultant data output can be so overwhelming as to leave coaches and sports scientists struggling to see significant patterns among the thousands and thousands of bits of data. This method appears to direct analysts to those important aspects of the data that shape winning and losing models; recent research had demonstrated that player profiles of perturbation shots are stable and differ from player to player (Hughes *et al.*, 2007a).

Simple harmonic motion

Simple harmonic motion is the simplest model of periodic motion and has a simple elegance to it.

Simple harmonic motion (SHM) refers to the periodic sinusoidal oscillation of an object or quantity. Take, for example, a mass suspended on a spring (see Figure 5.4). When displaced the mass will move up and down in SHM, under the forces of the tension in the spring and gravity. This motion is not dissimilar in rhythm to a squash player's movement around the 'T' (the centre of the court) during a rally. SHM is executed by any quantity obeying the differential equation:

Displacement:

$$Y = A\sin(\omega t).$$

This ordinary differential equation has an irregular singularity at ∞.

Hence the velocity, (dx/dt):

$$V = (dx/dt) = \omega A \cos(\omega t),$$

and the acceleration, (d^2x/dt^2):

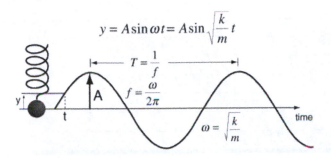

FIGURE 5.4 A schematic example of simple harmonic motion (SHM Website).

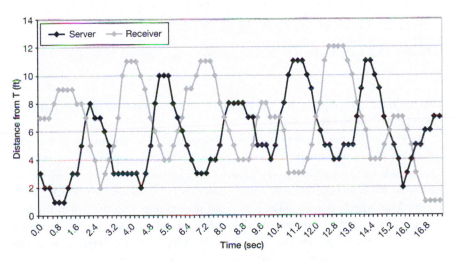

FIGURE 5.5 Distance from the 'T' (m) against time (s) graph for squash players.

Source: Peakman (2001).

$$a = (d^2x/dt^2)$$

$$= -\omega^2 A \sin(\omega t)$$

$$= -\omega^2 y$$

where the two constants, A and ω, are determined from the dynamic conditions.

If the basic principles of SHM are used as a model for the movement of a squash player in the game – with the 'T' the central focus of the court as the origin of movement – then we can examine some simple concepts. This is the simplest form of oscillating motion and is therefore a good place to start. There are immediate limitations in these ideas – that the 'T' is neither the geometrical centre of the court, and the player does not really follow the velocity patterns of classic SHM. A squash player will return to the 'T' and stop, retaining their balance to be able to move in any direction, while in SHM the oscillating particle attains maximum

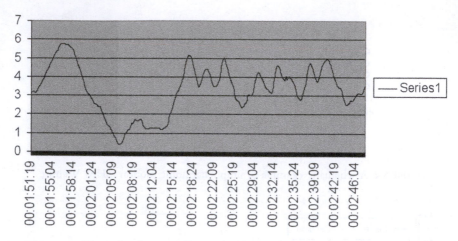

FIGURE 5.6 Example of a perturbation that was 'smoothed out' at time = 2.06:08.

velocity at the central point. It is surprising then how well the actual motion (Figure 5.5) matches the SHM model.

By examining the 'stability' of these constants A (the amplitude) and ω (the frequency of the movement) or T (the wavelength), it is hoped that we will get a reasonable fit to the model, and then be able to identify quantitatively where the variations become large enough to be classed as perturbations (Peakman, 2001; Figure 5.6). Squash coaches often talk about players imposing their own rhythms on the game – can this be measured by identifying specific values of ω, the frequency of play, for specific players and how does this vary against different opponents? This could be repeated in different individual and team sports.

Many physical systems undergoing small displacements, including any objects obeying Hooke's Law, exhibit SHM. This equation arises, for example, in the analysis of the flow of current in an electronic CL circuit (which contains a capacitor and an inductor). If a damping force such as friction is present, an additional term $\beta \, (dx/dt)$ must be added to the differential equation and motion dies out over time. Perhaps more complex models such as Damped SHM can be pursued in further research.

Critical incident and/or perturbation analysis seems to offer a way of making sense of all the masses of data that are available from an analysis of a team sport such as soccer – even a 'simple' sport such as squash will have 4000–6000 bits of data per match. The resultant data output can be so overwhelming as to leave coaches and sports scientists struggling to see significant patterns among the thousands and thousands of bits of data. This method appears to direct analysts to those important aspects of the data that shape winning and losing models.

5.5.3 *Statistical techniques*

Historically, the prediction of sports performance has been a concept usually reserved for those associated with the betting culture. However, in reality, each and every person involved within sport will subconsciously process information to predict sports performance. Performance prediction could be described as the ability to draw conclusions upon the outcome of future performance based upon the combined interaction of previously gathered information, knowledge or data. For players and coaches, predictions are often made about forthcoming opponents based upon previous encounters and known traits. Therefore, is it not reasonable to assume that with valid and reliable information, using the correct techniques, the accurate prediction of performance should be possible? From a sports science perspective, the most common approaches to performance prediction use large amounts of data and apply statistical techniques. Human predictions, however, are entirely derived from one's underpinning knowledge and subjective bias, although the 'experts' are able to accommodate a greater understanding and opportunity for the element of chance and uncertainty, unlike computerised models of performance prediction that are entirely statistically driven, such as multiple linear regression.

In an evaluation of human and computer-based prediction models for the 2003 Rugby World Cup (Table 5.1), O'Donoghue and Williams (2004) identified that the best human predictor performed better than any computer-based model, although the mean score of all the human predictions fell below each of the computer-based models that were used, unquestionably a result of the subjectivity within human prediction. Interestingly, in a similar study during the 2002 Soccer World Cup (O'Donoghue *et al.*, 2003), although the best computer-based models outperformed the human predictors once again, their overall effectiveness in predicting results was far inferior compared to the 2003 Rugby World Cup. Ironically, only the human-based focus group was able to predict four of the eight quarter-finalists and no method predicted more than one of the semi-finalists, whereas *all* of the computer-based models for the 2003 Rugby World Cup predicted seven of the eight quarter-finalists and three of the four semi-finalists.

However, this is understandable considering the inherent differences between soccer and rugby union. Very few upsets occur within rugby union and with only one drawn match during World Cup rugby from 1987 (O'Donoghue *et al.*, 2004), results generally go to form. Research by Garganta and Gonçalves (1996) led to the notion that among team sports, soccer presents one of the lowest success rates in the ratio of goals scored to the number of attacking actions performed, subsequently increasing the likelihood of drawn matches and upsets. This considered, unlike rugby union in which the number of points scored is far greater, the accurate prediction of soccer matches is far more difficult, a notion shared by O'Donoghue and Williams (2004) and demonstrated by O'Donoghue *et al.* (2003).

Making suggestions upon the types of data that should be used is difficult and ultimately reliant upon what is actually available. Historically, research in soccer, and similar team sports, that has attempted to identify the characteristics of a

TABLE 5.1 Marks awarded for each prediction

Method	Marks awarded					
	Group matches (40)	Quarter-finals (4)	Semi-finals (2)	3rd place play off (1)	Final (1)	Total (48)
Human-based methods						
Best individual human	39.00	4.00	2.00	1.00	0.00	46.00
Mean human prediction	35.63	3.45	1.17	0.26	0.31	40.66
Expert focus group	37.00	4.00	1.00	0.00	1.00	43.00
Computer-based methods						
Multiple linear regression (satisfies assumptions)	38.00	4.00	1.00	0.00	0.00	43.00
Multiple linear regression (violates assumptions)	38.00	4.00	1.00	0.00	1.00	44.00
Binary logistic regression	37.00	4.00	1.00	0.00	1.00	43.00
Neural networks with numeric input	37.00	4.00	1.00	0.00	1.00	43.00
Neural network with binary input – 4 middle layer nodes	34.00	3.00	1.00	0.00	1.00	39.00
Neural network with binary input – 8 middle layer nodes	34.00	4.00	1.00	0.00	1.00	40.00
Neural network with binary input – 16 middle layer nodes	36.00	4.00	1.00	0.00	1.00	42.00
Neural network with binary input – 32 middle layer nodes	37.00	4.00	1.00	0.00	1.00	43.00
Simulation program	38.50	4.00	1.00	0.00	1.00	44.50

successful team has used game-related performance indicators rather than factors such as distance travelled (Hughes *et al.*, 1988, Yamanaka *et al.*, 1993). By using process-orientated data, such as pass completion, shots on target and entries into the attacking third for example, a more accurate picture of a team's abilities would be created that directly relates to the dynamic processes involved in soccer. Although large databases of such information are available, the validity of the data in terms of defining successful performance is questionable and unsubstantiated. In order for performance prediction to move forward, not only within soccer, it is imperative that issues such as this are addressed, along with the continued development of valid and reliable methods of performance prediction.

By using multivariate linear regression (MLR), a number of conditions must be accepted in considering its use as a prediction tool. The method is not based upon any 'artificial learning' process in order to generate predictions and predicts each game on its own merit without consideration for other factors. The simulation package used by O'Donoghue and Williams (2004) favoured Brazil to win the 2002 World Cup, rather than France who were the strongest team in the tournament. The model took into consideration the probabilities of qualifying from the group stages and then progressing through the knock-outs against different ranked opposition and predicted that Brazil had a greater chance of winning the fixture against France, should they have actually qualified from the group stages, because of the events preceding the potential tie. However, MLR would simply identify that France had both a superior rank and far less travelling distance than Brazil and would predict France to win the tie. This simplistic approach of MLR and indeed other algorithmic methods such as binary logistic regression is their fundamental drawback, although the results of these research papers quoted proved that even the most simplistic approach can be relatively effective.

5.5.4 Artificial intelligence

Bartlett (2004) presented a broad overview of artificial intelligence (AI) encompassing speech recognition, natural language processing, computer vision (which would include online motion analysis systems that automatically track and assign markers, e.g. EVA real time, Vicon), and decision making. He suggested that the intelligent core of AI included:

- expert systems:
  - rule-based;
  - fuzzy;
  - frame-based; and
  - their uses.
- artificial neural networks (ANNs):
  - biological and artificial neural networks;
  - the Perceptron;
  - multilayer neural networks;

–   recurrent neural networks (we won't consider these);
–   self-organising neural networks; and
–   their uses.

This is a fascinating area of research and applied theory, and the potential developments here for performance analysts are limitless.

5.5.4.1 Expert systems

Rule-based expert systems

These are, effectively, a database combined with a knowledge base, 'reasoning' and a user interface. They can encompass a knowledge base that contains specific knowledge for 'domain', e.g. diagnosis of sports technique 'errors'. The 'reasoning' comes from rules that can be relations, recommendations, directives, strategies, or heuristics. They can include logic operations, just as a computer program will contain conditional operators. The inference engine 'reasons' by linking the rules with the facts, and finally, the explanation facilities explain how a conclusion was reached and why a specific fact is needed.

Uncertainty in expert systems

In most applications, knowledge rules based on simple logic, as in the mixed technique example, do not apply. This 'uncertainty' can be managed by (Bayesian) probability theory, e.g.

*   IF 'counter-rotation' is high
*   THEN 'technique' is mixed ($p = 0.8$).

This example was chosen to illustrate that much information is vague – 'high' in the above example has in recent research varied from 10 to 20 to as much as 30 to 40 degrees. This type of information is classed as 'fuzzy'.

Fuzzy expert systems

The difference between 'crisp' and 'fuzzy' knowledge is shown for fast bowling in Figure 5.7. This type of representation deals with fuzzy knowledge, which may be shown by linear or non-linear (e.g. sigmoidal) functions. Qualitative statements ('Hedges'), such as 'a little' or 'very' can be used to modify the fuzzy shapes. Domain knowledge can be interpreted by fuzzy rules, similar to those for rule-based systems but using fuzzy logic not simple logic. They offer great potential in quantifying the vagueness of much knowledge.

Frame-based expert systems

In these expert systems, knowledge is represented as 'frames', with 'attributes', rather as in many conventional databases. They 'structure' knowledge; for example, a frame-based system might contain a player's name, weight, height, age, position in last game, goals scored, passes made, tackles made, infringements and so on. By using 'object-oriented programming', frames communicate with each other by rules. Frames can belong to 'classes', e.g. forwards, midfielders, defenders, keepers.

Expert systems – advantages

- separate knowledge from processing, unlike conventional programmes;
- provide an explanation facility;
- can deal with incomplete and vague data;
- can model fuzzy human decision making;
- are good for diagnosis;
- 'Shells' for development of expert systems are widely available (e.g. add-ons to MATLAB).

Expert systems – disadvantages

- need to acquire knowledge from experts; this is a major problem;
- very domain-specific; the fast bowling system could not be used for javelin throwing;
- opaque relationships between rules;
- in general, do not have an ability to 'learn';
- have to manage conflicts between rules;
- ineffective rules searching – trawl through all rules in each cycle;
- relatively complex programs.

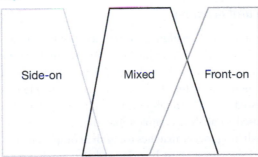

Fuzzy Fast Bowling Technique Classification

Crisp Fast Bowling Technique Classification

FIGURE 5.7 A comparison of 'crisp' and 'fuzzy' knowledge for fast bowling.

Source: Bartlett (2004).

Expert systems in performance analysis

Bartlett (2004) reported that a search of Medline with 'expert systems' yielded 480 references, but when these were redefined toward 'sport' or 'exercise' the results were reduced to nine strikes, and none of these was on sport. Expert systems in gait analysis offer a great deal more than any other areas of performance analysis. They have been shown to be relatively successful and can identify abnormalities that human observations missed.

The lack of applications in performance analysis of sport can be attributed to the fact that in sport the analyses are even more complex than gait analysis. There has been weak developmental motivation, as sport performance coaches and sport scientists are not expensive – they are poorly paid generally in comparison to the health profession. There are further difficulties because the analyses are often field-based, prohibiting, to date, automatic tracking. The great number and variety of sports create a large amount of various specialists – technique analysts, notational analysts, thus in turn making a broad expert domain. There is not a lot of data for technique analysis expert systems and comparatively fewer experts in each specific field than gait analysis.

It is still surprising that these types of expert systems have not been taken up and applied in the area of coaching. The type of diagnostic logic needed in the coaching of technique lends itself perfectly to the structure of rule-based expert systems. Perhaps this is an area that we can see developing hand in hand with coach development and education. In terms of modelling sports performance and for research purposes, other AI tools appear more promising.

5.5.4.2 Neural networks

The future of research within performance prediction undoubtedly lies in the development of artificial intelligence systems such as neural networking. In simplistic terms, an artificial neural network is a computer-simulated mathematical model of the neurons within the human brain that is able to learn from experience. It was suggested by O'Donoghue and Williams (2004) that neural networks are commonly used to analyse complex information and could ultimately be used as a tool for predicting soccer matches using the complex game-related data identified previously. However, it must be accepted that predicting the outcome of sports performance consistently and accurately is unlikely to be made possible even with the most sophisticated of computerised systems; after all, it is the unpredictability of sport that continues to capture the imagination of millions of people across the world.

The term neural network refers to a specific type of computational model, whose origins are found in the properties of neurons (i.e. nerve cells) and their interactions. Simply put, neurons receive inputs and send outputs in relay fashion, that is to say that the outputs serve as inputs to other neurons in the network (Figure 5.8). There are two main tasks that neural networks are used for, and these two tasks lend the specific characteristics to the two types of networks that service these tasks.

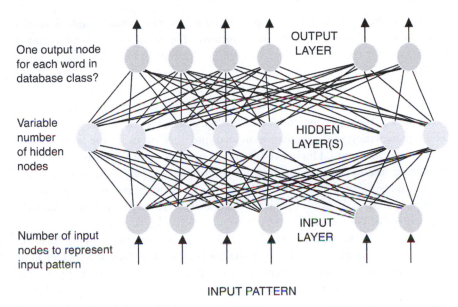

One output node
for each word in
database class?

OUTPUT
LAYER

Variable
number
of hidden
nodes

HIDDEN
LAYER(S)

Number of input
nodes to represent
input pattern

INPUT
LAYER

INPUT PATTERN

FIGURE 5.8 Neural network architecture: fully interconnected three-layer network.

The first task that neural networks can be used for is to recognise patterns, such as pictures, situations, processes, or any other types of structured objects. For this task, a special type of neural network is used which is called a Kohonen Feature Map (KFM). The characteristics of a KFM are that these networks are able to learn by forming clusters in response to a set of training patterns. These learning features allow the network to later identify other arbitrary patterns by associating these patterns to one of the already learned clusters within the network.

The second task that neural networks can be used for is in the selection of actions, in particular those actions that are identified as being optimal for given situations. One application of these tasks is the ability to make behavioural decisions in the context of sports games. For this task of selecting actions, a different type of network is used that often makes use of the attributes of 'feed forward' and 'back propagation' (Figure 5.8).

5.6 Current areas of research and support

Most of the support that is currently being offered to England Squash is based upon the work of Murray and Hughes (2001). During their research they offered England Squash various types of feedback from information gathered using the squash winner and error analysis technology (SWEAT) and the full analyses systems. Analyses ranging from simple winner and error ratios to complex rally ending patterns were produced from the computerised systems. Using the full analysis system (Brown and Hughes, 1995) they analysed five matches of a particular player and pooled the data from these five matches into a single database. From these data the system is able to produce up to 300 different distribution graphs from the different combinations of shots and positions. This is of course far too much information for coaches and players to use. So Murray and Hughes (2001), using feedback from coaches and players and their years of experience, condensed the information into bullet points that were used as a storyboard to accompany an edited video of the player. After further feedback the information was normalised, converted into percentages and condensed further onto a representation of the court. The representation of the court was divided into 16 sections (in the same manner as the SWEAT system, Hughes and Robertson, 1998) with the areas of the court containing unusual data analysed with respect to shot type. These profiles could be created for winners, errors, and N–1 and N–2 for winners and errors. The profiles were presented at a national squad and the players were very receptive of the style and content of the feedback.

The paper by Murray and Hughes (2001) was also the first to introduce the concept of momentum analysis. From the SWEAT analysis they already had all of the information concerning winners and errors during a particular match. By writing a new program they were able to give players a running score (momentum) during a match depending on the rally ending shots. A winning shot by a player was given a '+1' score, an error a '–1' score, and if the opponent hit the rally-end shot, or it was a let, the score stayed the same. From this information line graphs could be drawn to visually show any swings in momentum during a match. These lines graphs can also be coupled with data regarding rally length to highlight whether any swings in momentum are perhaps fitness related. This work was born from conversations with the SRA psychologist who was interested to see whether extremes of body language had any effect on the outcome of the next three or four rallies. By matching up positive or negative forms of body language on tape with points on the graph, the psychologist was then able to see how these physical outbursts affected the momentum of the players.

The research into momentum analysis was furthered by Hughes et al. (2006b) who analysed matches of elite squash players ($N = 8$ per player; six male and six female, all in top 40 in the world) to examine the length of the 'peaks' and 'troughs' of momentum in a match. Inevitably, large variations were found within each player's set of data, but all of these characteristics of the profiles stabilised to within 10 per cent of their respective means within six of the eight matches, for all the players. The data from each match were summated and the average positive and negative increases in momentum were calculated. A χ^2 analysis was used to test for inter-player differences and it was found that there were significant differences between patterns of peaks, peak lengths, troughs and trough lengths ($p < 0.05$). Also both the male and female, world #1 players had positive averages much higher than their peers (Figure 5.9).

Currently, the practical applications of these researches are being used with England Squash. Prior to the World Team Championships in November 2003 the England team were provided with player profiles of all possible future opposition, based on Hughes and Murray (2001). The only difference being that the profiles

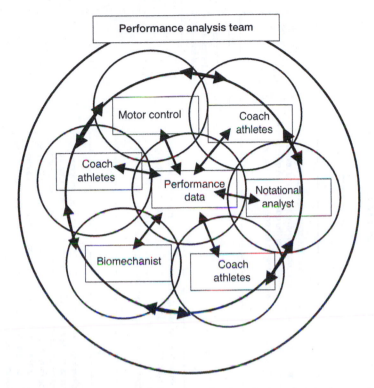

FIGURE 5.9 A digital systems approach to the data sharing that the interactive commercial systems have enabled for performance analysts working with coaches and athletes.

Source: Hughes, 2004a.

were created using the SWEAT analysis systems, rather than the full analysis system, due to time constraints and the large number of profiles that needed to be created. Compact discs containing edited video material of the unusual aspects of the relevant player profiles were provided to the players. They were created using the sports analysis package 'Focus'. Also English players competing in the World Championships or other major tournaments are provided with SWEAT analyses of their previous encounters with likely opponents and the respective momentum analyses of these matches (Figure 5.11).

This process is performed relatively quickly due to the large database of matches at the English Institute of Sport. The impressive use, and further recent developments, in feedback both for competition and training and coaching were presented by Murray and Hughes (2001) – an applied demonstration of the strengths and uses of the Focus, Quintic, Dartfish and SiliconCoach software, together with digital video, high-speed video and the best available VDUs for feedback. This 'digital' approach is represented schematically in Figure 5.9, and also exemplified by current approaches in badminton (See Figure 5.10).

Preparation	**Performance profiling** the starting point for tracking performance	Identify with the coach the areas of strength and areas for development for the player/pairs. This is information that the coaches will have already; it's just a case of making it accessible to me. This is set up using the performance profiling sheets distributed to the coaches. The results are then collated and put in an excel spreadsheet format where any changes can be monitored and updated. Do the coach and player agree on strengths and weaknesses?

↓

Technical analysis in Training and rehabilitation	Dartfish	Use of the Dartfish software to review technical aspect of training for players' personal development goals. This is set up courtside during training sessions. The players and coaches have access to review the technique as they progress through the session. Visual reinforcement assists the coach when giving feedback to the players, reduces the degree of discrepancy. This is available to the coaches and players whenever requested.

↔

Does any of the info here need to be fed back to the Physio/S&C? ↔

↔

Match analysis	★ Focus X2 ★ Notation Sheets ★ Match reports ★ Stats	**Monitors if the areas identified for development are improving in matches after training.** Templates can be individually designed so that the information being drawn out is specific to the player/pair being analysed. Every bit of information is not always a productive use of time. Files can be created and data can be produced for performances against specific pairs. This information can also be fed into opponent analysis.

Links can be made between technical and tactical analysis

↓

Review and feedback	★ CDs/DVDs ★ Review sessions with the coach	Relevant information and clips will be passed back to the player on a CD or DVD format depending on the size of the file. It is also possible to compress the data and send the information via email. Coach input is required to feedback to the player and me about which information to save for reviewing. From the analysis of the match, questions should be raised: Why did the player lose a certain match? What do they think, and do the results relate to this? Does the coach agree? Is it something that they have been working on in training? Should this aspect of training be included in the coaching plan? Can they use the strengths from this game in their next game? And so on…

FIGURE 5.10 Analysis guideline proposals for the Badminton Association of England players and coaches.

Source: Behan, 2006.

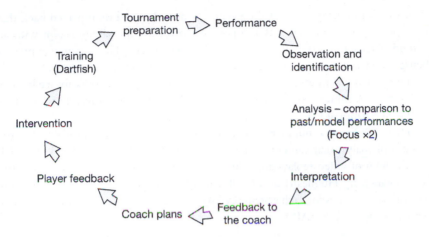

FIGURE 5.11 A schematic diagram of the analysis and feedback by the Badminton Association of England performance analyst.

Source: Behan, 2006.

One of the most exciting and potentially significant outgrowths of computerised sport analysis was the advent of interactive video technology. The ability of computers to control the video image has now made it possible to enhance existing sport specific analytical procedures. An inexpensive IBM based system was described by Franks, Nagelkerke and Goodman (1989). The system operates in conjunction with an IBM XT (or compatible) and requires a circuit board to be resident within the computer. The system was designed to interact with a video cassette recorder (VCR) that has a 34-pin remote control outlet (some Sony and Panasonic AG and NV series). The interaction between the computer and the VCR was outlined as well as the technical details of the circuit boards. In addition, several software programs were given that demonstrate the control features of the circuit board.

Franks and Nagelkerke (1988) developed such a system for the team sport of field hockey. The analysis system, described by Franks and Goodman (1986b), required a trained analyst to input, via a digitisation pad, the game-related data into a microcomputer. Following the field hockey game, a menu driven analysis program allowed the analyst to query the sequentially stored time–data pairs. Because of the historical nature of these game-related sequences of action, it was possible to perform both post-event and pre-event analysis on the data. That is to say, questions relating to what led up to a particular event or what followed a particular event could now be asked. In addition to presenting the sports analyst with digital and graphical data of team performance, the computer was also programmed to control and edit the videotape action of the game action.

The interactive video computer programme accessed from the stored database the times of all specific events such as goals, shots, set plays, etc. Then, from a menu of these events, the analyst could choose to view any or all of these events within one specific category. The computer was programmed to control the video such that it found the time of the event on the video and then played back that excerpt of game action. It was also possible to review the same excerpt with an extended 'lead in' or 'trail' time around that chosen event. This system is at present being tested and used by the Canadian national women's hockey team.

The system was modified for use to analyse and provide feedback for ice hockey and soccer. A number of professional ice hockey clubs are currently using it, as well as the national Canadian team.

There are now a number of commercial systems that are available for the notational analyst that can considerably enhance the power of feedback, through the medium of video replays and edited video clips. Some of the more successful are appraised by Hughes *et al.* (2002b); much more detail can be found on the appropriate websites for each system reviewed: SportsCode, Quintic, SiliconCoach, Tracksys and Purple VAIO.

5.7 Research into the methodology and theory of notational analysis

Recent research has reformed our ideas on reliability, performance indicators and performance profiling in notational analysis; also, statistical processes have come under close scrutiny, and have generally been found wanting. These are areas that will continue to develop to the good of the discipline and the confidence of the sports scientist, coach and athlete. If we consider the role of a notational analyst (Figure 5.9) in its general sense in relation to the data that the analyst is collecting, processing and analysing, then there are a number of mathematical skills that will be required to facilitate the steps in the processes (Figure 5.12):

1   defining performance indicators;
2   determining which are important;
3   establishing the reliability of the data collected;
4   ensuring that enough data have been collected to define stable performance profiles;
5   comparing sets of data;
6   modelling performances.

The recent advances made into the research and application of the mathematical and statistical techniques commonly used and required for these processes were discussed in detail by Hughes (2004b), and are further analysed in different chapters of this book.

5.8 Summary

To summarise the developments in computerised notational analysis, one can trace the innovative steps used in overcoming the two main problems of dealing with computers – data input and data output.

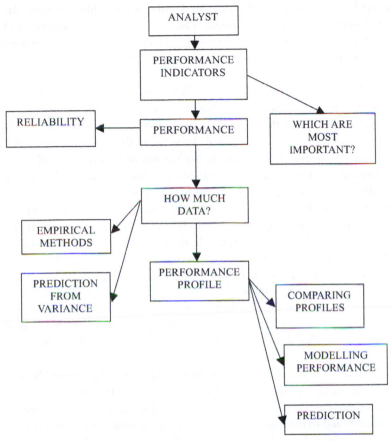

FIGURE 5.12 A schematic chart of the steps required in moving from data gathering to producing a performance profile.

Source: Hughes, 2004a.

The initial difficulty in using a computer is entering information. The traditional method is using the QWERTY keyboard. But, unless the operator possesses considerable skills, this can be a lengthy and boring task. By assigning codes to the different actions, positions or players that have some meaning to the operator, the key entry can be made easier. The next step is to assign areas of the keyboard to represent areas of the pitch, numbers for the players, and another section of the keyboard for the actions (see Hughes and Cunliffe, 1986). An alternative to this approach to this problem is to use a specifically designed keyboard (Franks *et al.*, 1983a; Fuller, 1990) that has key entry designed ergonomically to meet the particular needs of the sport under analysis.

The major innovation, however, in this area, that eased considerably the problems of data entry both in terms of skill requirements and learning time, was the introduction of the digitisation pad. In Britain most workers have utilised the

'Concept keyboard', while in Canada, Ian Franks, at his Centre for Sport Analysis at the University of British Columbia, Vancouver, has utilised another pad that has the trade name 'Power Pad' (Franks *et al.*, 1986). These are programmable, touch-sensitive pads, over which one can place an overlay that has a graphic representation of the pitch and aptly labelled keypad areas for the actions and the players. This considerably reduces the skill required for fast data entry, and the learning time required to gain this level of skill. These digitisation pads have gradually given way to the use of the Graphical User interface (the mouse) and using on-screen graphics, but this is not as quick as the use of the digitisation pads, because of their easy 'point and click' demands. But the mouse is universal, and a lot more convenient than trying to get the extra 'add-on' hardware to work which is not always 100 per cent compatible from country to country.

Another highlight that is still awaited is the introduction of voice entry of data into the computer. Although Taylor and Hughes (1988) were severely limited by the amounts of funding for their research, they were still able to demonstrate that this type of system can and will be used by the computer 'non-expert'. Although systems are expensive at the moment, computer technology is an environment of rapidly decreasing costs, even as the technology races ahead, so one can expect that this will be the next big step forward in the use of computers, in general, and sports systems in particular. It is strange, given the advance in electronic technology, that 15 years on from this research and the comments made above, that they are still true today.

Notational analysis, while having been the platform for considerable research, has its foundations in practical applications in sport. In these situations, it is imperative that the output is as immediate as possible and, perhaps more important, clear, concise and to the point. Consequently, the second strand of innovation that one can trace through the development of different systems is that of better output.

The first systems produced tables and tables of data, incorporated with statistical significance tests, that sport scientists had difficulty in interpreting: pity the coach or the athlete attempting to adopt these systems. Some researchers attempted to tackle the problem (Sanderson and Way, 1979), but not everyone would agree that this type of presentation was any easier to understand than the tables of data. Representations of frequency distributions across graphics of the playing area, traces of the path of the ball prior to a shot or a goal (Hughes and Cunliffe, 1986; Franks and Nagelkerke, 1988), and similar ploys, have made the output of some systems far more attractive and easier to understand. The system developed by Hughes and McGarry specifically tackled this problem and produced some 3-D colour graphics that presented the data in a compact form, very easy to assimilate. Finally the computer controlled video-interactive systems (Franks *et al.*, 1989) initiated the ideas that the users of analysis systems could utilise the potential of immediate analysis combined with the visual presentation of the feedback of the action. This has led now to the edited video image being the medium of feedback, the story-board of which is created by the detailed analyses provided by hand or computerised notation systems (or a combination of both) (see Murray and Hughes, 2001).

5.9 The future of notational analysis

In terms of technological development, notational analysis will undoubtedly move as rapidly as the developments in computer technology and video technology as we journey through the twenty-first century. The integration of these technological developments in computerised–video feedback will enable both detailed objective analysis of competition and the immediate presentation of the most important elements of play. Computerised systems on sale now enable the analysis, selection, compilation and re-presentation of any game on video to be processed in a matter of seconds. The coach can then use this facility as a visual aid to support the detailed analysis. Franks (1988) devised a more detailed model of the feedback process that could be possible with this type of technology. It is only 15 years later that the top professional clubs in sports, and some national governing bodies, are implementing these ideas fully.

As these systems are used more and more, and larger databases are created, a clearer understanding of each sport will follow. The mathematical approach, typified by Eom (1988) and McGarry and Franks (1994 and 1995), will make these systems more and more accurate in their predictions. At the moment the main functions of the systems are analysis, diagnosis and feedback – few sports have gathered enough data to allow prediction of optimum tactics in set situations. Where large databases have been collected (e.g. soccer and squash), models of the games have been created and this has enabled predictive assertions of winning tactics. This has led to some controversy, particularly in soccer, due to the lack of understanding of the statistics involved and their range of application. Nevertheless, the function of the systems could well change, particularly as the financial rewards in certain sports are providing such large incentives for success. The following glimpse (Franks, 1996, p. 254) into future integrated match analyses should help illustrate this point:

> The analysis from the match has been established and after reviewing a brief summary of the game statistics the coaching staff are concerned that late in the game crosses from the right side of the team's attack were being delivered behind the defenders and close to the opposing team's goalkeeper. The result being that the front strikers were not able to contact the ball despite making the correct approach runs (information also gained from the match summary). The coaching staff call for videodisc (immediate recovery) excerpts of each crossing opportunity from the right side of the field in the last 15 minutes of play. Along with this visual information, the computer retrieves other on-line information that is presented in the inset of the large projected video image. This information relates to the physiological condition of the player(s) under review leading up to the crossing opportunity. In addition a 3-D analysis of the crossing technique is presented as each cross is viewed. One player had been responsible for these crosses. Upon advice from the consulting exercise physiologist the coaching staff have concerns about the telemetered

respiration and heart rate of the player. A time–motion analysis of the player's movements in the second half of the game is called for, as well as a profile of the player's fitness level and physiotherapy report prior to the game. These are also retrieved from the same videodisc. After considering the information the coaching staff record their recommendations for team and individual improvement and move on to the next problem provided by a comparison of the predicted data and real data. A computer program running in the background is busy compiling instances of good performance (successful crosses) and poor performance that will make up an educational modelling programme for the individual player to view. Also the expert system of coaching practice is being queried about the most appropriate practice for remedial treatment of crossing in this specific setting. An individual fitness programme is prescribed when another expert system is queried. The final question that is asked of the mathematical model is 'given these changes are implemented, what is the likelihood that the number of crosses in the final fifteen minutes from the right side of the field will be more successful against our next opponent and what is their expected effect on match outcome?'

All aspects of the above scenario are either in place or are under investigation in notational analysis laboratories throughout the world.

Whether the most sophisticated and expensive of systems is being used, or a simple pen-and-paper analysis, as long as either system produces accurate, reliable results that are easy to understand, and they are based on performance indicators negotiated by the coach and the analyst, then coaches, athletes, sports scientists will gain objective, reliable data that will increase their insights into sport performance.

6

THE USE OF PERFORMANCE INDICATORS IN PERFORMANCE ANALYSIS

Mike Hughes and Roger Bartlett

6.1 Summary

The aims of this chapter are to examine the application of performance indicators in different sports and, using the different structural definitions of games, to make general recommendations about the use and application of these indicators. Formal games are classified into three categories: net and wall games, invasion games, and striking and fielding games. The different types of sports are also sub-categorised by the rules of scoring and ending the respective matches. These classes are analysed further, to enable definition of useful performance indicators and to examine similarities and differences in the analysis of the different categories of game. The indices of performance are sub-categorised into general match indicators, tactical indicators, technical indicators and biomechanical indicators. Different research examples and the accuracy of their presentation are discussed. We conclude that, to enable a full and objective interpretation of the data from the analysis of a performance, comparisons of data are vital. In addition, any analysis of the distribution of actions across the playing surface should also be presented normalised, or non-dimensionalised, to the total distribution of actions across the area. Other normalisations of performance indicators should also be used more widely in conjunction with the accepted forms of data analysis.

6.2 Introduction

Notational analysts and sport biomechanists are concerned with the analysis and improvement of sports performance. The practitioners of both make extensive use of video analysis and video-based technology. Recently, those involved in these two sub-disciplines of sport science have recognised some other commonalties that suggest that the two should grow closer together, collaborate more and share ideas, theories and methods. The formation of the British Olympic Association's Performance Analysis Steering Group, which brings together biomechanists and notational analysts, is one such example. The issues that are common to both biomechanists and notational analysts include optimising feedback to the performer and coach to improve performance (see Liebermann *et al.*, 2002; Smith and Loschner, 2002, both on this issue). Other common issues include the management of information complexity, addressing the reliability and validity of their data, and exploitation of the approaches and methods of artificial intelligence (see Lapham and Bartlett, 1995). The investigators from both disciplines study patterns of play involving the individual or 'constellations of individuals' (Shephard, 1999). One approach to theoretical-grounding that is similar to both of these elements of 'performance analysis' is the derivation of performance indicators (also called performance parameters by sport biomechanists) from flowcharts for notational analysis (see, for example, Hughes and Franks, 1997) or hierarchical technique models for biomechanics (see, for example, Hay and Reid, 1988).

A performance indicator is a selection, or combination, of action variables that aims to define some or all aspects of a performance. Clearly, to be useful, performance indicators should relate to successful performance or outcome. Biomechanical performance indicators are often linked to the outcome through hierarchical technique models, such as Figure 6.1, in which clear biomechanical relationships exist between the levels of the model (see also Lees, 2002). Mathematical modelling

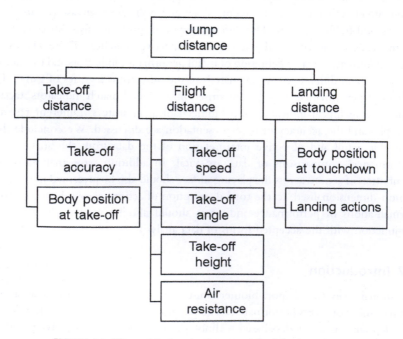

FIGURE 6.1 Hierarchical technique model of the long jump.

Source: Adapted from Hay and Reid, 1988.

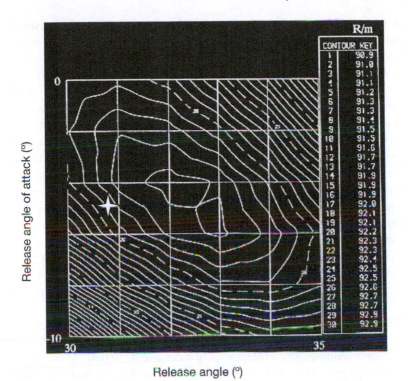

FIGURE 6.2 Contour map of the distance a javelin travels (R) as a function of two release parameters, with all others held constant. Release angle is the angle between the direction in which the javelin's centre of mass is travelling (the javelin's velocity vector) and the horizontal; release angle of attack is the angle from the javelin's long axis to its velocity vector at release. Contour lines (every fifth one numbered) are lines of constant R; the cross marks the maximal value of R (92.9 m). Any departure from that optimum results in a reduction in R.

Source: Adapted from Best *et al.*, 1995.

can often serve to reinforce this relationship, particularly in closed skills, as in Figure 6.2 (from Best *et al.*, 1995). In this figure, an optimal combination of two javelin release parameters (performance indicators), here release angle of attack and release angle, produces a maximum throw: departures from that optimum result in a decrement in distance thrown. Such modelling techniques have not yet been applied to team games.

Analysts and coaches use performance indicators to assess the performance of an individual, a team, or elements of a team. They are sometimes used in a comparative way, with opponents, other athletes or peer groups of athletes or teams, but often they are used in isolation as a measure of the performance of a team or individual alone.

Sport biomechanists have generally concentrated their analyses of performance on sports in which the movement technique is critical. Such sports involve predominantly closed skills and are classified as acrobatic (including gymnastics, trampolining, diving, freestyle skiing), athletic (including jumping and throwing) and cyclic (including running, swimming, skating and wheelchair racing) (Yeadon and Challis, 1992). The performance goal, or primary performance parameter (such as the distance jumped in the long jump) is initially partitioned into secondary performance parameters – such as the take-off, flight and landing distances in the long jump: these are sometimes based on phase analysis of the technique (e.g. Bartlett, 1999). In this example, these partial distances can be normalised by expressing them as ratios of the distance jumped – a similar approach is often used in the triple jump and, sometimes, in gymnastic vaults. The use of hierarchical technique models then allows these performance parameters to be related to the movements of the athlete that contribute to successful execution of the skill. All of these parameters and movement variables can be considered as performance indicators providing that they do meaningfully contribute to the performance. These performance indicators are usually kinematic variables or parameters, such as body segment speeds or angles. When trying to relate such indicators to the mechanisms of the movement, net joint reaction forces and moments and electromyographic (EMG) descriptors of muscle activation patterns are also used.

Sport biomechanists have paid far less attention to team sports, perhaps because of the perception that biomechanical interventions are less important in those sports than fitness training, psychological preparation and tactics. There are some exceptions to this. They include analyses of fast bowling in cricket (see Bartlett *et al.*, 1996), some studies of soccer skills (see Lees and Nolan, 1998) and limited studies of other games such as rugby and racquet sports. Even then, however, the focus is predominantly on isolated individual closed skills within the game. The lack of biomechanical analyses of team sports is regrettable, given that the most important requirement for success for any games player is skill – which is what most biomechanists try to understand and measure. The result is insufficient attention to the interaction of skill and successful play, clearly an important contribution to successful outcomes of games (Bartlett, 2000).

Notational analysis, on the other hand, has focused traditionally on team and match play sports, studying the interactions between players and the movements and behaviours of individual team members – mostly open skills. Few studies of acrobatic, athletic and cyclic sports exist from a notational analysis perspective, despite

TABLE 6.1 Published performance indicators used in notational analysis

Soccer:	Shots, Passes, Passing accuracy (see e.g. Hughes *et al.*, 1988; Winkler, 1996)
Rugby:	Turnovers, Tackles, Passes/Possession (see e.g. Carter, 1996)
Tennis:	Winners to errors ratio, Shots/Rally, Quality – service/return (see e.g. Taylor and Hughes, 1998)
Cricket:	Strike rate, Dismissal rate, Fielding efficiency (see e.g. Hughes and Bell, 1999)

the widespread use of dance notation systems. Clearly, however, notational analysis is far less relevant, if at all, to these sports than to team and match play sports. Notational analysts have focused on general match indicators, tactical indicators and technical indicators and have contributed to our understanding of the physiological, psychological, technical and tactical demands of many types of sports. For example, in tennis, performance of a player may be assessed by the distribution of winners and errors around the court. In soccer, one aspect of a team's performance may be appraised by the ratio of goals scored to shots attempted by the team. Other examples, taken from published research, are shown in Table 6.1.

These indicators can be categorised as either scoring indicators, or indicators of the quality of the performance. Examples of scoring indicators are goals, baskets, winners, errors, the ratios of winners to errors and goals to shots, and dismissal rates. Examples of quality indicators are turnovers, tackles, passes/possession, shots per rally, and strike rate. Both types of indicator have been used as a measure of positive or negative aspects of performance in the analysis of a particular sport.

If presented in isolation, a single set of data (indicators for a performance of an individual or a team) can give a distorted impression of a performance, by ignoring other, more or less important, variables. From our reviews of recent research and the work of many consultants, it is clear that many analysts do not give sufficient data from a performance to represent fully the significant events of that performance. Presenting data from both sets of performers is often not enough to inform on the performance. For example, if two rugby teams are playing and team A have had 12 turnovers (handling errors that lead to a change in possession) and team B have had eight turnovers, it would be tempting to assume that team B were having the better of the game. However if team A had 48 possessions and team B 24 possessions, then their relative turnovers with respect to possessions (turnovers/possessions, T/P) will be:

$$(T/P)_A = 1/4;$$

$$(T/P)_B = 1/3.$$

Now team A could be said to be performing better than team B because, although they have conceded more turnovers, they are making these errors once in four possessions whereas team B are making them in every three possessions.

The comparison of performances between teams, team members and within individuals is often facilitated if the performance indicators are expressed as ratios, as in the example above, such as winners to errors and goals to shots and the ratios of jump phases to overall jump distance. These proportions represent a binomial response variable (see Nevill et al., 2002, for appropriate analytical methods). These examples are clearly non-dimensional as they divide a measure (e.g. number of goals or phase jump distance) by a similar measure (number of shots or total jump distance). Similar non-dimensional ratios are formed by sport biomechanists by expressing forces acting on the performer as ratios to body weight, and by normalising EMG descriptors to the magnitude of that descriptor in a maximum voluntary contraction (MVC). More attention should be paid to this normalising, or non-dimensional, approach. For example, Stockill (1994) found a difference in the magnitudes and times of occurrence of peak segment speeds in senior and junior cricket fast bowlers. However, when the times were normalised to the time from the start of delivery to release, these ratio times of peak speeds were the same; the ratio speeds were also comparable. Therefore, the difference between the groups was not in timing or in different segmental significance but simply in speed of execution, a finding that is consistent with existing motor control literature (see, e.g. Newell and Corcos, 1993).

It is easy to see parallels with the use of non-dimensional analysis elsewhere; for example, indices such as the ratio of specific heats in high-speed flows, or non-dimensional groups such as Reynolds number in low speed fluid mechanics. When flow conditions are very complex, so that the equations of motion cannot easily be solved, fluid mechanists use dimensional analysis to predict how one variable may depend on several others. This is then used to direct the course of an experiment or the analysis of experimental results. Sport science has not reached this degree of sophistication in the application of analysis of performance, but there are certain empirical recommendations that can be explored. Few of the non-dimensional ratios in performance analysis relate to the importance of various forces, with the exception of expressing ratios of forces to body weight. Many of the important non-dimensional groups in fluid dynamics are force ratios, and some of these are important for biomechanical analysis. The Reynolds number is the ratio of inertia to viscous forces; it is important in any sport in which drag forces are significant or in which lift forces are used to generate propulsion or improve performance. These sports include swimming, ski jumping, skiing, throws of an aerodynamic object – such as the discus or javelin – and ball games in which the ball spins quickly (such as golf and tennis). The Froude number is the square root of the ratio of inertia to gravity forces; it is important in sports in which the body moving through the water makes waves, for example fast front crawl swimming, sailing and canoeing.

As we have noted above, biomechanists use measured forces, performance distances and segmental peak speeds to compare performances. However, far more meaningful comparisons may be obtained by using simple ratios of force to body weight, partial distances or speed ratios. However, we need to be careful to avoid information being lost by normalisation, which should be used to aid the evaluation of the measured results by adding relevant information. However, the most appropriate analysis of the results is best determined case-by-case and non-dimensionalising is not always appropriate. An example of the last statement was provided by Fleissig (2001), who proposed comparing ground reaction forces between baseball pitchers of widely varying ages by normalising forces (F) to body weight (W), to assess injury risk. However, tissue injury is related to the tissue stress (force/cross sectional area), which is proportional to F/l^2, where l is an appropriate tissue dimension, such as radius, whereas F/W is proportional to F/l^3.

Such incorrect use of normalisation shows that performance analysts have much to learn from allometric scaling (see e.g. Schmidt–Nielsen 1984).

Notational analysts use simple measures such as the number of shots per game in soccer. However, far more meaningful information is obtained from ratios such as: number of shots per game to number of shooting opportunities; number of shots per game on goal to number of shots per game; number of goals per game to number of shots per game (see Nevill *et al.*, 2002, for appropriate analytical methods for binomial response variables). In tennis, the winner and error distributions on their own are used to show relative strengths and weaknesses on the forehand and backhand; for example, 60 per cent errors on backhand and 40 per cent on forehand. However, such measures are meaningless unless expressed relative to the total shot distribution – the opponent could have been overloading the backhand (as is often the case) by 75 per cent to 25 per cent forehand: this dramatically changes the analysis. These simple examples demonstrate how misleading it can be to use only measured data to evaluate and analyse the complex factors that make for successful sports performance.

Performance indicators are also used in different ways. They have become increasingly popular in media coverage of sport, for example, possession, tackling and passing statistics in rugby and shot distribution patterns in cricket. They are also used in judging contests, in coaching and in other applications in sport science, such as monitoring team performance against that of rivals over a season in soccer (Olsen and Larsen, 1997). An interesting example of the usefulness of performance analysis is in ice hockey, where players are given a score after each game based on, for example, whether they scored or assisted and if the team scored or conceded when they were on the ice. These indicators are used both by the media and by the management when negotiating contracts. None of these applications is explicitly the focus of this chapter. The aims are rather to examine the application of performance indicators in different sports and, using the different structural definitions of games, to make general recommendations about the use and application of these indicators.

6.3 Analysis of game structures

Read and Edwards (1992) classified formal games into three categories, net and wall games, invasion games, and striking and fielding games, see Figure 6.3. This classification will be used in this paper as a starting point. The different types of sports are also sub-categorised by the rules of scoring or ending the respective matches. These classes will be examined further, to enable analysis of useful performance indicators and as a means of examining similarities and differences in the analysis of the different categories of game.

6.3.1 Net–wall games

Net games can be further sub-categorised into no-volley, bounce-and-volley and no-bounce games. Some examples of the more common sports that fall into these

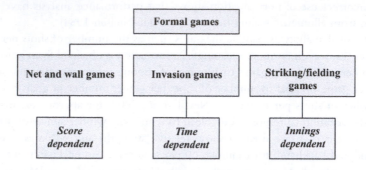

FIGURE 6.3 Game classification.

Source: After Read and Edwards, 1992.

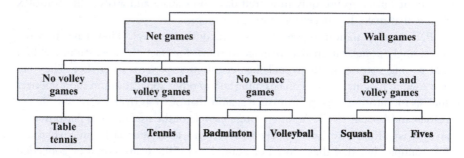

FIGURE 6.4 Sub-categorisation of net and wall games, with some common examples.

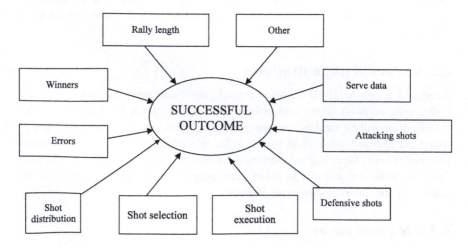

FIGURE 6.5 Some factors that contribute to success or improved performance in net and wall games.

classes are shown in Figure 6.4. The common wall games in Britain, squash and fives, are both bounce and volley games. There are many wall games from different parts of the world, each with their own rules that may well fall into the same sub-categories of the net games.

Despite the differences in the rules of these games, the performance indicators that have been used by different analysts are very similar. Figure 6.5 shows some of the different variables that contribute to success in all of these net and wall games.

The types of performance indicators that have been used in previous research further exemplify these variables; some are shown in Table 6.2. These general indicators have been classified as match descriptors, data that define the nature of the overall match, as well as biomechanical, technical and tactical. In some cases these categories are similar, somewhat inevitably, since match descriptors and tactics will depend upon technical strengths and weaknesses, but we feel that keeping the distinction between the two will be useful.

All these indicators have been used as ways of indexing performances, without reference to other normative data (such as previous performances or aggregated performances of peer opponents) and, in some cases, without reference to the opponents' data. The use of any of these variables in isolation is misleading.

6.3.1.1 Match classification indicators

Consider the example of a squash match that had 250 shots in 50 rallies. What can be said about the match other than that the ratio of shots per rally was 5? This, as a performance indicator, is meaningless without some other reference point. If elite players, for whom the average equivalent data were approximately 1000 shots and 100 rallies, had played this match, then these figures would suggest that something unusual had taken place. It would seem that one player has beaten the other player very easily. If, however, the match had been played by recreational players, then the figures would suggest that the match was closely contested as the values are close to the averages for that class of player. So the same data can give two totally different messages. Providing comparative data from samples of the same playing standard allows the best assessment of the important features of any performances.

The effectiveness of a serve in tennis will always depend upon the returning skills of the opponent; even aces will vary with the positioning, reflexes and skill of the other player. Consequently, presenting serve data without the opponents' complementary data can be misleading. Equally important is to present the data with a frame of reference, as discussed with the previous match classification data. If Goran Ivanisevich has made 14 aces in a match, compared to eight by his opponent, André Agassi, then this would seem to be a good performance for Ivanisevich and not so good for Agassi. If the average number of aces for elite players is six per match, then, by this standard, Ivanisevich is still having a good performance and Agassi is also playing well, relatively. This is true, with the aggregate of elite players as a standard of comparison, and this contrast is a sound way of assessing players' strengths and weaknesses. Another way of assessing a particular

TABLE 6.2 Categorisation of different performance indicators that have been used in analyses of net or wall games (some example papers indicated for each classification).

Match classification	Biomechanical	Technical	Tactical
No. of shots	Ball projection (release) velocity	Winners (W)	Shots/second
No. of rallies	Racket, bat or hand speed at impact	Winning shot distribution	Shots/rally
Scores	Kinematics of throwing or striking arm:	Error shot distribution	Shot types – distribution
Serve data:	• Pronation/supination	Serve data: etc.	Length of shot
• 1st serve winner	• Elbow extension		Winning shot distribution
• 2nd serve winner	Sequence of segment movements		Error shot distribution
	Weight transfer into shot or stroke		Opponents:
			• Winning shot distribution
			• Error shot distribution
For a review, see Hughes (1998b) See also (O'Donoghue and Liddle, 1998; Taylor and Hughes, 1998)	See, e.g. Bartlett et al. (1995); Tang et al. (1995); Kasai and Mori (1998); Bahamonde (2000); Marshall and Elliott (2000)	For a review, see Hughes (1998). See also McGarry and Franks (1994); Hughes and Robertson (1998)	For a review, see Hughes (1998). See also Furlong (1995); Hughes and Clarke (1995)

performance of an individual or team is to compare that performance with the aggregated profile of previous performances at this standard of play. Ivanisevich averages 16 aces per match; Agassi averages ten aces per match. Comparing the aces for this match to their individual averages of previous performances changes the interpretation of the data, with both underachieving in this part of the game. These data have been presented in three ways, relative to each other, relative to players of the same standard, and relative to their own profiles of previous performance. Each can give valuable comparisons, but it is important to remember that each of these comparisons elicit different interpretations of the quality of a performance. Consequently, to enable efficient interpretation of data, when using match classification indicators, it is very important to have comparative data from previous performances and also from peer group previous performances. Profiles of players will also vary depending upon whom they are playing; this too must be borne in mind when presenting information, ensuring that enough data are collected to present a normative profile (see previous chapter).

The above comparisons could be made even more meaningful by incorporating biomechanical indicators, such as hitting speeds and segmental velocities. More important information could be provided if biomechanists developed qualitative analyses that enabled the key features that contribute to a successful stroke to be recognised from direct observation. This happens, after all, in judging gymnastics and diving. Biomechanists have, to date, paid far too little attention to qualitative biomechanical analysis in their research, despite several well-known texts on the topic (e.g. Kreighbaum and Barthels, 1990; Knudsen and Morrison, 1997). These comments apply with equal validity to the technical and tactical indicators in racket sports, as well as to the other categories of games. The reliability and objectivity of measures based on human perceptions and judgements is clearly an issue. This needs to be addressed by validating such performance indicators against valid and reliable quantitative measures to which they are clearly related.

6.3.1.2 Technical indicators

Winners and errors are powerful indicators of technical competence and have often been used in research in notational analysis of net–wall games (Sanderson, 1983; Hughes, 1986; Brown and Hughes, 1995). However, there are dangers of mis-interpreting a performance if they are used in isolation. Sanderson (1983) used a winner:error ratio as a performance indicator. He found that, for all standards of play in squash, if the winner:error ratio for a particular player in a match was greater than one, then that player usually won. (This was achieved with English scoring and a 19-inch tin and when players were using wooden rackets.) Although this ratio is a good index of technique, it would be better used with data for both players, and the ratios should not be simplified nor decimalised. Winner:error ratios of 0.9 and 1.1 respectively tell that the first player is losing but little else about the match. However, if the ratios had been presented as 9/10 and 44/40, then it is clear that this is a long hard match for players of this standard (103 rallies). The first player is playing defensively, making few errors but few winners. The second player is playing more aggressively hitting many winners but also many errors. Perhaps the better way to present the processed data is as a combination of both forms, the former for an overview and the latter for more detail.

Rally end distributions, that is the frequencies of winners and errors in the different position cells across the court, have often been used to define technical strengths and weaknesses (O'Donoghue and Liddle, 1998; Hughes *et al.*, 2000d). The use of these distributions as indicators is valid as long as the overall distribution of shots across the court is evenly balanced on both sides of the court. However, this even distribution of shots across all the cells in a court rarely occurs in any net or wall game. For example, it could be that in a badminton match, player A has 20 drops from the backhand side of the court and 15 drops from the forehand. This would suggest that the backhand side of player A is the stronger and more aggressive flank. If, however, the overall total of shots on the backhand side was 120, and the equivalent total on the forehand was 60 shots, then the respective 'drops to total shots' ratios for each side are 20/120 − 1 drop in 6 shots; or 0.167 − and 15/60 − 1 drop in 4 shots; or 0.25. Again, it can be seen how this normalisation changes the interpretation of these data. Dispersions of winners and errors should be normalised to the totals of shots from those cells. It would be more accurate to represent the winner, or error, frequency, from particular position cells, as a ratio to the total number of shots from those cells.

Often rally end distributions are shot specific (Hughes, 1986; O'Donoghue and Liddle, 1998), for example a distribution of volley winners in different position cells of a tennis court. The distribution of these volleys will reflect the respective volleying skills of the player and will indicate the areas of the court where the strengths and weaknesses lie. However, the pattern of winners will also depend heavily on the overall distribution of shots and the total distribution of volleys. So, by the same argument that was used to explain the need for normalising the total shot distributions, the frequencies in this case should be standardised to the total distribution of volleys in each cell position and presented in both forms to give the complete picture.

6.3.1.3 Tactical indicators

Tactical performance indicators seek to reflect the relative importance of the use of pace, space, fitness and movement, and how players use these aspects of performance, of themselves and their opponents, targeting the technical strengths and weaknesses of the respective performers. These will be reflected in the ways that individuals and teams attack and defend, how they use the spaces in the playing surface and the variety of playing actions. The examples shown in Table 6.1 are representative of indicators used to identify these types of tactical play (Sanderson, 1983; McGarry and Franks, 1994).

The identification of the use of pace in net or wall games is not common; researchers have rarely used time bases to enable definition of the speed of play (Hughes and Clarke, 1995). When they are used, comparisons should be made to means of groups of peer performers. When players are trying to use perceived superior fitness in net or wall games, it will usually be reflected in the shots-per-rally indicators and the respective winner to error ratios. The latter will indicate which team or player is trying to sustain rallies in the hope of wearing down their opponents. Often the serve will be linked with control of the rally, sometimes this is through the scoring rules of the game. Therefore, linking the shots per rally to the respective serves is an additional way of using this indicator, which gives greater depth to the analysis and enables deeper insight into the tactics employed in the game. Comparing these values to means of groups of peer performers will yield greater insight into the respective performances. The assessment of the importance of technical strengths and weakness is done using similar indicators to those discussed in the previous section – and the same provisos for their use apply.

6.3.1.4 Biomechanical indicators

The biomechanics of racket sports has received much less attention than other aspects of these games. For example, the proceedings of the first two Congresses of Science and Racket Sports (Reilly et al., 1995; Lees et al., 1998) contain, respectively, five out of 44 and four out of 40 biomechanics papers. Five of these papers focused on tennis – one was a review; of the others, two were studies of the serve, one reported results on grip strength and one studied the effects of ball flight on several strokes. The emphasis on the serve reflects the closed nature of that skill compared with other skills – a trend that we shall see again for the other two categories of games discussed below. As we note below, biomechanical studies of the variability in stroke movement patterns and how these relate to the influence of opponents – and, in volleyball, the rest of the team – have received scant attention. Such studies in the future should afford great opportunities for collaboration between biomechanists and notational analysts.

Table 6.2 summarises some of the biomechanical performance indicators most often measured in net or wall games. These range from the descriptive – such as bat or hand speed at impact – to variables that relate more to mechanisms. The importance of segmental sequencing is more complex for racket arm movements than for kicking movements of the leg (see below). This is because of the supination–pronation of the radio-ulnar joints and the external–internal rotation of the humerus. Although the relevance of these long axis rotations was recognised two decades ago (e.g. Waddell and Gowitzke, 1977), it is only recently that their role in the proximal-to-distal sequence has been established (see Marshall and Elliott, 2000, for an overview). Their speed and timing could become important biomechanical performance indicators, although considerable scope remains for establishing the precise mechanisms that control and coordinate such strokes.

In all segmental analyses, the timing and speed of the segments should be normalised to the overall time of the stroke and the impact speed, so that we can ascertain whether differences between, for example, good, average and poor shots are due to timing differences or simply to speed.

Making detailed three-dimensional biomechanical measurements in racket sports – and many other games – is difficult and often impossible. It may also be unnecessary. If complex sports – such as gymnastics and diving – can be scored by judges in real-time (perhaps not always validly or reliably), then why cannot biomechanists develop and validate qualitative indicators of successful stroke production in tennis, other racket sports and other games? Coaches already use similar indicators when they coach technique. This is an area that demands far more attention by performance analysts, interacting with coaches and players, to develop sets of valid and reliable skill-related performance indicators that can be assessed qualitatively in a game, or from video, along with other performance indicators.

6.3.2 Invasion games

Invasion games can be sub-categorised into goal-throwing games, try-scoring games and goal-striking games. Figure 6.6 shows these and some examples of common sports that fall into these categories. Despite the differences in the rules of these games, the performance indicators that have been used by different analysts are very similar.

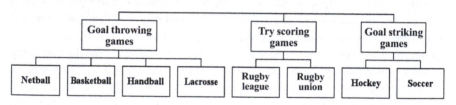

FIGURE 6.6 Sub-categorisation of invasive games, with some common examples.

As with net or wall games, we shall consider the different variables that contribute to an improved performance. Figure 6.7 shows some of the factors that contribute to success in soccer. Although the different invasion games have very similar types of performance indicators, the specific terms in each game, such as goal, try, basket, make a general list impracticable. Consequently, we have used soccer as an example, but the same types of indicators have been used in all the other invasion games, and are easily translated to other sports.

Some of the performance indicators that have been used in previous research in soccer are shown in Table 6.3. All these indicators have been, and are still, used as ways of indexing performances, without reference to other normative data and, in some cases, without reference to the opponents' data. As in the analysis of the

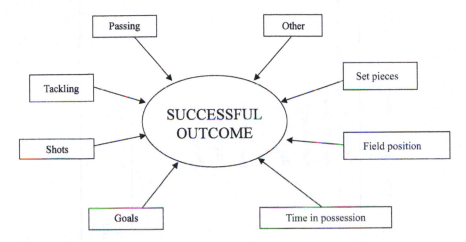

FIGURE 6.7 Some factors that contribute to success or improved performance in invasive games.

net or wall games, the indicators can be classified as match descriptors, and indices of biomechanical, technical and tactical performances.

6.3.2.1 Match indicators

Match indicators for invasion games give simple information to describe and define that particular performance. Such information differs from sport to sport but, inevitably, there are similarities – in soccer we have used examples such as scores, shots on and off target, corners and crosses. These can easily be translated to other sports. In rugby union, the equivalent indicators could be scores, penalties and drop goals – successful and otherwise – line-outs, incursions into the opponents' '22'. Similar examples could be inventoried for other invasion sports. The indicators for any of the invasion games can be seen to follow very similar rules of application to those of the net or wall games. Knowing the scores of the game will tell who won the match but, without knowing the average goals scored per match at this standard of play, it would not be possible to decide whether this was a high- or low-scoring performance. Similarly, the other match indicators can be seen to be potentially misleading without both the data of the opponents and the means of previous performances at this standard.

6.3.2.2 Technical indicators

Analysing and listing tactical indicators for invasion games such as shots on goal (soccer), missed shots at the basket (basketball), short corner conversions (field hockey), and so on, reflects the similarities again in the definition of these indicators. The differences in analyses will usually depend upon the questions the coaches have about their players, or the research question being posed.

TABLE 6.3 Categorisation of different performance indicators that have been used in analyses of soccer, an example of invasion games (some example papers indicated for each classification)

Match classification	Biomechanical	Technical	Tactical
Scores	Kicking	Passes to opposition	Passes/Possession
No. of shots on target	Ball projection velocity and spin	Tackles won and lost	Pace of attack
No. of shots off target	Kinematics and kinetics of kicking leg:	Shots off target	Shots
Corners etc.	• Energy transfers	Dribbles	Tackles won and lost
Crosses etc.	• Sequencing of joint actions	Lost control	Passing distribution
	• Net joint forces and moments	On target crosses	Length of passes
	Throw in	Off target crosses etc.	Dribbles etc.
	Ball release velocity		
	Kinematics of arms, including sequence of peak segment speeds		
For a review see Hughes (1993)	For a review, see Lees and Nolan (1998); see also Putnam (1993)	For a review see Hughes (1993); see also Pettit and Hughes (2001)	For a review see Hughes (1993); see also Pettit and Hughes (2001)

Accuracy in passing is a common technical indicator in all invasion games (Hughes *et al.*, 1988; Carter, 1996). Any error or success frequencies of a player, unit or team should be normalised to the total number of passes made by that player unit or team. Although it is a good index of technique for these sports, it should be used for both sets of players and, as explained above, the ratios could be presented first as simplified ratios or decimals and then as non-simplified, or non-decimalised, data. This will prevent any loss of information.

Loss of possession through any other action variables is another common way of assessing technical weaknesses in an invasion team, whether the action variable is catching (netball), free hits (field hockey), lineouts (rugby union), tackles (rugby league) and so on. These should all be linked to totals of actions involved so that they do represent indices of the error frequency of the particular action with respect to that action's total frequency.

Other indices of technical success or failure – shots on goal (soccer), missed shots at the basket (basketball), short corner conversions (field hockey), and so on – should also be normalised to these particular action totals. The total of this particular action variable could then be standardised by the overall number of possessions. This can also be seen to apply to all the indicators listed as examples used in research in soccer, and this rule should be applied to all technical indicators of invasion games.

6.3.2.3 Tactical indicators

Tactical performance indicators in invasion games seek to reflect the relative importance of teamwork, pace, fitness and movement, and targeting the technical strengths and weaknesses of the respective performers – very similar to those of the net or wall games. The examples shown in Table 6.3 are representative of indicators used in recent research to identify these types of tactical play; examples in soccer include Reep and Benjamin (1968), Hughes *et al.*, (1988), Partridge and Franks (1989a, b), Olsen and Larsen (1997), Garganta *et al.* (1997), Pettit and Hughes (2001). Similar examples in other invasion games could be cited for their respective tactical indicators.

The nature of these tactical indicators can be seen to be the same as those in Table 6.2, and the rules for their use follow the same logic. If two players, A and B, have four and six shots on goal respectively, it is not appropriate to report that player B is having the better performance. What are the respective totals of shot attempts? Player A could have had four shot attempts, while player B had 12 shot attempts, thus resulting in shooting indices of 4/4 and 6/12 shots on target per attempt respectively. Even this could be further analysed – how many shooting opportunities did each player have? Player A could have had a total of 12 opportunities but decided to pass eight times instead of shooting, player B shot on all 12 of the possible opportunities that were presented. Does this now indicate that player B was having the better game? Analysis of the errors could show that the passing options adopted by player A were deemed better tactically for the team. This would lead to further analysis and so on. As noted above, simple analysis of the data induces simple interpretation, which is not always appropriate in sport. The indicators in Table 6.3 should all be normalised to the respective action totals.

6.3.2.4 Biomechanical indicators

In soccer, biomechanists have focused almost exclusively on kicking. Other invasive sports have received far less attention, except for basketball, where most studies are of shooting skills (e.g. Miller and Bartlett, 1993; 1996). Soccer kicks occur in set pieces, such as penalties and free kicks, as well as in passing and shooting. Almost all of the reported studies are of maximum speed instep kicks of a stationary ball (Lees and Nolan, 1998). The many other kicks have been studied in far less detail, including passing – a crucial interaction between players, as noted above in the section on tactical performance indicators. The biomechanical performance indicators reported by researchers are summarised in Table 6.3. These vary – as with net or wall games – from the descriptive, such as ball projection velocity and spin, to those that cause the movements, such as net joint forces and moments. The sequencing of joint actions has also been studied, showing a clear proximal-to-distal kinematic sequence, unlike that for arm movements. This has led to the magnitudes and timings of segment peak speeds becoming recognised biomechanical performance indicators; their non-dimensionalising, i.e. normalising to ball speed or total duration of a phase of the movement (see below for cricket) has not yet been explored. Overall, the contribution of biomechanists to our understanding of various information-processing aspects of the game, including the control and coordination of movements, remains limited. One factor is the complexity of multi-segmental movements. This has led, *inter alia*, to different interpretations of the causes of segmental deceleration in kicks (see, e.g. Putnam, 1993), calling into question fundamental biomechanical tenets about proximal-to-distal sequencing and momentum transfer along segment chains. Marshall and Elliott (2000) have recently demonstrated the lack of a clear proximal-to-distal sequence in the tennis serve.

There has been far less research into other skills in the sport. Studies of heading have concentrated exclusively on injury risk factors rather than performance variables (see, for example, Shephard, 1999). The throw-in has received some attention; the main biomechanical performance indicators for this skill are summarised in Table 6.3. Goalkeeping skills, crucial to successful outcome, have been largely neglected by biomechanists.

Soccer is a team game in which individual skills have to fit within the tactical demands of the game. It is unfortunate – although understandable – that biomechanists have, to date, concentrated on the more closed skills, such as kicking a stationary ball and the throw-in. Considerable light might be shed on interactive aspects of the game if performance analysts could agree on, and then measure and validate, the important skill-related performance indicators in passing movements, tackling and dribbling. This could add rich skill descriptions to the other outcome-focused performance measures. Although in a cross, for example, the outcome might relate primarily to the positions of the ball, attackers and defenders, the execution of the crossing technique is hardly irrelevant. David Beckham is a supreme exponent of this skill mainly because he reproduces the skill consistently under pressure. Clearly, a cross is more difficult to analyse biomechanically than a kick or throw–in, but that should not prevent us from trying; after all, science does not progress by avoiding difficulties. As we have argued above, these measures should be qualitative so that they can be recognised in the game or from video by trained observers. They might include balance, in all these movements, minimising the foot-to-ball distance and its variability in dribbling and so on. Knudsen and Morrison (1997) advocated a 'critical factors'approach to qualitative skill analysis of soccer kicking (and other skills), each associated with observable clues. This approach might serve as a starting point for developing valid sets of qualitative skill indicators.

6.3.3 Striking and fielding games

These games can be sub-categorised into wicket games and base running games; Figure 6.8 shows these and some examples of common sports that fall within these categories. Despite the differences in the rules of these games, the performance indicators that have been used by different analysts are very similar. As with the approach to net or wall games, we consider the different variables that contribute to an improved performance. Figure 6.9 shows some of the factors that contribute to success in cricket, as an example of such games.

The types of performance indicators that have been used in previous research in cricket can also further exemplify these factors; some are shown in Table 6.4. All these indicators can be categorised by the same process used for the net or wall and invasion games.

6.3.3.1 Match indicators

The indicators to be discussed here for cricket can be seen to follow very similar rules of application to those of the net or wall games and invasion games. The interaction of the bowlers and the batters are the crux of the relative performances, a bowler having an outstanding performance can make an excellent batter appear ordinary and vice versa. Consequently, the match classification indicators can be seen to be potentially misleading without the opponents' data. As with all other sports, it is essential to place a team or individual performance in the context of previous performances; it is necessary then to compare each performance with the means of previous performances at this standard.

6.3.3.2 Technical indicators

These indicators for the example of cricket can be readily translated to other sports. They reflect the interactive nature of these sports – a batting performance is difficult

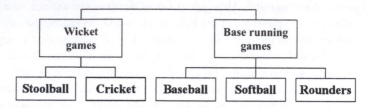

FIGURE 6.8 Sub-categorisation of striking and fielding games, with some common examples.

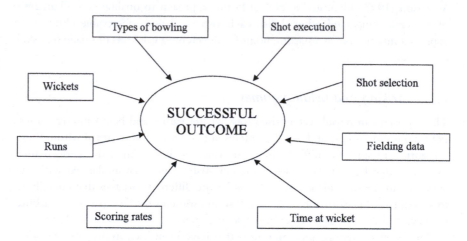

FIGURE 6.9 Some factors that contribute to success or improved performance in striking and fielding games.

to contextualise without some analysis of the bowling performance (and the fielding). Consequently, it can be seen that these variables are similar to the technical indicators discussed in the previous sections. The indices of technical success or failure, types of shot, type of ball, and so on, should also be normalised to either the particular action totals or the overall number of actions. This can also be seen to apply to all the indicators listed as examples used in research in striking and fielding games.

6.3.3.3 Tactical indicators

Some of the variables listed are a short-hand representation of the way actions have been analysed in cricket to interpret tactical decisions made by the players. The variables reflect the interaction of the batter and the bowler. For example, (Types of ball)$_{Shot}$ indicates the frequency of the different types of ball bowled that produced a particular shot made by a batsman. Similarly, (Types of shot)$_{Ball}$ indicates the frequency of the different types of shot made by a batsman from a particular

TABLE 6.4 Categorisation of different performance indicators that have been used in analyses of cricket, an example of striking and fielding games (some example papers indicated for each classification)

Match classification	Biomechanical	Technical	Tactical
Runs	*Batting*	Types of shot	(Types of ball)$_{Shot}$
Wickets	Timing of phases of stroke	Types of ball	(Types of shot)$_{Ball}$
Overs	Front foot movement, front knee angle and weight transfer in stroke	Types of dismissal	Field placing
Batting – individual data	Arm kinematics and grip force	Shot – position etc.	(Shots)$_{Field-Posn/Ball}$ etc.
Bowling – individual data	Pre- and post-impact bat and ball speed		
etc.	Kinetic variability		
	Bowling		
	Run-up speed and ball release speed		
	Class of technique (side-on, front-on, mixed) and shoulder counter-rotation in delivery stride		
See Hughes and Bell (2001)	See reviews by Bartlett *et al.* (1995); see also Cook and Strike (2000); Stretch *et al.* (2000), for a rare study of throwing in cricket	See Hughes and Bell (1999)	See Hughes and Bell (1999)

ball bowled. These could be further sub-divided into the areas of the pitch into which the batter hit the ball – depending upon the analyses.

These tactical indicators can be seen to be similar to those in Tables 6.2 and 6.3, and the rules for their use follow the same logic. The indicators shown in Table 6.4 should, as above, all be normalised to the respective action totals.

6.3.3.4 Biomechanical indicators

The two striking and fielding games that have attracted most attention from biomechanists are baseball and cricket, with pitching and bowling respectively being the most studied skills. This skill selection reflects the importance of these skills to the two games and their closed nature compared with batting and fielding skills. The latter of these presents far greater problems in data acquisition and the analysis of the former relies not only on the skills of the batter but also those of the bowler. The selection also reflects an interest in the causes of the overuse injuries that often affect fast bowlers and baseball pitchers. The incidence of low back injuries in cricket, for example, has been shown to be far more prevalent in mixed technique bowlers than in front-on or side-on bowlers (see Elliott *et al.*, 1996; Elliott, 2000).

Ball release speed is crucial to successful fast bowling performance. Biomechanical analysis of fast bowling has identified various indicators that contribute to ball release speed. These include run up speed and delivery stride length. The technique used (side-on, front-on or mixed) is mainly used in identifying injury risk; counter-rotation of the shoulders also affects the acceleration path of the ball and, possibly, its release speed (see also Table 6.4 and Bartlett *et al.*, 1996).

The sequence of segment peak speeds has received some attention although it is more constrained than in many sports by the rule that prohibits the extension of the delivery arm before release. Few studies have non-dimensionalised the peak speeds and their timing although, as noted in the introduction, this helps to identify whether differences between bowlers of different ages are due to speed or segmental coordination (Stockill, 1994).

There are far fewer studies of batting techniques in cricket; all of them do, however, focus on performance indicators rather than injury risk factors (see Stretch *et al.*, 2000, for a review). This research has concentrated on only a few of the many cricket strokes – the forward defensive and the front foot drives. The identified performance indicators are mostly kinematic, including the body position in the stance, the height of the backlift, the movements of the front foot and knee, and weight transfer. The kinematics of the arms and bat have also been measured, including pre- and post-impact bat (and ball) speeds. The grip force has also received some attention (Stretch *et al.*, 1998).

Many of these performance indicators have been shown to substantiate recognised coaching tips for the skill, but none has yet been shown to correlate with successful batting performance; more research into batting skill will be needed before such associations emerge. No non-dimensional indicators have been studied to date; this type of analysis could help to identify whether differences between similar strokes are due to different segmental recruitment patterns or simply faster execution. Although Stretch *et al.* (1998) did measure variability in grip force, no attempt has been made to 'establish the role of compensatory variability in the skill of striking a moving cricket ball with a moving cricket bat' (Stretch *et al.*, 2000, p. 718). This would mark an important step forward for biomechanists involved in performance analysis, as it would begin to identify interactions between the bowler and the batsman.

Such interactions are a key feature of games. For example, if a batter intends to play a cover drive to the boundary but instead hits the ball directly to extra cover or edges a catch to the slips, was the ball too good, could the batter not read cues or is there a technique defect? If the last of these, what is the problem? This approach could be developed to include the effects of field placement on the selection and successful execution of batting strokes and to evaluate fielding and catching skills.

6.4 Summary and conclusions

Through an analysis of game structures and the performance indicators used in recent research in performance analysis, basic rules emerge in the application of performance indicators to any sport. In every case, success or failure in a performance is relative, either to the opposition or to previous performances of the team or individual. To enable a full and objective interpretation of the data from the analysis of a performance, it is necessary to compare the collected data to aggregated data of a peer group of teams, or individuals, that compete at an appropriate standard. In addition, any analysis of the distribution of actions across the playing surface must be normalised with respect to the total distribution of actions across the area.

Performance indicators, expressed as non-dimensional ratios, can have the advantage of being independent of any units that are used; furthermore, they are implicitly independent of any one variable. Mathematics, fluid dynamics and physics in general have shown the benefits of using these types of parameters to define particular environments. They also enable, as in the example of bowling in cricket, an insight into differences between performers that can be obscure in the raw data. The particular applications of non-dimensional analysis are common in fluid dynamics, which offers empirical clues to the solution of multivariate problems that cannot easily be solved mathematically. Sport is even more complex, the result of interacting human behaviours; to apply simplistic analyses of raw sports data can be highly misleading. Further research could examine how normative profiles are established – how much data is required to define reliably a profile and how this varies with the different types of data involved in any analysis profile. Hughes *et al.* (2001) have completed an empirical study but this area needs more exploration and understanding.

Many of the most important aspects of team performance cannot be 'teased out' by biomechanists or match analysts working alone – a combined research approach is needed. This is particularly important for information processing – both in movement control and decision making. We should move rapidly to incorporate into such analyses qualitative biomechanical indicators that contribute to a successful movement. These should be identified interactively by biomechanists, notational analysts and coaches, sport-by-sport and movement-by-movement, and validated against detailed biomechanical measurements in controlled conditions. Biomechanists and notational analysts, along with experts in other sports science disciplines – particularly motor control – should also seek to agree on, and measure, those performance indicators that are important from this perspective.

For the different types of games considered, it has become clear that the classification of the different action variables being used as performance indicators follow rules that transcend the different sports. The selection and use of these performance indicators depend upon the research questions being posed, but it is clear that certain guidelines will ensure a more clear and accurate interpretation of these data. These are summarised below.

Match classification

Always compare with opponents' data and, where possible, with aggregated data from peer performances.

Biomechanical

Compare with previous performances and with team members, opponents and those of a similar standard. As well as presenting the original data analysis, consider presenting normalised data when a maximum or overall value both exists and is important or when inter-individual or intra-individual across-time comparisons are to be made.

Technical/Tactical

The technical and tactical variables should be treated in the same way. Always normalise the action variables with the total frequency of that action variable or, in some instances, the total frequency of all actions, and present these data with the raw frequency or processed data.

Most of the research community in performance analysis have not followed these simple guidelines to date. We feel that the utility of performance analysis could be considerably enhanced if its practitioners agreed and implemented such conventions in the future.

7

SPORTS ANALYSIS

Mike Hughes

The aim of this chapter is to provide an insight into how different sports can be broken down into a series of decisions represented by a limited number of actions and their possible outcomes. These logical progressions provide the inherent structure within each sport. The construction of flowcharts of different sports is examined, together with the definition of key events in these respective sports. The next step is to design a data collection and data processing system, so anyone interested in designing a notation system should read this chapter first.

7.1 Introduction

Before discussing the work and research done in the field of notational analysis, including both manual and computerised systems, it is necessary to explore methods of applying analysis to sport in general. As stated in previous chapters, the very essence of coaching athletes is to instigate an observable change in behaviour. Methods of analysis used to measure these changes form the central focus of the remaining sections of this chapter. Objective performance measures should serve as the basis for future planning in any coaching process. While it is clear that both the quantification of performance and the assessment of qualitative aspects of performance are required, it would seem from the current research in these fields (see sections 2.2, 2.3), that the former has been largely ignored, and the latter has many inherent weaknesses. This section therefore focuses on measures of performance that can be collected in order to analyse quantitatively the performance of an athletic event. First, analysis systems will be discussed with a view to applying them generally to either team sports or individual sports. In later chapters these systems are then extended into data recording systems. Current research work, both pure and applied, is reviewed and assessed. Finally the recent extension of these systems by the development of fast and inexpensive microcomputers will form the nucleus of the final sections of the book.

7.2 Creating flowcharts

The information that is available during a game is diverse and extensive. Continuous action and a dynamic environment make objective data collection difficult. Any quantitative analysis must therefore be structured. As there are so many ways in which to collect information about any sport, there are two very important points that should be considered:

a) consult with the best technical expert (i.e. coach) of the game to be analysed; and

b) make sure that what is required from the analysis system has been completely determined before starting anything else – i.e. the potential use of the information should guide how the system will be designed.

The first step is to create a 'flowchart' or logical structure of the game itself. This means defining the possible actions in the game and linking these actions with the possible outcomes, thus describing the sequential path the game can take. This is more easily explained by example. In a team sport such as field hockey, Franks and Goodman (1984) described the game very simply by a two state model. Either 'our' team has possession or the opposing team has possession of the ball. This would be the top of what Franks and Goodman termed 'the hierarchy'. They then proposed that the next level of questions in the hierarchy would be:

1 Where on the field did our team gain and lose possession?
2 Can these areas be easily identified (e.g. field divided into six areas)?

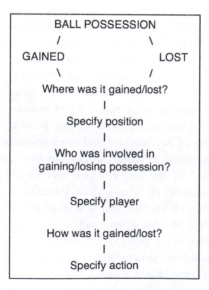

FIGURE 7.1 Hierarchical structure of a model for representing events that take place in a team game such as field hockey, soccer, basketball, water polo, etc.

3   Who on the team gained or lost possession?
4   How was possession gained and lost (e.g. was it from a tackle, an interception, foul, etc.)?

These questions can be included in the hierarchical structure as indicated in Figure 7.1 (Note: For those interested in reading around the subject further, Franks, Wilberg and Fishburne (1982) developed a series of detailed and more complex structures in which they modelled the decision-making processes of athletes engaged in team games. This work is very interesting from a modelling point of view, but as it approaches the problem from a perceptual point of view on behalf of the player, rather than an analytical view from the coach, it is not directly applicable here. However, it does provide a basis for a more thorough understanding of how to build up hierarchical structures).

The questions posed above in Figure 7.1 can yield extremely useful information, although this level of analysis is obviously very simple. It is best to anticipate the form in which you wish to look at your data. Simple tabulated records are often the easiest to produce, and are easily translated to pictorial representations that are always easier to assimilate. More detailed analyses might be concerned with the techniques individuals used during performance. It might also include physiological and psychological parameters that are mapped along a time axis during the performance. No matter how simple or complicated your intended analysis, always start as simply as possible and gradually add other actions and their outcomes bit by bit – in computing terminology this would be termed the addition of more 'sub-routines'.

Franks and Goodman (1984) go on to suggest a simple series of steps or tasks in the evaluation of performance. The first one is based upon the above analysis and states:

TASK 1:   Describe your sport from a general level to a specific focus.

The next step outlined by Franks and Goodman is fundamental in forming any evaluative analysis system:

TASK 2:   Prioritise key factors of performance.

The final step in the process being:

TASK 3:   Devise a recording method that is efficient and easy to learn.

The first two steps are discussed further with more examples in this chapter; the third task is given separate consideration in Chapter 8.

Consider our simple analysis of the team sport above, Figure 7.1; this can be made more sophisticated by considering in more detail the possible actions and their respective outcomes (Figure 7.2). These actions and outcomes can then be incorporated into a model for the events taking place in this team game, which happens to be soccer, but which could easily be transposed to any team sport. This is shown in Figure 7.3.

ACTION	OUTCOME	EFFECT ON POSSESSION
Pass	Good	Retained
	Bad	Lost
Shot	Wide	Lost
	High	Lost
	Blocked	Retained or Lost
	Saved	Lost
	Goal	Lost
Cross	Good	Retained
	Bad	Lost
Corner Kick	Good	Retained
	Bad	Lost
Goal Kick	Good	Retained
	Bad	Lost
Throw-in	Good	Retained
	Bad	Lost
Gk.'s Throw	Good	Retained
	Bad	Lost
Gk.'s Kick	Good	Retained
	Bad	Lost

Free Kick – Pass, Shot, etc. and their subsequent routines.

Penalty – Shot (subsequent routines).

FIGURE 7.2 Some actions, and their respective outcomes, for soccer.

The natural sequential logic of the game can be followed. As possession is gained by one of the players, a number of choices of actions are presented to the player. The choice, and the outcome of the action, determines whether this side retains possession, scores a goal, gives away a free kick, etc. Inevitably this system can be made more sophisticated still, that is always possible with any system. For example the dribble, run, tackle, foul, etc. have not been included, nor have any actions when not in possession. The difficult decision to make in designing this type of model is knowing when the limitations of the model are acceptable within the terms of reference of the desired data.

The core elements – 'Player', 'Position', 'Action' – in Figure 7.3 can be seen to be fundamental to analysis systems. If 'Time' is also included, then this would represent the most complex of systems. These elements are rarely included in all systems – for example if we were analysing the attacking patterns of a hockey team,

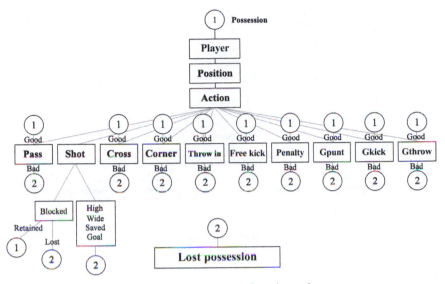

FIGURE 7.3 Simple schematic flowchart of soccer.

we would not need to record the players' identities – only the position on the pitch, the action and any outcomes (if any). If we were examining the work-rate of a player then all we would be recording would be the position, the action (stand, walk, jog, run, etc.) and possibly the time. These basic elements form the heart of any analysis of a sport.

Consider the game of squash as another example. This is a field-invasive individual racket sport. Other than the definition of the playing area, the logic of this game could as easily be applied to tennis or to badminton, which are non-field-invasive. The system in Figure 7.5 shows the simple logic needed to record and analyse the key elements of the performance. To include the scoring system would require considerable additions to this flowchart. The basis of the 'English' scoring (a similar system is used in badminton) is that the server receives a point

FIGURE 7.4 Core elements of any analysis system of performance.

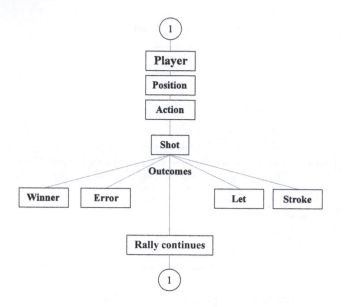

FIGURE 7.5 A simple flowchart for squash.

if he/she wins the rally. If the non-server, 'handout' wins the rally, he/she does not receive a point. The winner of the rally serves for the start of the next rally. This simple logic to the game of squash is complicated a little by the concept of 'lets' and 'strokes'. A 'let' is when one player impedes the other in the process of his/her shot; this results in the rally being played again, no change in score, same server. A 'stroke' is given against a player when he/she prevents the opponent from hitting the front wall with a direct shot or prevents a winner. (The concept is a little more complicated than this, as all squash players will testify, but this explanation should suffice for non-combatants.) So a 'stroke' given against a player is equivalent to the player conceding an error.

Creating the model for the logic of the sequence of the shot production and respective positions is relatively straight forward, see Figure 7.5. If the shot is a winner then that player serves the next rally. Whoever hits an error, or receives a 'stroke' adjudged against him/her, does not serve the next rally. The 'let' ball decision results in the rally starting again. If none of these conditions applies then the ball is still in play and the other player strikes his/her shot from the notated court position. In most simple systems for racket sports, analysts will start with a 'winner/error' analysis – recording the type of shots that were winners or errors and where on the court they were played.

One way of incorporating the logic of the scoring, and who serves, into the model of the action, is to keep the definition of the server and non-server throughout the rally. This helps clarify whether the score is increased at the end of the rally or not, depending upon who won. The selection of actions or, in this case, shots, to be inserted into these models, as in the previous examples, is determined by the detail of complexity required by the data collection. Sanderson and Way (1979) used a relatively complex menu of shots that included:

- Straight drive cross court drive;
- Straight drop cross court drop;
- Volley drive volley cross drive;
- Volley drop volley cross drop;
- Boast volley boast;
- Lob cross court lob;
- Others.

Included in 'others' were infrequent shots such as crossangles, cork–screw lobs, skid boasts, back wall boasts, shots behind the player's back, etc. Perhaps this selection of shots does not look too complex at first sight, but consider these facts. Sanderson and Way divided the court into 28 cells for definition of position. In the course of one match they would record in the region of 4500 items of information. Processing this data would take another 40 person–hours of work. In addition, the learning time to use the system 'in-match' was 5–8 hours. This was a complex system; despite its apparent simplicity, it produced the data that its designers required. But it is only too easy to gather too much data – be sure that your system gathers only the data needed. The recording system is discussed in detail in Chapter 8.

Franks and Goodman (1986b), working with David Hart and John MacMaster, both of the Canadian Water Polo Association, developed a flow diagram of water polo. The design was attack-based, whereby the events, the player responsible, and the reason, are recorded. By using this flow diagram, a computer program was constructed so that the whole history of the game was stored and produced for analysis. This system is further discussed later in this chapter and also in Chapter 8.

7.3 Levels of analysis – the team, subsidiary units and individuals

Although there are many facets of the team's performance that could be described, there are only a limited set of priority elements that serve a useful function with a view to improving performance. In deciding upon which information is useful, Franks, Goodman and Miller (1983a) suggested that the coach should be guided by three elements:

1   coaching philosophy
2   primary objectives of the game
3   database of past games.

For example, if a game objective has roots in the principle of possession, then the important questions to be answered should relate to possession (i.e. total number of possessions; where on the playing surface possession was lost and won; who was responsible for winning and losing possession; etc.). Coaching philosophy may also dictate certain defensive or offensive strategies to implement at critical time periods during a game. If this is the case, then the analysis should be directed towards objective counts of defensive or offensive behaviours during these periods of play. It should be noted that Franks *et al.* contend that 'The most important of these three elements is the formation of a data base of past games. With such a data base it is possible to fomulate a predictive model' (1983a p. 4).

If one knew how, where and when goals or points were scored in past games, a probablistic model could be constructed to aid future training and performance. Technical and tactical training could then be directed towards the high-probability events. Coaching could then be directed at gradually modelling a team to more fully fitting a winning profile.

After all the significant game related questions have been defined by the technical expert it is necessary to decide upon the level of analysis that is needed. Figure 7.5 illustrates a primary level of team analysis. The example extends the soccer model already used but it must again be emphasised that this can be equally applied to other team games. Four areas are considered for information gathering: possession, passing, shooting and set pieces. However, within each of these categories more detail is available. For example, when a shot is taken, this analysis should not only reveal whether the shot was on or off target, but also, if it was on target, was it saved or was it a goal? Further information about the off-target shooting could also be gathered – was it high, wide or high and wide? This type of information is extremely important and should greatly influence subsequent coaching practices.

According to Franks *et al.* (1983b), the information gained from set pieces (i.e. corner kicks, throw-ins and free-kicks) should be relative to some prescribed definition of success or failure. Coaches should have expectations of performance at set pieces in a game such as soccer. Other games will have similar structured phases where similar definitions of performance should be met, e.g. American football, yardage on a running play; field hockey, percentage of short corners converted to goals; rugby league, number of tackles made by specific positions, etc. The definition of performance in each case will depend upon the personal philosophy of the coach in relation to her/his sport. These expectations should be made clear to the players and should be practised. For example, a free kick that is awarded in the defending third of the field should be delivered in less than three moves to the attacking third of the field, whereas a free kick that is awarded in the attacking third of the field should result in a strike on goal in less than three moves. If these expectations are not met then the set piece is registered as a failure. According to Franks *et al.* (1983b), it is important to note that these definitions of success and failure should be continually upgraded to correspond to the level of performance and realistic expectations of the coach. If the definitions are unrealistic then the evaluation will not be sensitive to the performance changes.

A detailed analysis of an individual player is illustrated in Figure 7.6. It would take a very detailed and comprehensive recording system, involving a battery of

---

SOCCER EXAMPLE

1. POSSESSION INFORMATION

    a) Total possessions

    b) Where possessions were won and lost:
        Defending 1/3, Mid-field 1/3, Attacking 1/3

2. PASSING INFORMATION

    a) Square passes

    b) Back passes

    c) Forward passes

    d) Consecutive passes

3. SHOOTING INFORMATION

    a) Opportunity

    b) On target

    c) Off target

    d) Blocked

    e) Shooting angle

4. SET PIECE INFORMATION

    a) Corner kick

    b) Free kick

    c) Throw in

FIGURE 7.6 Primary level game analysis – team.

Source: Franks and Goodman, 1984.

experts, to gather the data for this sort of analysis. Franks *et al.* have, however, provided a very complete example of the way to go about defining the type of data required for an individual analysis. The player has two distinct categories of performance that can be evaluated: these are on the ball, and off the ball behaviour. These behaviours could be recorded in a cumulative fashion, e.g. number of defensive recovery runs, or given a success/failure rating, e.g. 20 successful square short passes and ten unsuccessful short passes gives a success/failure ratio of 2:1.

The area of the field in which events occur could, and should, be included in these computations to give the necessary spatial dimensions to the analysis. The division of the area of the pitch is again subject to the detail required: a simple division of the pitch into six equal areas would give a definition of the attacking, midfield

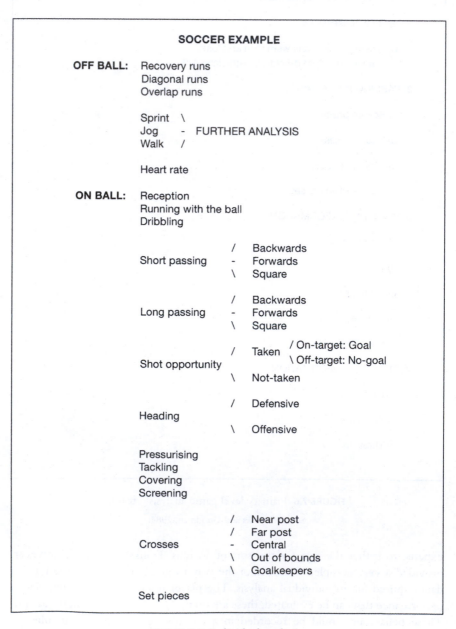

FIGURE 7.7 Individual analysis.

Source: Franks and Goodman, 1984.

and defending one third of the pitch. Other studies have used a finer definition overall, and then a finer definition yet again in the penalty area (Church and Hughes, 1986; Hughes *et al.*, 1988), so that these areas of specific interest have a finer degree of detail to them. Finally, further data relative to physiological requirements can be accessed in methods of measuring heart rate, and physiological requirements can be accessed in methods of measuring heart rate and blood lactates during and/or after game action. These measures can be correlated to technical data and then inferences can be made about the complete performance of individuals within a team game.

The way of applying these analyses, demonstrated in this example, should be applied to units in a team as well as the whole team or individuals. The efficiency of attacking, midfield or defensive groups of players within a team can be assessed. This is one objective way of selecting the best combinations of players within the tactical sub-groupings within a team, and monitoring their continued performance.

For sports such as tennis, golf, martial arts, etc., individual levels of analysis can be applied, using similar logical analyses as those shown in Figure 7.7.

7.4 Summary

Logical analysis of the form and function of the events taking place in a sport is necessary before any analysis can take place. Franks and Goodman (1986b) outlined three steps in forming any analysis system:

TASK 1: Describe your sport from a general level to a specific focus.
TASK 2: Prioritise key factors of performance.
TASK 3: Devise a recording method that is efficient and easy to learn.

By elucidating tasks 1 and 2, the creation of a notation system becomes an easy and logical progression. Practising these logical definitions is not difficult but it is a skill that becomes easier and easier with practice.

The more complex the sport, team games such as soccer or American football for example, then the more care that must be taken in deciding exactly what is required of the system: which units of the team, or individuals are to be analysed, which actions and events have the most relevance and so on.

The next step in analysis logic is to decide the level at which the analysis will take place. If it is a team game, then what units of the team are going to be analysed? Or are individuals to be monitored? Or the whole team? This type of decision does not apply in individual sports, but the level or degree of detail of output must be decided – and it is vital that these decisions are made early in the analytical process.

8

HOW DO WE DESIGN SIMPLE SYSTEMS?

How to develop a notation system

Mike Hughes

8.1 Introduction

The aim of this chapter is to enable you to begin to understand how hand notation systems are developed. No matter how simple or complicated you wish to make it – the same underlying principles apply. If you are hoping to develop a computerised system, the same logical process must be followed, so this section is a vital part of that developmental process too. Again, if you wish to go further down this design route then read Chapters 5 and 6 in Hughes and Franks (2004).

8.2 Data collection systems

There are several types of data collection systems that can be roughly divided into three categories, by the nature of the data collected:

a) scatter diagrams;
b) frequency tables; and
c) sequential systems.

8.2.1 Scatter diagrams

Scatter diagrams are usually simple and are most often used to gather data in-event and enable immediate feedback for the coach and athlete. They are usually used in the form of drawing a schematic representation of the playing surface of the sport in which you are interested on a sheet of paper, and then notating on this the actions of interest, at the position at which they took place (player number too?). For example, consider a soccer coach wanting to know where a football team loses possession – a simple plan of the pitch enables the recording of these positions (Figure 8.1).

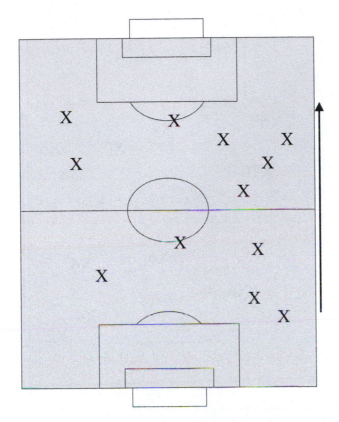

FIGURE 8.1 A simple scatter diagram for recording position of loss of possession for soccer.

What else does the coach need to know – which of the players is offending most? This system can be made a little more sophisticated by adding the number of the player who lost possession (Figure 8.2).

What else might we need to know about our problem of loss of possession? Perhaps the actions that the players are executing might give us more insight into the relative merits of the performance of the players involved (Figure 8.3).

So let us also record the actions involved, for this we will need a simple definition of the most common actions and some symbols:

What action?

- P – Pass
- D – Dribble
- C – Cross
- S – Shot
- K – Clear

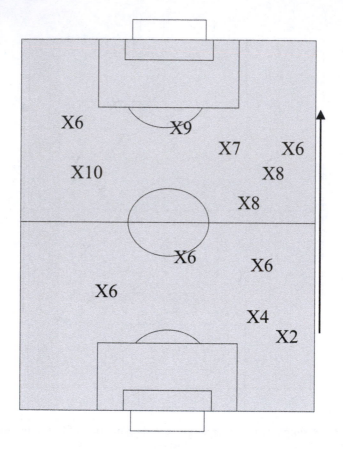

FIGURE 8.2 A simple scatter diagram for recording position of loss of possession, and the player involved, for soccer.

Figure 8.2 shows an example of this form of data gathering. Because this is more complicated, to be able to do this at match speed might take a little practice. Scatter diagrams have a number of immediate advantages:

- simple, quick;
- accurate – can be quite accurate if you practise a lot;
- usually 'in-event';
- immediate feedback;
- usually no need to process data;
- do not know the order of events – no 'sequentiality'.

But it must be noted that there are dangers in interpretation of these simple forms of data, not only because usually their accuracy is not very high, but also the simple data can only yield simple analyses. Attempts at further depth to analyses will only lead to problems.

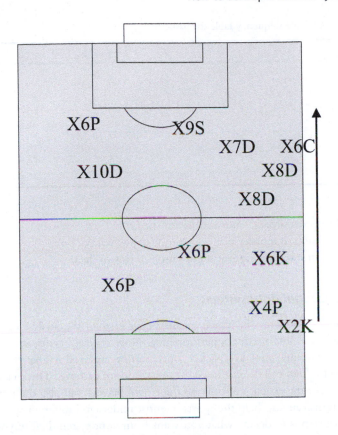

FIGURE 8.3 A simple scatter diagram for recording position of loss of possession, and the player and the action involved, for soccer.

8.2.2 Frequency tables

Frequency tables are another commonly used form of data gathering that enables quick, simple analyses of performance of athletes and teams. Let us consider an example of a basketball coach wanting to know which players have made which actions during a game. By using a frequency table such as that shown in Table 8.1, the analyst can easily record the frequency of each of the actions by the players in the squad.

Like scatter diagrams, frequency tables have some obvious advantages and disadvantages:

- simple, quick;
- accurate – can be accurate with practice;
- usually 'in-event';
- immediate feedback;

TABLE 8.1 A simple frequency table for basketball

Actions	1	2	3	4	5	6 . . .
Pass	///////		///	////		
Dribble	///		/	//		
2-pt shot	////		////	//		
3-pt shot	//			/		
Assist	////		////	/		
Lost poss.	/		//			

- need to process data – not usually too bad;
- do not know the order of events – no 'sequentiality';
- dangers in interpretation of these simple forms of data.

8.2.3 Sequential data systems

Recording the sequence in which events occur enables the analyst to go to far greater depths in interpreting a performance. Now critical events, such as a shot at goal or a winning shot in a racket sport, can be analysed so that those events that led up to them can be examined for repetitions of patterns. These can be very informative for the coach, not only on their own players, but also the opposition. These patterns can also help the sports scientist understand different sports.

The first step is to decide what you want from your system before you design the system.

This does sound a little odd but the reason for this lies in the fact that notation systems provide masses of data. Unless you have a crystal clear idea about what data you wish to collect, then you will find that your system will collect confusing, and sometimes irrelevant, information. Keep in mind the old adage about not seeing the wood for the trees. Time spent working on what form(s) your output might take can save a great deal of frustration later. Most importantly, it also simplifies the job of defining input. Having once decided what you want, the process of designing your data collection system is simple and straightforward. Often the most difficult part is making sense from the mass of data – this is true for all analysis systems. The simplest way of starting is to consider a basic example. A field hockey coach may wish to have more information about the shooting patterns, or lack of them, for her/his team. Consequently, this coach will need an output from this system consisting of:

1 position of the pass preceding the shot (the assist);
2 player who made the pass;
3 type of pass;
4 position from which the shot was taken;

5   which player made the shot;
6   outcome of the shot, i.e. goal, save, block, miss (wide), miss (high), corner
    . . . etc.

(Note: If field hockey is not a game with which you are familiar, this method will as easily apply to any field-invasive team sport such as basketball, soccer, water polo, lacrosse, etc.)

The data needed to be notated in this example is relatively simple. The next step is to assign notation symbols for each of the above variables. First, divide the pitch into segments or cells and give each one a code – this could be either a number or a letter, but there are usually advantages in using specifically one or the other. Deciding upon how the playing surface should be divided is not always as simple as it might appear. Using small cells does enable fine definition of the positions at which actions take place, but the more cells you have the more data you have to collect in order to have significant numbers of actions in each cell. If in doubt, err on the side of simplicity – the most influential research on soccer was done with the pitch divided into three, the defending third, the middle third and the attacking third. The hockey pitch in Figure 8.4 is at the other extreme of definition with a large number of position cells.

As position, player, action and so on are notated it is often useful to have the codes entered in the system alternating from letter to number to letter; this makes interpretation of the data much simpler. Any saving that can be made in the number of items entered, can also mean a large saving in time – often the difference in being able to notate 'in match' or not. It is easy to identify players by their shirt number (if they have one of course), but if there are more than nine in a team or squad then you have to note two digits instead of one. Some systems in the past have employed letters for the players '10' and '11'. In Figure 8.3, letters have been used to differentiate between respective areas of the pitch rather than numbers. The significance of this is that, for each of the areas in Figure 8.3, there is only a single item of information required to be written down, irrespective of which area. This may sound trivial, but when systems can be recording thousands of items of data, each small saving in design, at the developmental stage, will increase the effectiveness of the system many times over.

So let us assume that the coach has decided to use letters for pitch cell divisions and numbers for the players of the team. Does the coding of position cells in Figure 8.4 seem a reasonable layout? A number of potential problems present themselves. The use of letters 'I', 'L' and 'O' could present some translational problems later. Most notation is done at speed, 'I' and 'L' can easily be confused both with each other and the number '1', and of course the letters 'O' and 'Q' with zero, '0'.

The main problem now with the representation of the playing area in Figure 8.4 is one of definition. Will these pitch divisions give the coach sufficient information on the significant areas of the pitch from which his team are shooting well or poorly? It would seem unlikely. In this situation, previous researchers have used unequal divisions of the playing areas, making the definition finer in the areas

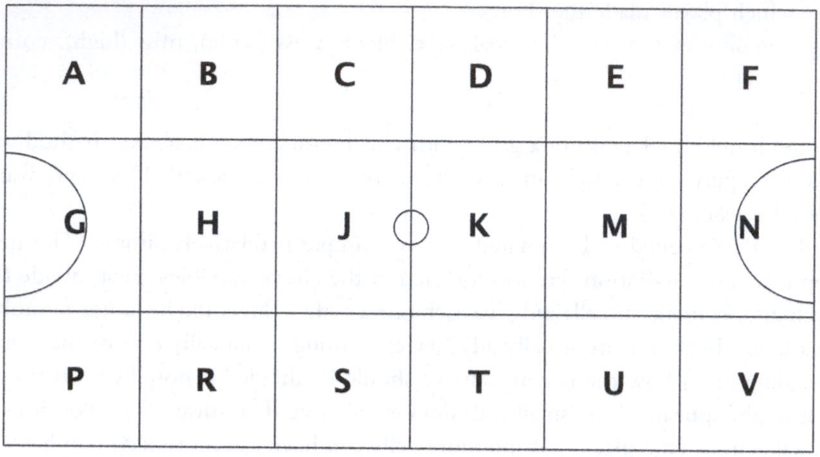

A	**B**	**C**	**D**	**E**	**F**
G	**H**	**J**	**K**	**M**	**N**
P	**R**	**S**	**T**	**U**	**V**

FIGURE 8.4 A definition of position on a representation of a field hockey pitch.

of most interest. In this example this will be around the goal. There are a number of ways of doing this: below is one simple way using a representation of just half the playing area – this does however negate the possibility of notating shots at goal from the player's own half.

Another way of doing this would be to use arcs from the goal as shown in Figure 8.5. This has been used in a number of systems, both in basketball and soccer, to good effect. In both games there is an optimum area from which to shoot that is more easily defined in this way.

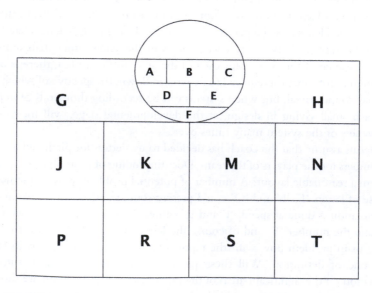

FIGURE 8.5 A definition of position on a representation of a field hockey pitch oriented to analysing attacking moves.

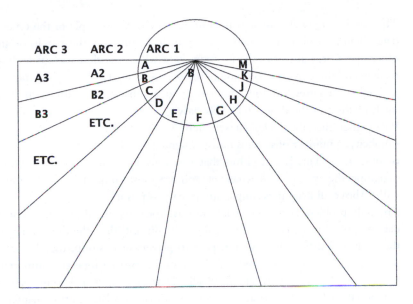

FIGURE 8.6 Another definition of position on a representation of a field hockey pitch oriented to analysing attacking moves.

For our example let us assume that the coach is using the area representation shown in Figure 8.5, and that players are identified by their shirt numbers. The two actions that we are notating are the pass and the shot. There are four different types of pass that our coach has defined:

- F   Flick
- P   Push
- A   Arial
- H   Hit

Now we only have to decide on the possible outcomes of the other action variable, the shot, and we have a notation system. The coach has decided at this stage not to differentiate between types of shot, so it is the outcome of the shots that need coding. As we are writing letter and then number as we notate position and player, let us use a letter code for the action outcome. A number of systems involve specifically invented symbols but, for the sake of keeping this example simple, let us stick to recognised numeric and alphanumeric symbols. A simple code would be:

- G   GOAL
- S   Saved
- W   Wide
- H   High
- B   Blocked
- R   Rebound

- The coach is now able to start notating a match. An example of the type of data obtained will be as shown in Chapter 9. In this way the coach, or any other operator, can record the position from which the shot was made, who made it and the outcome. Because of the way that the data have been entered, a number, a letter, another number, and a separate line for each shot, interpretation of the data is relatively easy.

- Remember that the codes chosen here in this example were chosen for simplicity, a number of systems utilise invented symbols that represent actions or outcomes. This is a decision that can only be made by the individual designing the system. Use whatever you are most comfortable and familiar with. Above all keep it as simple and as easy as possible.

- The only problem facing the coach now is processing the data. First, enough data will need to be collected to make it significant, then the distribution of the shots and their assists, with respect to players or position, together with their outcome, can be explored. This form of data processing is very important in most forms of analysis and feedback. Data analysis is a difficult part of notational analysis – a separate section is devoted to it later in this chapter.

- Table 8.1 makes it easy to record the above data, there is less chance of becoming confused, and it is easier to interpret the data once recorded. It also makes it easier for someone else to understand the data collection system, should that be desirable. Decide who is likely to use your system, if it is only for your own use only spend as much time 'dressing it up' as is necessary.

- N.B. Always remember that when other people either use your system or are presented with the data from your system, they will tend to judge the whole system by its appearance.

8.3 Data collection systems in general

What can we learn in general terms about notational analysis from our example? In the most general form of notation the following parameters are being recorded:

1   position
2   player
3   action – and the subsequent outcome(s)
4   time.

This is the most general situation possible in any match analysis, in most notation systems only two or three of these variables will be necessary. In individual sports, such as squash, tennis or gymnastics, the notation of which player is involved becomes easier. In team sports it becomes more difficult, depending upon the analysis and the form of the output. In certain situations, perhaps where the movements of one particular player are being recorded, it will be unnecessary to record that player because the notation is only about the one performer. The time variable is not used as frequently as the other variables in notation systems; it increases the complexity considerably, but there are some analyses that will require it. Analyses where velocities, accelerations and/or rates of work are the desired output from the data will use a time base. Reilly and Thomas (1976) completed what can be regarded now as a classical study of motion analysis in soccer, by using a combination of hand notation, with stop watches and audio tape recorders. Position and action are nearly always involved in notation systems, although there are examples of systems not using one or other of these two. In summary then, most systems will use two or three of the above variables, there are very few instances where it is necessary to use all four.

In our example we recorded position, player and then the outcome of the action (shot). The beginning and end of each sequence were indicated by using a new line for each event.

Position: the way in which the position was defined in the example was as good a way as any in going about recording positional data. The needs of the system often dictate the definition required within the system. Obviously the finer the definition the more accurate the information, *but* the finer the definition the more data will need to be collected to make it significant. Be careful not to submerge yourself in too much data or too much data collection – notation is not an end in itself, the end product has to justify the time spent on it. Notating position is always a compromise between accuracy and having manageable data.

Player: recording which player executed the action cannot be very different in more sophisticated systems. In individual sports the system may only be notating one player at a time, so differentiation will not be necessary.

Action: what made our example a relatively simple one was that we were considering only two actions – the assist and the shot. But even so, the system still required four different types of pass (assist) and five possible outcomes of the shot to be notated. These again could have been more complicated since it may be useful to know whether possession was regained after the save or the block. Consider then the complexity of the situation when defining all the possible actions, and their respective outcomes, in a game such as soccer or hockey or basketball. It is this logical and structured analysis, coupled with a clear idea of the salient information that is required from the game, that forms the nucleus of any notation system. A sound system that will produce consistent and meaningful data must be based on a careful analysis of the sport to be notated. It is most important to be able to understand the logic of the game structure of the sport under study – Chapter 7 is devoted to sport analysis.

The most important aspect of defining any action, or outcome, is ensuring that the 'operational definition' of this term is clear and unambiguous. The operational definition of the action and outcomes enable you, and others, to consistently interpret events in the same way. We have found, with experience, that any problem with reliability (repeatability) of data gathering is nearly always associated with the clarity of the operational definitions.

A few notes to remember:

1   You must have a clear idea what information you want from the system.
2   Make the data collection, and the data processing, as simple as possible to start with. Build the complexity of your system in easy stages, adding on to what you know works and to what you can handle.
3   Test your system on a small part of a match or event using video. In this way you can practise and improve your notation skills, and also find out how accurate you are. Then practise some more, after that my advice is to practise some more. There is nothing worse than notating for half an hour, getting in a muddle and then realising you have made a mess of the whole thing (always after you have promised a detailed analysis to someone important).
4   Having tested the system, does it collect the data you wanted? It is easy to be carried away with the design stage, adding on little bits here and collecting a little more information there, until the whole structure has assumed gargantuan proportions, and does not fulfil the original aims defined at the start.
5   The more complex your system the longer it will take to learn. In addition, the amount of output increases immensely, which means considerably more work processing the data. For example, the notation system developed by Sanderson and Way (1979) involved 5–8 hours learning time and also required 40 hours of work to process the data of a single match. Remember:

> KEEP IT SIMPLE

> You can always add to your system and build up its complexity as you grow in experience, confidence and speed – and, most importantly, fully process the data output and decide on additional forms of output before adding extra sub-routines to your system.

6   Once you have arrived at the final version of your system – you find this out by continually testing the system to examine whether the data that you can gather provides the answers to the questions that you have about your sport – then you must test its reliability. This is not necessarily a complicated process, but it is very important to know the accuracy of your system. We have devoted a whole chapter to it (see Chapter 10).

9

EXAMPLES OF NOTATION SYSTEMS

Mike Hughes

9.1 Introduction

The best way to appreciate the intricacies of notational analysis is to examine systems for the sport(s) in which you are interested, or sports that are similar. Presented here are a number of examples of different systems for different sports. They have been devised by students of notational analysis and are therefore of differing levels of complexity and sophistication – but there are always lessons to be learned even from the simplest of systems. The explanations and analyses are completed by beginners at notational analysis; coaches of these sports should not therefore be irritated at some of the simplistic levels of analysis for the respective sports. The encouraging aspect about these examples is the amount of information that the systems provide – even the simplest of these. Examples 9.21–9.22 are for individual sports, while examples 9.31–9.34 are for team games. More examples can be found in the first version of the book – *Notational Analysis of Sport*, by Hughes and Franks (1997).

9.2 Individual sports

9.2.1 A notation system for tennis

This system, for the notation and analysis of data for tennis, was designed to gather basic information on winners and errors. The court was divided up into sections as shown in Figure 9.1. Six sections were chosen in order to keep the recording of position, and its subsequent analysis, as simple as possible. A singles match was to be notated, which reduced the court size, removing the need for the tram-lines, simplifying the system.

Symbols were allocated for the basic shots to be recorded, these were as follows:

S   =   Serve
F   =   Forehand drive
B   =   Backhand drive
V   =   Forehand volley
BV =   Backhand volley
L   =   Forehand lob
BL =   Backhand lob
Sm =   Smash

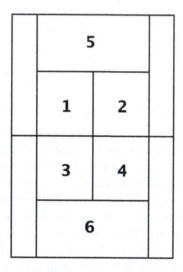

FIGURE 9.1 Division of the court into six cells for analysis of tennis.

Having established shot symbols, it was then necessary to devise 'result of shot' symbols, i.e. whether the shot was a winner, or whether a mistake was made. These were as follows:

- A dot ('.') following a shot symbol indicates that the shot was played into the net.
- An arrow ('→') following a shot symbol indicates that the ball was played out of court.
- A shot symbol followed by 'W', indicates that the shot was either an outright winner or that the opponents shot following this one was a mistake.
- A single line indicates the end of a point.
- A double line indicates the end of a game.
- A triple line indicates the end of a set.

For the actual notation purposes, the construction of simple columns was used. One vertical column for each player. The play was notated by alternating from each column as the shots were played until the conclusion of the point. A single line was then drawn across both columns and the winning players last shot ringed. An example of a game notated using this system is shown in Figures 9.2a and 9.2b.

Smith	Jones
S4	F2
B6	L1
Sm →	

FIGURE 9.2A Notation of data using the system for tennis.

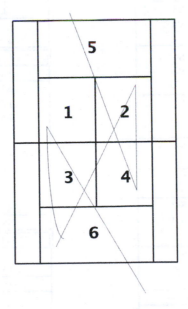

FIGURE 9.2B Schematic representation of data used in example in Figure 9.2a.

Description of point:

Smith served the ball wide and Jones returned the serve with a forehand that landed short. Smith moved in to play a deep cross-court backhand causing Jones to play a defensive backhand lob. This lob was not a good one and Smith had the chance to smash the ball, but he hit the ball out of court. Jones won the point and the score was 0–15.

The match chosen for analysis was the 1989 Ladies Wimbledon Final between Steffi Graf and Martina Navratilova. This selection was made to incorporate a wide variety of shots while at the same time displaying constructive rallies to analyse, but which did not continue for too long as is the case with some women's matches, i.e. making notation strenuous.

WIMBLEDON LADIES FINAL 1989
Steffi Graf v Martina Navritilova

First Set (Graf won, 6-2)

STEFFI	MARTINA		STEFFI	MARTINA
	S4			S3
B2	V3		B.	
F1 W	V →			S4
	S3		B.	
B2	V4			S3
B2 W			B →	
	S4		1-0	
F5	V4		S4	B →
F2	V3 W		S3	B5
	S3		F6	F2
B.			F6	B5
	S4		F4 W	
B2 W	V.		S4 W	
	S3		S3	F5
F5	V6 W		F4	B5
	S4		L	Sm2 W
F5	L6 W		S4	B.
XF →			1-1	
	S3			S1
F1	V4		F3 W	
F2 W			ETC.	
	S4 →			
	S3 W			
B.				

FIGURE 9.3 Example of the tennis data gathering system.

Also the choice of a grass court surface would produce an exciting game without creating very short rallies as displayed in a men's game, with one player hitting a fast serve that results in either a mistake or an outright winner from his opponent.

The aim of the notation was to devise a system that was simple enough to notate a match live without the use of video cameras. Therefore, although this match was viewed from video, it was notated continuously without pausing or rewinding the tape. An example of part of the notation is shown in Figure 9.3.

9.2.1.1 Results

A simple analysis of the data from this match is presented, more information could have been obtained from the data given more time.

STEFFI GRAF

Mistakes	NET	=	1 FOREHAND
			4 BACKHANDS
	OUT	=	2 FOREHANDS
			3 BACKHANDS
			2 BACKHAND LOBS
Outright Winners		=	5 FOREHANDS
			4 BACKHANDS
			1 SERVE
			1 LOB

Points lost:

Unforced errors	Navratilova winners
12	12

MARTINA NAVRATILOVA

Mistakes	NET	=	3 FOREHANDS
			5 BACKHANDS
			4 VOLLEYS
			1 DOUBLE FAULT
	OUT	=	4 FOREHANDS
			4 BACKHANDS
			1 VOLLEY
Outright winners		=	1 FOREHAND
			8 VOLLEYS
			2 SMASHES
			1 SERVE

Points lost:

Unforced errors	Graf winners
23	11

SUMMARY OF RESULTS

If a performance indicator is defined as:

$$\text{Tennis ratio} \quad = \quad \frac{\text{Number of errors}}{\text{Number of winners}}$$

Graf	Tennis ratio	=	12/11 (or nearly 1/1)
Navratilova	Tennis ratio	=	23 : 12 (or nearly 2 : 1)

9.2.1.2 Discussion and conclusions

Analysis of the results showed that in this particular match, the loser i.e. Martina Navratilova had a ratio of nearly 2:1 for unforced errors to winners. The players analysed were of the highest playing standard currently competing and therefore made relatively few unforced errors. Also, the fast grass court made rallies shorter than usual with many more winners played, in contrast to the 'waiting game' played on slow clay courts. Another reason for Navratilova's results could be related to the nature of her game. She plays a high-powered attacking game aiming to control play from the net position as soon as possible. Consequently her mistakes occurred in trying to get to that position but once there, very few unforced errors occurred and points were won by outright volley winners or by passing shots played by Graf.

9.2.2 A notation system for boxing

First, the types of punches have to be identified, together with other behaviour variables considered to be the important in defining a boxing match. These were considered to be:

(i)   jabs
(ii)   hooks
(iii)   upper cuts
(iv)   misses (complete)
(v)   front body punches
(vi)   side body punches
(vii)   holding
(viii) hit guard (partial miss)
(ix)   foul punching
(x)   ducking
(xi)   on ropes
(xii)   knockdown
(xiii) knock out
(xv)   technical K.O.
(xvi)   points decision.

As it can be seen, there are numerous actions which constitute,

- offensive information
- defensive information
- positional information
- fight outcome.

These provided too many variables to notate using a hand system as many or all could be occurring simultaneously. It is suggested that, if both boxers are to be notated, only offensive actions and specific key features could be recorded. These could be identified as:

- jabs
- misses
- knockdowns
- hooks
- body shots
- uppercuts
- holding.

The system was now progressed to separating these factors into left and right sides depending on which side the punch was thrown from. (Knock downs remained universal as the final punch would be recorded.) The symbol denoting the jab, aims to represent the jab itself i.e. a straight punch. Hence the symbol used was a straight line. The dash was placed either side depending on where it was thrown from, the left or right. This reasoning was then followed for the construction of the other symbols. Thus the notation shown in Table 9.1 was devised.

TABLE 9.1 Symbols used in the data gathering system for boxing

Left	Right	Punch
-]	[-	Jab
(	)	Hook
UL	UR	Upper cut
m	m	Miss
B	B	Body punch
<	>	Holding
v	v	Knock down

For example, a boxer while holding his opponent with his left arm produces an uppercut that misses with his right; it would be notated as:

    < URm

TABLE 9.2 Example data from the Tyson–Bruno fight (1989) using the data gathering system for boxing

Tyson	Bruno	Tyson	Bruno	Tyson	Bruno
-]			<		<URm
	-]		<UR		<URm
(	)		<UR		<URm
)			<)m		<)m
	)		<UR		)
	)		<)	-]	
	)		<)m	(	
(			<)		<UR
BUR	<)		)		<UR
	<)		<)		<UR
(		(	<)	(m	
-]			<)		<(
)		-]			)m
(m		)			-]
URm			<>		-]
	V		UR	(	
(	<		)	)m	
	<		-]		-]
)		)		(m	
<)	<)		<)		-]
<)	<)		<)	)m	
	(		<)		)
)		(	<)	(	

A chart (see Table 9.2) was then devised to record a fight on which the punches of each boxer could be notated in sequential order.

This format of a vertical linear layout remains common in hand systems as it enables quickly translated and stored records. One line of the chart corresponds to one punch from each boxer. In situations where punches were thrown simultaneously, both were recorded on the same line to indicate they occurred within the time space of one punch.

It was decided that certain characteristics of a fight which might ease the notation task were as follows:

1   a heavyweight match in which the 'punch rate' is considerably slower than lower weight categories;
2   a fight which is relatively short in duration, so massive amounts of raw data are not produced.

The chosen match was: Mike Tyson *vs* Frank Bruno held in 1989 at the Hilton International, Las Vegas. This was a five-round fight between two heavyweight boxers.

Notating the fight involved first watching the fight through completely, to get a 'feeling' of punch speed, and of any anomalies that may exist in their boxing style. Then, the fight was notated using the pause function on the video and, at instances when numerous punches were thrown within a very short period, a frame by frame analysis was used. The raw data were then collated by frequency tallies (see Figures 9.4 and 9.5). Summary totals could then be calculated and represented graphically (see results).

9.2.2.1 Collated raw data

TABLE 9.3 Collated data of total punches thrown

	Tyson	Bruno
Round 1	38	68
Round 2	36	54
Round 3	27	47
Round 4	32	24
Round 5	48	23
Total	181	216

TABLE 9.4 Analysis of the number of types of punches thrown by both boxers

Punch	Tyson		Bruno	
	Number	% of total	Number	% of total
Jab	40	22	45	21
Upper cut	22	12	29	13
Hook	66	37	72	36
Body	16	9	19	9
Miss	37	20	46	21

9.2.2.2 Results

From the results we can see that Bruno threw 55 per cent of the punches; however, if these are broken down round by round, we see that in the first three rounds he threw more than Tyson, and in Rounds 4 and 5 Tyson threw more than Bruno (Table 9.3). This suggests that he was tiring and was failing to counter punch. So the fight was essentially lost in rounds 4 and 5.

Both boxers had almost identical punch compositions (see Table 9.4) with Bruno missing 1 per cent more than Tyson. However, during the fight Bruno was cautioned for holding. This is illustrated by Table 9.5 which shows the percentage of punches made while holding. Bruno made 41 per cent of his punches while holding compared with Tyson's 4 per cent. This is probably a reflection of Bruno

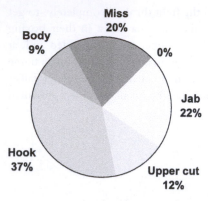

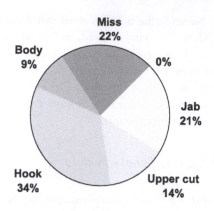

FIGURE 9.4 Distribution of the types of punches thrown by Tyson in the Bruno–Tyson match (1989).

FIGURE 9.5 Distribution of the types of punches thrown by Bruno in the Bruno–Tyson match (1989).

TABLE 9.5 The number of punches thrown while holding

Tyson	Bruno
8	89

TABLE 9.6 The number of jabs thrown in each round

	Tyson	Bruno
Round 1	5	9
Round 2	8	21
Round 3	8	20
Round 4	15	7
Round 5	6	5
Total	42	62

trying to punch 'inside' Tyson, i.e. by staying close you have less chance of being knocked out with one punch which is characteristic of Tyson's fights. This was therefore intentional and probably not due to fatigue alone.

Bruno has a reputation for his jabs, which intimidate his opponents. In the first three rounds his jabbing more than doubled those of Tyson (Table 9.6 and Figure 9.6). However, from then on the number of his jabs decreased dramatically and Tyson's increased. The final round contained roughly the same number of jabs thrown by each opponent. This was probably due to Bruno having only the strength to produce jabs and Tyson trying to finish the fight off with hooks and uppercuts, which are more powerful punches. All the statistics tend to suggest that the fight was won in rounds four and five.

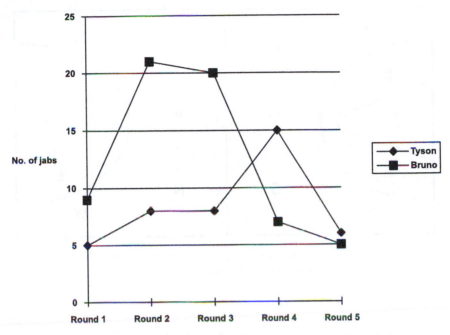

FIGURE 9.6 Distribution of jabs on a round-by-round analysis by both fighters (Bruno–Tyson, 1989).

9.2.2.3 Conclusions

1   This simple system does enable the notation of a boxing match by a post-event analysis of video. While acknowledging that the results describe the basic techniques employed by a boxer during a match, one must recognise that the notation in itself was very simplified and somewhat crude, and did not address many essential aspects of a fight, namely positional information, defensive information and subjective measures of power and accuracy (which may require the knowledge of a skilled coach).
2   Considering the speed of boxing matches, it was almost impossible to notate a fight live. The use of video and playback was therefore essential.

However, some very simple and basic information clearly maps the progress of the fight and gives a quantitative analysis of the progress of the two boxers during the bout.

9.3 Team sports

9.3.1 A notation system for basketball

The schematic representation of a basketball court, in Figure 9.7, shows the court position used in the notation. In basketball a team squad consists of ten team

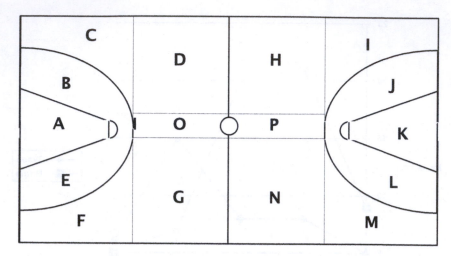

FIGURE 9.7 Schematic representation of the basketball court in order to define position cells for a data gathering system.

members, five on the court at any one time. For the purpose of this notation the players were assigned numbers in the range from 4 to 14 (1, 2 and 3 were not used to avoid confusion with the letters I, Z and B), although some teams, and all American ones, often use numbers such as 33, 42 etc.

The actions under consideration in this hand notation and the symbols used to represent them are listed as follows:

Actions	Symbol		
Tip off	TO		
Dribble	D		
Drive	V		
Shot	S	B/M	(Basket good – B)
Lay up	L	B/M	(Basket missed – M)
Rebound	R		
Pass	P		
Fastbreak	F		
Foul	FL	time	The time
Free throws	FT	time	the action
Turnover	T	time	occurred
Substitution	SB	time	should be
Out of court	O	time	recorded
Sideline ball	SL		
Base line ball	BL		

These symbols, together with the player number and his position on the court, are written down in columns in a table in the following manner.

      6   G   P

i.e. player No. 6, in position cell G, passed the ball.

TABLE 9.7 A demonstration of how the notation system works

Team A	Time	Team B
TO 6 P		
H 7 D		
I 7 P		
K 13 S M		
		K 4 R
		K 4 D
		L 4 P
	2:20	N 13 FL (5)
		SL–N 13 P
		N 10 P
	2:59	T
C 6 P		
I 13 L B	3:01	
2-0		
		BL-K 4 P
		I O
	3:05	SB-4/6
		SL-I 6 P
	Etc.	

The following is an explanation of the events notated in Table 9.7.

Line	Comments
1	The tip off was won by 6 who passed.
2	No. 7 received the ball in H and dribbled
3	to I where the ball was passed
4	to No. 13 in K who shot and missed.
5	Team B: No. 4 rebounded in K,
6	dribbled from K
7	to L where the ball was passed
8	to No. 13 in N who was fouled by No. 5.
9	No. 13 took a side line ball in N passing
10	to No. 10 in N who dribbled

11   to O where the ball was passed.
12   Turnover – after 2 mins 59 secs.
13   No. 6 intercepted the ball in C and passed
14   to No. 13 in I who scored a lay-up.
15   The running score is 2–0, time 3 mins 01 sec.
16   Base line ball in K is passed by No. 4,
17   the ball goes out of court in I.
18   Substitution: No. 6 comes on for No. 4.
19   Side line ball in I is passed by No. 6.

9.3.1.1 Conclusion and discussion

A coach or analyst can use this very simple notation system to gather performance data of individual players or the whole team. It can be used to analyse from which side of the court the most successful attacks come; what success rate the team and individuals achieve at rebounds, (do they win more than they lose?); how successful they are in the majority of freethrows; is there any increase in success rate/ performance after a time out etc. The coach can then assess the strengths and weaknesses of the individuals and the team, or their opponents, and be able to make an attempt at correcting them.

This type of system is very easily changed to suit any team sport, redefining the playing surface, the number of players and the actions, and their outcomes, accordingly.

9.3.2 A notation system for soccer

The aim of this notation system was to notate the distribution ability of a right full back in soccer.

9.3.2.1 Method

Notation occurred each time the subject, the right full back of Brook House FC, appeared to play or distribute the ball. The following symbols and meanings were used in order for the system to function.

Passes/Clearances/Shots	Distances	Symbols
By foot	< 10 yards	F1
	10–30 yards	F2
	> 30 yards	F3
By head	< 10 yards	H1
	10–30 yards	H2
	> 30 yards	H3
By hand	< 10 yards	T1
(i.e. throw–in)	10–30	T2
	> 30	T3

- clearances – above symbols preceded by 'C', e.g. CF2 is a clearance by foot of 10–30 yards (it should be noted that clearances were neither counted as completed or uncompleted passes);
- shots – above symbols for feet or head preceded by i.e. 'F' for a goal and 'X' for a miss;
- completed pass – above symbols for feet, head or hand;
- uncompleted pass – above symbols for feet, head or hand, *circled*;
- the time elapsed of the half was also recorded at the end of each piece of information.

Therefore, an example of notated data is as follows:

CH3 12, 37

This refers to a clearance by head of a distance of 30 yards or more, that occurred after 12 mins 37 secs of the half. These data were then recorded in columns on a prepared data collection sheet.

9.3.2.2 Results

The data were collected over 45 minutes (one half) of a 'local Sunday football league' match.

Match information date = 29/10/89   Start = 12.09 pm

1st half of Bow & Arrow FC   vs   Brook House FC
(Black and white stripes)   (Royal blue and navy stripes)

Half-time score 1–3

The data were obtained by notating the first half of the above match and processing the data in a very simple way. From these results the following analysis was carried out.

9.3.2.3 Analysis

1) Number of touches of the ball = 29

2) Number of touches of the ball by each method
    i)   Number of foot contacts = 21
    ii) Number of headed contacts = 3
    iii) Number of throw-ins = 5

3) Percentage of touches by each method:-
    i)   Feet = 21/29 = 72.4%
    ii) Head = 3/29 = 10.4%
    iii) Throw-ins = 5/29 = 17.2%

4) Number of incomplete passes (i.e. errors), signified by circled symbol = 9

5) Number of errors by each method
   i)   Feet = 8
   ii) Head = 0
   iii) Throw-ins = 1

6) Percentage of errors by each method
   i)   Feet = 8/9 = 88.9%
   ii) Head = 0/9 = 0%
   iii) Throw-ins = 11.1%

7) Distribution at the various distances:

   A) Total analysis
      i)   Total < 10 yards = 14
           (By foot = 12, By head = 1, Throw-in = 1)
      ii) Total 10–30 yards = 11
           (By foot = 5, By head = 2, Throw-in = 4)
      iii) Total > 30 yards = 4
           (By foot = 4, By head = 0, Throw-in = 0)

      TOTAL: 29

      Percentages of this total analysis, A i)–iii):
           < 10 yards = 48.3%
           (By foot = 85.7%, head = 7.1 per cent, Throw-in = 7.1%)
           10–30 yards = 37.9%
           (By foot = 45.5%, head = 18.2%, Throw-in = 37.4%)
           > 30 yards = 13.8%
           (By foot = 100%)

   B) Completed pass analysis (not including clearances):
      i)   Total < 10 yards = 3
           (By foot = 2, By head = 0, Throw-in = 1)
      ii) Total 10–30 yards = 6
           (By foot = 3, By head = 0, Throw-in = 3)
      iii) Total > 30 yards = 2
           (By foot = 2, By head = 0, Throw-in = 0)

      TOTAL: 11

      Percentages of completed pass analysis, B i)–iii):
           Total < 10 yards = 27.3%
           (By foot = 66.7%, Throw-in = 33.3%)
           Total 10–30 yards = 54.6%
           (By foot = 50%, Throw-in = 50%)
           Total > 30 yards = 18.2%
           (By foot = 100%)

C) Uncompleted pass analysis (not including clearances):-
   i)   Total < 10 yards = 6
        (By foot = 6)
   ii) Total 10–30 yards = 2
        (By foot = 1, Throw–in = 1)
   iii) Total > 30 yards = 1
        (By foot = 1)

   TOTAL: 9

   Percentages of uncompleted pass analysis, C i)–iii):
        Total < 10 yards = 66.7%
        (By foot = 100%)
        Total 10–30 yards = 22.2%
        (By foot = 50%, Throw–in = 50%)
        Total > 30 yards = 11.1%
        (By foot = 100%)

8) Ratio: completed passes to total number of passes = 11/20 = 0.55
   Ratio: uncompleted passes to total number of passes = 9/20 = 0.45
   (N.B., doesn't include clearances)

9) Clearance study:

   A)   Total number of clearances = 9

   B)   Total number of clearances at each distance:
        i)   Total < 10 yards = 5
             (By foot = 4, By head = 1)
        ii) Total 10–30 yards = 3
             (By foot = 1, By head = 2)
        iii) Total > 30 yards = 1
             (By foot = 1)

   Percentages of B) i)–iii):

        Total < 10 yards = 55.6%
         (By foot = 80%, By head = 20%)
        Total 10–30 yards = 33.3%
        (By foot = 33.3%, By head = 66.7)
        Total > 30 yards = 11.1%
        (By foot = 100%)

10) Outline of the subject's activity:

	Section	No. of	Successful Touches	Unsuccessful	Clears
i)	0–5 min.	2	1	1	0
ii)	5–10 min.	2	0	1	0
iii)	10–15 min.	4	1	2	1
iv)	15–20 min.	4	1	1	2

v)	20–25 min.	3	3	0	0
vi)	25–30 min.	3	1	2	0
vii)	30–35 min.	1	0	0	1
viii)	35–40 min.	3	1	0	2
ix)	40–45 min.	4	3★	1	0
x)	45–50 min.	3	0	1	2

(★including one successful attempt at goal)

See Figures 9.8–9.11 for a visual representation of some of the data.

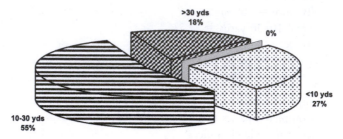

FIGURE 9.8 Representation of the number of completed passes.

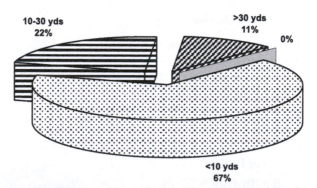

FIGURE 9.9 Representation of the number of incomplete passes.

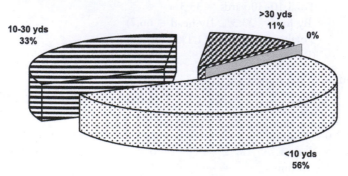

FIGURE 9.10 Representation of the clearances.

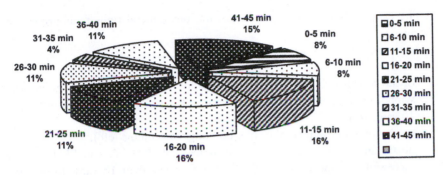

FIGURE 9.11 Representation of the percentage of activities throughout the first half.

9.3.2.4 Discussion

Just one half of a soccer match does not produce anything like a significant amount of data about which conclusions can be drawn, but this example does give ideas about analysing and presenting data. A few statements can be made about these interpretations. The majority of the full-back 'touches', 72.4 per cent, were performed by the foot. But this percentage led to a larger amount of errors, 88.9 per cent, being by foot contact. There was a roughly equal distribution of passes performed over distances of less than 10 yards and between 10 and 30 yards, 48.3 per cent and 37.9 per cent respectively. Despite this almost equal distribution, the subject was twice as successful at passing over a distance of between 10 and 30 yards as one of less than 10 yards. This success over the intermediate distance (10–30 yards) is mirrored by the fact that the subject committed only 1/5 of the total errors committed over the distance. From the analysis it was found that the subject performed 10 per cent more completed passes (not including clearances) than uncompleted passes (not including clearances).

Analysis of the clearances the subject performed shows that the majority were carried out over the short distance of less than 10 yards. As the 'direction of distribution' was not recorded (see adjustments) this aspect of clearance distance is difficult to interpret, but a part explanation could be that the full back plays near to the touchline and so a safe clearance will be over this touchline, which in many situations will be less than 10 yards from the point of play. The subject's intense periods of involvement were evenly spread throughout the half, with no one 'five minute section' having no activity. A more general observation is of the small contribution that heading made to the subject's play, but this could be explained by the opposition employing two small forwards and subsequently not playing the ball to them in the air.

It would be interesting to see whether these statements still held true with six to eight matches of data. Many of these points are somewhat subjective as they are made on the basis of only one short data collection session. It could be that all of the points made came about due to the context of the game, and a completely different set of remarks could have occurred if a different game had been notated.

The exercise did however produce some recommendations to improve the system.

Adjustments to the system:

1   divide foot passes into left foot or right foot passes – therefore the present symbol would be proceeded by a 'L' or a 'R', e.g. F1L, = a left foot pass of 10 yards or less;

2   notate fouls and indiscretions (i.e. bookings or sendings-off);

3   notate attempts on goal with a separate symbol = 'S', e.g. SF1L, ! = a successful attempt at goal with the left foot less than 10 yards from goal; SH1, X = an unsuccessful attempt at goal with the head less than 10 yards from goal;

4   notation of tackles could be introduced – but this is moving away from the aim of notating the 'distribution ability' of a full back;

5   notation with the aid of a grid – the grid could be designed by measuring the length and width of a pitch and dividing it into nine equal areas (see Figure 9.12), and then notation of positional data from where the full back passes, and to where the passes go, becomes possible.

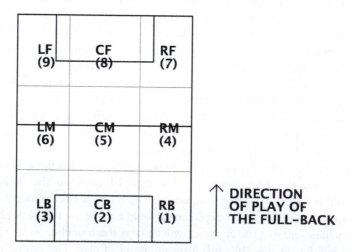

FIGURE 9.12 Schematic diagram of a soccer pitch showing suggested divisions of the playing area into a grid for notation.

This grid adjustment could lead to two methods of notating:

i)   produce printed sheets of the grid and for each piece of notation draw a line from the origin of the pass (i.e. position of full back) to its destination, and on the same sheet include the appropriate symbol and time as before; or

ii) similar to the original system notating in columns, the following type of codes could be used:

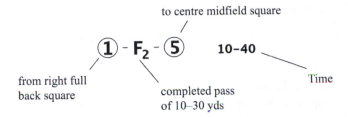

to centre midfield square

(1) - F_2 - (5) 10–40

from right full
back square

completed pass
of 10–30 yds

Time

Method i) would be more accurate as the exact position and not just the square would be notated. But it would require one sheet for each piece of information notated. Also learning time would be much longer and 'logging time' for each action would be longer and more complicated.

9.3.3 A notation system for netball

A netball team consists of seven players. Each player has a limited area within which to operate. Every player is allocated a specific role in the game that corresponds to the area in which they operate. The object of the game is to attempt to score as many goals as possible. To achieve this requires team cohesion, cooperation and understanding between all the team members. A skilful game of netball relies on effective passing to maintain possession of the ball.

9.3.3.1 Method

Before outlining the system, it is necessary to ensure that you understand the basic rules of the game.

Essential rules of netball:

Like any other team game netball has its own specific set of rules that must be adhered to throughout the match. Before a system of notational analysis can be designed it is important to be familiar with these rules:

1   There is a three-second limit on the time it takes a team member to pass the ball or attempt a shot at goal.
2   The ball must be caught or touched in each third of the court during play.
3   The centre pass must be caught or touched by a player allowed in the centre third of the court (Figure 9.13).
4   When a ball goes out of court it can only be thrown-in by a player allowed in that particular area.
5   Only the goal-shooter or goal-attack can score a goal. The ball must also have been wholly caught within the goal circle.
6   A player must keep within the limits of area prescribed by her position.

9.3.3.2 Notation symbols

The symbols to be used will record the following:

i)   the team member in possession of the ball and the position on the court where they received the ball;
ii) what happens at the end of the passing sequence before reverting back to the centre pass or change of possession;
iii) out-of-court shots where the ball has been passed outside the side line.

Each player wears a vest with letters representing their roles (each one is self-explanatory):

GK = goal-keeper
GD = goal defence
WD = wing defence
C   = centre
WA = wing attack
GA = goal attack
GS = goal shooter

The court is divided into five areas so that a simple view of the path of the ball can be deduced (Figure 9.13).

1 = goal circle
2 = goal third
3 = centre third
4 = goal third
5 = goal circle

Each player has a prescribed playing area – these are designated in Table 9.8.

9.3.3.3 Actions

\/ = goal scored (should be followed by a centre pass)
X   = goal attempted but missed
O   = out-of-court shot (the appropriate team is given a free throw from the side line where the ball went out)
C   = centre pass (no court position number is added since it is always taken from within the centre circle).

Continued notation within the column implies a successful pass.

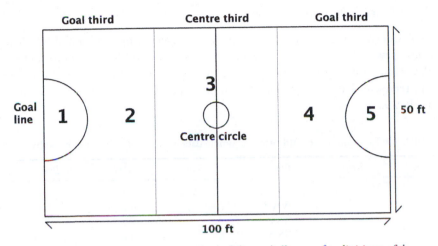

FIGURE 9.13 Schematic representation of the netball court for divisions of the playing surface.

TABLE 9.8 Each player has designated areas within which they must play

Player	Areas for team playing from area 1 towards area 5		
GK	1	2	
GD	1	2	3
WD	2	3	
C	2	3	4
WA		3	4
GA	3	4	5
GS		4	5

9.3.3.4 The record sheet

It is necessary for the recording sheet to contain descriptive details of the match or practice session so that the information obtained is available for analysis, and future reference if required.

1   match or practice session
2   venue
3   date
4   (if possible) names of players.

The recording sheet consists of vertical columns under the headings of red and blue (referring to the team colours). Play is recorded in the appropriate column according to the team in possession of the ball. Play is recorded from the top to the bottom of the column. The score is shown at the left side of each column.

9.3.3.5 Recording a sequence:

Each sequence begins with the centre pass represented by the symbol 'C'. The centre pass is always taken from within the centre circle. Play continues and the player and position are notated. The sequence is completed when a goal is scored and represented by the symbol 'V'. An example of a record sheet is shown in Table 9.9.

TABLE 9.9 Example of a record sheet for simple data gathering for notation of netball

Score	Red	Blue	Score	Red	Blue
		C		O	
		WA 3		GD 4	
		GA4		WD 3	
		GS 5		C 3	
		X		O	GK 2
		GS 5			O
0–1		\/		WA 3	
	C			C 3	
	WA 3			GA 2	
	C 2			GS 1	
	GS 1		2–1	\/	
1–1	\/				
	C			etc.	

9.3.3.6 Results

The results (see Table 9.10) showed that the red team were more successful at retaining possession once they had got it. The red team averaged three passes per possession and had only two passing errors. Both passing errors were caused by the red centre player passing the ball out of court.

TABLE 9.10 Data processed from a notated netball match (part only)

	Red	Blue
No. of possessions	7	10
No. of passes	21	16
Average sequence	21/7 = 3	16/10 = 1.6
No. of passing errors	2	4

The blue team had more possessions but that did not compensate for their passing errors since they only managed 1.6 passes per possession and incurred more passing errors. From this short example of data few conclusions can be drawn about the play – much more data is needed. But the notation exercise enabled an assessment of the notation system. By examining the record sheet there are several factors that can be analysed without a great deal of effort:

1   The number of possessions by each team. A possession is defined as a single player or sequence of players following each other simultaneously in the team's column on the record sheet.

2   Related to the number of possessions is the number of passing errors induced by a team and the frequency of passing errors by a particular player. To obtain a percentage of passing errors it would be necessary to evaluate the number of touches by that player. It is then also possible for the coach to assess whether the team is making good use of all the players in the team although this is somewhat dependent on their accessibility at the time. The latter information would need to be combined with the coach's own subjective observations.

   A passing error would be defined as the ball changing possession or going out of court. A touch would be defined as the ball actually being caught and passed or must being touched as it travelled through the air.

3   It is possible to calculate the average number of passes in a sequence. This is important when assessing the path of the ball particularly from the centre pass to an attempt at goal. A common strategy outlined in books is a three–pass attack down the centre although a two-pass attack is possible. The greater the number of passes incurred the greater the opportunity for defenders to break the attack.

4   A percentage success rate of goals by the goal shooter and goal attack can be calculated. It allows the coach to assess which, or whether both, players need goal-shooting practice.

5   When analysing who attempted the most shots at goal it could be beneficial to work backwards and see the shots leading to the attempt. With sufficient data it may be possible to outline a common attacking strategy.

Although the record sheet appears 'simplistic' a great deal of information can be gleaned from it. It is possible to assemble a quick summary after the match. Given more time, more detailed information may be extracted. Once the notation is sufficiently rehearsed it is easy to modify the system to take into consideration a number of other factors.

9.3.3.7 Possible improvements:

1   The court could be subdivided into smaller sections to outline a more accurate path of the ball that can then be transferred to plans of play. For example, this would be useful when tracing the path of the ball from centre pass – a common strategy advocated in coaching books is an attack down the centre. By recording the team's patterns with their centre pass, the coach can conclude whether the centre line attacking strategy is successful for them or whether the team tends to play more down one side than the other. On the other

hand, having more position cells will mean that more matches will have to be analysed to produce significant amounts of data in all the cells.

2   Players can be penalised for foot-faults, but this is not a common occurrence in experienced players. So it would be only relevant when notating novices.

3   A throw-up is called for when a player of each team gains possession of the ball equally at the same time. A throw-up is then called for and the success of gaining possession by a particular team could be notated.

9.3.4 A motion analysis of work-rate in different positional roles in field hockey

9.3.4.1 Aim

The aim of this investigation is to analyse the overall movement patterns of elite male field hockey players. Furthermore, it aims to compare and contrast the difference in movement patterns with a player's position.

9.3.4.2 Hypothesis

Null hypothesis (H_0)
There will be no significant difference in the movement patterns of field hockey players in relation to their position.

Experimental hypothesis (H_1)
There will be a significant difference in the movement patterns of field hockey players in relation to player position.

9.3.4.3 Devising the method

The analysis of team games has tended to be more of a subjective and qualitative nature, and is characterised by observational techniques relying on the coach's evaluation of the game. An objective and quantitative paradigm should lead to a greater insight into the physiological demands of invasive games.

There are indicators of the physiological demands of hockey players, including heart rate response (Carter, 1996; Boddington *et al.*, 2001), distance covered (Rebelo and Soares, 1996a) and work–rest ratios (Lothian and Farrally, 1994; O'Donoghue and Parker, 2001). The most interesting time–motion analysis studies have been in the movement patterns of different positional roles (Reilly and Thomas, 1976; Herbert and Tong, 1996.)

According to Hughes and Franks (2004), any statistics being gathered from a dynamic environment, such as field hockey, can be difficult to obtain. Therefore, any quantitative analysis must be structured – for example, a flow chart. Franks and Goodman (1984) produced a hierarchical structure for initiating a notational system (cited Hughes and Franks, 2004) (Figure 9.14).

FIGURE 9.14 Hierarchical structure representing events that take place in team games.
Source: Frank and Goodmann, 1984.

9.3.4.5 Pilot system

A pilot study was carried out for approximately ten minutes. From conducting the pilot study, strengths and weaknesses of the system could be identified. It demonstrated that although the system collected great amounts of data, the system was too complex. The difficult decision is knowing when the limitations of a hand notation are acceptable within the terms of reference of the desired data collection. The hand notation was revised and evaluated, thus allowing a more effective methodology to be utilised (see Table 9.11).

9.3.4.6 Finalised method

The male hockey match recorded ($N = 1$) was of international standard between Spain and Germany in the semi final of the World Cup 2006. The location of the camera is unknown, but assume its location is approximately the halfway line. The game was viewed once for each discipline ($N = 3$ (1 forward, 1 midfield and 1 defence)) for a total of three players and for the duration of 20 minutes.

Due to lack of technological equipment, movement classifications were timed with a stopwatch, and by a random sampling method Spain was selected to be the team of focus. In addition, the recording of data required two operators and movements patterns were operationally defined.

By adopting both Hughes and Franks' (2004) and Franks and Goodman's (1984) theories, a simple flow chart was devised appropriate for this investigation (Figure 9.15.)

TABLE 9.11 Short-hand symbols

Movement	Short-hand symbol
Stationary	O
Walking	W
Jogging	J
Shuffling	Ø
Sprinting	⋆
Game-related activity	G

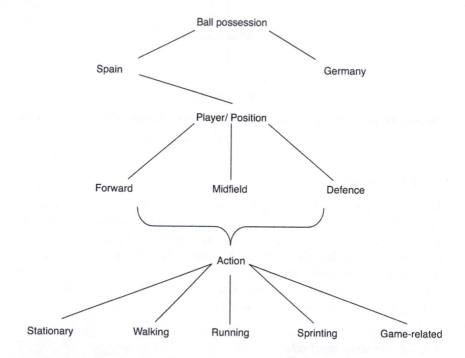

FIGURE 9.15 Hierarchical model of time–motion analysis in field hockey.

9.3.4.7 Limitations

There will be limitations placed upon this investigation such as a time and word limit, and lack of technological equipment, which prevents the investigation going into too great a depth.

Former type error occurs when an operator unintentionally enters incorrect data, for example, uses the wrong short-hand symbol. The chance of error possibilities occurring is heightened within this study due to there being two operators.

Due to the continuous nature of running, it is difficult to strictly classify its movement into discrete categories such as sprinting and jogging. Therefore, the study is subjective, thus affecting the reliability and repeatability of this notation.

9.3.4.8 Operational definitions

Stationary

Standing, sitting, lying or stretching – activity that portrays little exhaustive movement.

Walking (forwards, backwards, lateral)

The back foot does not leave the floor until the front foot makes contact with the ground. This movement is slow in nature.

Running (forwards, backwards)

This is a slow running movement without obvious exhaustive effort.

Sprinting

Explosive movement that involves rapid extension of the hip and knee. There is obvious acceleration.

Game-related activity

This is any time during the game where the player is either in contact with the ball or attempting to come in contact with the ball; hitting, dribbling, tackling, channelling, side line balls, free hits, passing etc.

9.3.4.9 Reliability

The repeatability and accuracy of a study is a central facet to notational analysis. Hughes (1998b) found that within analysing 72 research papers, 70 per cent of investigations did not report any reliability study. A simple inter–operator test for reliability was performed using an equation suggested by Hughes (1998):

$$\sum \frac{\mathrm{mod}\left(V_1 - V_2\right)}{V_{mean}} \times 100\%$$

V_1 and V_2 are variables, V_{mean} is their mean, mod is short for modulus, and Σ means 'sum of'. The calculation will give a percentage error for each variable and operator. Significance level was set at 5 per cent. If a value is $p > 5$ it is assumed that the test is not significant, therefore not reliable.

From the results illustrated in both Table 9.12 and Figure 9.16 it can be identified that the overall reliability of the system was 1.01 per cent suggesting that the system

TABLE 9.12 Data from a field hockey game notated once by two operators for 20 minutes, presented as an inter-reliability analysis

	Operator 1 V_1	Operator 2 V_2	Percentage error (%)
Sprinting	4.71	4.11	13.6
Running	4.55	5.36	16.4
Walking	4.78	5.01	4.7
Shuffling	1.85	2.24	19
Stationary	3.5	3.28	6.4
Game–related activity	2.26	1.89	17.8
	Overall percentage error		12.9

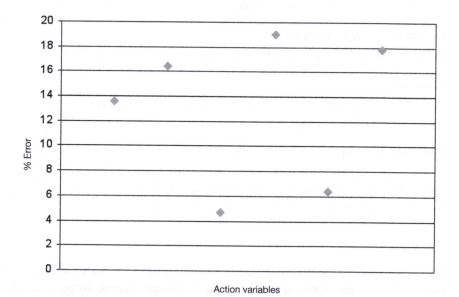

FIGURE 9.16 The overall data from the reliability study

is reliable. However, when analysing the discrete values, there are large discrepancies within the data. For example, the least significant value is 19 per cent for shuffling. The most significant value was walking 4.7 per cent. This emphasises the subjective nature of the investigation. Also, dynamic activities such as shuffling and sprinting are more arduous to identify than walking and stationary movements. This heightens the importance of operational definitions.

Using computerised methods such as the CAPTAIN system (McLaughlin and O'Donoghue, 2004) may increase the reliability of future time–motion analysis systems.

TABLE 9.13 Movement patterns of a forward

FORWARD	
Movement	*Time (minutes)*
Sprinting	5.57
Running	5.23
Walking	5.07
Shuffling	1.05
Stationary	3.08
TOTAL	20
Game-related activity	1.28

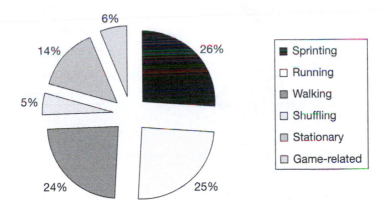

FIGURE 9.17 Pie chart displaying movement pattern breakdown of a forward.

9.3.4.10 Results

From both Table 9.13 and Figure 9.17, it is illustrated that a forward position in hockey spent 5.57 minutes (26 per cent) of the twenty minutes of performance sprinting. This is followed by 5.23 minutes running, and 5.07 minutes walking.

It can be assumed that a forward may sprint and run more often during a game as it is their short duration bursts of activities into space that create through balls, and therefore attacking opportunities. In contrast, only 1.28 minutes of the game was spent doing game-related activity. This suggests how the results may be influenced by the state of play, for example, if Spain had less possession, or more defensive play.

TABLE 9.14 Movement patterns of a midfielder

MIDFIELD	
Movement	*Time (minutes)*
Sprinting	5.24
Running	6.41
Walking	3.52
Shuffling	2.01
Stationary	2.82
TOTAL	20
Game-related activity	3.07

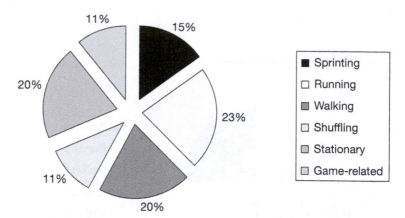

FIGURE 9.18 Pie chart displaying movement pattern breakdown of a midfielder.

Table 9.14 and Figure 9.18 show the results of the movement patterns of a specific midfield hockey player. In comparison, the midfield player spent a longer duration in a wider range of activities than the forward. This may be because of the specific role of a midfield player: they create links with the defence and forwards, therefore adopt both an attacking role consisting of short duration bursts of activity (23 per cent running), and defending play consisting of shuffling (11 per cent) movements associated with channelling and tackling. Furthermore, this may suggest why the midfield player has more game-related activity, 3.07 minutes.

The movement patterns of a defender, as show in Table 9.15 and Figure 9.19 are similar to that of a midfield player (9 per cent of activity was spent shuffling which is associated with tackling and channelling movements typical of a defender). This is in complete contrast to a forward who spent only 5 per cent of the game shuffling. Furthermore, the defending and midfield positions spent more time in game-related activity, suggesting the team was adopting a defending strategy rather than attacking.

TABLE 9.15 Movement patterns of a defender

DEFENCE	
Movement	Time (minutes)
Sprinting	3.37
Running	5.01
Walking	4.55
Shuffling	2.48
Stationary	4.59
TOTAL	20
Game-related activity	2.42

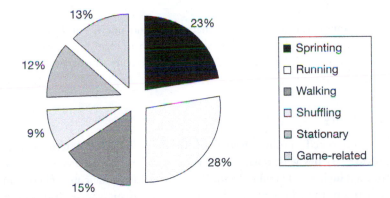

FIGURE 9.19 Pie chart displaying movement pattern breakdown of a defender.

TABLE 9.16 Independent T-test results

	Forward/ Midfield	Forward/ Defence	Midfield/ Defence
P-Value	0.846	0.791	0.903

TABLE 9.17 Movement patterns for an average hockey player

Movement	Mean and standard deviation
Sprinting	4.71 ± 1.18
Running	4.55 ± 0.75
Walking	4.78 ± 0.79
Shuffling	1.85 ± 0.73
Stationary	3.5 ± 0.96
Game-related activity	2.26 ± 0.91

A simple independent T-test was carried out upon three groups of paired data (Table 9.16). The significance level was set at 0.5. The results illustrate that there is no significant difference in the movement patterns of field hockey players in relation to their position (Table 9.17).

9.3.4.11 Application

Measurement parameters such as heart rate, body temperature and respirometers are impractical during competitive play. Time–motion analysis aids the coach in assessing the physiological demands of a performer: its most important application is to assist the coach in devising an accurate fitness programme that will train the specific physiological systems that are in high demand during competition.

9.3.4.12 Conclusion

From this study it can be concluded that there is no significant difference in the movement patterns of elite male field hockey players in relation to position. Future research must be carried out both reliably and effectively in order to solidify such conclusions as this one.

9.4 Summary

As previously stated in other chapters of this book, notation systems such as this can provide coaches with reliable, calculated data to provide precise feedback to performers (Hughes and Franks, 2004). By evaluating important and effective aspects of competition, the adoption of a rational and systematic approach to improving performance and reducing the unpredictability of a team can be applied to coaching practices (Lyle, 2002).

9.4.1 Recommendations for further research

The following are recommendations for future research investigations within the area of time–motion analysis of field hockey:

1 the inclusion of heart rate monitors;
2 blood lactate measurements;
3 the effect of score line upon work-rate;
4 group efficacy beliefs and work-rate.

10

ANALYSIS OF NOTATION DATA

Reliability

Mike Hughes

10.1 Introduction

The key factor in any research that uses new equipment is the repeatability and accuracy of this equipment. In most performance analysis papers the researchers are presenting systems that have been specifically designed for that experiment. It was the exception (Hughes *et al.*, 1989; Wilson and Barnes, 1998) rather than the rule that most papers presenting new systems produce evidence of systematised testing of the reliability of these new systems. In a number of studies, parametric techniques were used with data that were non-parametric; although, in some cases, the means of the data sets appeared ordinal, they were often means of nominal data and therefore the use of a parametric test put the conclusions at risk.

There are many similarities in the nature of the data generated by experiments in performance analysis of sport. Although Atkinson and Nevill (1998) have produced a definitive summary of reliability techniques in sports medicine, there has been no similar attempt to make recommendations in the use of techniques in performance analysis for solving some of the common problems associated with these types of data. Since Hughes *et al.* (2002a) produced their paper on reliability and statistical processes, the presentation of reliability, and the application of correct statistical techniques, has improved immensely. Some of the issues that were perceived as being causes for uncertainty are explained below.

- It is vital that the reliability of a system is demonstrated clearly and in a way that is compatible with the intended analyses of the data. The data must be tested in the same way and to the same depth that it will be processed in the subsequent analyses. In some cases the reliability studies were executed on summary data, and the system was then assumed to be reliable for all of the other types of more detailed data analyses that were produced.

- In general, the work of Bland and Altman (1986) has transformed the attitude of sport scientists to testing reliability; can similar techniques be applied to non-parametric data?
- It is clear that just applying a test of differences about the mean or median (t-test, Anova, Mann Whitney, Kruskal-Wallis, Chi-square, etc.) is not enough, and a measure of absolute differences of the means or medians should also be applied.
- The most common form of data analysis in notation studies is recording frequencies of actions and their respective positions on the performance area; these are then presented as sums or totals in each respective area. What are the effects of cumulative errors nullifying each other, so that the overall totals appear less incorrect than they actually are?
- The application of parametric statistical techniques is often misused in performance analysis – how does this affect the confidence of the conclusions to say something about the data, with respect to more appropriate non-parametric tests?

By using practical examples from research, this chapter aims to investigate these issues associated with reliability studies and subsequent analyses in performance analysis.

10.2 The nature of the data, the depth of analysis

10.2.1 Sample data

As a test of inter-operator reliability, a squash match was notated in-event, by two experienced analysts. A computerised system was used. The match was analysed live, rather than from videotape. It was a match in the team World Cup, played in Holland, July 1999. Both analysts had already gathered data for four matches that day and were therefore tired: errors could be expected. Both recorded the match from similar positions from behind the court, both using similar laptop computers with which they were very familiar. The data input system required the number of shots in each rally, the outcome, which player made the rally ending shot, the type of shot and from which position on the court this shot was struck (the court was divided into 16 position cells, coded by number). The system stored the data of each rally sequentially in the 'Access' database and, as part of the system, there was specifically written software to process the data into graphical output for feedback to coaches and athletes. The 'raw' data in the database was used, rather than the processed output that no longer retained the sequential nature of the data, as this enabled certain questions to be posed that could not otherwise be answered from the processed data.

Analysing the total shots in each analysis of the match indicates a 100 per cent accuracy between the two operators (Table 10.1). The analysis of the different totals of shots in each game demonstrates how adding frequency data from two or more

TABLE 10.1 The total shots per game

	Shots per game		
	Analyst 1	Analyst 2	% Difference
Game 1	789	792	0.38
Game 2	439	435	0.91
Game 3	457	458	0.21
TOTAL	1,685	1,685	0

sources can hide differences. The different totals now indicate that there are errors but they are still all less than 1 per cent. This is a very simple example, and more complex data analyses are demonstrated below; adding data together in this way will lead to masking 'true' error figures. The results will always depend upon the relative depth of analysis that is applied to the sequentiality of the data and also the definition of the terms involved in percentage error. Let us examine different ways of analysing these types of data. Percentage differences are a simple but effective way to measure the absolute difference between sets of data.

10.2.2 The sequential nature of data

It is becoming more and more clear that the first step in a reliability study should always be to compare the raw data of the study, if this is possible, in their original form. Sometimes, in the case of preprogrammed computer systems, this is not always possible. The raw data sets in this example from squash, two sets of columns, were scanned and it was seen that they were of different lengths. One of the sets of data had a series of null data that occupied a row of data. This could have been a software error, an operator error or a combination of both. This row was deleted and the two sets of data were of equal length. This process was repeated four times until the differences in the data were within the expected range from operator errors. So the data had five errors in non-matching lines of data due to either operator or software error. The two data sets then appeared to match in length and content. The respective shot and/or error totals had not indicated these errors.

10.3 Consistency of percentage difference calculations

Consider now the simple concept of calculating the percentage difference in the repeatability of counting the number of shots in each rally. We have already seen the different values obtained by using the game totals and the match total. Let us examine some of the different possible interpretations of 'percentage difference'.

- There were 20 lines of data in which there were differences between the data sets, errors made, in counting the lengths of the rallies. There was an (adjusted) total of 105 rallies in the match, so the percentage error, based upon the number of lines with differences in them, and the five mismatches, could be stated as 24.1 per cent of the number of rallies.

- The differences of the 20 error measurements totalled 37 shots, 1.85 shots/line. The average rally length was 16.2 shots, so the average percentage error per average rally length was 1.85/16.2 = 11.4 per cent.
- When each error was calculated as a percentage of the length of that particular rally, then the error on the length of the rally (1.85/9.25) averaged a 20.0 per cent error of the length of the respective rally.
- However, taking into account all the rallies, then by calculating:

$$\sum \frac{\text{mod}\left(V_1 - V_2\right)}{V_{\text{TOTmean}}} \times 100\%$$

where 'mod' is the modulus and 'Σ' indicates the 'sum of', the overall percentage error figure for rally length comes out as 2.1 per cent, and V_{TOTmean} is the mean of the total variables measured.

By examining the data at different levels, and using different definitions for the calculations involved, then very different values for the percentage error of the rally length have been obtained. There are no right and/or wrong answers in these scenarios, but it does emphasise the necessity for analysts to be very explicit when presenting these types of data analyses, so that their audience can clearly understand what is meant by the definition of 'percentage error' presented.

10.4 Processing data

Let us consider another example from these data. It would be expected, from experience of previous work in performance analysis, that a notation of position would result in the largest source of errors in this process. The positions were defined in a 16-cell distribution across the court (see Figure 10.1). Figures 10.2 and 10.3 show the data, a correlation was performed on the two adjusted sets of data ($r = 0.998$; adjusted $r = 0.987$), indicating strong reliability.

Comparing each pair of positions in each data line (Table 10.2) tallied the differences in position. The total number of differences is 34 in 104 measurements, which would seem to support Bland and Altman's (1986) statement that correlation alone is not sufficient to test reliability. The value of the differences was noted to examine how many were perceptual errors and how many were likely to be typographical errors. The data in the shaded areas of Table 10.2 are attributed to typographical errors, as differences of 1, 3, 4 or 5 can be attributed to perceptual differences of the two analysts. There were 34 differences in 104 rallies in total, i.e. percentage error of 32.7 per cent, of which 31 were perceptual (29.8 per cent) and three were typographical (2.9 per cent).

By summing each column, the number of rally ending shots played in each position in the court, gives the totals shown in Figures 10.2 and 10.3. This is the

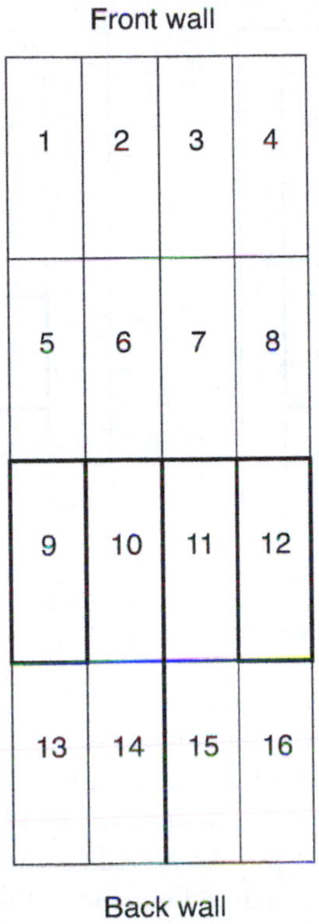

Front wall

FIGURE 10.1 The definition of positional cells across the squash court area.

TABLE 10.2 The arithmetic differences in the
positions recorded by the two analysts.

Value of the difference	Frequency
−11	1
−8	1
−4	7
−3	2
−1	4
0	70
1	7
4	10
5	1
11	1
Total	104

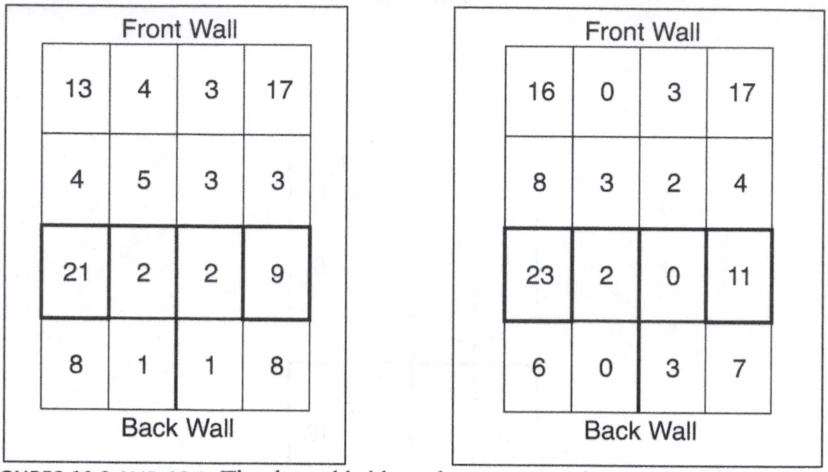

Front Wall			
13	4	3	17
4	5	3	3
21	2	2	9
8	1	1	8
Back Wall			

Front Wall			
16	0	3	17
8	3	2	4
23	2	0	11
6	0	3	7
Back Wall			

FIGURES 10.2 AND 10.3 The data added by column to give the positional frequency of rally ending shots in the example squash match data.

way an analyst will usually add up the data to present patterns of play across a playing surface. Between these two sets of data there are 27 (26 per cent error) differences; from the data checked sequentially there were 34 (32.7 per cent error). The seven errors were missed due to the process of adding the data, effectively eliminating some mistakes from the sum. Adding frequencies has masked errors again; this is a very dangerous contaminant of reliability tests of data of this nature, particularly where there are large amounts of data, c.f. the percentage errors of the total numbers of shots per game and per match.

A Chi-square test of independence was used and a value of $\chi = 11.16$ ($df = 15$) was obtained.

10.5 Visual interpretation of the data (a modified Bland and Altman plot)

A modified Bland and Altman plot was constructed for the variable – number of shots in a rally (Figure 10.4). But what does this plot mean with this type of data? The range of errors across the mean (16.2) was found to be ± 2, i.e. percentage error of 12 per cent. The normal process is to include on the graph an indication of the range of $\pm 1.96 \star S.D.$ to demonstrate how the data varied about the mean. The mean of the data is 16.2 shots with a standard deviation of 12.88, to plot these data as a Bland and Altman range is meaningless. The range is $\pm 1.96 \star S.D. = \pm 25.2$ shots, but a range of ± 25.2 is obviously unacceptable. Confidence levels can be calculated (Bland and Altman, 1986), but perhaps in notation studies with non-parametric data we have to reconsider the logic behind the idea of these plots. The abscissa, with parametric data such as these, is different. This is not a continuous scale; each of the items (in this case the length of rally) is different – they are not

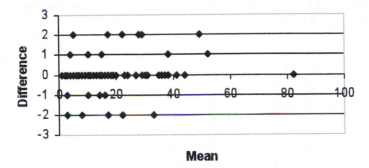

FIGURE 10.4 A Bland and Altman plot of the differences in rally length plotted against the mean of the rally length from the two tests.

related in any simple way. Better to modify the graph to meet the same ideas of Bland and Altman – how much of the data falls within the range of accuracy set by the researcher (usually less than 5 per cent error, but it may be 10 per cent or 15 per cent depending on the nature of the data)?

Instead of plotting the differences in measurements on the same subjects against their means (a continuous scale), let us consider summing the differences found and non-dimensionalising them with the sum of all the readings taken. Multiplying this by 100 will then, in effect, give a plot of percentage errors. Hence, by calculating and plotting:

$$\sum \frac{mod\ (V_1 - V_2)}{V_{TOTmean}} \times 100\%$$

against each variable reading, then the data should fall within the range of percentage error already indicated acceptable by the researcher. Let us examine a more complex reliability study.

10.5.1 Sample data

Consider an example from rugby union. Five analysts were to undertake an analysis of the recent World Cup and all five notated the same match twice each, so that data were available for intra- and inter-operator reliability studies. The data for the frequencies of the simple variable actions of tackle, pass, ruck, kick, scrum and line are shown in Table 10.3. An accepted way of testing these operators would be to use Chi-square and percentage differences for the intra-operator tests, and to use Kruskal-Wallis and percentage differences for the inter-operator tests. The Chi-square and Kruskal-Wallis tests reflect the shape of the data sets rather than the actual differences and so there is a need for a second simple difference test. However, care must be taken with the percentage difference test, in both its definition and application.

TABLE 10.3 Data from a rugby match notated twice by five different operators and presented as an intra–operator reliability analysis.

Operators	L		S		I		G		O	
	V_1	V_2	V_1	V_2	V_1	V_2	V_1	V_2	V_1	V_2
Tackle	51	53	53	55	54	49	53	56	53	55
Pass	102	108	97	99	94	97	98	99	99	97
Kick	39	40	38	39	39	38	39	41	37	39
Ruck	49	49	50	51	49	46	51	49	44	49
Scrum	6	6	6	6	6	6	6	6	6	6
Line	14	15	14	14	14	15	14	15	14	15
$\Sigma\text{Mod}[V_1-V_2]$	10		6		13		9		12	
$[\Sigma V_1+V_2]/2$	264.5		261		258.5		263.5		260	
% Error overall	3.8		2.3		5.0		3.4		4.6	

The overall percentage differences in Table 10.3 show a satisfactory analysis, all of the operators scoring 5 per cent or less. They are presented in Figure 10.5 as a plot of $(\Sigma(\text{mod}[V_1 - V_2])/V_{\text{mean}})*100$ % for each operator. As the expected limits of agreement in this study were 5 per cent, then all the data should fall below this line. There is a similarity in presenting the data in this way with that of the Bland and Altman plot, the visual power of the chart is its ability to immediately identify those measurements that are in danger of transgressing the limits of agreements.

The processed data in Table 10.4 is the intra–operator test for reliability of each of the separate variables with the difference between tests 1 and 2 shown as a percentage of the respective operator's mean for that particular variable. The error percentages for each of the variables vary much more, as would be expected, depending upon the degree of difficulty of recognition of the defined action. This variation may depend upon the accuracy of the operational definition of that action

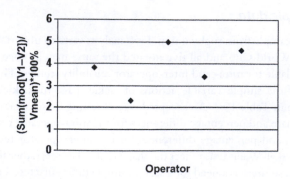

FIGURE 10.5 The overall data from the reliability study, the intra–operator test, presented as a function of the accuracy of each operator.

TABLE 10.4 Data from a rugby match notated twice by five different operators and the differences for each operator expressed as a percentage of the respective mean

	L	S	I	G	O
Tackle	3.8	3.7	9.7	5.5	3.7
Pass	5.7	2.0	3.1	1.0	2.0
Kick	2.5	2.6	2.6	2.5	5.3
Ruck	0	2.0	4.0	4.0	10.8
Scrum	0	0	0	0	0
Line	6.9	0	6.9	6.9	6.9

by the operators, the quantity of training of the operators, or it may be that there are accepted difficulties in observation of that particular variable.

Some observations are more difficult to make than others: for example in rugby union, deciding when a maul becomes a ruck; or, using the previous example, the identification of position in a squash match. It is logical then to have different levels of expected accuracy for different variables. Some research papers have argued for different levels of accuracy to be acceptable, because of the nature of the data they were measuring (Hughes and Franks, 1991; Wilson and Barnes, 1998).

These data were then plotted as percentages against each of the actions in Figure 10.6a. They can also be plotted against each of the operators (see Figure 10.6b) to test which of the operators are more, or least, reliable and by how much. These charts are very useful, highlighting which variables are most contributing to violations of the levels of expected reliability.

10.6 Conclusions

It was found that many research papers in performance analysis present no reliability tests whatsoever and, when they do, they apply inappropriate statistical processes for these tests, and the subsequent data processing. Many research papers have used parametric tests in the past – these were found to be slightly less sensitive than the non–parametric tests, and they did not respond to large differences within the data. Further, the generally accepted tests for comparing sets of non–parametric data, Chi–square analysis and Kruskal–Wallis, were found to be insensitive to relatively large changes within the data. It would seem that a simple percentage calculation gives the best indicator of reliability, but it was demonstrated that these tests can also lead to errors and confusion. The following conditions should be applied.

- The data should initially retain its sequentiality and be cross–checked item against item.
- Any data processing should be carefully examined as these processes can mask original observation errors.

(a)

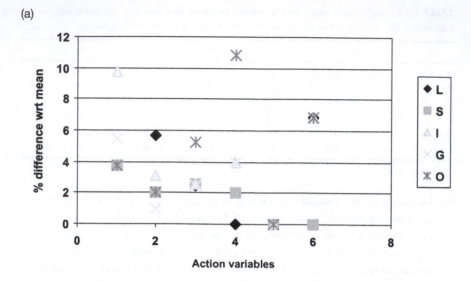

(b)

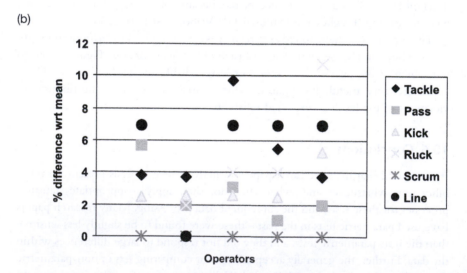

FIGURES 10.6A AND 10.6B The data from the reliability study, the intra–operator test, presented as a function of the action variables and the operators.

- The reliability test should be examined to the same depth of analysis as the subsequent data processing, rather than just being performed on some of the summary data.
- Careful definition of the variables involved in the percentage calculation is necessary to avoid confusion in the mind of the reader, and also to prevent any compromise of the reliability study.
- It is recommended that a calculation based upon

$$\sum \frac{\text{mod}\left(V_1 - V_2\right)}{V_{\text{TOTmean}}} \times 100\%$$

(where V_1 and V_2 are variables, V_{mean} their mean, mod is short for modulus and Σ means 'sum of') is used to calculate percentage error for each variable involved in the observation system, and these are plotted against each variable, and each operator. This will give a powerful and immediate visual image of the reliability tests.

It is recommended that further work examine the problems of sufficiency of data, first, to ensure that the data for reliability is significant, and also to confirm that the data present in a 'performance profile' have reached stable means.

11

QUALITATIVE BIOMECHANICAL ANALYSIS OF TECHNIQUE

Adrian Lees and Mark Robinson

11.1 Introduction

In this chapter we aim to provide an essential background into the recommended approaches for identifying and diagnosing faults in performance through either a *phase analysis model*, which is sequential in nature and based on the use of movement principles, or through a *performance outcome model*, which is hierarchical in nature and based on the mechanical relationships underpinning performance.

Qualitative biomechanical analysis is a method used to evaluate technique in the performance of sports skills. It uses observation and can be supplemented with a visual recording such as video with playback facilities such as single frame, slow motion and repeated viewing. It relies on a knowledge of the relevant sport and sports skill, as well as biomechanical knowledge such as 'analysis models' and 'principles of movement'. It also requires an ability to integrate these sources of information as a part of the evaluation process.

Technique is defined in general terms as the 'way of doing' and the technique used in the performance of a specific sports skill can be defined as the way in which that sports skill is performed. Good technique is a prerequisite of good performance so it is sensible to attempt to understand 'good technique' for individual sports skills. The advantage of qualitative analysis is that an analysis can be undertaken quickly without recourse to expensive, time-consuming and often restrictive methods characterised by contemporary quantitative methods. A further advantage is that a sports skill can be analysed holistically, something that is quite difficult to do using quantitative methods.

Technique is analysed mostly with reference to specific individual sports skills, which are single or sequential in nature, rather than with the wider aspects of sports and games where tactics and strategy are often influencing factors. The skills that are most amenable to technique analysis are:

- event skills that themselves constitute a sporting event, such as:
  - the high jump in athletics
  - a springboard dive
  - a vault in gymnastics
  - a shot put in athletics;
- major skills that are dominant in a sport, such as:
  - the hurdle clearance in sprint hurdles
  - a move during the floor exercise in gymnastics
  - a golf swing
  - bowling in cricket;
- minor skills that are important to the overall performance but do not dominate the sport or game, such as:
  - a kick in soccer
  - a serve in tennis
  - a spike in volleyball
  - a throw in water polo.

Technique analysis has two stages: the first is based on observation and its purpose is to *identify and diagnose faults* in performance, i.e. the causes of any discrepancies between the actual and desired performances of a sports skill or its outcome. The second is *remediation*, which is based on instruction and its purpose is to try to eradicate these discrepancies. This chapter will only be concerned with the first of these issues, as the process of feedback is itself a complex area worthy of further study. In practice, teachers and coaches develop their own methods of feedback and remediation, based on their experiences within the teaching and coaching fields and common practice within each sport.

The recommended approaches for identifying and diagnosing faults in performance are through the use of either *phase analysis*, which is sequential in nature, and based on the use of movement principles, or through *performance outcome*, which is hierarchical in nature and based on the mechanical relationships under-pinning performance.

11.2 Phase analysis

11.2.1 The phase analysis model

Phase analysis begins with the descriptive process of dividing up a movement into relevant parts so that attention can be focused on the technique used in each part. Some authors identify three main phases to a skill (*retraction*, *action* and *follow through*), while others identify four main phases (those above but preceded by a *preparation* phase), a recognition that the start of a movement may also influence the way a movement is performed (e.g. in a soccer kick the distance away from the ball and angle of approach are relevant factors to performance; in golf, the stance, how the club is held and position of the feet relative to the ball are also relevant factors).

Some authors identify more than four phases but these are often sub-phases of the four main phases mentioned above. Most authors acknowledge that phases can be further broken down into *sub-phases* and that the distinction between one phase or sub-phase and another is arbitrary and determined by the particular skill and the needs of the analyst. Nevertheless, this process of breaking a skill down into its functional parts is an important first analytical step.

The *preparation phase* describes the way in which the performer sets or prepares for the performance of the skill. For example, as noted above, it may relate to the start position and/or the way the ball is placed in a soccer penalty kick, or the way the club is held and/or ball placed on the tee in a golf drive. The *retraction phase* refers to the withdrawal of, typically, the arm or leg prior to beginning the main effort of performance. For example, in kicking, the kicking leg is drawn back, and in tennis this is represented by the backswing. The *action phase* is where the main effort of the movement takes place. For example, forward motion in executing a tennis serve, or the throwing action when propelling a javelin. The *follow-through phase* allows the movement to be slowed down under control and is thought to be necessary to avoid injury that might occur as a result of rapid limb deceleration. Some examples are given in Table 11.1. As noted above, the phase analysis model requires the phases and sub-phases, if appropriate, to be identified and each described. Some examples of sub-phases are given in Table 11.2.

The description of phases and sub-phases should identify *key moments, critical features* and *movement principles*. *Key moments* are those points in time in which an important event occurs or action is performed related to the 'way of doing'. One important event in striking sports is impact, which is a key moment. However, actions such as toe-off, foot-strike, maximum knee flexion, or minimum elbow angle, to name a few, would all define a key moment of the technique. *Critical features* are observable aspects of a movement and define a major characteristic of that movement. They refer to body or limb position (e.g. when catching a ball – crouch with arms and legs flexed; for a tennis serve – the 'back-scratch' position of the racket in the backswing), and motions (e.g. when catching a ball – give or retract the hands with the ball). It is worth noting that critical features are often related to coaching points and often are expressions of selected underlying movement principles (dealt with below). In some cases critical features may also be key moments. *Movement principles* complete the phase analysis model and are dealt with separately below. The phase analysis model is given schematically in Table 11.3.

Movement principles are based on mechanical relationships that have been developed over time to include multi-segment interactions and biological characteristics of the human musculoskeletal system. A movement principle is a description of how to achieve a specific movement outcome based on sound mechanical and/or biological principles and is used to help to understand and evaluate how sports skills are performed.

Movement principles can be classified according to the general outcomes that they are associated with. These outcomes are *speed* production, *force* production, movement *coordination* and some that relate to *specific* circumstances. Speed and

TABLE 11.1 Examples of the four phases of selected skills

Event/skill	Preparation	Retraction	Action	Follow-through
long jump	run up	body adjustments during penultimate stride to touch-down	take-off, from the moment of touch-down to take-off	flight from take-off and landing
golf swing	correct grip and stance	backswing	downswing	follow through
soccer penalty kick	run up	retraction of kicking leg	forward swing of kicking leg and contact	follow through

TABLE 11.2 Examples of the sub-phases for the action phase of selected skills

Event/skill	Action phase	Sub-phase 1	Sub-phase 2	Sub-phase 3
long jump	take-off	compression (knee flexion)	extension (knee extension)	—
golf swing	downswing	weight shift: initiation of movement with the hips	wrist locked and arms rotate as single unit	wrist unlocks and arms rotate as a double unit
penalty kick	forward swing of kicking leg	hips rotate forwards and leg flexes at knee	knee extends to contact	—

TABLE 11.3 Schematic template for a phase analysis model

Phase description	Preparation	Retraction	Action	Follow-through
Phase description[a]				
Sub-phase description[a]				
Key moments[b]				
Critical features[c]				
Movement principles[d]				

a   Each space under each phase should contain a brief description of the phase and (if appropriate) the sub-phase.
b   Key moments are often related to the start and end of a phase or sub-phase.
c   Critical features are often related to key coaching points.
d   Movement principles can be identified by their abbreviated title (see text).

force principles are based on mechanical relationships such as Newton's Second Law and principles such as the conservation of momentum. These equations are not detailed here to preserve the 'qualitative' nature of this chapter, but can be found in any good biomechanics text. Coordination principles are based on multi-segment interactions and have mechanical or biological foundations. This group of principles reflect the more complex operation of the human body and the inclusion of biological principles is an acknowledgement of the biological factors that determine complex human movement. Specific performance principles are where a number of interacting mechanical factors are commonly encountered, such as in the flight of projectiles, and these can be defined specifically.

There is no general agreement as to the number – or even the names – of movement principles. Some authors have identified as many as 53 movement principles, while others as few as six (Lees, 2002), which leads to a 'chaos of terminology' (Knudson, 2007) further complicating the issue. The higher number tends to reflect the specific mechanical principles while the lower number tends to reflect the more general principles (e.g. Bartlett, 2007). There have been some attempts to reduce the larger number of principles to a manageable form as 'core concepts' (Knudson and Morrison, 2002) that contain a mixture of mechanical, multi-segment and biological principles and that provide some use in a practical context. Table 11.4 is a list of those relevant to most sports and suitable for a qualitative biomechanical analysis of performance; they are explained in detail in the appendix to this chapter. They are not definitive but are thought to cover most sports skills.

When using these principles it's important to realise that in some cases these may overlap. For example, in a kick, tennis serve or golf swing, C2 PDS (proximal-to-distal sequence) also produces high end point speed (S4 EPS). Both principles apply but in a temporal sequence one occurs before the other. Indeed, in this example, one *causes* the other. Care must be taken not to include principles when there is no requirement for their maximum or optimal use. For example, in both kicking and long jumping, running takes place but it is only in the latter that maximum speed is required for performance and where the principle S1 applies. Uncertainties in the application of movement principles can be minimised by gaining experience of their use.

TABLE 11.4 Table of movement principles with codes

Speed	Force	Coordination		Specific performance
S1	F1	C1	AR	P1
S2	F2 ROM	C2	PDS	P2
S3	F3	C3		
S4 EPS	F4	C4	SSC	
	F5			
	F6			
	F7			

11.2.2 An application of the phase analysis model

A soccer penalty kick is used to illustrate how the phase analysis model and movement principles are used. The kick would typically be recorded on video and be available for repeat viewing, and inspection of individual frames. A series of still images have been extracted from such a video and presented in Figure 11.1a, b, covering the kick from take-off kicking leg on the last stride to follow-through.

In the phase analysis template (Table 11.5), each phase is identified along with the relevant sub-phases, key moments, critical features and movement principles. The movement principles can be the abbreviated names as suggested in Table 11.4. It can be seen from this analysis that several movement principles may apply at the same time. Some of these movement principles can be more easily appreciated by drawing appropriate indications on the images. For example, in Figure 11.2 the stretch shorten cycle, range of motion and action–reaction principles are easily appreciated from annotations to the images. Once a phase analysis model is completed, the coach is then able to view performances of the skill with a knowledge of what to look for in the movement (critical features) and how these relate to the mechanical performance of the skill (movement principles). For example, if a player needs to improve kick speed, then the coach would reasonably look at the range of motion achieved as indicated by the length of last stride, the degree of retraction of the hips and the use of the contralateral arm. Once these aspects of technique have been improved, the coach may then focus on the coordination of the movement, specifically the proximal-to-distal sequence of the movement and the general speed of execution which would improve the effect of the stretch–shorten cycle. Once these characteristics of technique have been developed, further improvement in performance may well come from the development of muscle strength characteristics. One should note that as strength changes so too may the technique, therefore a continual monitoring of technique used should always be made.

11.3 Performance outcome

11.3.1 The performance outcome model

An alternative approach to the phase analysis model is to analyse the factors that influence performance. By focusing on those factors, it is claimed that faults and limiting factors in performance can be identified. The most influential of these is the Hay and Reid model (Hay and Reid, 1982). The model was first developed for use in qualitative analysis but has also found widespread use in quantitative analysis to assist biomechanists identify important variables for quantification (Chow and Knudson, 2011) and for determining relationships between individual variables and performance outcome. The model does not address aspects of technique (the way of doing) directly, but the mechanical relationships that govern performance. In that sense, the model is more closely linked with movement principles and one

FIGURE 11.1A Still images of a penalty kick in soccer: (a) take-off from the kicking leg, (b) last stride, (c) touch-down support leg, (d) maximum knee flexion of kicking leg.

FIGURE 11.1B Still images of a penalty kick in soccer: (e) contact, (f) contact rear view, (g) post-impact, (h) follow-through.

TABLE 11.5 Phase analysis model template for the soccer kick

Phase description	Preparation (run up)			Retraction (of kicking leg)	Action (swing of kicking leg)		Follow-through	
Sub-phase description	1 Place ball and withdraw	2 Approach strides	3 (Fig. 11.2a) Last stride	1 SL placement of (11.2b) KL hip extension (11.2c)	1 (Fig. 11.2d) KL hip forward KL knee flexes	2 (Fig. 11.2e) KL knee extends	1 (Fig. 11.2g) KL knee full extension	2 (Fig 11.2h) KL knee flexes
Key moments			KL take-off	KL max hip extension (11.2c)	KL max knee flexion	Impact	KL knee fully extended	
Critical features			Stride length	KL hip extension (11.2c) Opposing arm back (11.2d)	KL max knee flexion	Body posture at impact	KL knee fully extended Opposing arm forwards	
Movement principles			ROM	ROM, SSC (stretch), AR	PDS	PDS, SSC (shorten), EPS	AR	

FIGURE 11.2 Selected images from the soccer kick with indications of important movement principles. (a) Illustration of the stretch arc (stretch shorten cycle principle), retraction of the hips and the hip–shoulder separation (both ROM – range of motion principle) and the simultaneous retraction of the kicking leg and opposite arm (AR – action reaction principle). (b) Illustration of the shorten arc (SSC – stretch–shorten cycle principle) in the follow-through.

may view it as a more direct and systematic approach to the identification of the mechanical principles that govern performance. The model is constructed as a hierarchy of factors on which the result (outcome) of the performance is dependent (Figure 11.3). The rules that govern the construction of a model for a particular skill is that each of the factors in the model should be completely determined by those factors that appear immediately below it either (1) from an algebraic relationship (such as addition) or (2) from a known mechanical relationship.

As noted above, the performance outcome model does not address issues of technique directly. For example, in a golf drive, the model will tell us that the speed of the club head must be high at impact but not how to achieve it. Information on how to use the arms and club as a two-lever system, weight shift and hip–shoulder rotation are beyond the scope of the model. In other words, the model is able to identify factors relevant to performance but not aspects of

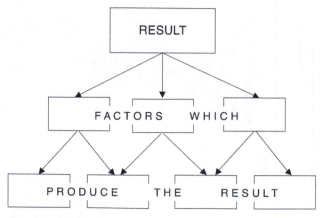

FIGURE 11.3 The Hay and Reid performance outcome model.

technique relevant to these factors. Nevertheless, the Hay and Reid model would appear to be valuable for identifying a range of factors influencing performance and providing a framework within which technique can be discussed. In this sense, it is not an alternative model for technique analysis but is complementary to other methods.

11.3.2 An application of the performance outcome model

The long jump is used to illustrate how the performance outcome model can be used (Figure 11.4). The measure of performance in the long jump is the official distance jumped. As the athlete must take off in front of the foul line, athletes often give themselves a margin of safety by taking off a few centimetres in front of it. This distance is known as the distance lost at take-off. When the athlete leaves the ground and becomes a projectile the distance covered is known as the flight distance. A small distance is lost on landing (the landing distance) as the heels (or backside) make a mark in the sand in front of where the centre of mass would intersect the ground. The actual distance jumped is determined by the take-off distance + flight distance − the landing distance. This is an example of rule 1. Of these three distances, the most important is the flight distance, so this is taken for consideration at the next level of analysis. In flight, the body is a projectile and so the flight distance is governed by the mechanical relationships that determine projectile flight. These mechanical relationships are the height, velocity and angle of projection at release (see performance principle P1). For practical reasons, it is more convenient to combine the velocity and angle together and to use their components in the vertical and horizontal directions. Thus, in this example, the three projectile parameters used are height, horizontal velocity and vertical velocity of the centre of mass at release. This is an example of rule 2, which is based on mechanical relationships. A full hierarchical analysis for the long jump is given in Figure 11.4 (but also see Bartlett, 2007, for a more detailed development). Note that only the main factors are followed through. Nevertheless, the model is quite comprehensive and has been used by the authors to provide scientific support for international long jumpers. The model clearly identifies what needs to be measured through biomechanical analysis. For example, the horizontal velocity of the centre of mass at touch-down and take-off are key factors. These factors can be measured from motion analysis during competition. This provides a strong rationale for the provision of biomechanical services during competitive events. If one wants to measure factors deeper into the hierarchy, such as force, then the model implies that force measurements need to be made. So far, this has not been done in high-level competition and it may never be done. This type of information is therefore only gained in a training environment. The implication is that suitably instrumented training environments need to be available to provide comprehensive support to high-level athletes. Finally, we need to return to the issue of how this model can be used to analyse technique. Implicit in the model is the need to quantify the factors identified. This is the role of biomechanists but once this is done then the

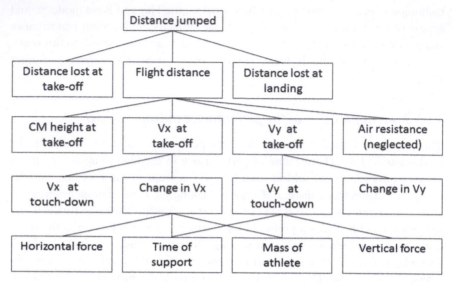

FIGURE 11.4 Performance outcome model for the long jump. (See text for further explanation.) CM, centre of mass; Vx, horizontal velocity; Vy, vertical velocity.

results of their analyses can be used with the model to provide advice on aspects of technique. For example, it is clear in the model that performance is dependent on the horizontal velocity. Thus, it is also clear that maximising this will be advantageous. It is also apparent from the model that vertical velocity is important, but the only place that vertical velocity can be generated is at take-off. Thus, attention should be focused on the actions of take-off and the actions leading up to take-off. This then implies that a more detailed investigation of the technique during this phase is warranted, and that it may be approached using the phase analysis model described in detail above.

11.4 Recent thoughts and developments

The scope of qualitative analysis is greater than outlined above. Texts on the topic (Knudson, 2007; Bartlett, 2007) emphasise wider issues such as the preparation, observation, evaluation, diagnosis and intervention skills required to undertake a complete qualitative analysis with the purpose of improving 'performance'. This emphasises the origin of qualitative analysis, which was in the coaching arena where its application was to aid the coaching process. Its formalisation as noted above is still relevant to this group, but is also appropriate to the professionalisation of the sport biomechanists whose services are now sought by national governing bodies of sport in many countries. The reader is encouraged to consult these two texts for a wider appreciation of the method.

While texts have focused on the wider issues, researchers have attempted to solve other problems. One in particular that is worth noting is the concept of 'technical level'. Any skill may be performed badly or well and as beginners learn they tend to move from a poor to a good demonstration of the skill. The research issue is whether this progress can be determined using qualitative analysis. Marqués-Bruna et al. (2007) attempted to determine the technical proficiency of 187 boys and girls aged 6–11 years, and 31 male and female adults in a stationary ball kicking task. Phase analysis was used to divide the event into five relevant components and for each, three levels of technical proficiency were defined and scored. For example, the first component was the approach and was classified as straight (1 point), angled (2 points) and curved (3 points). The other components were opposite arm movement, foot placement, contact pattern and follow through. The highest technical level was associated with a mature skilled kick and the greater technical proficiency was associated with a higher score. The results were clearly able to distinguish between ages and sexes with older children demonstrating a higher technical proficiency than younger children, and boys showing a higher technical proficiency than girls. These differences were evident in each component as well as overall. Interestingly, the adults were little better than the 11-year-old boys. This novel approach introduced a new concept into the literature and has shown it can be sensitive to skill development of children on a large scale. Such an analysis using quantitative analysis would be impossible.

Finally, it's worth commenting on the advancement of computer technology. The introduction of low-cost video analysis facilitated qualitative analysis, but this is now several decades old. The introduction and portability of low-cost computers, smartphones and tablets have enabled qualitative analysis to progress. There are an increasing number of anecdotal reports of people using video analysis apps on a smartphone or tablet to undertake their own qualitative analyses. This allows them to also annotate onto the video and provide instant feedback to the performer. The difficulty for the wider use of these possibilities is the need to have the biomechanical and technique knowledge to be able to provide meaningful interpretation of the video in the context of the skill. Publications such as this chapter hope to help fill this need.

11.5 Conclusion

This chapter has sought to introduce the methods relevant to the qualitative analysis of sports skills. Qualitative analysis is appropriate to the biomechanical analysis of sports technique and two major approaches have been identified for this. The phase analysis model is appealing in that it is based on a sequential breakdown of performance, performed from visual images gained, typically, from video analysis. By identifying phases and sub-phases of movement, the key moments and critical features, it is possible to identify the principles that govern performance. Using these principles, faults can be diagnosed from which it is hoped that performance can be improved. In order to use this model effectively, a sound knowledge of movement principles is needed. These are not readily available in the literature so the opportunity has been taken to outline them in this chapter. In contrast, the second approach is based on performance outcome. This leads to a hierarchical model of performance that identifies the relationships and mechanical factors that govern performance. It is implicit in this model that many of these factors need to be measured quantitatively. This is something that we have to rely on others to do, but based on their information it is possible to gain an insight into the key factors that influence performance and attend to these directly (such as the importance of approach speed in the long jump) or to use this information to guide a more 'technique' orientated analysis using the previous phase analysis model. The tools provided in this chapter should enable the enthusiastic student of sports science to undertake an effective analysis of sports technique using qualitative methods.

11.6 Appendix

11.6.1 Movement principles

11.6.1.1 A1 Speed (S) principles

These are a range of movement principles that relate to the generation of speed in a part or the whole of the body.

(S1) Whole body running speed

Running speed is increased gradually through sequential drives of the legs. The increase in speed with each stride is greatest at low speeds and reduces as whole body speed increases. Maximum running speed is achieved after about 40–50 m of sprinting. Therefore, to reach maximum speed, a person must be able to sprint for at least this distance. Some consequences of this are (a) running speed is often controlled by the performer due to the complexity of the skill and/or the high forces involved. In these cases the speed is kept sub-maximal in order to complete the skill and (b) in field games players are unlikely to reach their top running speed over a 10–15 m sprint, therefore their ability to accelerate is important.

(S2) Whole body rotational speed

Rotational movements of the whole body are completed more rapidly by bringing the limbs closer to the body's axis of rotation. For example, in a somersault the trampolinist rotates more rapidly when tucked; in a pirouette the ice skater rotates more rapidly when the arms are brought close to the body; in a squash backhand stroke the action phase begins with the racket arm close to the body so that the whole body can rotate into the movement before extending the racket arm. Conversely, extending the limbs slows the body down. This is done not only to slow down the rotation but to allow the performer more time to make a good landing. For example, stretching the arms above the head after a gymnastic vault slows the forward rotation of the gymnast; opening out after a tucked somersault slows the rotation of a trampolinist.

(S3) Limb rotational speed

To rotate a limb (e.g. arms or leg) rapidly requires the limb to be flexed and held close to the body. For example, in sprinting the leg is flexed tightly during the recovery part of the cycle. In a tennis serve the racket arm is flexed to achieve a back-scratch position (a critical feature); in golf the arm and club are in a flexed position at the top of the downswing.

(S4) End point speed (EPS)

A high end point speed requires a large distance from the axis of rotation to the end point. Consequently, at impact (or release) the limb is at or close to full extension. For example, when striking in sports such as tennis, golf, baseball and cricket the action phase begins with the limb and implement held close to the body and as the phase develops the end point (hand, foot, racket head, club head) is allowed to move away from the axis of rotation, thus increasing its distance of rotation.

11.6.1.2 A2 Force (F) principles

These are a range of movement principles that relate to the generation of force used to achieve a specific movement outcome.

(F1) Maximum force production

To produce the maximum effective force, a firm base is required on which to push. For example, in throwing events such as shot and javelin the action phase occurs when the delivery foot is in firm contact with the ground; in jumping events such as long, triple and high jump a firm surface is always used to push from. Conversely, if the surface moves the effective force produced is reduced. For example, soft surfaces – such as turf and sand – are more difficult to run and jump on due to the deformation of the surface. In tennis serving, the server is often seen to come off the ground. Is this an exception? Not really. To gain maximum racket head speed the server extends the legs (generating maximal effective force) and it is only after this that the player throws the racket head towards the ball. This combination of vigorous movements directed vertically causes the body to lift off the ground. Other principles are also used in the performance of this skill in order to achieve high end point speed (see C2 and C4 below).

(F2) Range of motion (ROM)

Muscle force can be applied for longer, the greater the limb's range of motion. Consequently, there is a possibility of achieving a greater effect by contracting muscle over a greater range of motion. For example, in running, as speed increases, the stride length increases, which occurs due to the greater extension (i.e. range of motion) of the leg during the drive-off. One implication of this principle, is that if the joint has greater flexibility, it is likely that this will allow a greater force-producing range of motion leading to enhanced performance. Consequently, there is thought to be a performance aspect to flexibility training.

(F3) Change of running direction

A change in direction of motion when running is produced by applying a force at right angles (perpendicular) to the current direction of motion. For example, in a side step or swerve made by a player in field games the foot is placed so as to maximise the friction force applied to the surface. This friction force should be directed perpendicular to the current direction of motion and *not* towards the intended direction of motion.

(F4) Impact – stationary ball or object

When hitting a stationary ball or object, the implement making the impact must move in the direction it is intended that the ball or object being hit should go to. For example, when taking a penalty kick, a goalkeeper can sometimes guess correctly the direction of the ball by carefully watching the motion of the kicker's foot as it moves to strike the ball.

(F5) Impact – moving ball or object

When hitting a moving ball or object, the striking implement must move in such a direction as to take into account the motion of the moving object. It will always be the case that the direction of the striking implement at impact will be different from that to which the ball or object subsequently goes. This divergence is related to the mass and speed of the two objects respectively (and another expression of principle F3 above). If, when heading a moving ball or making a cricket, baseball or tennis shot, the implement is swung to drive it in the direction of intended motion the ball will *not* travel in this direction.

(F6) Stability

Objects are more stable if they have a wide base and low centre of mass. For example, in wrestling – at the start of a competition wrestlers spread their legs and lower their centre of mass to provide a stable base. Stability is a 'statics' concept. Beware of 'dynamic stability' which is a 'dynamics' concept, beyond the scope of this chapter and probably not appropriate for a qualitative approach.

(F7) Resistance to motion in fluids

Resistance to motion when moving through air or water is reduced by reducing the area presented to the on-coming air or water (known as the cross-sectional area) and making a more streamlined shape. For example, in cycling, handle bars that are lowered and extended forward enable the cyclist to adopt a smaller cross-sectional area and more streamlined shape. Conversely, resistance is increased by increasing the cross-sectional area and making the shape less streamlined. For example, in swimming, the area of hand can be increased by the use of a hand paddle.

11.6.1.3 A3 Coordination (C) principles

These are a range of movement principles that relate to the coordination of motion between segments so as to achieve maximal or optimal performance.

(C1) Action–reaction: simultaneous movements of opposing limbs (AR)

The movement of one limb or body part helps the movement of the opposite (or contralateral) limb or body part. For example, in walking, running and sprinting, as one leg comes forward the contralateral arm also comes forward; an effective sprint start is one in which the arms drive vigorously to aid the force generation of the opposite leg – a good coaching point is that 'the arms drive the legs'; in hurdling (crossing over the hurdle) the lift of the lead leg is helped by bringing the opposite arm forward as far as possible; in pike movements in gymnastics, trampoline and diving, the performance of the pike is aided if the upper and lower body are brought together at the same time – the movement of one is helped by the movement of another; when heading a soccer ball the same pike movement is produced which increases the speed with which the head makes contact with the ball.

(C2) Proximal-to-distal sequence of movements (PDS)

This is used when producing high-speed movements. Many skills require a coordinated sequence of rotational movements to achieve a high end point velocity. This is achieved by rotating the large segments close (proximal) to the body first and terminating in the rotation of the segment farthest (distal) from the body. For example, in most throwing/striking/kicking skills, the action often starts with a step forward with the leg contralateral to the throwing/striking/kicking arm or leg, which has the effect of opening the hips. It continues with the hips rotating forward and is then followed by the trunk, shoulders and finally the elbow, hand and implement. The speed of the rotation of the earlier segment is built upon by the next segment, so as to build up the speed of the end point sequentially. Rotation of the distal segments causes the end point to move away from the axis of rotation, thus increasing the distance of rotation (see speed principle S4).

(C3) Simultaneous joint movements for force/power production

Simultaneous joint movements are used when producing forceful or powerful actions for a linked body segment chain that includes several of the major joints of the body. To ensure that this link system provides a firm base (see force principle F1) it is important that the muscle groups operate simultaneously. Therefore, forceful/powerful movements require muscles about joints to act synchronously. For example, when jumping for height, the hip and knee muscles act simultaneously to generate high force; in the shot put, the drive from the trunk and legs occurs simultaneously; in the bench press, the muscles activating the shoulder and elbow joint act together; in the sprint start, the hip, knee and ankle joint extend together.

Detailed biomechanical analysis has shown that, in some cases, even though the muscles act synchronously, the joints do not extend synchronously. Typically in the vertical jump, the ankle joint extends after the hip and knee joints generate their main effort. As the ankle joint is weaker than these other two joints, its role is to maintain a firm base for the other stronger joints as they produce their effort. Once this diminishes, the ankle, which is kept in a position of flexion, extends making its contribution to the movement. The sequence of joint motion is a reflection of the relative strength and function of the joints rather than a violation of the principle.

(C4) Stretch–shorten cycle (SSC)

Many actions involve a pre-stretching of the muscles and tendons which aids performance by enabling the highest muscle forces to be built up at the beginning of the movement. Consider a throw (or jump) in which the starting position is in the squat position. When the muscles begin to shorten, their force develops gradually. As this force develops, the movement velocity increases as does the speed of shortening of the muscles, which are now less capable of generating force (as determined by the force–velocity relationship for muscle). The net effect is that the movement is less able to increase speed further. If the muscles are pre-stretched by a counter-movement, the muscles are fully active at the beginning of the upward movement. This means that as they begin the upward movement, they are generating their maximum effort. The muscle and tendon 'stretch' should be quickly followed by the 'shorten' in order to maximise this effect.

11.6.1.4 A4 Specific performance (P) principles

These are a range of movement principles that identify the underlying factors relevant to specific aspects of performance.

(P1) Flight and projectile motion

An object that moves through the air under the influence of gravity is called a projectile. The outcome of projectile motion is often the range, but sometimes the height reached and time of flight are important performance measures. The mechanical factors determining projectile motion are the height, angle and speed of release, with the speed of release being the most important. The effects of air resistance can be important in many situations, particularly those where the ball is light, the relative velocity of the wind is high, or the object is shaped so as to have aerodynamic properties. The flight path of the projectile is modified accordingly and this as well as more complex effects (e.g. spin) needs to be taken into account.

(P2) Speed–accuracy trade off

In the performance of many skills, the outcome is determined by both speed and accuracy. It is generally found that as the demands for accuracy increase, the speed of the movement decreases. For example, when kicking a football for accuracy (e.g. a penalty kick), a hard–hit shot is less accurately placed than one hit less hard; in a basketball shot, the greater the distance of the throw the less chance the ball will go into the basket; in the long jump approach, jumpers need to hit the take-off board accurately so there is a tendency to reduce their speed close to touch-down.

12

APPLIED MOTION ANALYSIS

(a) Athalie Redwood-Brown and (b) Michael T. Hughes, Jo Clubb and Ben Pollard

(A) SYSTEMS OF MEASUREMENT IN TIME-MOTION ANALYSIS – A CASE STUDY OF SOCCER

Athalie Redwood-Brown

12A.1 Introduction

Soccer is a high-intensity intermittent sport that provides unique challenges for coaches and sports scientists alike with regard to tracking performance changes across matches (Gregson *et al.*, 2010). Being able to identify both the physiological and technical demands on players during game play is essential to enable coaches to adapt training and recovery strategies accordingly, to ensure adequate preparation to achieve optimal performance (Drust *et al.*, 2007; Carling *et al.*, 2009). A number of studies (Reilly and Thomas, 1976; MacLeod *et al.*, 2009; Rampinini *et al.*, 2009) have investigated the activity profiles of soccer players in an attempt to understand the demands placed upon them during matches. Methods used to analyse player movement have progressed rapidly from manual notation systems (Reilly and Thomas, 1976) to human operated computer based systems (O'Donoghue and Tenga, 2001) and more recently automatic player tracking with limited need for human interaction (Di Salvo *et al.*, 2006; 2009; Gamble *et al.*, 2007; O'Donoghue and Robinson 2009). Such video-based time–motion analysis has been applied widely in the soccer world providing useful information regarding the work capacity of players during competitive matches (Krustrup *et al.*, 2003; Mohr *et al.*, 2003; Rampinini *et al.*, 2007). Over the past 15 years the influx of computer-based technology has allowed new methods of assessing movement in soccer; such as multiple camera methods (Di Salvo *et al.*, 2009; Rampinini *et al.*, 2007; 2009), global positioning system (GPS) (Kirkendall *et al.*, 2004; Coutts and Duffield 2010; Edgecomb and Norton 2006) and systems using microprocessor technology (Frencken *et al.*, 2010).

More recently, fully automated tracking systems such as TRACAB, with no human operator input, have introduced the concept of live tracking during games (Carling *et al.*, 2009). Such physical performance data related to the activity profile of players has become so sophisticated that performance analysts can now retrieve data corresponding to specific speed zones to evaluate the performance of various players. Data relating to the activity profile of players has been used to give indications of training effects (Reilly, 2003), injury (Rahnama *et al.*, 2002) and fatigue (Bangsbo *et al.*, 1991). Companies such as Prozone (Leeds, UK), Amisco (Nice, France), TRACAB (Stockholm, Sweden) and Sportstec (Warriewood, Australia) have all provided systems to the commercial market that allow tracking data to be collected and used for post-match analysis. Computer-based coding systems have also been available for live analysis and half-time review such as Focus (Elite Sports Analysis, Fife, Scotland), Dartfish (Fribourg, Switzerland), Digital Soccer (Italy) and SportsCode (SportsTec, Warriewood, Australia). The aim of this chapter is to highlight the development of player tracking, in terms of capturing both event data and player movement.

12A.2 Manual notation systems

Notation systems are often recommended as an inexpensive way of providing an insight into the physiological and technical demands of game play by recording and quantifying player movement patterns that are characterised as skilled performance (Duthie *et al.*, 2003). Notational analysis has been used in numerous studies to investigate performance characteristics and activity patterns in various sports such as soccer (Wright *et al.*, 2011; Duthie *et al.*, 2003), rugby (Quarrie and Hopkins, 2007, Jones *et al.*, 2004a; Vaz *et al.*, 2012), squash (McGarry, 2006; McGarry *et al.*, 1999), basketball (Tavares and Gomes, 2003; Bourbousson *et al.*, 2010), hockey (Sunderland *et al.*, 2006), tennis (O'Donoghue and Ingram, 2001) and badminton (Blomqvist *et al.*, 1998a). Specifically, soccer has received an abundance of interest from notational analysis research in a number of areas including passing (Scoulding *et al.*, 2004; Ridgewell, 2011); possession play (Jones *et al.*, 2004a); behavioural incidence and outcomes (Taylor *et al.*, 2008); successful versus unsuccessful teams (Lago, 2007); match location (Tucker *et al.*, 2005); offensive and defensive variables (Luhtanen *et al.*, 2002); and individual and unit behaviours (Taylor *et al.*, 2005; Redwood-Brown *et al.*, 2012a).

These notation systems generally involve either pre-recorded or live video feed to 'tag' game events. This enables such events to be stored and either exported into other programmes to analyse or, if the system permits, analysed and presented within the programme itself (Ridgewell, 2011). A number of systems exist on the commercial market that enable such analysis (SportsCode, Sportstec, Warriewood, Australia; Dartfish, Fribourg, Switzerland; Focus, Elite Sports Analysis, Fife,

Scotland; Digital Soccer, Italy), all with varying features and associated costs. The main benefit of manually operated systems compared to automated systems is the vastly reduced costs in gathering data; however, due to the speed at which team games are played, collecting large amounts of live data can be difficult, incurring numerous errors (Barris and Button, 2008). Therefore, although manual notation systems are convenient, practical and usually inexpensive, the validity and reliability of such systems has been questioned (Barris and Button, 2008). The following section details some of the most utilised computerised notation systems in soccer together with research that has been conducted using such systems.

12A.3 Computerised generic systems

12A.3.1 Sportstec – SportsCode

Sportstec (Warriewood, Australia) provides a number of products aimed at coaches across a variety of sports. The most popular product, SportsCode, is used extensively in soccer and rugby for both in-game and post-game analysis. SportsCode is primarily a tool for notating and editing video game footage, enabling the user to edit and code the recorded game with the help of the program. The data can then be stored in a database and events can be categorised and recalled systematically through the program. It is a relatively inexpensive and flexible product that can be used with limited training in virtually all sporting environments. However, the product does rely heavily on human operators to produce, edit and analyse the data, which can result in a number of problems with reliability, validity and ultimately time to complete the process (Franks and Miller, 1986). SportsCode is also only available on an Apple Mac computer and thus can be challenging for analysts who have been used to a PC platform or require extra resources (e.g. new laptops) to run the program. SportsCode is however an affordable system for smaller clubs who are unable to afford computer-based systems.

Numerous studies have used SportsCode to investigate performance variables; Ridgewell (2011) used SportsCode Elite to investigate passing patterns before and after scoring in the 2010 FIFA World Cup. The system was specifically used to create a performance matrix to record the total number of passes (successful and unsuccessful) as well as the number of possessions made in the different territorial zones. Ridgewell (2011) concluded that scoring teams had significantly lower possession in both the attacking and middle thirds compared to the average for the half, and the conceding team significantly increased possession in both the middle and attacking thirds after a goal while significantly reducing possession in its own defensive third. Chinchilla Mira *et al.* (2012) used SportsCode (V8) to investigate how males and females differed in their use of offensive zones in elite beach volleyball. Twenty players (ten female and ten male) who took part in the European Beach Volleyball Championship 2005 and 2006 were observed across eight matches. By splitting the court into six zones the system was used to notate which zones the players used most frequently. Differences were found in both the zones used –

men used zones 1, 2, 4 and 5, whereas women used zones 1 and 5 more – and in the percentage of times the players were observed coming to the net – men came to the net more frequently (7.73 per cent) than the women (5.53 per cent). Russell *et al.* (2011) used SportsCode to compare the demands of a soccer match simulation session (SMS – 90 minutes of soccer-specific movement including passing, dribbling and shooting skills) with those of a competitive match. Using predefined operational definitions, player movement was characterised within the system as either walking, jogging, striding/dribbling or backwards and presented as percentages in each modality. Intra-reliability was evaluated by analysing both the physical player movement and skill demands of one player throughout one 90-minute match on two separate occasions. The system allowed differences between the two observations to be highlighted. These were 0 per cent for on-ball skills and 1.3 per cent (walking), 0.2 per cent (jogging), 9.8 per cent (striding), 3.0 per cent (sprinting/dribbling) and 5.2 per cent (backwards jogging). No differences existed between trials for mean heart rate, peak heart rate and blood glucose concentrations, thus suggesting the SMS replicates the physiological demands of match-play while including technical actions.

12A.3.2 Digital soccer

Panini Digital, formerly known as Digital Soccer (Brescia, Italy) provides analyses of football games using a technological station with a broadcast feed and a human operator. The human operator registers time, position and technical movements whenever a player gets the ball via voice recording (www.paninigroup.com/business-areas/panini-digital.html). The system also offers game analyses, team reports, preview analyses and game video analyses. Although the company stresses their process is based on scientific rigour, no computer vision technology is used to produce any of the data and thus human error could be a major factor in its reliability and validity as an analysis tool as it is heavily dependent on the experience and accuracy of the operators (Barris and Button, 2008). No published research to date has been conducted using this system of data coding.

12A.3.3 Dartfish and Focus X2

Basic video analysis systems such as Dartfish (Fribourg, Switzerland), Digital Soccer (Italy) and Focus (Elite Sports Analysis, Fife, Scotland) are aimed at coaches and athletes to help provide feedback on important game events (Barris and Button, 2008). They allow input of video to enable the user to time-code specific (predetermined) events alongside the video. Focus X2 (Elite Sport Analysis, United Kingdom) is used more as a tool for coaching and education, where users can zoom in on key events in detail, as well as showing multiple images simultaneously. Although the system is capable of tagging key events in a similar way to SportsCode and Dartfish, its strength lies in the ability to show video from various angles and annotate video to create educational or motivational clips (Carrozza *et al.*, 2011).

The voice recognition function is a unique feature of the Focus X2 system, which has been empirically tested for reliability and accuracy for the live and post-match coding of football at championship level (Court, 2007). However, Hughes *et al.* (2011) found the Focus X2 manual (mouse) system more efficient in both real-time and lapsed time than the voice recognition system when comparing the accuracy of both systems during live squash matches.

Dartfish has similar features to the Focus X2 software, but has the added benefit of two separate sections, one for analytics and one for tagging. The analytics enables users to calculate angles, distances and trace trajectories of player movement, as well as assessing detailed aspects of performance such as muscle imbalances in the prevention of injury (Carrozza *et al.*, 2011). More recently, Dartfish has added the ability to integrate data from other monitoring systems such as heart rate monitors, tachometers, dynamometers, EMG, GPS and ergometers. However, neither system currently provides tracking information, and all input comes from the end user (Barris and Button, 2008). All three systems are simple to use and set up and can be extremely cost effective, although their validity and reliability is heavily dependent on the ability and experience of the end user (Hughes and Franks, 2005). However, both Focus (Jovanovic *et al.*, 2011) and Dartfish (Young *et al.*, 2010; Padulo *et al.*, 2012) have been used in a number of studies to collect game event data and shown good intra- and inter-reliability.

12A.3.4 MatchViewer – ProZone

ProZone MatchViewer is a more sophisticated notation system that enables on-the-ball events to be notated using a computer-led process (Di Salvo *et al.*, 2006; Valter *et al.*, 2008). The event, the time of event, the players involved and pitch location, using X/Y coordinates, are notated for each game event recorded. This allows event details to be recorded and associated with frames within match videos in a similar way to other commercial systems such as Focus X2 (Elite Sports Analysis, Fife, Scotland) and SportsCode (Sportstec, Warriewood, Australia). The added benefit of the MatchViewer system is the ability to specify pitch location of events to give tactical as well as technical outputs at player level (Bradley *et al.*, 2007). The multiple levels at which the data is collected also allows for inter-game and inter-player comparison and interactive information such as passing matrices and player formation strategy (Di Salvo *et al.*, 2009). Although the data is collected manually and inputted by a team of human operators, a number of studies have tested this system for validity and reliability. Bradley *et al.* (2007) tested the reliability of the Prozone MatchViewer system and found high levels of inter-observer reliability; however, this was attributed to the quantity of user training and the strict use of the system's precise operational event definitions. The most common source of error was found when one observer considered an event to be a single event, while the other considered it to be composed of two separate events (e.g. touches). However, the largest error occurred when entering event position;

95 per cent of the events were agreed by the two observers to within 8.5 m with a mean absolute error of 3.6 m (Bradley *et al.*, 2007). Although this study reported the system as reliable when operated by observers who had undergone the necessary training (Bradley *et al.*, 2007) the large positional errors may be considered differently when compared to more recent tracking technologies. Both Valter *et al.* (2006) and O'Donoghue and Robinson (2009) in their respective studies have also found event data compiled by Prozone MatchViewer to be valid and reliable.

Although reliability of the system has been tested (Di Salvo *et al.*, 2009; O'Donoghue and Robinson 2009), there is still some doubt over the quality of the data due to the volume of human validation needed. And, as O'Donoghue (2007) highlights, if coaches and players are making important decisions about how they will prepare for competition using such data, it is important that the data is reliable and accurate.

12A.3.5 OPTA – Sportsdata

OPTA Sportsdata has been the world leader in collecting, compiling, analysing, storing, distributing and supplying live sports data on a wide variety of sports for the last 20 years. Over 40 sports are analysed by OPTA providing data for the betting industry, broadcasting, online and mobile media, print publishers, sponsors and brands, professional clubs and governing bodies (Optasports, 2013). Although OPTA works with a variety of sports their primary focus has been within soccer. OPTA has two main products within the soccer industry for performance analysis; OPTA Client System and OPTA Pro. OPTA's unique infrastructure enables over 40 soccer leagues to be analysed by their extensive team of analysts, producing some of the most comprehensive scouting and recruitment data in the business. Their core strength, however, lies in their depth of data with over 2000 events collected per game that can be packaged to suit the end user (OPTA, 2012). This depth of match data has helped to advance both the field of performance analysis and academic research investigating event data.

Within OPTA's system, analysts use a set of rigid definitions to code every possible type of ball touch and on-the-ball activity within the match. Analysts are familiarised with the definitions and short-cut keys used for recording events to ensure reliability of the data. There is still a large amount of subjectivity when using the system; however, the strict training processes undertaken by analysts ensure that ambiguity across events is limited (OPTA, 2012). The OPTA Client System has also recently been investigated in terms of its reliability in collecting live soccer match statistics (Liu *et al.*, 2013). Liu *et al.* (2013) tested the OPTA *Client system* using data from a game in the 2012–13 Spanish soccer league. A team of experienced operators independently coded the game both in relation to the event and the time it took place. Results indicated a good level of agreement (kappa values were 0.92 and 0.94) with an average difference of event time $0.06\pm0.04s$

suggesting that the OPTA Client system is reliable as a tool to collect live soccer data by trained operators.

A number of studies have also used data provided by OPTA to analyse soccer performance. Oberstone (2009) used multiple regression analysis to establish the most important performance variables for success in the 2007–08 English Premier League season. Results also found significant differences between top (teams that finished in the top four positions in the league), middle (middle 12 teams in the league) and bottom (teams that finished in the bottom four positions in the league) teams across 13 of the performance variables. Tunaru and Viney (2010) used OPTA data to establish a framework for estimating a player's financial worth. The model aimed to explore patterns of performance for individual players or teams on which value for money could be attributed, a valuable tool for any club or manager. Most recently, Collet (2013) used OPTA data across multiple soccer leagues to analyse the impact of possession time on overall team success. Results found that while possession time and passing predicted team success in domestic leagues, both variables were poor predictors of success once team quality and home advantage were accounted for. The impact of possession time was even less in national teams' tournaments and the Champions League.

Although data supplied by OPTA has been accessible for academic study, the research has only just scratched the surface in terms of analysing the data that is available. Although OPTA boasts the largest collection of event data, it currently does not provide tracking solutions, which are fundamental to analysing the movement patterns of players during the game (Carling *et al.*, 2008) limiting its application as an all-in-one tool for professional soccer clubs.

12A.4 Human operated/video-based semi-automatic player tracking systems

Semi-automatic player tracking systems are used by sports professionals to provide objective and reliable movement data. Unlike manual notation systems, these systems have the ability to track a large number of players within the same game (Di Salvo *et al.*, 2009; Gregson *et al.*, 2010) and thus allow researchers to investigate both team and individual player performance. Out of all the team sports soccer has received the most attention with regard to video-based time–motion analysis (Bangsbo *et al.*, 1991; Krustrup *et al.*, 2003; Mohr *et al.*, 2003; Reilly and Thomas, 1976). Such analyses have provided a wealth of information regarding player movement with regard to distances covered at high intensity in relation to: playing position (Reilly and Thomas, 1976), standard of competition (Rampinini *et al.*, 2007), physical capacity of the players (Mohr *et al.*, 2003) and physical performance of the opposition. The following sub-section details some of the key software programs that are commercially available to track player performance in soccer as well as research that has used such programs to collect data.

12A.4.1 Sport Universal – Amisco

Sport Universal's major product Amisco Pro enables users to view player movements, as well as tactical and technical performance data (Liebermann *et al.*, 2002). Using the system's analytics function users can compare individual players and teams across a host of performance measures (Amisco Pro, Nice, France). The Amisco system (Amisco Pro, Nice, France) uses a series of video cameras and sensors (approximately 4–6) installed around the playing surface to track player movement. This is achieved through sophisticated software that compares predicted trajectory paths of both the players and the ball with the data acquired via the multi-camera system (Liebermann *et al.*, 2002). Through this process an interactive representation of player actions is generated via graphical reconstruction and thus provides digital replays of all players and the ball from a range of positions. The system tracks all 22 players at a rate of up to 25Hz (Amisco, Nice, France) while human operators note all game events such as fouls, off-sides and cautions that occur during the game (Liebermann *et al.*, 2002). Its functionality and applicability make it a useful tool to investigate game performance (Liebermann *et al.*, 2002), and it has been used to track player activity profiles in a number of studies (Di Salvo *et al.*, 2009; Randers *et al.*, 2010). Although such studies have enabled coaches and researchers to evaluate player movement, the lack of a formal validation of the system may bring into question the reliability of the data. The volume of data generated by the system means that only trained analysts who are able to extract relevant data are able to effectively use the system. The positioning of the camera system also means it is not portable and is thus limited to the stadium in which it is fixed, which makes it a costly system to install and utilise (Liebermann *et al.*, 2002).

12A.4.2 Prozone 3

PROZONE® offers a semi-automatic tracking system able to analyse movement patterns quantifying both motion characteristics and work-rate ratios of professional football players during games (Prozone, Leeds, UK). The system uses a number of fixed cameras, positioned strategically around the stadium to produce a complete view of the pitch. To ensure accuracy, occlusion, resolution and resilience each area of the pitch is covered by at least two cameras (Di Salvo *et al.*, 2006). The primary capture equipment consists of a high-specification server and Prozone's unique capture software: PZ Stadium Manager® (Prozone, Leeds, UK). PZ Stadium Manager® acquires the relevant videos from the frame grabbers (located on the server) and converts them to AVI-MJPEGs. On receipt of the video files, human operators transfer the media onto dedicated file servers which instigate the automatic tracking of the videos (Di Salvo *et al.*, 2006). Each video is tracked independently, determining image coordinates and continuous trajectories for each player. Once the automatic tracking is complete, the output from all eight cameras is automatically combined to produce a single dataset. The video's image coordinates can then be converted into world pitch coordinates via a calibration process (computer vision homography) (Di Salvo *et al.*, 2006). The final stage of this process involves quality control operators identifying each player (by start position, position during the game and correspondence with the outside broadcast (OB) feed) and verifying that the trajectories identified for each player remain constant to that actual player (Prozone, Leeds, UK). During periods throughout the game, the trajectory is re-identified on the computer tracking system, checking the movement of each player during the game.

In order to test the system's tracking accuracy, Di Salvo and his colleagues (2006) conducted a validity study on the Prozone system. Four separate tests were completed across a number of speeds and distances and compared to a measured benchmark. The mean differences and limits of agreement between the two systems ranged from 0.05 to 0.23kmh^{-1} and 0.05 to 0.85kmh^{-1} respectively, with the coefficient of variation (CV) ranging from 0.2 to 1.3 per cent. Although the study highlighted Prozone to be a valid system for tracking player movement, with only 30 individual runs tracked, this is not a true reflection of the number of runs conducted during a standard soccer match and thus further testing of this system should be undertaken. As well as testing the accuracy of the system to track player speeds and distances, O'Donoghue and Robinson (2009) investigated its ability to track the location of path changes and transitions between different areas of the pitch. Their observations supported the system's accuracy in tracking player movement; however, as with previous validation studies, only a small portion of the game was tested.

Although Di Salvo and colleagues (2006; 2009) have reported this system as reliable with good inter- and intra-operator agreement for the distances covered at different speed ranges (Di Salvo *et al.*, 2006; 2009), they reported that as much as 42 per cent of player time was required to undergo a verification process in order to achieve the required level of accuracy. This can be a lengthy process, resulting in client clubs waiting as long as 24 hours for match data after the final whistle (O'Donoghue and Robinson, 2009). A lot of manual work is also required to register all the relevant events that occur during the game, such as free kicks, corners and passes (Mylvaganam *et al.*, 2002). Although a time-consuming process, the system does enable all 22 players to be tracked simultaneously with no disruption or necessity to wear tracking devices. Although previous camera-based systems have successfully tracked players, they were unable to track more than one player at a time (Castagna *et al.*, 2004) and generally required a large investment from human operators to follow the individual analysed during the course of the game. The advantage of the Prozone system is the possibility of tracking each single individual participating in the game (players and referees) and the ability to quantify their motion patterns at the same time. The major disadvantage, however, resides in the high costs (approximately £100k a year) and the necessity of installing multiple fixed cameras and a computerised network with a dedicated operator to run the data collection and analysis element (Di Salvo *et al.*, 2006). The fixed installation also means the system is not portable and thus clubs are only guaranteed their data from home games. Although Prozone was acquired by the Sport Universal brand (owners of Amisco) in 2011, the processes used to capture data at this point have remained independent.

12A.4.3 LucentVision

LucentVision uses similar technology to both Prozone and Amisco, but in tennis. The system uses multiple cameras positioned around the court (four on the side and two at the ends of the court) to track the motion of the tennis ball in 3D (Pingali et al., 2000). With balls speeds of up to 225 kmph, ball tracking using this method enables virtual replays and other visualisations that enable the ball trajectory to be viewed from any position. This also records a variety of numerical statistics; for example, the changing speed of the ball during its trajectory (Pingali et al., 2000). The system, which is also able to track player motion, is mainly used in broadcast where computer vision techniques are used to track each player's movement in real-time. Real-time tracking is also applied to the ball on all serves, giving its three-dimensional trajectory and speed throughout its motion (Pingali et al., 2000). A major strength of this system is the ability to scale the number of cameras to track multiple objects; however, as yet no trials in soccer have taken place and no validation of the system's accuracy has been conducted. No research to date has been conducted using this system.

To overcome the costs and set-up logistics of multiple camera systems, global positioning systems (GPS) have been employed as an alternative to track player movement (Witte and Wilson, 2004). This has proved valuable in sports such as hockey and rugby; however, during league soccer matches players are not allowed to wear any device, thus making it impossible to use GPS systems to measure performance during competitive games of elite players outside friendly matches. Their use in training and in non-league/cup matches, however, has provided coaches and managers with valuable information regarding player performances (e.g. Macutkiewicz and Sunderland, 2011; MacLeod et al., 2007; Cahill et al., 2013). Their use in other sports such as hockey and rugby (where the units are permitted during match play) has also provided some useful information regarding player movement patterns in invasion games.

12A.5 Global positioning systems

Global positioning systems were originally designed for military use, but in the 1980s they became commercially available, although deliberate error (selective availability) was incorporated into the systems to guard against them being used inappropriately (Larson et al., 2003). In 2000 the selective availability was reduced, thus increasing the accuracy of the non-differential GPS systems as they were consequently named (Witte and Wilson, 2004). In team sports GPS has been employed to monitor a number of performance-related activities such as work-rate of players (Macutkiewicz and Sunderland, 2011; MacLeod *et al.*, 2007), fatigue (Wisbey *et al.*, 2009), training loads and player movement during games (Gabbet, 2010). The technology uses operational satellites that orbit the Earth to send signals to GPS receivers here on Earth (Larson *et al.*, 2003). Once activated, the GPS receiver continually sends and receives signals from the satellites; by synchronising the time of the satellites with the atomic clock, the receiver can measure the distance travelled by each signal. Using a minimum of four satellites, the system calculates the distance measured using complex algorithms to determine the position of the receiver (Larson *et al.*, 2003; Townshend *et al.*, 2008). Sampling frequencies of commercially available GPS units can range from 1 Hz or 5 Hz for older systems, to newer systems that, although not extensively tested, have been proposed to be more sensitive to movement sampling at 10 Hz (Catapult MinimaxV4.0, Scoresby, Australia) or 15 Hz (GPSports SPI Elite, Canberra, Australia). The units are generally worn either on the player's upper back inside a neoprene pouch attached to a harness around the player's shoulders, or inside another pouch sewn into a sleeveless undershirt (Wisbey *et al.*, 2009).

Schutz and Chambaz (1997) were the first to investigate the use of GPS for monitoring human activity and since then a number of studies (Witte and Wilson, 2004; Townshend *et al.*, 2008; Gabbett, 2010; Portas *et al.*, 2010; Macutkiewicz and Sunderland, 2011; Cahill *et al.*, 2013) have used GPS to provide an insight for coaches and managers on player movement during game play and training. Although there is limited research in elite soccer (due to the inability to use GPS in competitive matches), GPS has been used extensively to monitor player movement in other invasion games.

Gabbet (2010) used GPS (MinimaxX Catapult Innovations, Melbourne, Australia) sampling at 5 Hz to investigate the physical demands of elite women's hockey players during both training and competitive match situations. He found that players spent more time in the low intensity category (0–1 ms^{-1}) than the medium (1–3 ms^{-1} and 3–5 ms^{-1}) or high (5–7 ms^{-1} and.7 ms^{-1}) category during game-based training than in the actual competitive game situation, suggesting players work harder during competitive matches than in training. Macutkiewicz and Sunderland (2011) investigated the activity profiles of elite women's hockey players during match-play in relation to playing position. Twenty-five players were analysed over 13 international games using GPS (GPSports SPI Elite, Canberra, Australia). They found forwards spent a greater percentage of time running, fast running and sprinting, and less time walking compared to midfield players or defenders. Although the low-intensity activity reported by Macutkiewicz and Sunderland (2011) was below that found in previous studies (97 per cent, Boddington *et al.*, 2001; 95 per cent, MacLeod *et al.*, 2007; and 92 per cent, Spencer *et al.*, 2004) this was the first study to provide a detailed positional analysis, using GPS, of the distances covered and time spent performing various activities during a match. Cahill *et al.* (2013) displayed similar findings in Premiership Rugby players where the running intensities of players differed depending on positions. Such findings may have implications for match strategies and training, allowing the physical demands of the game to be better replicated during training sessions. With some systems it is also possible for coaches to monitor players live both in terms of their movement profiles and heart rate (Wisbey *et al.*, 2009). This immediate feedback is important to allow coaches to adjust training intensities, for example of players coming back from injury and perhaps more importantly in match play to make tactical changes around players who are suffering from fatigue (Wisbey *et al.*, 2009).

A number of studies have attempted to measure the accuracy of GPS in team sports (Macleod *et al.* 2007; 2009; Coutts and Duffield, 2010; Portas *et al.*, 2010) with most concluding that GPS technology provides accurate measures of speed and distance covered during the activity categories identified in team sports. Specifically, validity for GPS has demonstrated CV ranging from 1.3 to 3.1 per cent and mean difference ±limits of agreement of 0.0 ± 0.9 kmh^{-1} (MacLeod *et al.*, 2009; Portas *et al.*, 2010). Coutts and Duffield (2010) used two male participants to access the accuracy of a 1 Hz GPS system with a built-in accelerometer. The participants were instructed to move around a circuit consisting of high intermittent exercise, including changes of direction and speed. Although the GPS showed an acceptable level of accuracy, it was suggested that without an accelerometer built in, the system would have failed to track players when signal strength dropped below an acceptable range. Coutts and Duffield (2010) concluded that the GPS units alone were not sufficient to accurately track player movement. However, more recently a number of higher sample frequency units have become available that have shown increases in both accuracy and reliability for measuring distance (Varley *et al.*, 2012). Varley *et al.* (2012) assessed the validity and reliability of both a 5 and 10 Hz GPS for measuring instantaneous velocity during acceleration, deceleration, and constant velocity while straight-line running. They found the 10 Hz GPS devices were up to six times more reliable for measuring instantaneous velocity than the 5 Hz units (coefficient of variation 1.9–6.0 per cent).

Gray *et al.* (2010) state that despite relatively few independent studies focusing on the validity and reliability of GPS technology during match-specific conditions, they are gaining popularity in a number of sports as a means for coaches to assess specific movement demands of their athletes in both training and competition. Given the number of clubs using GPS systems in training to monitor player movement, it is important that the systems used on match day are able to report data with the same or better accuracy for training and match day comparisons (Randers *et al.*, 2010). Even with higher frequency GPS, which has been shown to be more sensitive for detecting changes in performance in team sports (Castellano *et al.*, 2011; Varley *et al.*, 2012), coaches must account for the inherent match-to-match variation, reported when using these devices (Randers *et al.*, 2010). Studies have also shown problems when systems are used in built-up areas (Williams and Morgan, 2009). As many stadiums, especially in football, are enclosed or in close proximity to other buildings, constricting satellite signals, this may pose problems, even if GPS units were permitted for use during match play.

12A.6 Automatic player tracking systems

With no human operators needed to gather data, automated tracking allows a greater amount of time to be spent on real-time analysis investigating tactical and technical aspects of play. Automatic tracking in this way allows sports science and medical personnel to make detailed observations of player movement in order to evaluate agility and injury risk respectively (O'Donoghue and Robinson, 2009). In addition, having this information live during matches can allow the appropriate personnel to assess whether players are performing to their individual targets, informing tactical aspects of play such as substitutions, which can be critical during a game (Hirotsu and Wright, 2002). The cost of image processing technology and fixed installation is generally much higher than using GPS systems which are relatively inexpensive and do not require a fixed base (e.g. stadium) on which to place cameras (MacLeod *et al.*, 2009; Witte and Wilson, 2004). However, if the intervention is able to assist in injury prevention by highlighting player movement issues live during a game, a large part of the cost of the technology could be justified, especially if the overall incidence of injury in a team is reduced (O'Donoghue and Robinson, 2009). Due to the fully automated nature of the systems, a greater volume of data can be collected on individual player movement, allowing more relative analysis responding to movements that may involve sharp turns or cutting movement, associated with ankle and other such injuries (Simpson *et al.*, 1992). The following sub-section details some of the key automatic tracking systems currently available in the commercial market for tracking player movement.

12A.6.1 Venatrack

Venatrack's Visual-AI technology (Venatrack, Slough, UK) allows players to be monitored in real-time (at 25 Hz) providing identification through recognition algorithms (based on x, y, z coordinates for hands, feet, head and the pelvis and shoulder lines; Venatrack, UK). Between 24 and 28 high definition (HD) colour cameras are installed in each stadium to maximise accuracy. As visual acuity of any camera image based system is limited by the number of video pixels provided to either the human operator (in the case of most semi-automated systems) or the computer algorithm (in the case of the Venatrack system), using a greater number of cameras results in a greater number of pixels with which to quantify the pitch area and thus provides a greater accuracy for measuring each point. Venatrack's automated system therefore uses 28 HD cameras in up to ten locations compared to most semi-automated systems that use between four and ten HD cameras in up to four locations (Di Salvo *et al.*, 2006; O'Donoghue and Robinson, 2009). Accordingly, the estimated visual acuity for the current system is in the range 5–25 mm compared to previous systems which are estimated at between 500 mm and 1500 mm depending on the region of the pitch. The camera's position, orientation and field of vision are determined and fixed when installed using a Theodolite (Nikon NPL 362, Japan). The cameras are thus positioned to give a full view of the pitch using the system's unique configuration coordinates (unique to each ground). This allows each position on the pitch/player to be covered by at least five cameras at any one time (Venatrack Ltd, UK). Calibration of the automatic tracking system is completed by a team of technical experts. Although the system is fixed for the duration of the game, only eight of the 28 cameras are permanently fixed due to their location (generally on the stadium roof). Each installation process takes up to four hours, with a further two hours required for calibration to be completed. The running and installation costs are comparable to both the Prozone and Amisco systems but with much less human operation once calibrated, therefore reducing the delay on data extraction. The cost of image processing technology and fixed installation is generally much higher than using other more portable positioning systems such as GPS which are relatively inexpensive and do not require a stadium for camera positions (Libermann *et al.*, 2002; O'Donoghue and Robinson, 2009). However, having immediate feedback on player performances has many potential benefits that would arguably outweigh the initial costs of installation. In order to test the accuracy and reliability of the system, Redwood-Brown *et al.* (2012b) conducted a validation study comparing the system to calibrated speed gates within a stadium environment. The mean differences and limits of agreement between the two systems ranged from 0.07 to 0.64 kmh^{-1}, with the CV ranging from 0.2 to 2.8 per cent. Pearson correlations (r) among timing gate speed and automated tracking speed were ≥ 0.99 ($p < 0.001$), except the 20 m sprint, with 90° turn ($r > 0.7$) (Redwood-Brown *et al.*, 2012b). The results of this study suggest that the automated system (Venatrack) is a valid real-time motion analysis system for tracking player movements during soccer.

At the time of publication the Venatrack system was not currently available on the commercial market.

12A.6.2 Orad – CamTrack

Orad's CamTrack product uses real-time image processing and 3D graphics to produce content for TV broadcasters, sports sponsorship and internet markets (www.orad.tv). Their software permits the broadcaster to display live and replayed footage with graphics and animation that can be integrated into the match environment giving the appearance of a real-time environment (Williams, 2007). A process of calibration is required prior to the match footage that involves identifying set positions within the stadium. This allows the software to calculate where and how on the sports ground the graphics should appear. Using image processing technology the software transforms a flat two-dimensional video into a 3D graphical representation (www.orad.tv). The camera can then 'navigate' around the 3D world, permitting the end user to view the match from a variety of angles within the game (Williams, 2007). Due to the complex process of data transformation, the replay is generally only used to show short clips and replays. There is also a great deal of human verification required as clips are rendered at around 50 times per second. CamTrack can provide a lot of statistical information about the course of the game, such as area covered by each player, as well as accumulated distances and speeds. The system can also plot player trails and measure distances between players, which may be useful for tactical game feedback (www.orad.tv).

12A.6.3 TRACAB

TRACAB is a semi-automatic computerised player tracking system (TRACAB Image Tracking System™, Solna, Sweden) that uses a multiple camera system to passively track player movement in real-time. Using eight pairs of cameras, the video stream captured by the cameras is analysed by the TRACAB Image Tracking System™, capturing player movement at 25 Hz. This generates x, y, z coordinates as well as speed and acceleration for all objects (Lago-Peñas et al., 2012). The system has been found to measure player location to less than 0.1 m (Castellano et al., 2011) making it an accurate and useful tool for player analysis. Lago-Peñas and his colleagues (2012) used the TRACAB system to characterise match activity profiles of 432 top-class outfield soccer players during the 31 matches of the UEFA EURO 2008. The overall distance covered by each player was recorded as well as a minute-by-minute breakdown of work-rate over time (distance divided by effective time played). Results indicated that midfield players covered a significantly greater total distance than both defenders and forwards ($p < 0.01$). Significantly more distance was covered in the first half compared to the second (5136 ± 468 m vs 5063 ± 461 m, $p < 0.01$). However, this difference may be explained by the fact that the effective playing time of the first half was significantly greater than the corresponding one for the second half of the match (27.4 ± 2.2 min vs. 26.9 ± 2.4 min, $p < 0.05$). The findings suggest that the TRACAB system was a suitable and accurate system for calculating player work-rate specifically when considering more precise information such as effective playing time.

12A.7 Sensor technology companies

12A.7.1 Trakus

The Trakus system, more commonly known as Digital Sports, uses microwave receivers that analyse the signal emitted from special transmitters worn by players/performers to instantaneously capture the movement of athletes and objects during sporting events (Perš et al., 2002). The main aim of the system is to provide real-time digital sports content for TV broadcasts, the internet and other social media. However, the system has since become available as a tool for coaches and managers to use to evaluate performance in sports such as ice hockey, golf and motor sports (Setterwall, 2003). The system can provide metrics such as location, speed, acceleration, endurance and intensity. It can also graphically reconstruct how plays unfold and create selective views of a game from any angle. As all players need to wear special sensors to capture data, this technique is not currently allowed in many sports (Perš *et al.*, 2002), although it may be possible to develop such technologies for future use. However, to-date no development to the author's knowledge has taken place in this area.

12A.8 Comparison studies

Although validations have taken place on some of the tracking products available on the market, studies comparing the systems with one another have been limited. Recently, however, Randers *et al.* (2010) found significant differences between various time–motion analysis systems with regard to the output they produced for distances covered at various speeds. He compared a video-based time–motion analysis system, a semi-automatic multiple-camera system, and two commercially available GPS systems (GPS1–5 Hz and GPS 2–1 Hz). Total distance covered ranged from 10.83 ± 0.77 km (semi-automatic multiple-camera system) to 9.51 ± 0.74 km (video-based time-motion analysis system) and high intensity running distances ranged from 2.65 ± 0.53 km (semi-automatic multiple-camera system) to 1.61 ± 0.37 km (video-based time–motion analysis system). Although correlations were found between systems, a number of differences were also found. Specifically, the GPS1 system measured more walking than the multi-camera system ($p < 0.001$) and time–motion analysis system ($p < 0.001$); the multi-camera system recorded a longer total running distance ($p < 0.001$) compared with the other three systems (although no differences between the latter three systems were found). The multi-camera system also measured more ($p < 0.001$) high-intensity running than the other three systems. Differences were also found between the two GPS systems in terms of distance covered (GPS1 = 10.76 ± 0.80; GPS2 = 9.64 ± 0.93; $p < 0.001$). Randers *et al.* (2010) suggested that although each of the respective systems may have been able to detect trends in player movement over a game, the absolute reported values for running distances seem to be highly dependent on the system and these differences should be taken into account when comparing results collected with different systems. Given the results presented by Randers *et al.* (2010) it is not surprising that at present no gold standard test in soccer has been found to track player movement. This has generally been attributed to the unpredictable nature and variability in the sport (O'Donoghue, 2004) and the lack of agreement about the speed ranges to be used to represent different classes of movement, such as walking, jogging, running and sprinting (Carling *et al.*, 2008). It may, however, be more useful to establish which system is the most accurate and reliable for measuring player movement to create a gold standard.

Edgecomb and Norton (2006) compared two GPS systems (GPS-1 5HZ and GPS-2 1HZ GPSports) with a manual computer-based tracking system (CBT; TRAKERPerformance, Sportstec, Warriewood, Australia) to investigate player movement patterns during competitive Australian football games. A number of methods were used to determine the validity and reliability of the systems for tracking the total distance covered by the players; including multiple cameras, multiple observers and validated comparisons with calibrated objects; comparisons were also made between the systems. The results indicated that the CBT overestimated total distances by an average of 5.8 per cent, whereas the GPS system overestimated by 4 per cent. Although the GPS system showed slightly better accuracy compared to the test variable used by trained operators, the CBT system was found to be as accurate as the GPS (Edgecomb and Norton, 2006).

Aughey and Falloon (2010) also used GPS (GPSports MinimaxX) to compare player motion data of Australian football players both in real-time and post-game. They found real-time data were significantly different to post-game data for jogging (4.2–5.0 ms^{-1}), running (5.0–6.9 ms^{-1}), sprinting (6.9–10.0 ms^{-1}) and total distance (CV = 6.4–19.6 per cent). It was unclear from the study specifically why such large differences occurred between the real-time and post-game data; however, in order for the performance data to be used live, the signal strength must be greater than the noise created (Aughley and Fallon, 2009). This was only achieved during the jog and total distance measures, although it was not thought to completely explain the differences observed. Therefore, Aughley and Fallon (2009) suggest that great caution should be applied when using real-time data to monitor performance, especially if targets are set for players using post-game data.

Harley et al. (2011) compared data derived from both match play and training situations using a semi-automated video analysis system (Prozone) and GPS respectively. Six elite-level soccer players were analysed during a competitive match using semi-automated video analysis (ProZone®) and GPS (MinimaxX) simultaneously. The GPS reported higher values than the Prozone system for total distances (GPS: 1755.4 ± 245.4 m; Prozone: 1631.3 ± 239.5 m; $p < 0.05$) and Prozone reported higher values for sprinting distance (SPR) and high-intensity running (HIR > 4.0 ms^{-1}) than GPS (SPR: PZ, 34.1 ± 24.0 m; GPS: 20.3 ± 15.8 m; HIR: Prozone, 368.1 ± 129.8 m; GPS: 317.0 ± 92.5 m; $p < 0.05$). Although attempts have been made to compare semi-automated and automated tracking systems in a controlled environment to understand which system is more valid for assessing player movement, as yet no such study has been conducted. Tracking data from such systems has been compared; however, due to the commercial implications of highlighting such results it has been difficult to gain the relevant permissions to publish such data.

12A.9 Conclusions

At present no fully automated valid '3D' system is currently commercially available to the soccer market that tracks live, and requires no human operator; therefore the amount of information that is currently analysed in real-time within clubs is limited by the method of collecting the data, rather than the way in which the data is used. Information that is produced 'live' during games by current providers has had its validity questioned, and is based somewhat on human perception and observation where it is proposed that on average 42 per cent of player tracking is manually verified in the case of some systems (Di Salvo et al., 2009). More research is needed to evaluate such methods of player tracking as it is essential that the data is reliable and valid if it is to be used to make important game decisions (Drust *et al.*, 2007).

Comparisons between tracking systems used by professional clubs, such as Prozone and Amisco and new GPS 15 Hz systems (GPS Sports) should be undertaken to enable coaches and sports scientists to compare player movement data. Similarly, using professional players would support the use of such a system in the professional field. As Carling *et al.* (2008) suggested more relevant movements should also be included in validation studies to best replicate 'in–game' players' movements to ensure match play can be accurately reported.

(B) SOME PRACTICAL NOTES ON GPS SYSTEMS

Michael T. Hughes, Jo Clubb and Ben Pollard

12B.1 Introduction – inside the GPS unit

Most practitioners, especially those working in team sports, are exposed to GPS technology. It can seem like a little black box that spits out streams of data; data that we are expected to translate for coaches and players. As scientists it is essential we understand the inner workings of the technology we employ, the methodologies behind the numbers and the limitations and errors associated with them.

GPS units can contain a number of components including the satellite receiver, accelerometer, magnetometer, gyroscope and a battery, and here I will focus on the two currently most associated with calculating the data we use (satellite and accelerometer).

FIGURE 12B.1 A global positioning satellite docking station and units.

Source: Courtesy of GPSports.

12B.2 GPS

Global positioning satellite receivers can provide data based on point to point location analysis. There are 24–30 satellites orbiting the Earth, originally part of the USA's military programme and now accessed by many everyday objects, including car sat navs and GPS watches, and units for sport and exercise. A receiver needs to lock onto three or more satellites, calculate the distance to each and therefore determine its own location via trilateration.

Satellite visibility affects the signal strength, the more satellites the receiver can 'see' the better the quality of data, hence why data can be poor when using GPS in stadiums, as the stands block access to multiple satellites. Data quality can also be affected by tall buildings, terrain and foliage, atmospheric conditions, electronic interference and satellite geometry, all of which can cause 'positional dilution of precision'.

The frequency of the GPS unit dictates how many sampling points per second are registered, i.e. 5 Hz represents 5 per second. These discreet data points are joined up to estimate the path of the individual so in theory a higher sampling rate should provide data closer to the actual path travelled. However, not all is what it seems when it comes to GPS frequency. Some of the higher advertised frequencies, i.e. 15 Hz are not necessarily derived from 15 GPS data points per second but from interpolated data. This is a 10 Hz GPS sampling rate supplemented with accelerometer data in an attempt to improve the reliability of the tracking data.

There is debate regarding the optimal sampling frequency of GPS. With a higher resolution of data collection, some points may not represent true human movement plus the error associated with each point could be amplified by a greater sampling frequency. On the other hand, more data points may help to improve the collection of smaller, more intense movement such as accelerations and decelerations.

The validity and reliability findings of GPS studies and different sampling frequencies will be discussed further on.

12B.3 Accelerometer

GPS units contain tri-axis accelerometers, meaning that they measure a composite vector magnitude by calculating the total of proper accelerations across three axes; x, y and z. When a unit is stationary they will measure 0 g across the x and z plane but a gravitational force of −1 g (or 9.8 m/s/s) in the y (vertical) axis due to the Earth's standard acceleration due to gravity.

I like to think of using accelerometers on 'thrill rides' as the movement of the body due to g forces is exaggerated:

- When you are thrown from left to right by side-on crashes during the bumper cars, the g force acts along the x axis.
- The g force from a vertical freefall on Disney's Tower of Terror or The Detonator at Thorpe Park act in the y axis.

- Being driven straight forward into a tunnel on Aerosmith's limo in Disney's Rock n Roller Coaster throws your body backward by the g force acting along the z axis.
- The best rollercoasters of course exert g force along all of the axes!!

Accelerometers can be found in a variety of everyday objects, including Wii remotes, pedometers and smartphones. A great 'app', called Accelerometer-Visual, displays tri-axial readings and is a useful tool in understanding the behaviour of an accelerometer.

Unlike GPS receivers, it is widely accepted that the greater frequency of an accelerometer is beneficial, given that they are attempting to capture all movement and force going through the unit. There are currently 100 Hz tri-axial accelerometers integrated into the newest GPS units, measuring up to 16 g on each axis.

The use of accelerometers in quantifying the forces elicited on the body, through impact and/or collisions, is a very interesting area of research.

12B.4 GPS validity and reliability – a collection of independent research findings

GPS technology provides coaches, sport scientists and athletes with the opportunity to collect individual physical data that have not previously been available and on a basis that is time efficient, relatively low cost, non-invasive and potentially in real-time. As well as the practical benefits, there has been a surge in uptake in elite sport, probably due to those in the elite setting wanting to gain a competitive advantage and/or not fall behind their opposition. Although it first became available to the sports industry in 2003, little validation research was published until 6–7 years later. Given the increase in popularity, GPS technology had been exposed to the high-performance team sport environment, before thorough research had been conducted into data accuracy and global definitions of metrics. This pattern endures as manufacturers release new models and firmware updates ahead of academic research.

It was a surprising struggle to find a collection of the independent publications from the literature readily available on the internet (published literature reviews aside); Table 12.1 contains my selection of some of the research.

The complexity of validity and reliability of the technology to quantify movement demands is significant and stating an across-the-board conclusion is impossible due to the variation of manufacturers, models, sampling frequency and algorithms, plus the different parameters, task designs, criterion measures and statistical analysis employed in the research. Consequently, practitioners working with GPS must take steps to understand the validity and reliability of their own devices within their own setting and usage. Caution is strongly advised if using models and systems interchangeably.

The demands of the movement significantly influence the accuracy of the data collected, with trends in reduced accuracy, with increases in velocity, decreases in

TABLE 12.1 Independent research findings in GPS

Citation	Manufacturer Model Sampling freq.	Course design	Parameter(s)	Criterion measure(s)	Conclusion excerpt
Edgecomb and Norton, 2006	GPSports SPI-10 1 Hz	Predetermined marked circuit	Distance	Trundle wheel	GPS overestimated true distance travelled by players (average < 7%). There is relatively large error when small distances are involved (< 200 m) but these become less over longer movement patterns (> 2 km)
Macleod et al., 2009	GPSports SPI Elite 1 Hz	Simulated team sport (hockey) circuit	Distance and speed	Trundle wheel and timing gates	Valid tool for measuring speed and distance during hockey
Coutts and Duffield, 2010	GPSports SPI-10, SPI Elite and WiSPI 1 Hz	Simulated team sport circuit	Total distance, high intensity distance (> 14.4 km/hr), very high intensity running distance (> 20 km/hr) and peak speed during 20 m sprint	Measuring tape and timing gates	Accurate and reliable information on total distance travelled during team sport running patterns; however data from different devices should not be used interchangeably. 1 Hz may not provide accurate information regarding high intensity activities, especially if they are completed over a non-linear path
Gray et al., 2010	GPSports WI SPI Elite 1 Hz	Linear and non-linear (including curved) 200 m courses	Distance across different movement velocities and mean and peak velocities	Actual distance using total station EDM/theodolite	GPS distance demonstrates reduced validity in non-linear movement patterns, including curved or circular paths, as movement intensity increases … Although 1-Hz GPS receivers should be considered a reliable tool for measuring distance travelled by athletes in field-based team sports, multiple changes in direction at high speed may reduce both reliability and validity
Jennings et al., 2010	Catapult MinimaxX 1 & 5 Hz	Straight line running and change of direction courses at various self-selected speeds and simulated team sport circuit	Distance across different movement velocities	Measuring tape and goniometer for change of direction sections, and timing gates	The reliability and validity of GPS to estimate longer distances appears to be acceptable (< 10%). However, currently available GPS systems maybe limited for the assessment of brief, high speed straight line running, accelerations or efforts involving a change of direction. An increased sample rate improves the reliability and validity

Reference	GPS unit	Activity	Measures	Criterion	Findings
Portas et al., 2010	Catapult MinimaxX 1 & 5 Hz	Linear, multi-directional and soccer specific courses	Distance	Trundle wheel and tape measured distance	Both methods produced valid and reliable measures of linear motion and could be used to precisely quantify total distance motion in linear sport activity such as running. For multi-directional motion, both 1-Hz and 5-Hz were valid and reliable in less challenging scenarios but not in the more complex where reliability decreased . . . presently NdGPS is incapable of detecting small but practically important changes (SWC)
Waldron et al., 2011	GPSports SPI-Pro 5 Hz	Straight line sprinting	Distance, peak speed and proper acceleration (integrated accelerometry)	Measuring tape and timing gates	GPS devices (5 Hz, SPI-Pro) can be used to quantify small, yet practically significant changes in sprint performance, particularly with reference to measures of peak speed in young rugby players. However, it appears that calculations made using either a GPS device or timing gates can differ markedly
Varley et al., 2012	Catapult MinimaxX V2.0 5 Hz MinimaxX V4.0 10 Hz	Straight line running	Acceleration, deceleration and constant velocity	Instantaneous velocity using a tripod mounted laser	Superior validity and inter-unit reliability of V4.0 Minimax compared with the older V2.0 units . . . The latest V4.0 units sampling at 10 Hz provide sufficient accuracy to quantify the acceleration, deceleration and constant velocity running phases in team sports
Johnston et al., 2012	Catapult MinimaxX V2.5 5 Hz	Simulated team sport circuit (Coutts and Duffield, 2010) and flying 50 m sprint	Total distance, peak speed, player load, distance covered/ time spent/number of efforts across different movement velocities	Measuring tape and timing gates	This study demonstrated that 5-Hz GPS units are capable of measuring the fundamental movement demands of TD and peak speed. However, because of the levels of reliability revealed in this study of 5-Hz GPS units it is recommended that they are only used to measure the distance covered, time spent, and number of efforts performed at different speed zones at low speeds
Buchheit et al., 2013*	GPSports SPI-ProX and SPI-ProX2 15 Hz (although looks like the 5 Hz model in the pic?)	Simulated match running activities; data collected during training sessions	Total distance, distance >14.4 km/hr, distance > 25.1 km/hr, peak speed, accelerations and decelerations	Reliability was assessed between model, unit and software update	Very large variations in common GPS measures (particularly accelerations and decelerations) between models and units from the same manufacturer. Analysis of same data files with different software versions showed substantial differences in the occurrence in accelerations and decelerations

* For more on the Buchheit et al. (2013) paper see: http://sportsdiscovery.net/journal/2014/03/09/monitoring-with-gps-time-to-slow-down/

Environment	Unit	Movement Demand
• Satellite visibilty • Environmental conditions • Surroundings • Location	• Manufacturer • Model • Sampling frequency • Chipsets • Software version	• Velocity • Task assessed • Complexity • Duration • Parameter

FIGURE 12B.2 Factors influencing GPS reliability.

task duration and increases in the complexity of the movement path (i.e. non-linear/curved/multidirectional). Of course these are the kinds of movements that are arguably of most interest in team sports – short, high intensity sprints/accelerations/decelerations/change of directions. Although research has shown this error can be improved with increased sampling frequency, limitations remain. We must question whether we are accurately capturing the most crucial movements relating to loading through the body and possible impact on the game.

As well as sampling frequency we have to consider the variation between manufacturers, models, hardware, software etc. I find it really interesting to see that the manufacturers covered in this sample of literature are limited to only two of the leading manufacturers; I would certainly be interested to read the independent findings into the others (if these even exist?!). Martin Buchheit's (2013) study showed substantial differences in outputs from the same data files using different software versions, so care must be given in the applied world to whether, when and how we run the updates. Finally, there are also environmental factors that can affect the quality of data (http://sportsdiscovery.net/journal/2014/03/14/inside-the-gps-unit/) (see Figure 12B.2).

While the research moves on to explore new ventures – small-sided games, metabolic power, accelerometer data for collision sports to name but a few – it is essential we do not forget the foundation of accuracy of the technology. As well as the research cited above there are a number of review papers that further summarise the findings of GPS validity plus the potential applications of the technology: Aughey (2011); Cummins *et al.* (2013); Dellaserra *et al.* (2014).

12B.5 GPS application to rugby

GPS technology has been available and used in elite professional rugby for around 8 years. Throughout this period, hardware, software, popularity and understanding of its capabilities have increased considerably.

12B.5.1 Uses

Each rugby team, as in many other sports, will use GPS differently whether due to budget, the user, the previous user, the head strength and conditioning coach or the head coach. In general, the uses of GPS in order of direct relevant use are:

Rehab running:
Running at a set pace (i.e. percentage of maximum speed) and for a set distance can be of use to a medical team to rehabilitate an injured athlete. As a player progresses, his running sessions may objectively reflect the running demands of the game. Real-time feedback of rehabilitation sessions can be very valuable to adjust the session there and then.

Monitor training volume and intensity:
Training sessions can be viewed objectively from a movement perspective regarding the volume (typically total distance) and intensity of a session (typically metres per minute). If there is a priority from a physical perspective of the load or stimulus that the session should evoke, the outputs from the GPS (which variables discussed later) can help analyse whether this has occurred (post analysis) or is occurring (looking at the data real-time). This data can be compared to normative stats from specific sessions and provide data for meso- and macro-cycles from a loading perspective.

Assessing training performance:

a)   running conditioning/conditioning games: individuals or positions can be compared for running performance during sessions where movement is the main priority;
b)   rugby sessions: comparisons can be made between individuals of similar position with the outputs from the GPS showing their work-rate from a movement perspective.

Assessing match performance and match 'load':
These are two areas that are debatable and there is a lack of research stating links between match GPS data and subsequent performance, or fatigue from the GPS 'load' post game.

a)   Performance: outputs require to be analysed to see whether there are correlations and relationships with i) team performance via win/loss, points scored/conceded, team specific internal ratings etc. and ii) individual performance via positive contributions, coach ratings etc.
b)   Load: outputs from the GPS also require to be correlated to physical status in the days post game. This obviously requires a robust valid and reliable method of monitoring physical status whether by subjective measures, biomechanical or neuromuscular.

12B.5.2 Key variables

With software now being able to output over a hundred different variables from the GPS unit there is much discussion between users as to which variables to focus on and how to display them. The simplest way to answer this is:

a) ensure you know what each variable is telling you;
b) ensure you know what question you want answering, e.g the outputs that you may prioritise for a rehab run (% max. speed, no. of efforts over 70/80/90%, number of accelerations/decelerations in certain zones) may be different from conditioning game (metres per minute, distance over jogging speed, number of accelerations, number of efforts over 70% max speed).

Do you want to know what the *volume* of the session was?

- total distance;
- distance over a certain percentage max. or speed. If you wanted to look at distance not walking it is estimated at 1.5 m/s or ~20% of average max. speed. Self-selected jogging speed has been reported at 3 m/s via GPS, and 3.88 m/s via timing gates.

Obviously this does not ascertain all that is involved in a rugby session re volume. This may be total time, rate of perceived expiration (RPE), no. of scrums/lineouts/kicks/collisions.

Do you want to know what the *intensity* of the session was?

- metres per minute is very commonly used;
- distance over jogging speed per minute;
- accelerations per minute;
- repeated high intensity efforts; these is where you can set the software to recognise when there has been repeated efforts of your choice, i.e. a sprint, acceleration and impact of a certain level within a certain time period.

Obviously this does not ascertain all that is involved in a rugby session as regards intensity. This may be total RPE, heart rate (HR) mins in certain zones, work to rest ratios, and all of the above with regard to volume per minute. An appreciation of what GPS can and cannot do helps in understanding the potential of GPS unit technology – that it cannot answer all questions about sports but it can support their analyses.

When considering percentage maximum speed zones, think about whether to individualise these. Is it best to give the same cut-off to all players, as that is what may affect performance on the pitch vs each other, *or* do you go off percentage of individualised maximum speeds to merit an effort that is vastly different to execute from a tighthead prop to a winger?

12B.5.3 Research

Although there are a number of research papers regarding GPS use in AFL, soccer and rugby league, there is actually limited research published regarding elite rugby union. There are descriptive papers of average distance sprinted: 6–9 m and 15 m for forwards, and 13–15 m and 20 m sprinting distances for backs, respectively. A recent paper looking at French international players using Amisco showed that mean acceleration was significantly higher in the first half versus the second half when all players were analysed together. The only positional group that was actually significant in decrease was the back row, who also showed the highest mean acceleration (Lacome *et al.*, 2014). Cahill *et al.* (2013) examined GPS data collected from a number of premiership rugby clubs. They found that scrum halves covered the most distance of all players, and openside flankers the most of all forwards. They also found that as much as 9.8 minutes can be spent in static exertion alone.

12B.6 Summary

GPS can provide objective data to solve answers to rugby players and staff in certain situations. In others they will support the answer to what you are trying to solve, and in some they may even sidetrack you from what the answer is. There will be questions posed from a physical performance standpoint, whether from head coaches, strength and conditioning coaches, or medical teams, where thought is required as to how best to answer them. The user can pick the outputs available to them to answer these.

13

PROBABILITY ANALYSIS OF NOTATED EVENTS IN SPORTS CONTESTS

Skill and chance

Tim McGarry

In this chapter we:

*   present some examples to introduce the idea that the behaviours and outcomes in sports contests can be analysed on the basis of chance (or probability); and
*   demonstrate that consideration of various aspects of sports contests from the perspective of chance is a useful way of investigating and informing on sports behaviours.

13.1 Introduction

On first consideration from sports experience, a viewpoint that sports actions and sports outcomes might be thought of on the basis of chance might seem questionable if not objectionable. In the following sections, however, we demonstrate with select examples that consideration of sports behaviours from the perspective of chance using probability analysis is a useful and common method for describing and analysing sports contests with the aim of advancing game understanding. Hereafter, the term sports contests is used to describe an adversarial contest between two opponents. Other types of sports contests excluded from this definition may also be viewed, however, from the perspective of chance and investigated using probability analysis.

13.2 Skill and chance

The words skill and chance may appear to some to be a contradiction of terms when combined in the same phrase. They are not. In terms of probability analysis, chance refers to uncertainty, so chance may be defined and quantified as the probability, or percentage likelihood, of a future occurrence. (Probability and percentage are the same measure except that probability is reported between values of 0 and 1 and percentage between values of 0 and 100.) Thus, chance is not a euphemism for fortune (good luck) or misfortune (bad luck), an interpretation in common usage when referencing outcomes in terms of chance, nor should it be taken to indicate equal likelihood of outcome, as in a 50 : 50 split for instance, although an equal probability of two outcomes is not excluded in this same consideration.

Skill refers to the ability to produce an action that attains a desired future outcome with a high degree of probability (or chance). Thus, a definition of skilled action can be quantified as the ability (or probability) of the willed action to achieve its intended outcome. To illustrate this basic concept of skilled action, consider two penalty kick takers in football (soccer) with, all other considerations aside, scoring probabilities of 0.9 and 0.8, respectively. The first player in possession of the higher scoring probability is more skilful at taking penalty kicks than the second player with the lower scoring probability, by definition, as the first is more likely than the second to score on any given penalty kick. In this example, whether either player will score or miss on any given penalty kick remains unknown until the outcome is observed, even though both players are more likely than not to score, given that their respective scoring probabilities both exceed a half.

To repeat, the likelihood (or chance) of a player scoring in the above example on any given penalty kick, or any given number of penalty kicks, is quantified in their scoring probabilities, with higher probabilities referencing higher skilled behaviours. Put simply, skilled actions win out more often than not, and with increasing likelihood over the long run, as expected. This conclusion with regard to skilled action indicates that they can indeed be quantified on the basis of chance using probability.

13.3 Probability: stationarity and independence

In later sections we report on some investigations of sports behaviour using probability analysis. First, we present two important concepts for probability analysis, those of stationarity and independence. Stationarity refers to the assumption that the probability of an event, or occurrence, does not change from instant to instant. That is, the event probability remains constant across the time frame under investigation. In a sequence of coin tosses, for instance, stationarity applies if the probability of a 'heads' (or 'tails') is the same from one coin toss to the next. For example, if the probability of a heads is a half then it remains so from trial to trial. In this same coin toss example, independence applies if the outcome of a given event, or occurrence, does not affect the outcome of a next event, or occurrence. For example, if the result of the first coin toss is heads, the result of the second coin toss is just as likely to be heads or tails as it was on the first coin toss. Thus, the second coin toss is not affected by the result of the first coin toss. Similarly, the outcome of the third coin toss in the sequence is unaffected by the second outcome, and so on. While it might seem from the example presented that stationarity and independence speak to the same properties, suffice to say that, while complementary, the properties of stationarity and independence are not the same as we shall see later.

13.4 Taking a random walk in a field of probabilities

To illustrate the use of probability for analysis purposes consider a sequence of three coin tosses, assuming stationarity and independence, with the probability of heads (p) and tails (q) on any coin toss being equal, as expected (i.e. $p = q = 0.5$). Since the probabilities of all possible outcomes must sum to one, it follows that if p or q is known, then the other is known also (i.e. $p = 1 - q$ and $q = 1 - p$). Each of the possible outcomes from a sequence of three coin tosses, together with the paths, or probability sequences, that lead to these outcomes are presented in Figure 13.1. Starting at the sequence of coin tosses we take a random walk through Figure 13.1. The first coin toss yields heads with probability p_1 or tails with probability q_1. The integer subscript following the probability notation indicates the trial number in the trial sequence for purposes of tracking convenience. Should the random walk on the first trial take the upper path then the outcome of the first coin toss is heads (p_1), whereas tails results from taking the lower path (q_1). Which path is taken in this instance is determined, or at least quantified, by chance (or probability), hence the reference to a random walk. The random walk depicts the new state of the system under investigation with the first state represented in one of two nodes (H or T) depending on the outcome of the coin toss. The random walk then continues from its present state and follows the respective upper or lower paths in similar fashion to the second state now represented in one of four nodes (HH, HT, TH or TT). The process continues in like fashion until the sequence of events, three coin tosses in our example, is completed as represented in one of eight nodes (HHH, HHT, HTH, HTT, THH, THT, TTH or TTT).

From Figure 13.1, we find eight possible outcomes for a three coin toss sequence ($2^3 = 8$) as expected, but we also can follow the paths, or the random walk sequences, that produce each of the eight distinct outcomes. For example, if the upper path is followed on all three trials then the outcome of the three coin toss sequence is three heads (HHH), and since the probability of the outcome is expressed in the random walk that produced it, the probability of getting three heads from three coin tosses is $p^3 = 0.5^3 = 0.125$. In this example, since $p_1 = p_2 = p_3$ the $p_1 p_2 p_3$ term in Figure 13.1 may be simplified to p^3 and similarly for q^3. To restate, if we want to know the probability of obtaining three heads from three trials, we can determine the random walk that produces this particular outcome and use that information to find the answer. The probability of getting three heads *or* three tails from three coin tosses is likewise obtained in similar fashion. To quantify the chance of obtaining either outcome we must take two random walks as appropriate (p^3 and q^3). Since $p^3 = 0.125$ and $q^3 = 0.125$, the probablility of getting three heads or three tails from three coin tosses is therefore 0.25 ($p^3 + q^3$). Similarly, the probabililty of getting two tails from three coin tosses is $3pq^2 = 3(0.5)(0.5^2) =$

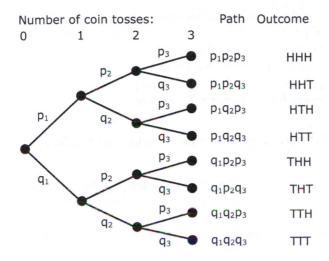

Number of coin tosses:				Path	Outcome

FIGURE 13.1 Probability structure depicting a sequence of three coin tosses. p and q denote the probability of heads and tails, respectively. The subscripts 1, 2 and 3 denote the first, second and third trial in the probability sequence, respectively. H = Heads. T = Tails. The outcome list details the outcome of the three trials, and the path list denotes the path, or probability sequence, that produced that particular outcome.

0.375, a result obtained from taking all possible random walks that lead to the outcome of two tails ($p_1q_2q_3 + q_1p_2q_3 + q_1q_2p_3 = 3pq^2$), that is those random walks denoted by the q^2 term. In this way, the information contained in all possible random walks is sufficient to answer whatever questions are posed regarding any combination of possible outcomes from three coin tosses.

The foregoing demonstrates that the probability of a given outcome can be obtained by accounting for all of the different random walks by which that outcome may be reached. In design, a simple example comprising eight (2^3) probability sequences was presented by which the random walks necessary for any given outcome could be identified quite easily by enumeration. Longer sequences of probability chains render this approach impractical, however, as well as being increasingly subject to error on the part of the enumerator. Imagine using enumeration for instance to determine the probability of getting eight heads from a sequence of ten coin tosses yielding 1024 (2^{10}) probability sequences or random walks. Fortunately, mathematical formulae may be used in replacement of enumeration though, importantly, both methods achieve the same result in the same way. For instance, in a system comprising two event probabilities (p and q) as per the coin toss example used, the probability of getting eight heads from ten coin tosses is obtained quite readily from the binomial theorem (or binomial series). In example, the binomial series for the three coin tosses is $(p + q)^3 = p^3 + 3p^2q + 3pq^2 + q^3$. Similarly, as shown in Figure 13.1, enumerating each possible outcome from the three coin toss sequence presented yields $p_1p_2p_3$, $p_1p_2q_3$, $p_1q_2p_3$, $p_1q_2q_3$, $q_1p_2p_3$,

$q_1p_2q_3$, $q_1q_2p_3$ and $q_1q_2q_3$ which when expressed as a sum of all possible outcomes gives $p^3 + 3p^2q + 3pq^2 + q^3$. To revisit the question of the probability of obtaining two tails from three coin tosses then, we may therefore simply obtain the q^2 term from the binomial series ($3pq^2$) and compute accordingly. Similar computational principles apply to the probability of obtaining eight heads from ten coin tosses, if desired. So much for coin tosses. Our interest is in sports contests.

13.5 Investigating sports contests using probability analysis

There are quite a few examples of authors using probability analysis to investigate sports contests, including analysing the design and resulting efficacy of tournament structures, with the game outcome of win and loss serving as the event probabilities. Tied outcomes may be included in the probability analysis if required. Regarding efficacy of tournament designs, the argument is that better tournament stuctures will yield increased probabilities of the better players or teams ranking higher in the final placings. Similar examples include analysing scoring systems in a given sport, with the outcome of a point win or point loss of some type, say, serving as the event probability. Again, the better scoring systems should increase the chances of the better players or teams achieving winning outcomes.

Identifying optimised decision-making strategies in the aim of maximising a winning outcome offers another example of applying probability analysis in a sports context. In particular, baseball has long been replete with game statistics and these data may be used, for instance, to inform player selection and assignment of individual players to specific positions on the basis of their playing statistics for maximising team output using a mathematical approach known as the Hungarian algorithm, as well as making value-based decisions on player trades informed by player statistics, as popularised quite recently in the 'Moneyball' account. For reasons of focus, however, we will skip the details of the authors and the specifics of their contributions to probability analysis as applied to these various aspects of sport behaviour and instead offer a couple of select examples using probability analysis for investigating football game behaviours.

In writing the article for the first edition of this textbook (McGarry, 2008), an example of applied probability analysis of sports behaviours in squash contests was offered by investigating the shot sequences in squash rallies and their associated behavioural outcomes of winner, error and let, resulting ultimately in game and match outcomes of win and loss. In this revised version, an example of applied probability analysis of sports behaviours in football is offered; first, in reference to applying probability analysis for identifying an optimised game strategy for winning a penalty shoot-out and, second, in reference to a seminal article published in 1968 by Reep and Benjamin using binomial series analysis to report on frequencies of passing sequences leading to goal attempts. Then, as with the first edition, a now abbreviated consideration of analysing sports behaviours in squash contests as a stochastic (probability) process is presented to demonstrate the important requirement of invariant data properties that underpin applying probability analysis for informing sports behaviour.

13.6 Football: identifying optimised game strategies for the penalty shoot-out

As with coin tosses, the outcome of a penalty shoot-out can be quantified in terms of chance, or probabilities and, as such, the penalty shoot-out is sometimes referred to in colloquial terms as a lottery. The implication in use of this reference of lottery, for me at least, is that the outcome of a penalty shoot-out is attributed to the hands of fate and not to the feet and hands of the players. To continue the lottery analogy, as the chances of winning a lottery increases with increasing purchases of additional tickets, so the odds of winning a penalty shoot-out increases with increasing the skilled actions of penalty takers and penalty stoppers by advance preparation (practice). Identifying an optimised line-up sequence for the penalty takers may also increase the likelihood of achieving a winning outcome.

Some decisions taken in sports contests can be made ahead of time by advance planning. In football, the penalty shoot-out is used to break tied games in knock-out competition and the selection and placement in the line-up sequence of the five (or more) penalty takers presents a good example for a priori decision-making by the coaching staff. From the binomial series, with p and q representing the probability of scoring and not scoring on a penalty kick respectively, the list of all possible outcomes from five penalty kicks is $p^5 + 5p^4q + 10p^3q^2 + 10p^2q^3 + 5pq^4 + q^5$. Thus, the probability of scoring five goals from five penalty kicks is p^5, that of four goals is $5p^4q$, that of three goals is $10p^3q^2$, that of two goals is $10p^2q^3$, that of one goal is $5pq^4$ and that of zero goals is q^5. As before, since p represents the probability of scoring on a penalty kick, the number of goals scored from five penalty kicks is indexed in the p superscript. The practical significance attached to increasing the probabilities of the penalty takers on a given team scoring (p), and also increasing the probabilities of penalty kick stopping by the goalkeepers (q) on the scoring tally and, consequently, on winning a penalty shoot-out can be quantified using the above formula. Increasing these respective probabilities of p and q can be achieved through dedicated and deliberate practice (training).

The skill of taking a penalty kick is quantified in the scoring probability which varies among individual players. The probability of a given player scoring on a given penalty kick is furthermore expected to be influenced by the importance attached to scoring on that single attempt. One might argue that each penalty kick in a penalty shoot-out comprising five penalty kicks is of equal importance but this position holds only when penalty kicks are independent of each other. If the penalty kicks are not independent, however, then a reconsideration of probability points towards the penalty kicks assuming increasing importance as the line-up sequence progresses, that is the second penalty kick is more important than the first, the third penalty kick more important than the second, and so on. The importance of a point in tennis was quantified by Morris (1977) as the probability of winning a game given the point is won minus the probability of winning a game given that the point is lost. This same concept of importance applied to a penalty shoot-out confirms increasing importance of penalty kicks as the line-up sequence advances as later misses assume increasing costs towards a winning outcome. For example, a miss at a scoreline of 5–4 has more negative consequences than a miss at 4–3 which in turn has more negative consequences than a miss at 3–2 and so on. (Note: in this consideration, the assumption of independence is rejected for the reasons just expressed, whereas the assumption of stationarity is retained – i.e. the probability of a given player in a given line-up position for a given scoreline condition remains unchanged from trial to trial, as described below, even though the probabilities themselves are determined by the player and game circumstances.)

Given that the five penalty takers selected for a penalty shoot-out will have different scoring probabilities, and given that penalty kicks later in the line-up sequence assume increasing importance, the question begs regarding the optimised placement of the penalty takers in the line-up order. For example, to which penalty kick position should the best penalty taker be assigned, to the first penalty kick to maximise the prospects of getting off to a good start, or to the fifth penalty kick which is the most important should the penalty shoot-out advance to that stage, or to the third penalty kick which guarantees that the player will take a penalty kick in the shoot-out but at a more important stage than the first penalty kick? This question of an optimised line-up sequence for five penalty takers in a shoot-out was addressed by McGarry and Franks (2000) using computer simulation techniques.

Probability analysis of the penalty shoot-out was undertaken using various assumptions. Specifically, that the five penalty takers assumed different scoring probabilities with the best penalty taker awarded the highest scoring probability and least variability, the next best penalty taker awarded the second highest scoring probability and second least variability and so on, together with the best penalty taker being the most resistant to reduced scoring probability as the importance attached to a penalty kick increases, the second best penalty taker being the second most resistant to reduced scoring probability and so on. The latter assumption of reduced scoring probabilities was designed to address skill degradation brought on by psychological stress (pressure) associated with the importance attached to any given penalty kick as a result of earlier outcomes as represented in the scoreline.

Given the above assumptions, the outcome of all possible line-up sequences for both teams was assessed using computer simulation techniques. There are 120 (5!) possible line-up orders for both teams yielding 14,400 (120^2) ways in which two teams may contest a penalty shoot-out. The results from repeated computer simulations reported the optimised placement of penalty takers in the line-up sequence for a penalty shoot-out as 5–4–3–2–1, that is the fifth best penalty taker should take the first penalty kick, the fourth best penalty taker the second penalty kick and so on. These results hold for the initial set of conditions applied based on the assumptions reported, and different initial conditions will produce different optimised line-up strategies. Regardless of the particular optimised line-up order used for the first five penalty takers, it follows that the continued optimum strategy going into 'sudden death', a reference to the penalty shoot-out progressing beyond five kicks apiece, is to assign the next best penalty taker to the next penalty kick. Thus, the sixth best penalty taker is assigned the sixth penalty kick, the seventh best penalty taker the seventh penalty kick and so on. This recommended optimised line-up sequence of 5–4–3–2–1–6–7 etc. applies for both teams regardless of which team wins the coin toss and hence takes the first penalty kick.

The example from the penalty shoot-out described above exemplifies the fact that some decisions that must be made in a particular sport context can be foreseen and hence taken ahead of time for purposes of optimised decision making. Further implications for sports practice arise if an optimised line-up order for a penalty shoot-out identified in advance is to be implemented in sports competition, whatever the particular decision taken on the line-up sequence to be used. For instance, following a tied game at the end of extra time the coaching staff must identify the best five penalty takers from the available players on the field of play at that time. In practice, this requires a priori ranking of the penalty taking abilities of each squad player (p). The goalkeepers should be subject to the same ranking process (q). The intelligent use of substitutions, including goalkeepers, in consideration of a pending penalty shoot-out should also be given serious consideration depending on the circumstances. Tournament results demonstrate the penalty shoot-out is an important determinant of progress in knock-out football competition and, as such, should be given due attention and advance preparation by both coaching staff and players if a team is to have serious design on winning a tournament competition.

13.7 Football: the negative binomial distribution of passing sequences and the shot-to-goal ratio

Football has a long history of match analysis going back to Reep and Benjamin (1968). These authors reported behaviour analysis from an extensive data set collected from English league and World Cup matches obtained from 1953 through 1967. These data, recorded using systematic pen-and-paper observation methods, included the frequencies of passing sequences of different lengths, shots at goal and goals scored. The frequency of passing sequences, reported in tabular form by Reep and Benjamin (1968), are presented in Figure 13.2 (from McGarry and Franks, 2003), with the frequencies of passing sequences greater than seven passes excluded. The x-axis reports the length of unbroken passing sequences, that is the number of consecutive passes within a team before the chain was broken by interception by the opponent or the ball going out of play. The y-axis represents the frequencies of their occurrence expressed as a proportion of the total number of frequencies from that data set. The games from which these data were obtained, as reported by Reep and Benjamin (1968), are presented in parentheses (see legend, Figure 13.2).

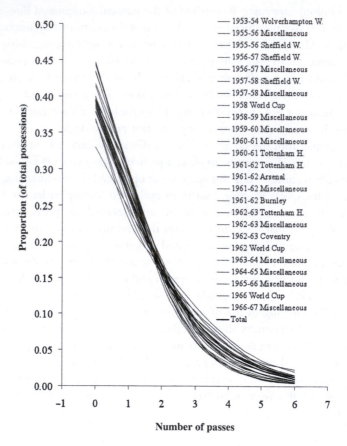

FIGURE 13.2 Negative binomial distribution of the number of passing sequences in soccer. The data were first reported in Reep and Benjamin (1968).

From Figure 13.2, increasingly lower frequencies of passing sequences for longer lengths are observed, as expected, given the increasing likelihood of the passing sequence being broken as its length increases. As reported by Reep and Benjamin, these frequency data for the passing sequences conform to a negative binomial function description taking the form p_0, p_1, p_2 and so on to p_n. The terms p_0, p_1, p_2 through p_n represent the probabilities of the different lengths of passes, from zero, one, two through n passes, respectively. The negative binomial distribution description for the passing sequences (Reep and Benjamin, 1968), together with the approximate 1:10 ratio of goals to shots reported, led these authors to assert the observation that chance (probability) exerts significant influence on the outcome of a football match. These results were to have profound impact on some aspects of English football (also see Hughes and Franks, 2005).

That behavioural events in a football game may be described using a probability structure led to the deliberate use of 'direct play' (or 'long-ball' game) by some coaches in English football. This term is used to describe a style of play that looks to assault the opposing team with direct attacks once possession of the ball has been won, a method of play that stands in contrast to the alternative approach that aims to retain ball possession while seeking opportunities on which to launch an attack. The merits and demerits of both approaches were the subject of contested debate within football for some years, although the former approach for direct play now seems to have lost traction for some. To my knowledge at least, there is no reporting of a fundamental shift from the findings first reported by Reep and Benjamin, however.

Using direct play as a tactical game strategy is based on the negative binomial distribution description of passing sequences and the stable approximate 1:10 ratio of goals to shots. The probability data indicate that increasing the frequencies of shots at goal increases the goals scored, and since most shots at goal stem from shorter passing sequences – approximately 80 per cent of shots at goal derive from three passes or fewer (Reep and Benjamin, 1968) – the direct playing of passes into and within the scoring zone is therefore predicted to maximise the frequency of shots at goal and, consequently, the amount of goals scored. The strategy of direct play, furthermore, has the additional benefit of decreasing the chances of a team losing possession in the defending half of the field, an important tactical aim, given that the opposing team will oftentimes win possession in the attacking half of the field before proceeding to a goal scoring attempt. For example, approximately half of the shooting opportunities from the 1953–67 data were generated as a result of regained possession in the attacking half of the field (Reep and Benjamin, 1968). These general findings were found to hold for newer data sets many years on from their first reporting (e.g. Franks, 1988; Reep, 1989). These same behavioural patterns in football may or may not continue to the present day, given the noted shift in recent years to possession-based approaches by some coaches and teams. Future data analysis from the last few years is required to inform on this particular comment. In more general terms, nonetheless, playing the percentages may well be an appropriate game strategy in the long-run average providing that the percentages demonstrate invariant properties, that is the behavioural data probabilities from the past repeat in the future.

13.8 On the requirement for invariant data for probability analysis of sports behaviour

The main idea behind an objective accounting of sports behaviour using quantitative data in sports practice is to describe sports performance for purposes of providing information-based feedback to inform the decision-making processes of players and coaches. Thus, the data provide a behavioural description of past sports performance but their application in sports practice is used in prescriptive fashion to influence future decisions and actions, be that to identify and correct for past errors using remedial practices, to facilitate desired sports behaviours associated with winning outcomes and/or to inform on player selection, contract extensions and/or player transfers, among other examples. The long-accepted sports practice of scouting both assumes and requires invariant patterns across behavioural data from past to future. The previous two sections both also require invariant data if their interpretations and recommended applications for sports practice are to have merit.

The direct style of play in football offers a classic example of how future game strategies can be identified and designed on the basis of past information (data). As noted, however, the data on which identified future sports decisions are predicted must remain invariant if these sports applications from past to future are to be valid. The large amount of football data reported in Reep and Benjamin (1968) has been demonstrated to meet this important criterion of invariant behaviour. Keep in mind, however, that while invariant sports performance data are required for appropriate information transfer from past observations to future applications, they do not necessitate it, meaning that there is no guarantee that identified interpretations are valid on the basis of invariant data.

Identifying game strategies for future use from past (existing) information offers an example of the important requirement of invariant behaviour, with predictions, or expectations, derived from past to future on the following reasoning. The same (or similar) behavioural tendencies are predicted in future under the same (or similar) context as observed in the past, thus, future sports performances can be (and are) predicted with good accuracy from past data on the basis of probabilities. This said, while the presence of invariant sports behaviour is key for appropriate information transfer and hence consequent application from past behaviour to future behaviour, a demonstration of invariant data in the scientific literature is often found wanting. In this regard, invariant data in sports contests may be sought on different levels of analysis, from individual players or teams through to many players or teams, as well as from individual games to many games.

The behavioural actions and behavioural outcomes in sports contests can be investigated using probabilities, providing the data demonstrate invariant features. On the supposition of invariant behaviours in squash contests, McGarry and Franks (1996c) investigated high-level squash match-play contests using probability analysis in search of identifying playing signatures of game behaviour. The term signature was selected to indicate specific patterned behavioural game profiles unique to each individual. These behavioural signatures were quantified using two probability matrices for each player, a shot selection matrix describing the probabilities of a shot by a given player depending on the previous shot by the opponent, and a shot outcome matrix describing the probabilites of a rally outcome (winner, error or let) depending on the shot made by that same player. These two probability matrices are exemplified in Tables 13.1 and 13.2.

Tables 13.1 and 13.2 present frequency data for shot selections and shot outcomes from which probability profiles can be obtained. From Table 13.1, we observe one drive (A) for a given player in response to a serve (S) from the opponent. Similarly, two cross-court boasts (D), nine long volleys (I) and 12 cross-court long volleys (J) were produced in response to a total of 24 serves (S) by the opponent.

TABLE 13.1 Frequency shot selection profile for an individual player

Shot selection (player)	Previous shot (opponent)														Total
	S	A	B	C	E	F	G	H	I	J	K	L	M	N	
Drive (A)	1	56	24	1	6	2	3	1	1	17	7	—	—	1	6	126
XC–Drive (B)	—	34	11	2	5	—	4	—	—	13	4	1	—	—	3	77
Boast (C)	—	—	—	—	2	1	—	—	—	—	2	—	—	—	1	6
XC–Boast (D)	2	19	9	—	4	—	—	1	—	4	4	—	—	1	2	46
Drop (E)	—	6	2	—	18	11	6	3	2	—	—	—	—	—	2	50
XC–Drop (F)	—	2	—	1	4	1	1	1	1	1	1	—	—	—	—	13
Volley[Short] (G)	—	14	7	—	—	—	—	—	—	1	4	—	—	—	5	31
XC–Volley[Short] (H)	—	6	—	—	—	—	—	—	—	1	1	—	—	—	—	8
Volley[Long] (I)	9	1	2	—	—	—	—	—	—	—	—	—	—	2	12	26
XC–Volley[Long] (J)	12	10	2	—	—	—	—	—	—	2	3	—	—	—	2	31
Volley-Boast (K)	—	—	1	—	—	—	—	—	—	—	—	—	—	—	—	1
XC–Volley-Boast (L)	—	5	—	—	—	—	—	—	—	—	—	—	—	—	—	5
Lob (M)	—	—	—	—	—	1	—	—	—	—	—	—	—	—	—	1
XC–Lob (N)	—	—	—	1	1	2	3	1	1	—	—	1	—	—	—	9
Total	24	153	58	5	40	18	17	7	4	39	26	2	4	33		430

Note: The shot codes for the opponent are found in parentheses in the list of shots for the player.

TABLE 13.2 Frequency shot-outcome profile for an individual player

Outcome	Current shot (player)															Total
	S	A	B	C	D	E	F	G	H	I	J	K	L	M	N	
Unconditional winner	–	1	1	–	–	4	4	3	–	–	–	–	–	–	–	13
Conditional winner	–	4	–	3	1	10	1	2	2	2	1	–	–	–	–	26
Unforced error	–	2	1	–	2	4	–	2	–	–	–	–	1	–	–	12
Forced error	–	–	–	1	1	1	–	–	–	–	–	–	–	–	–	3
Let	–	3	1	–	–	2	–	1	–	4	–	–	–	–	–	11
Total	–	10	3	4	4	21	5	8	2	6	1	–	1	–	–	65

Note: See Table 13.1 for a list of shot codes.

In this way the probability of a selected shot response for the player in response to a serve (S), or any other shot type (A through N) by the opponent can be determined from the frequency matrix. The opponent also has a frequency shot selection profile (not shown) from which his (her) shot response selection probabilities to the player can likewise be determined. Thus, a sequence of shots made by the player and opponent can be reconstructed from the respective shot selection profiles on the basis of probability. The frequency shot outcome profile (Table 13.2) functions in similar manner to the shot selection profiles. For the same given player, we find one unconditional winner, four conditional winners, two unforced errors and three lets (neutral outcomes) assigned to the drive shot (A) for that same player for a total of ten outcomes. Again, the opponent likewise is assigned a shot outcome profile from past observations (not shown). The probability of a given outcome is assigned to each shot selected as a rally shot sequence is constructed. For example, from the data presented in Tables 13.1 and 13.2, the 126 drive shots (A) from the player produced ten outcomes meaning that the probability of an outcome assigned to a drive (A) by that player is 0.079 (10/126). Thus, in the sequence of shots reconstructed from the shot selection profiles for a given rally, the rally ends when a given shot is assigned a rally outcome. The process repeats rally by rally until a winning score is reached for a squash game and squash match (five games).

The foregoing describes how squash game behaviour was considered as a stochastic (probability) process with the likelihood of a selected shot type by a given player, together with its associated outcome in any given rally sequence, quantified using probability depending on the antecedent shot by the opponent. The reasoning underpinning identifying signature behaviours was that these playing profiles (or probability matrices) are expected to contain important information, not only for prediciting future game outcomes on the basis of past performances, but also in identifiying specific optimised playing profiles depending on the playing signature of an opponent. For example, if four players compete in separate semi-final matches, say, then the outcome of the final match can be predicted from the playing signatures of the two semi-final winnners. Furthermore, optimised game strategies for a given finalist can be identified by changing shot selection probabilities and the consequent outcomes predicted based on the playing signature of the other finalist – that is, assuming that the playing signature of the opponent itself remains unchanged and instead approximates invariant behaviour as described in the probability data.

This investigation using probability analysis to identify playing signatures for purposes of prediction and optimisation yielded mixed results. In short, the shot selection probabilities of a player tended to be more invariant when competing against the same opponent in different matches. When competing against different opponents, however, a player demonstrated increased variability in shot selection probabilities although invariant data properties increased when the context of the antecedent shot was more detailed, for example if court location from where a shot by the opponent was played was taken into account. These findings indicate that behavioural context for a given action is an important consideration for increased reliability (stability) of information transfer from one sports contest to the next. Beyond this observation, however, the playing signature for a given player was more varied than anticipated when competing against different opponents, effectively then questioning the assumption of invariant behaviours for individual players across different time frames, particularly when competing against changing opponents. Thus, the playing signatures as first supposed are not really signatures per se, at least not on a match-by-match basis. Instead, the playing profiles (probability matrices) are influenced by the interactions with the different opponents. Statistical considerations suggest that increasing the amount of data under analysis by increasing the number of matches recorded should lead to increased invariant behaviours observed and hence more reliable detection of playing behaviour signatures. This said, the time span of the data collected should be considered if the findings from probability analysis are to be applied usefully for identifying individualised optimised game strategies for increasing the future likelihood of producing winning outcomes.

13.9 Summary

Various aspects of sports contests have been considered on the basis of chance as described in formal terms using probability analysis. The analysis of sports behaviours using probability analysis is commonplace in scientific literature and represents a good basis for describing and explaining the behaviours and outcomes of sports contests. This observation is perhaps unsurprising, given the widespread applications of statistics regarding risk management using probabilities in many different fields, for instance, actuarial tables, insurance statistics, health statistics, stock market forecasts, sports betting, etc. Indeed, the behaviours in sports contests appear good candidates for this type of analysis, not least since game strategies are often designed on the basis of future expectations, as exemplified in the use of game strategies based on future expectations derived from percentage play approaches. This said, some important considerations for using probability analysis were outlined in terms of requiring invariant data for appropriate information transfer from past to future, indicating that investigating sports behaviours and outcomes using probability analysis, at least at the level of game-to-game behaviour, is not as straightforward as might otherwise be imagined. Given the transient, contextual and unique conditions in which sports behaviours are always produced, it is perhaps unfortunate that the usefulness of statistics and probabilities for informing on sports performances at a formal level of understanding appears better geared to the long term rather than the short term, as well as more to generalities than to specifics. That said, an understanding of the restrictions and applications of probability analysis for describing sports behaviour and informing subsequent decision making affords competitive advantage to the knowledgeable sports coach and/or support staff.

14

DYNAMIC SYSTEMS AND 'PERTURBATIONS'

Matthew Robins and Mike Hughes

14.1 Introduction

Although sports performance analysis often defies a clear, conceptual definition (see Hughes, 2004a), it can be broadly considered to be the science relating to the collection, synthesis, interpretation and communication of performance data gathered during training and/or competition. This chapter is concerned with outlining a dominant motor control theory that can aid the explanation and interpretation of performance analysis data – dynamic systems theory. In addition, dynamic systems theory can act as a valuable theoretical framework by which to (1) study emerging patterns of coordination between players and (2) analyse critical incidents during sports competition. These critical incidents take the form of perturbations, defined as events that disrupt the normal flow and rhythm of a game, and that can lead to goal scoring opportunities. As such, the study of inter-personal coordination and perturbations represents fruitful lines of scientific enquiry allowing both researchers and practitioners alike to gain an understanding of how successful attacking outcomes, e.g. shots and goals, can be generated, or in turn, nullified. Therefore, the purpose of this chapter is to define dynamic systems, outline their relevance to sports performance analysis, and identify and explain how inter-personal coordination and 'perturbations' can be examined during sport competition.

14.2 What is a dynamic system?

In the first instance, it is important to clearly define a dynamic system and outline its utility and application to sports performance analysis. Broadly speaking, dynamic systems theory is a theory of action, and a dynamic system is considered to be any system that evolves over time (Kay, 1988). In other words, it is a theory concerned with understanding how patterns of coordination emerge from complex systems, and ultimately how coordinated behaviour changes over a particular time course (see Newell, 2003), e.g. over the course of a competitive match. By complex systems we mean those systems that are comprised of many different constituent parts. Examples of complex systems include: the human body, which is composed of a multitude of joints and muscles, and sports competition, which involves the continuous interaction and coordination of individuals on a 'sports field'. Dynamic systems theory is multidisciplinary in nature, integrating ideas from numerous scientific disciplines, such as physics, mathematics, biology and psychology (Davids *et al.*, 2003a). It has been applied to a number of scientific fields including; motor development (e.g. Thelen, 1985; Newell *et al.*, 2003), sports medicine (e.g. Davids *et al.*, 2003a), physical therapy (Harbourne and Stergiou, 2009), motor skill learning (e.g. Schöner *et al.*, 1992; Zanone and Kelso, 1997; Newell *et al.*, 2003; Hong and Newell, 2006), as well as more recently performance analysis, in the form of multi-individual (social) systems such as inter-personal coordination (Schmidt *et al.*, 1990; Riley, *et al.*, 2011) and player–player, or, attacker–defender interactions during sports competition (e.g. Grehaigne *et al.*, 1997; McGarry *et al.*, 2002; Walter *et al.*, 2007; Correia *et al.*, 2011; Passos *et al.*, 2011). This latter application has grown in prominence over recent years (e.g. Bartlett *et al.*, 2012), and is of particular relevance to the current chapter. The application of dynamic systems theory to these diverse scientific sub-disciplines is facilitated by an important and attractive feature of the theory. That is, the central principles of dynamical systems theory can be used to explain the emergence of coordinated behaviour, regardless of system structure. This approach is a particular strength because it provides a credible theoretical framework for how a wide variety of systems exhibit the same type of behaviour, irrespective of how different their internal structures may be (Beek and Beek, 1989).

The apparent need for dynamic systems theory has emerged because sports performance analysis research has been criticised for being overly descriptive (see Glazier, 2010) and too heavily focused on discrete behaviours of teams and/or individuals (Vilar *et al.*, 2012). Consequently, much of the emphasis has been given to the four core 'observation elements' that are used to document on-the-ball behaviours: player, action, location, time. Hence, the utilisation of dynamic systems theory has been argued to afford 'explanatory power' of sports performance data, offering the 'why' and the 'how' to supplement the 'who', 'what', 'where' and 'when' (see Correia *et al.*, 2013). In addition, using continuous variables, ones that capture the collective behaviour of the team over a particular phase of the match, e.g. a team possession, have recently become eminent areas of study (Bartlett *et al.*, 2012; Vilar *et al.*, 2013). This alternative approach to analysis corroborates the recommendations of McGarry (2009) who argued that future sports performance analysis research should examine, among other things, player–player interactions and behaviours both on-the-ball and off-the-ball, thereby providing appropriate context and a more holistic understanding of sporting competition.

However, the challenges facing the promotion of dynamic systems theory as a valued theoretical framework were surmised perfectly by Lewis (2000, p. 36) who, in attempting to debunk the key principles of dynamic systems theory, stated: 'Many developmentalists are intrigued by the DS (dynamic systems) approach but they do not fully understand it, and their confusion is exacerbated by the new and competing terminologies, conceptual ambiguities, and methodological disagreements that pervade DS writings.' Although this quote specifically relates to the field of motor development it is also relevant to sports performance analysis, and is extremely poignant in light of the influx of articles advocating its use (e.g. Glazier, 2010; Vilar *et al.*, 2012; Correia *et al.*, 2013). As such, owing to the applied nature of sports performance analysis, greater accessibility is needed with regard to the key principles of dynamic systems, with clear signposts provided as to how the theory can advance the discipline and aid both researchers and applied practitioners. This will help bridge the gap between theory and practice (Glazier and Robins, 2013), which is especially important considering the views of Cardinale (2011) who stated: 'the disconnect between academia and sport is getting bigger and bigger every day.' Consequently, the purpose of the following section is to decipher the central tenets of dynamic systems theory and offer clear examples as to how the theory relates to applied practice.

14.3 The features of a dynamic system

Dynamic systems theory is 'plagued' by an abundance of terms and principles, e.g. attractors, multi-stability, bifurcations, critical fluctuations and hysteresis, which often discourage readers from outside of the field of motor control. Although a detailed overview of all scientific terminology of dynamic systems theory is beyond the scope of this chapter (for a review of the aforementioned terms, see Bardy *et al.*, 2002), three of the central principles of dynamic systems theory will now be critically explored: (1) synergies, (2) self-organisation and (3) constraints. Readers are also referred to the work of Glazier and Robins (2013) who outline the value of the constraints-led approach (an adjunct to dynamical systems theory) to sports performance analysis research and practice. According to dynamic systems theory, system complexity is harnessed through the development of synergies, functional couplings between interacting macro- or micro-components (for a review on synergies, see Lee, 1984; Turvey, 2007). From a technique analysis perspective, these macro-components could be the different body segments contributing towards the execution of a given motor skill, e.g. a throwing or kicking action, whereas from the perspective of sports competition, macro-components could be the individuals or units (defence/midfield/attack) on the playing field. The formation of synergies, also known as coordinative structures, ultimately governs the emergence of stable patterns of behaviour. During early stages of learning the patterns of coordination appear rather 'chaotic' and variable. This can be exemplified by the common adage of 'bees around a honey pot' or 'chasing the egg'. This phrase captures the organisational properties of team invasion games played by young children, whose primary tendency is to simply follow/chase the ball. However, with practice 'order is restored' and the appropriate spatial and temporal patterning between individuals emerges, and consequently, a stable, organised offensive/defensive structure. Something akin to what you would expect from watching a professional soccer match. Furthermore, as a consequence of practice and learning, a characteristic feature of synergies is the interdependency and compensatory adjustments between components (see Latash *et al.*, 2002). For instance, if a single component introduces an error into the 'output', other components contributing to the synergy can attenuate this error by adjusting their relative contributions. A classic example can be derived from soccer whereby if one player moves out of position e.g. a left-back, the other defensive players within the unit, e.g. centre-backs and right back, can move accordingly to try to 'offset' the positional error with the goal of preserving a balanced and organised defensive structure.

Synergies are suggested to be guided and influenced by the process of self-organisation. Beek *et al.* (1995, p. 577) acknowledged that the concept of self-organisation is sometimes 'interpreted by some movement scientists as a kind of mystical ability, according to which movements come out of the blue'. For example, Kelso and Schöner (1988, p. 30) refer to self-organisation as 'the structure of change in structure that occurs spontaneously in open systems', whereas Kelso (1995, p. 94) states that 'in open dynamic systems, spatial, temporal, and functional patterns arise spontaneously in a self-organised fashion'. Beek *et al.* (1995, p. 577) offer a more detailed definition of self-organisation, and in doing so recognise two important properties of dynamic systems – stability and flexibility:

> The notion of self-organisation implies that coordinated movements are the orderly products of complex organisations that are composed of a very large number of interacting elements and that may adapt in a flexible manner to changing internal and external conditions by adopting a different coordination pattern without any explicit prescription of this pattern.

Importantly, self-organisation does not operate in isolation; it is governed by several different constraints acting on the system. The constraints-led approach primarily came to prominence with Newell's (1986) model of constraints, which was latterly revised by Newell and Jordan (2007). Since its inception, the constraints-led approach has been popularised by the work of Davids and colleagues (e.g. Davids *et al.*, 2003b; Chow *et al.*, 2006; Davids *et al.*, 2008; Glazier and Davids, 2009; Renshaw *et al.*, 2010; Hristovski *et al.*, 2011; Renshaw *et al.*, 2011). Within Newell's (1986) original constraints framework, constraints were broadly categorised as those pertaining to the organism (individual), the task, and the environment. Furthermore, Newell (1986) classically defined a constraint as a characteristic of the task, environment or organism that either facilitates or restricts movement. For instance, constraints either allow individuals to explore the available 'movement space', or alternatively, constrain the system to a narrow range of possible solutions. In other words, constraints set boundaries or limits within a dynamic system (Clark, 1995). From a biomechanical perspective, this could relate to the range of motion (e.g.

Higuchi *et al.*, 2003) or movement variability (e.g. Robins *et al.*, 2006) exhibited by particular joints. In the context of sports competition, ball possession may determine whether the system of players explores or constrains the available movement space. For instance, teams typically 'expand' or 'contract' when in and out of possession respectively (see Bartlett *et al.*, 2012). As such, there are clear links here between the theory and the principles of play of the sport, i.e. the attacking principles of play in soccer: width, mobility, support etc., thereby facilitating the exploration of the available playing space. In contrast, the defensive team operate a compact structure both within and between units, e.g. defence and midfield, thereby reducing any permitted space that attacking players can exploit.

It is important to note that the constraints of the organism, task and environment do not operate in isolation, they interact and channel the search towards the emergence of functional, coordinated behaviour. Organismic constraints refer to those properties of the individual. Broadly speaking, organismic constraints are those constraints imposed physiologically, morphologically or psychologically (McGinnis and Newell, 1982). To account for the diverse nature of organismic constraints, two sub-classes of organismic constraints have been proposed: structural and functional constraints. Structural constraints are those properties of the individual that change very slowly with time, whereas functional constraints concern those properties that change over a more rapid timescale. Examples of structural constraints include, among others, height, mass, body composition, anthropometrics, strength, flexibility, genetic make-up and task expertise. Conversely, functional organismic constraints include those psychological and physiological factors that change over much shorter time frames, such as anxiety, self-confidence, motivation and neuro-muscular fatigue. Environmental constraints are considered to be any physical properties that are external to the organism (Newell and Jordan, 2007). Consequently, environmental constraints tend to be global and non-performer specific. Examples of environmental constraints include ambient light, wind, altitude, ambient temperature. Socialisation also constitutes an important environmental constraint, encompassing factors such as peer groups and societal expectations (McGinnis and Newell, 1982; Chow *et al.*, 2006). The final category of constraint relates to that of the task. Task constraints can be sub-divided into two sub-classes: (1) the goal of the task and (2) the rules specifying a particular movement pattern to satisfy a goal (Newell and Jordan, 2007). Examples of task constraints could include shooting distance during a basketball match (e.g. Robins *et al.*, 2006), or imposing a one-touch rule within a simulated football match during a training session.

The important question to pose at this stage is how do dynamic systems theory and the associated principles of self-organisation and constraints relate to applied practice within sports performance analysis? First, let's address the concept of self-organisation. This concept is captured perfectly (and implicitly) by Steve Brown, First Team Analyst at Everton Football Club, who, when commenting on the club's approach to opposition analysis, stated:

You'll see that individual changes and personnel changes affect their (opponent's) weaknesses or strengths or the way they play. For example, there are some fullbacks that like to stay in position irrespective of which team they are playing in, but there are some fullbacks that want to go in tight. It doesn't look like a definitive instruction to go tight, but a natural tendency and it's important to pick those things up really.

(Brown, 2012)

The crucial element of the quote is that it is 'a natural tendency' to go tight. In relation to dynamic systems theory, the team self-organised to produce this particular pattern of coordinated behaviour. This implies that the personnel of the team, and each player's physical prowess and movement capabilities, act as an important organismic constraint shaping the resultant spacing and coordination between players. In this case, the full-back 'naturally' wanted to go tight towards his fellow centre back. This may consequently provide crucial information that could inform opposition tactics and exploit tactical weaknesses, and provides a clear link between theory and applied practice. With regard to constraints, the location of a competitive sporting event, such as playing at home or away, can be considered an environmental constraint, and has been shown to affect both technical and tactical behaviour in soccer (Tucker et al., 2005). Altitude and ambient temperature are obviously particularly poignant environmental constraints within international competitions. One such example, is the Estadio Hernando Siles, home to the Bolivian national soccer team, which is located at an altitude in excess of 3,500 metres. Fatigue (Rampinini et al., 2009) and situational factors such as quality of opposition and match status (see Taylor et al., 2008; 2010; Lago, 2009; Lago-Ballesteros et al., 2012) also represent important constraints that affect the collective behaviour of the team. For instance, Taylor et al. (2010) reported an interactive effect between match location and match status on the frequency of passes performed. In addition, the location of passes also changed as a function of both match status and match location.

To date, this chapter has aimed to outline the importance of dynamic systems theory, deciphered some of the central principles and established links between the theory and applied practice. The following sections will now systematically review two of the dominant lines of empirical research that can be aided and explained using dynamic systems theory: inter-personal coordination and perturbations. Each of these avenues of research will now be discussed in turn.

14.4 Inter-personal coordination

The study of inter-personal coordination is based upon past research relating to bimanual rhythmic coordination (e.g. Kelso et al., 1981; Scholz and Kelso, 1989; Scholz and Kelso, 1990). Bimanual rhythmic coordination involves the synchronous oscillation of body segments, typically the index fingers, at varying movement frequencies. Furthermore, the findings derived from bimanual rhythmic coordination tasks formed much of the empirical support for the aforementioned features of dynamic systems theory. Briefly, during bimanual rhythmic coordination there are two stable patterns of coordination; an in-phase pattern and an anti-phase pattern. The in-phase pattern involves the simultaneous flexion/extension of right and left limb/fingers, whereas an anti-phase pattern means one limb/finger is flexing while the other limb/finger is extending. One of the seminal studies concerning bimanual rhythmic coordination was conducted by Scholz and Kelso (1989), whereby participants were required to rhythmically oscillate their index fingers in either an in-phase or anti-phase mode of coordination. A metronome was used to regulate movement frequency, and after a period of 10 s, the metronome pulse increased incrementally by 0.2 Hz. It was found that the in-phase pattern of coordination was more stable than the anti-phase pattern of coordination. This finding was a consequence of the observed transition from anti-phase to in-phase mode of coordination as oscillatory speed increased, i.e. the system self-organised. However, there was no such change from in-phase to anti-phase with increased movement speed. The in-phase pattern persisted regardless of any change in oscillatory speed. Interestingly, increases in movement variability, termed critical fluctuations, subserved the transition from anti-phase to in-phase pattern of coordination. Hence, movement variability appeared to possess a functional role in permitting a new pattern of coordination to emerge. Corroborating data have been found for human stance (see Bardy *et al.*, 2002).

Importantly, these characteristics of bimanual rhythmic coordination also translate to inter-personal coordination (see Schmidt *et al.*, 1990; Turvey, 2007). Consequently, performance analysis research has begun to explore inter-personal coordination during dyadic sports such as tennis (Palut and Zanone, 2005), squash (McGarry *et al.*, 1999; McGarry, 2006; McGarry and Walter, 2007), as well as attacker–defender interactions during simulated 1 v 1 (Passos *et al.*, 2008) or 4 v 2 + 2, i.e. four attackers against two defensive lines, each comprising two players (Passos *et al.*, 2011), scenarios in rugby union. First, let's address inter-personal coordination during dyadic sports such as tennis and squash. These sports are referred to as dyadic sports because they involve two individuals who form a pairing or coupling. Tennis and squash share commonalities with bimanual rhythmic coordination, but unlike bimanual coordination that requires the oscillation of index fingers, players in tennis and squash oscillate either along the baseline or to and from the 'T' respectively. Hence, the same dynamic system principles governing inter/intra-limb coordination apply to inter-personal coordination. Empirical support for sport competition as a dynamic system was provided by the seminal study of McGarry *et al.* (1999). McGarry and co-workers (1999) tracked the movement of squash players during a rally, and computed their radial distance with respect to the 'T'. The coordination pattern between the two competing squash players was shown to be anti-phase. That is, one player was moving towards and/or located near to the 'T' while the other player was moving away and/or located away from the 'T'. Players then made oscillating movements to and from the 'T' in an alternating fashion. Furthermore, McGarry *et al.* (1999, p. 309) postulated that:

> There is little evidence from the phase relation data that the system moves between stable behaviour and unstable behaviour, or indeed between two stable behaviours via instability; rather, the system is anti-phase stable and subject to fluctuations (variance) that probe the system.

Consequently, unlike bimanual rhythmic coordination that had two patterns of coordination (in-phase and anti-phase) – a phenomenon known as multi-stability – the dyadic relationship between competing squash players only had one discernible pattern of coordination. In addition, this pattern of coordination could be perturbed, thereby introducing fluctuations (see section 14.5). These findings have been corroborated more recently by both McGarry (2006) and Walter *et al.* (2007) who both observed an anti-phase pattern of coordination existed between squash players.

As well as looking at dyadic sports such as racket sports, research has also examined attacker–defender interactions during simulated 1 v 1 (Passos *et al.*, 2008) or 4 v 2 (Passos *et al.*, 2011) sub-phases in rugby union. For instance, Passos *et al.* (2008) examined attacker–defender interactions using measures of interpersonal distance and relative velocity. The two-dimensional coordinates of each player were extracted from each of two cameras and three-dimensional coordinates derived. Interpersonal distance (distance between attacker and defender) and relative velocity (speed of attacker – speed of defender) were then examined with regard to three outcomes: clean try, tackle with attacker passing defender, and effective tackle. The key finding to emerge was that a successful outcome could be predicted if interpersonal distance achieved a critical value less than 4 m, and, relative velocity was equal to or exceeded 1 m/s. Although this study built upon the existing research by using dynamic systems theory to study attacker–defender interactions in rugby union, it could be argued that the practical implications were rather limited. For instance, for a successful try to be scored the interpersonal distance *has* to be less than 4 m, i.e. the attacker *must* pass the defender. In addition, relative velocity is crucial because the higher the relative velocity, the greater the velocity of the attacker in comparison to the defender. Consequently, the ball carrier will then have greater momentum by which to either evade the defender or break through an intended tackle. Greater relative velocity is a common tactic employed by rugby union players because attacking players are routinely encouraged to 'win the space' or 'win the collision'. Greater velocity is one such variable that contributes to achieving such a positive outcome, as well as, obviously, the mass of the individual. Winger Jonah Lomu demonstrated this to excellent effect during his career as a New Zealand All Black. Building upon a 1 v 1 scenario, Passos *et al.* (2011) examined functional coupling within attacking players during a 4 v 2 sub-phase. Inter-personal distance was again quantified, but this time between the group of four attackers. In addition, interpersonal coordination tendencies were calculated using a running correlation, i.e. the distances of each attacker to the try line were correlated for each trial, e.g. attacker 1 correlated with attacker 2, and so on, with the strength of the coupling assessed using explained variance (r^2). The authors reported that the interpersonal distance for the attacking players ranged from 2 to 5 m, and r^2 values exceeded 0.9 for 92 per cent of the dyadic relationships between two attackers. Hence, the strength of coupling between two attackers within the sub-group was very strong. Consequently, and as you would expect, the attacking players were highly coordinated during their pursuit to pass the defenders to the try line.

With the developments in technology, such as the use of multi-camera tracking systems, e.g. ProZone (Di Salvo *et al.*, 2006) and Amisco (Randers *et al.*, 2010), global positioning systems, e.g. Catapult (Johnston *et al.*, 2012), and local positioning systems (Frencken *et al.*, 2011; Sathyan *et al.*, 2012), player coordinate data during actual sports competition is now more accessible. Subsequently, empirical research has now begun to use these data collection techniques to explore interpersonal coordination within team sport invasion games such as soccer (Bartlett *et al.*, 2012; Vilar *et al.*, 2013; Goncalves *et al.*, 2014). However, it should be noted that methods of digitisation and software automatic tracking are also used, such as that undertaken within futsal (Travassos *et al.*, 2011) and basketball (Bourbousson *et al.*, 2010), respectively. There are a number of different methods used to capture the collective behaviour of a team (for a review see Duarte *et al.*, 2012). For instance, Vilar *et al.* (2013) quantified the numerical dominance held by teams within seven sectors on the pitch, i.e. +1-player was denoted if Team 1 had one more player in a particular zone than Team 2. The seven sectors included: left-front, centre-front, right-front, centre-middle, left-back, centre-back and right-back. Vilar *et al.* (2013, p. 83) reported that 'local numerical dominance played a key role in offensive and defensive success'. However, it could again be argued that the practical implications of these findings for the coaching process are rather limited. For instance, creating an overload in attack, or providing support and cover in defence are common tactical traits encouraged by football coaches. With that said, the number of times a team had numerical dominance within a attack, i.e. quantifying the number of overloads created, could provide useful information if the team failed to capitalise upon those overloads — in other words, if the team drew or lost the match yet created significantly more overload situations within the game than their opposition. The coach could therefore examine the reason(s) for the poor conversion rate of overloads into chances and/or goals. Therefore, future research that uses dynamic systems theory as a theoretical framework by which to analyse inter-personal coordination should consider the depth of analysis undertaken, ensuring that the analysis can be more effectively linked to the attacking/defending principles of play, and be useful and informative for coaches and performance analysts.

An alternative approach to studying inter-personal coordination within team sport invasion games, and that may yield useful insights, has been to use variables such as the centroid, stretch index and surface area (e.g. Bourbousson *et al.*, 2010; Bartlett *et al.*, 2012; Clemente *et al.*, 2013). These variables are quantified using the x and y coordinate data for each player. It would be first useful to operationally define each term. Within soccer, the centroid is simply the team's 'average position', calculated from the mean of the ten outfield players' positions. The goalkeeper is excluded so as not to skew the data. The stretch index is the mean distance of the players from the team centroid. This measure consequently takes into account the distance of all players with respect to the team centroid, and can be quantified as a single radial measure, or separated out into horizontal (SIx) and vertical (SIy) components (see Bartlett *et al.*, 2012). In contrast to the stretch index, the surface area is the total space (also referred to as the convex hull) covered by the team (see Frencken *et al.*, 2011; Moura *et al.*, 2013). These variables provide a useful insight into the collective organisation of competing teams, allowing the identification of the relative expansion or contraction of intra-team spacing. This is typically examined in relation to positive (e.g. shots, goals) and negative (e.g. losses of possession) outcomes. For instance, Bartlett *et al.* (2012) analysed five 11-a-side soccer games from the group stage of the European Champions League. The team centroid and measures of team dispersion, e.g. stretch index and surface area, were calculated for both teams and correlations between the two teams performed for each of the respective variables using a Pearson product moment correlation coefficient. High positive correlations were found between the team centroids for attacking and defending teams for all types of attack observed, although the correlation was weaker across the pitch (touchline to touchline) ($r = 0.756 - 0.918$) than along it (goal to goal) ($r = 0.931 - 0.994$). Contradictory to small-sided games (Frencken *et al.*, 2011), no crossing of the centroids of the two teams occurred along the pitch for any of the 14 goals sampled. Negative correlation coefficients were found for the teams' surface area, i.e. attacking team 'expanded' while the defending team 'contracted'. Perhaps the most interesting finding was that there were no discernible differences in coordination dynamics between possessions that resulted in a positive or negative outcome. Furthermore, successful attacks did not show less stable coordination dynamics (smaller correlation coefficients) between the team centroids or dispersion measures. However, this could be because the aforementioned variables were quantified using *all* members of the team, and therefore not sufficiently sensitive to detect subtle variations in player movement.

Consequently, using smaller sub-sets of the team, i.e. within unit, e.g. defence or midfield, and/or between unit, e.g. defence and midfield, may yield more informative, practically relevant findings. This approach of using smaller sub-sets of players was employed by Goncalves *et al.* (2014), who quantified unit-specific centroids, i.e. defender centroid, midfielder centroid etc., during a simulated 11-a-side soccer match. In addition, Goncalves and co-workers also calculated the absolute distance from each player to each of the respective centroids. The key findings to emerge were that the midfield players exhibited the strongest within-unit coupling, evidenced by lower values of distance with respect to their centroid. In contrast, forwards demonstrated much higher distances relative to their centroid. The authors commendably interpreted these results in relation to key principles of play, i.e. optimising support play and options within midfield, hence midfielders remain closer together. Conversely, forwards increase their distance from one another looking to create space, generate unpredictable situations and/or cause imbalance from within the opposition defence. However, future research is certainly warranted that follows the example of Goncalves *et al.* (2014), analysing the coordination dynamics of team sub-sets, e.g. defence, midfield, attack, with respect to differing possession outcomes, and makes clear associations between the theoretical insights of dynamic systems theory and the resultant sporting principles of play.

A complementary area of study that can be examined either in conjunction with inter-personal coordination or completed independently is that of perturbations. The research relating to perturbations will now be systematically reviewed.

14.5 Perturbations

Perturbations are a relatively recent development and an extension of the ways in which we analyse sport in general. Perturbations are those incidents that disrupt the normal flow and rhythm of a game and can lead to scoring opportunities. Furthermore, from a dynamic systems perspective, perturbations are used to destabilise the organisation/coordination dynamics of the opposing team. It could be identified, e.g. in soccer, as a penetrating pass, a dribble, or a change of pace, or indeed any skill, that creates a disruption in the defence that might enable an attacker a shooting opportunity. In some cases this disruption of the defence may not result in a shooting opportunity, due to defensive skills and/or a lack of skill in attack, which has been defined as a 'critical incident', e.g. a winner in squash, a shot at goal in soccer, a shot on basket in basketball. Perturbations are relatively intuitive and comparatively easier to quantify than other measures associated with dynamic systems theory. Hence, it is an easy way of approaching this subject and can yield some fascinating and applied results. Work by Downey (1992) commented on this type of disturbance and instability found in competitive squash and tennis.

> A particularly weak or strong shot, forces a disturbance that places one player at a recognised disadvantage to the other, say in a displaced court location. The rally then exhibits a different behaviour characteristic that may ultimately result in a rally outcome. Therefore, the strong or weak shot is thought to have caused a consequent perturbation, a resulting instability in the pattern of play and, sometimes, a significant outcome. This same theory can be applied to soccer by performing an incisive forward pass that will cause instability to the system.

Perturbations were studied in squash initially because it has an easily identified rhythm to the rallies. In squash, a perturbation may be either a very skilful shot by one player or a weak shot by the other, the result being that one player is under severe pressure. This pressure may be relieved by good defence or very quick movement to re-establish the original rhythm of the rally. In other situations the pressure will build up to lead to the end of the rally with a winning shot by one player or an error by the other. A perturbation that leads to a critical incident in a rally would result in a winning point. Research by McGarry and Franks (1995) has shown strong evidence that perturbations exist in squash. Analysis of those individual shots that cause a perturbation show good agreement between observers, which lends compelling evidence as to their actual existence.

Earlier work by McGarry and Franks (1994) also attempted to predict the outcome of future matches with the aid of critical incidents. Some of the ideas of McGarry and Franks (1994) can be related to the perturbation incidents that occur during football, with the normal rhythm of one side attacking and then the opposing side attacking, resulting in no shots on goal being defined as a stable system. When a critical incident occurs, in this case a shot, then the system must have therefore become unstable. So all shots must be preceded by a point in play where a perturbation happens as a result of skilful play by an attacker or a mistake by a defender. So a way of identifying perturbations would be to define the moment of skill, or lack of it, when the normal rhythm is disrupted by an attack that results in an attempt on goal (shot or header).

Hughes et al. (2000c) determined and identified perturbations that occur during English Premier division football which disrupt the normal flow and lead to goal scoring opportunities. Furthermore, Hughes et al. (2000c) extended their work by applying the same methodology to the European Championships 1996, comparing successful and unsuccessful teams and examining some individual team profiles. By tracing back from the shot on goal, Hughes et al. (2000c) trained their observers on tracing the perturbations that led to the shots on goal. They categorised these attacking skills, or defensive lapses, that contributed to this critical phase of play. However, they did not analyse the perturbations that do not result in a critical incident. After relatively short training they demonstrated that perturbations could be reliably identified. These findings support those of Hodges et al. (1998) who investigated whether system disturbances in squash could be reliably detected across observers of different skill level. Specifically, the task was for observers to identify shots that perturb the system from stability to instability and from instability to stability. The study found that both novice and expert squash players could reliably identify system perturbations, although there was higher agreement within expert groups.

Hughes et al. (2000b) raised an important fact that not all perturbations are followed by a critical incident, and sometimes play can revert to its normal rhythm. Also, not all critical incidents are preceded by perturbations, sometimes a player may just miss-hit a ball. Furthermore, McGarry et al. (1999) found evidence of multiple perturbations showing that the system does recover from instability in some cases, and reverts again to stability as evidenced by the next perturbation in the same rally.

In light of these insights, and developing from their earlier work on British league football, Hughes et al. (2001) analysed how international teams stabilised or 'smoothed out' the perturbations. Hughes et al. (2001) identified three categories of perturbation that did not lead to shots on goal: actions by the player in possession, actions by the receiver and interceptions. Although Hughes et al. (2001,

p. 32) highlighted the requirement for improved technical skill, by combining the data of many teams the conclusions provided little benefit for coaches of specific teams and highlighted the need for analysis of individual 'team "signatures"'.

Summarising, previous research has confirmed the existence and definition of perturbations in soccer, and has identified the opportunity for the profiling of individual teams (Hughes *et al.*, 2000a, 2001). Identifying the strengths and weaknesses of specific teams may provide coaches with information to improve their own team's strategies, while also providing a tactical advantage gained from predicting opposition patterns of play. Profiling by perturbations reduces the amount of data being analysed, restricting the data sets to those actions that disrupt the defence and lead to critical incidents. In an average game of soccer there are about 4000 bits of data to analyse, by just analysing the perturbations, it reduces this data set to about 400. All the researchers in soccer and squash ended up using similar methods and sets of variables to classify perturbations; let us examine their methods, because they can certainly be applied to any soccer team, and those of the researchers and analysts working in squash. There are other sports that can be investigated in terms of their perturbations: rugby union, volleyball, field hockey, tennis and so on, but by examining these two key sports we can hopefully demonstrate the power of these types of analyses.

14.5.1 Methods in soccer

Hughes *et al.* (2000b) decided that a shot must be preceded by a perturbation. Consequently, if a video of a match were analysed, using the shots as a starting point, and rewinding the action to the point at which possession was gained, then between that point and the shot there must occur a perturbation. This was used as a method of training the observers in this and subsequent studies. Through analysing a series of games, a general idea of the categories of attacking and defensive skills required to define perturbations was compiled. A table was designed and used for a number of games. Gradually those variables that were not yielding significant amounts of data during a match were either discarded or combined with others until the final system was accepted. The variables for the perturbations were categorised into 12 types of causes, and have been used by a series of different researchers:

> ATTACKING: run, dribble, pass, skill, tackle, run off the ball;
> DEFENDING: lost contol, mis tackle, bad pass, positioning, deflection, foul.

The system was then used for a number of matches to ensure that any training effects were eliminated. Although a number of colleagues and researchers have expanded these 12 actions, they have always ended up reducing back to the same list.

Subsequent validation studies were undertaken by Hughes *et al.* (2000a; 2000c and 2001) to test intra–observer reliability using a match taken from the top English division. In each test the match used for these tests was notated on three separate occasions with sufficient time between in order to produce the fairest results. It was found that perturbations were consistently identified and classified, and an inter-rater ANOVA test on the three sets of data produced an $r = 0.995$ ($p < 0.01$).

14.5.2 Methods in squash

A hand notation system for squash was devised, in order to develop performance profiles using perturbations of elite male squash players. The system produced data (see Figure 14.1), including whether a perturbation occurred for or against the player, where in the rally it occurred, the shot and cell from which it occurred, and whether or not the rally regained stability and after how many shots. In addition, the rally end shot, cell and total number of shots in the rally were also recorded as the rally end shot could be considered the ultimate perturbation. Once the data were gathered, they were compared to England Squash SWEAT (squash winner and error analysis technology) data, for each player, and where they played their winners and errors from and where their opponents played them.

The squash court was divided into a 4 × 4 cell, labelled 1–16 (Figure 14.2); this was the same as that used by Murray and Hughes (2001). Intra-observer reliability was performed to ensure that the researcher was correctly identifying perturbations. One game was analysed on three separate occasions; the results gathered were put

Rally number	Pertur-bation for	Pertur-bation against	Number of shots in rally at that point	Cell	Shot	Gain stability?	How many shots?	Rally end shot?	Winner/error	Cell	Player	Total number of shots

FIGURE 14.1 Hand notation system used for collecting perturbation data.

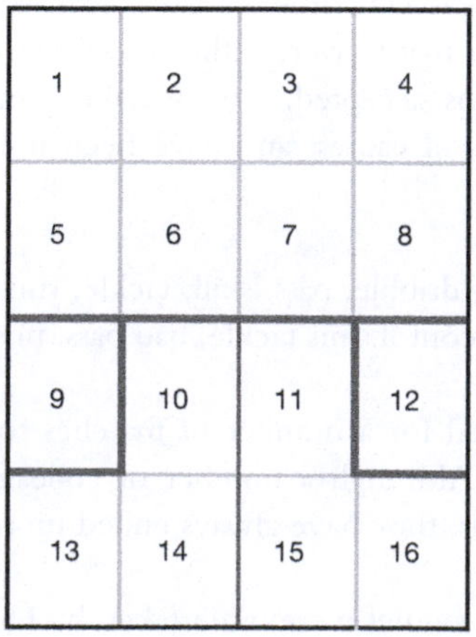

FIGURE 14.2 Squash court cell, used to record position of shot.

into spreadsheets and compared using percentage differences (Hughes *et al.*, 2000d). For this study, an error difference of 10 per cent was deemed acceptable.

14.5.3 Results in soccer

Although the pass skill has both the highest frequency of shots and produced the most goals by far, and this is followed by the run skill, the most efficient skill in terms of conversion of shots into goals is the defensive error 'lost control'. This had a conversion ratio of 5.5:1. The higher number of passing perturbations leading to shots could be the result of the high standard of play found in the Premier League, where attempts on goal are more frequently created from attacking skills as opposed to coming from defensive errors. This is substantiated by finding that 55.5 per cent of all attempts resulted from the pass, run, dribble and skill categories, which are all associated with positive, creative play. Whereas the areas of mistimed tackle, out of position, lost control and bad pass produced 28.8 per cent of attempts on goal. When examining the ratio of attempts against goals scored, the perturbation that produced the best ratio was that of lost control – a goal was found to result from every 5.5 losses of control that led to shots on goal. The reason for this is probably due to the fact that if someone in a key defensive position loses control of the ball then the dislocation of the defence is going to be extreme because of the surprise element (Table 14.1).

TABLE 14.1 Goals and the number of perturbation skills

Perturbation	Frequency	No. of goals	Ratio
Run	88	6	14.7
Pass	153	18	8.5
Tackle	17	3	5.7
Dribble	65	5	13
Skill	27	0	–
Change of pace	16	0	–
Miss tackle	21	2	10.5
Foul	34	6	5.7
Deflection	27	2	13.5
Out of position	65	2	32.5
Lost Control	22	4	5.5
Bad pass	65	2	32.5
TOTAL	600	50	12

TABLE 14.2 Number of shots for the successful and unsuccessful teams

	Top five	Bottom five
Total number of attempts on goal	158	116
Average number of attempts per game	17.6	12.9

Tables 14.2 and 14.3 show a comparison of data from five successful (top five in the league) and five unsuccessful (bottom five in the league) teams. The results were gained from nine analysed games for each of the two categories.

The successful category of teams produced goals from seven out of 12 skill areas, whereas the unsuccessful category produced goals from two out of 12 skills. It is clear that the successful sides are producing more shots which, in turn, would be expected to relate to more goals scored. The top five teams scored a total of 16 goals whereas the bottom five teams managed only four goals for the nine matches observed. The fact that more successful sides will produce a greater number of shots is reinforced by Hughes *et al.* (1988) in his study of the 1986 World Cup. The top five teams chosen produced a ratio of goals per shots of 9.9:1. This is better than the overall ratio for all teams in the study and points to the fact the successful teams not only produce more shots but also more frequently convert those chances into goals. However, the unsuccessful teams (bottom five) displayed a very poor ratio of 29 shots per goal scored, three times that of the expected value (one goal roughly every ten shots), displaying the inability to turn chances into goals.

When analysing positive and creative play (i.e. pass, run, dribble and skill) it is found that the bottom five teams actually produce a higher percentage of their own total of shots from this group of perturbations than the average for the 20 matches and that of the top five teams: 59.5 per cent of shots resulted from this area for the bottom teams compared with 55.5 per cent for the 20 matches and 55.1 per cent for the top five teams. Furthermore, the bottom teams produced twice as many shots resulting from the skill category. Therefore, the way in which shots or attempts on goal are created does not seem to inhibit these teams, so there

TABLE 14.3 Perturbation variables for the successful and unsuccessful team with the ensuing shots, goals and shot/goal ratios

Perturbations	Top five			Bottom five		
	Shots	Goals	Ratio	Shots	Goals	Ratio
Tackle	4	0	–	1	0	–
Run	22	2	11:1	15	1	15:1
Pass	38	5	7.6:1	35	3	11.6:1
Dribble	22	3	7.3:1	10	0	–
Skill	5	0	–	9	0	–
Change of pace	1	0	–	2	0	–
Miss tackle	4	0	–	2	0	–
Foul	13	2	6.5:1	6	0	–
Deflection	7	1	7:1	4	0	–
Out of position	18	1	18:1	15	0	–
Lost control	10	2	5:1	2	0	–
Bad pass	14	0	–	15	0	–
TOTAL	158	16	9.9:1	116	4	29:1

must be a different contributing factor. A clue may be when the categories of lost control, foul and tackle are considered. The top five sides displayed a ratio of a goal scored for every five losses of control; however, the bottom five sides only produced shots resulting from two instances of lost control. No goals are scored from the other perturbation categories either – it would seem that this dysfunction of scoring is a result of lack of pressure from this standard of team on their opponents' defence, failing to capitalise on defensive errors. Where the perturbations are caused by defensive errors, then, mainly, these can be expected to occur deep in the pitch and close to the goals. From this area a higher number of shots are expected to result in goals as found by Olsen (1988) who recorded 90 per cent of goals scored within a distance of 16 m of the goal.

As stated earlier, these errors (also including bad pass, mistimed tackle and out of position) occur at a low percentage in this particular standard of football, the lost control category was only responsible for 3.7 per cent of all attempts on goal. Therefore, if these defensive mistakes can be decreased the high percentage of goals from this area can also be decreased. Closely behind 'lost control' for producing the best goal/shot ratios were the areas of foul and tackle, which both produced a goal every 5.7 attempts resulting from their respective areas. A high ratio of goals would be expected from the foul category due to the large numbers of shots resulting from free kicks awarded close to the opposition's goal. Also, due to the high standard of play, and individual skill found in the Premier League, most sides will include a player who is accomplished at taking such free kicks. The fact that penalty kicks were included as resulting from the foul category must be taken into account. These points may explain why such a good ratio was obtained. When discussing the tackle category it must be remembered that a tackle was defined as 'dispossessing an opponent', therefore the same factors apply as with those found in lost control. A defender is dispossessed and the attacker is left with a shooting chance.

The results showed that both the pass and run perturbations supplied 241 attempts on goal and 24 goals scored, which equates to 40.2 per cent of all shots (displaying the reliance on teams to play in that particular style) and 48 per cent of goals scored in this particular study. The two skills of pass and run are interlinked, because if an attacker makes a good penetrating run, the player still has to be found with an accurate pass for the move to be successful. This philosophy can be very successful and is used by some of the best footballing teams in the world, for example, Brazil, Italy and Holland. The top five teams also show another important difference from the bottom teams when noting the fact that goals were attained from seven out of the 12 categories of perturbations, whereas the unsuccessful teams utilised only two categories when achieving goal scoring success. This may reflect a wider range of tactical awareness to be able to change the direction and type of attacks in order to achieve success when needed. It seems that if one style of play is not producing goals the successful teams are able to change tactics and still produce a high frequency of shots on goal.

Possible team 'signatures' (patterns of play) were identified and used in predicting future match outcomes, which may aid coaches in identifying their own team's

TABLE 14.4 Occurrences of perturbations and the general categories of actions that caused the smoothing out of the critical incidents

Actions	Matches															Tot	x_m	σ
	1	2	3	4	5	6	7	8	9	10	11	12	13	14	15			
Possess	89	84	71	55	85	49	92	102	99	81	44	59	58	59	49	1076	72	19
Defence	88	59	56	68	87	62	84	107	88	98	86	50	50	40	36	1059	71	21
Receipt	11	31	19	28	25	28	21	24	19	34	22	27	25	30	32	376	25	6
Fouls	3	4	4	5	11	8	15	24	16	6	27	3	2	5	4	137	9	8

strengths and weaknesses and exploiting an opposing team's weakness (e.g. a team concedes a high proportion of goals from lost control). So, perturbations may aid coaches in improving defensive and attacking strategies from a tactical advantage gained from predicting how an opposing side plays.

14.5.3.1 Perturbations not leading to shots on goal

Hughes *et al.* (2001) decided to extend this research by confirming that perturbations can be reliably identified in soccer without recourse to the method of 'backtracking' from a shot at goal and determining the skill variables by which these 'non-critical incident' perturbations are most commonly smoothed out.

The data were taken from Euro96; 15 matches were analysed in detail but can be summarised in three areas: player in possession, defensive actions, intended recipient actions. In addition, fouling by defenders gave away free kicks, which, in one sense, gives another type of perturbation to the attacking side (Table 14.4).

The distribution of unsuccessful perturbations, and their outcomes, varied over the 15 matches. The amount of action variables ranged from 257 to 129. These are the numbers of actions, not perturbations. The perturbations per match averaged 88.2 ($\pm$ 22.1), so that together with the number of perturbations that led to shots on goal, 30.0 (Hughes *et al.*, 1998), the total number of perturbations per match is 118.2. This is a high number and interestingly only one in four, approximately, produces a critical incident – a shot on goal.

The matches with the highest amounts of actions were the games between Portugal and Croatia, and England and Holland. This was probably due to the attacking style employed by these teams, all using short, close controlled passing patterns, which can be very aggressive in terms of attacking football.

Passing by the player in possession was found to be the most frequent reason for the 'smoothing out' of the perturbation – 46.7 per cent of the action variables of the player in possession, about two-thirds of these being inaccurate, the rest

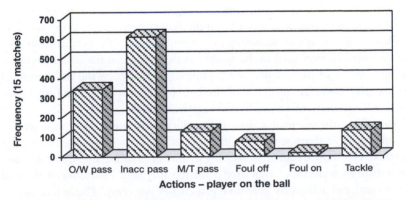

FIGURE 14.3 The frequency of actions by the player on the ball that led to perturbations being smoothed out.

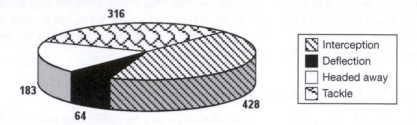

FIGURE 14.4 The frequency of actions by the defence that led to perturbations being smoothed out.

being overhit or mistimed. The most common defensive contributions to the smoothing out of the perturbation were interceptions (428 (44 per cent) of the defensive actions) and different types of tackle (316 (32 per cent) of the defensive actions). The actions of the intended recipients were not as important as the other two categories but nevertheless they accounted for 15 per cent of the overall errors causing the smoothing, the most common being the loss of control variable (208 (61 per cent) of the recipient actions).

The actions of the passing player (see Figure 14.3) are dominated by the inaccuracy of the passes made, accounting for a total of 83 per cent of the 1076 actions made by the player on the ball. A number of these will be made while playing under pressure from the defence, and also, a large number of these passes will have a high risk quality. Nevertheless this is a rewarding area of practice from which coaches and athletes can profit.

The analysis of the different errors in passing showed that the actual accuracy of the passing is more important than the over-weight pass or the mistimed pass. This is surely an area for far more technical work by players, in all positions. Perhaps further work could analyse the contribution by the respective positions in the team, highlighting those positions that are more susceptible to allowing the perturbation chance to slip away, having created the opportunity in the first case.

The fact that the defensive action with the highest frequency is the interception (Figure 14.4) is not surprising, given the high frequencies of the passing variables of the player in possession contributing to the eradication of the perturbation. But part of this must be attributed to the quality of the actions of the defensive team. The relative effect of the defence was compared by analysing the interaction of the passing player and the recipient of the ball, but it is necessary to first discuss the relative frequencies of actions by the recipient player.

By identifying the essential actions that nullify the perturbations in soccer, it was possible to give teams specific profiles of variables that identify winning and losing traits. The most frequent of action variables accounting for smoothing out the perturbations were those associated with the player in possession of the ball (46.7 per cent) and actions by defensive players (41 per cent). The inaccuracy of the pass by the player in possession accounted for 62 per cent of the passing variables. The interception by the defence was strongly interlinked with the inaccurate passing and was the highest frequency of the defensive actions by far (68 per cent). Although the actions by the recipient were comparatively less frequent (12 per cent overall), this is a most important skill, being that much closer to the critical incident, the strike on goal. The most common of the actions of the recipient players was the loss of control. All these actions causing the attack to break down indicate the specific skills for more technical work by the coaches and athletes in the sport.

14.5.3.2 Creating a performance profile using perturbations in soccer – a case study of Arsenal (Hughes and Reed, 2005)

Attacking perturbations

The highest frequency of goals occurred between minutes 31 and 45, and 61 and 75, although when the data were contextualised using shot:goal ratios, the most efficient period was the middle third of the second half (minutes 61–75) when, on average every 2.2 shots resulted in a goal (Figure 14.5) although 20 shots occurred during the first 15 minutes of the match, only two of those resulted in a goal. Perhaps as Luxbacher and Klein (1993) suggested, the high ratio could be the result of high concentration of the defending goalkeeper at the start of the game, or that the attacking players require time to settle into the match as Hughes (1980) proposed. A reversal of these factors may also explain the favourable attacking ratios later in the game; as attackers become relaxed and gain confidence, so the defence lose concentration, allowing greater opportunity to score. A graphic representation of these data is displayed in Figure 14.5.

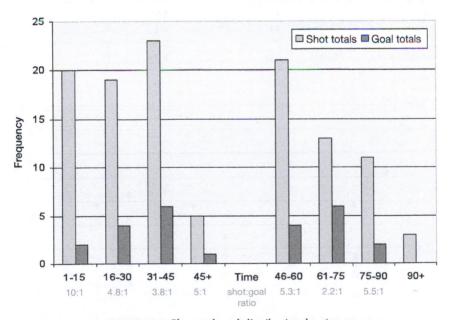

FIGURE 14.5 Shot and goal distribution by time.

A total of 58.3 per cent of all shots occurred in the first half of the matches analysed, suggesting Arsenal endeavour to create a lead in the first half of games upon which they will consolidate in the second period, a strategy explained by Gray and Drewett (1999).

These data serve to highlight Arsenal's strengths and weaknesses rather than suggest future strategies; (for example) just because a team concede from every four shots during a period of the game does not mean that Arsenal should attempt to shoot (and expect to score) from unrealistic positions during that time. Instead, these data could provide information to help coaching staff develop the fitness/concentration of players during specific periods of the match.

Table 14.5 describes the distribution of all shots by nature (i.e. game state – winning, losing or drawing); although the highest frequency of shots occurred when drawing, contextualisation of data revealed shots occur almost twice as frequently when losing as winning. An average of 70 minutes per goal (with a shot:goal ratio of 7:1) when winning, contrasts with an average of 28 minutes per goal when losing (shot:goal ratio of 5:1), thus providing further evidence that Arsenal consolidate (show a reluctance to attack) matches when a lead has been established.

TABLE 14.5 Distribution of shots by nature (i.e. game state – winning, losing or drawing)

Game nature	Time	Shots	Goals	Average mins p/shot	Average mins p/goal	Shot: goal ratio
Winning	420	41	6	10.2	70	7:1
Drawing	402	44	10	9.1	40.2	4:1
Behind	168	29	6	5.8	28	5:1
Overall	990	115	22	8.7	45	5:1

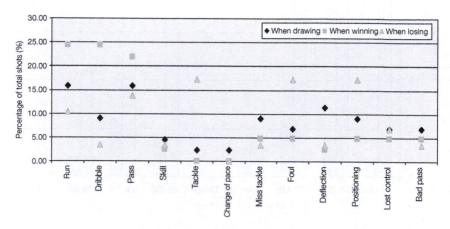

FIGURE 14.6 Distribution of Arsenal perturbations by nature.

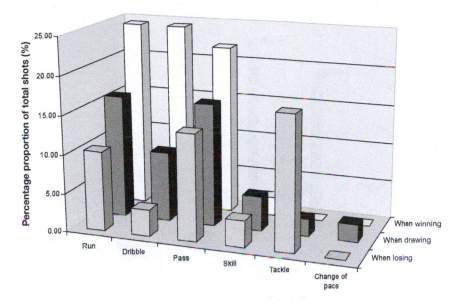

FIGURE 14.7 Proportion of attacking perturbations by nature.

Figures 14.6 and 14.7 describe the distribution of perturbations by nature; when winning, 71 per cent of all shots are created by just three perturbations; running (24.4 per cent), dribbling (24.4 per cent) and passing (22.0 per cent). When losing, the tackle, foul and positioning perturbations supplied 17.4 per cent of shots each, compared to the minimal contribution (< 5 per cent) they make when the team is winning.

A chi-square test of the data revealed significant differences between the patterns of play when winning, losing and drawing. It is apparent that Arsenal are reluctant to dribble with the ball when trailing (perhaps for fear of losing possession), and pressurise the opposition to dispossess them of the ball, induce fouls and exploit bad positioning. These data support the assertions of a number of coaching texts (Gray and Drewett, 1999; Hughes, 1980) that suggested winning teams will have great pressure exerted on their defence, and are therefore expected to concede a greater number of scoring opportunities than when pressure is reduced. In contrast, when winning matches Arsenal almost exclusively used passing, running and dribbling to create shots on goal; this could be the result of increased confidence and composure, or simply indicative of a high standard of play where attempts are more frequently created than resulting from defensive errors. These data support assertions by Hughes *et al.* (1997) that successful teams display a wide range of tactical awareness; when one style of play is not producing goals the team is able to change tactics to produce goal scoring opportunities.

Analysis of location data revealed a strong central preference for attack; 71.9 per cent of all perturbations occur in areas 5 and 6 (Figure 14.8). There is a small

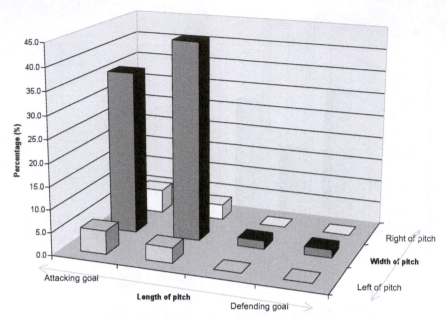

FIGURE 14.8 Location of perturbations in attack.

variation between the first and second halves, with 6.3 per cent of second half perturbations originating in Arsenal's own half, compared to 1.5 per cent in the first half. These data support the earlier suggestion made in this paper, that Arsenal spend the second half of games defending a lead and therefore play more football in their own half.

Perturbations in defence

From the 11 matches used to compile a normative profile in defence, a total of 97 shots on goal were observed, of which 14 resulted in goals (Table 14.6). Goals were scored, on average, from every 7.5 shots. Although this is a higher ratio than that observed for Arsenal in attack, the ratio compares favourably with that presented by Reep and Benjamin (1968) who recorded approximate shot to goal ratios of 10:1. The multitude of teams that formed the analysis of opposition play explained the higher ratio compared to Arsenal's shots: the opposition teams had a poorer standard of player compared to that of Arsenal.

The perturbation that produced the highest frequency of goal attempts was the pass skill, which produced 27 shots (27.8 per cent) (Table 14.6). The lost control perturbation again had a low shot to goal ratio (2:1); perhaps because these losses of possession occur nearer the goal, presenting a better chance of scoring than may occur through other perturbations. Yet the skill with the greatest scoring efficiency is run, suggesting that Arsenal fail to mark players running with/without the ball into Arsenal territory. Because the pass and run perturbations are interlinked

TABLE 14.6 Goals and the frequency of perturbation skills in defence

Perturbation	Frequency	No. of goals	Ratio
Run	4	3	1.3:1
Dribble	4	1	4:1
Pass	27	1	27:1
Skill	4	0	–
Tackle	5	0	–
Change of pace	0	0	–
Miss tackle	11	0	–
Foul	9	1	9:1
Deflection	4	1	4:1
Positioning	16	5	3.2:1
Lost control	2	1	2:1
Bad pass	11	0	–
Total	97	13	7.5:1

(as discussed previously in section 14.53) the high ratio for passing (27:1) and low for running (1.3:1) must be treated with caution. However, these data and conclusions highlight Arsenal's strengths and weaknesses, which may aid coaches in improving defensive and attacking strategies for future performances.

Figure 14.11 demonstrates the analysis of shots and goals over each period of play; from a total of 97 shots on goal, 41 per cent occurred during the first half of matches. The highest frequency of goals occurred between minutes 0 and 15 and 75 and 90, although when the data were contextualised, the most efficient goal scoring period was the first 15 minutes of the game when, on average every 3.5 shots resulted in a goal. In an interesting contrast to attacking shots, where the highest ratio was observed, Arsenal appear to show vulnerability at the start of the match; perhaps resulting from a lack of confidence/concentration, or, as Gray and Drewett (1999) suggested, the high motivation of the opposition players in the first 15 minutes.

Although 20 shots occurred during the first 15 minutes of the second half, only two of those resulted in a goal; perhaps these data could be the result of higher concentration from the Arsenal goalkeeper and defenders at the start of the second half. A total of 58.8 per cent of all opposition shots occurred in the second half of the matches analysed. These data suggests that Arsenal placed less urgency on attack during these periods, perhaps having established a lead while the opposition are forced to chase the game.

These data serve to highlight Arsenal's strengths and weaknesses rather than suggesting future strategies; for example, just because a team concede from every four shots during a period of the game does not mean the opposition should attempt to shoot (and expect to score) from unrealistic positions during that time. Instead, these data should be used to complement other analysis before presentation is made to the coaching staff.

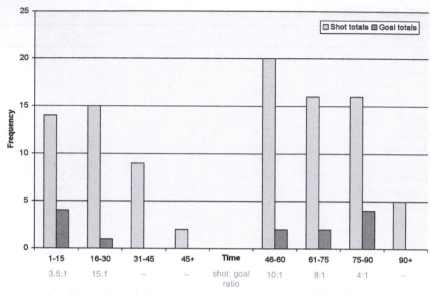

FIGURE 14.9 Shot and goal distribution over time.

TABLE 14.7 Distribution of shots of the opposition by nature (i.e. game state – winning, losing or drawing)

Game nature	Time	Shots	Goals	Average mins p/shot	Average mins p/goal	Shot: goal ratio
Winning	168	9	0	18.7	–	–
Drawing	402	33	9	12.2	44.7	4:1
Behind	364	49	4	7.4	91	13:1
Overall	990	97	13	10.2	71.9	7:1

Table 14.7 describes the distribution of all shots by nature; the highest frequency of shots occurred when Arsenal's opposition were losing. Further analysis to contextualise the data revealed the average time between shots varied by nature, with shot frequency when losing 2.5 times that when winning. An average of 91 minutes per goal (with a shot:goal ratio of 7:1) when losing, contrasts with an average of 44.7 minutes per goal when drawing (shot:goal ratio of 4:1), therefore suggesting Arsenal dominate possession when losing, preventing the opposition an opportunity to extend their lead.

Figure 14.10 details the distribution of perturbations by nature; when winning, 38.5 per cent of all shots are created by the pass perturbation compared to 15 per cent of shots when drawing. The attacking strategy of Arsenal's opposition shows less variation by nature than Arsenal had exhibited, suggesting the tactical awareness described by Hughes *et al.* (1997) is lacked by the opposition teams. Because this

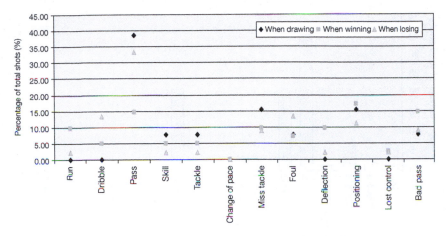

FIGURE 14.10 Distribution of opposition perturbations by nature.

study analysed a multitude of teams, differentiation between the contrasting styles of opposition is impossible; the data represent a general trend of the opposition play. A chi-square test revealed significant differences between the patterns of play for all game states, with the greatest statistical variation occurring between drawing and losing.

When trailing, the opposition used dribbling (14 per cent) perturbations more frequently, and relied less upon skill and tackle. While these data provide little team-specific accuracy, it is interesting to contrast Arsenal's reluctance to dribble with the opposition enthusiasm to do so when losing.

14.5.4 General results in squash

Murray *et al.* (2008) analysed data for both men and women, and used the perturbation data to define and complement performance profiles for individual players. From the results (Figure 14.11) it is evident that drop (34.7 per cent), volley drop (18.3 per cent) and boast (20.7 per cent) are the three main shots that cause perturbations in a squash match. These findings are very similar to Hughes (1985; 2000a) who concluded that boast, straight drop and volley short are the three main shots to move an opponent to the front of the court. By comparing these two findings it can be suggested that players going short more often than not cause perturbations.

This study found that once a perturbation occurred, it was more than likely to lead to a critical incident rather than regain stability; these findings are consistent with Hodges *et al.* (1998) and McGarry *et al.* (2002) who found that the shots that cause instability are key athletic behaviours in determining the rally outcome and causing critical incidents. While conducting this study the researcher noted that as the match progressed, players became fatigued and the rallies were less likely to stabilise. If a rally did stabilise then the majority of the time it only stabilised once,

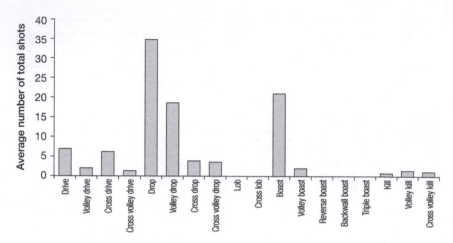

FIGURE 14.11 Type of shot that caused a perturbation when playing a squash match.

and took between one and three shots to stabilise. Although on one occasion a rally stabilised seven times before a critical incident occurred. It could also happen that a rally lost its rhythm for 11 plus shots before regaining stability. These findings support McGarry *et al.* (1999) that there is evidence of multiple perturbations and that rallies go from stability to instability.

Hughes *et al.* (2000c) also found that not all perturbations lead to critical incidents, and that some rallies do stabilise. They also concluded that not all critical incidents are preceded by a perturbation. This was also found in this investigation. The researcher stated that a perturbation only occurred if the player actually went for the shot. In some cases a player played a good shot, which the other player did not go for, meaning a critical incident occurred without a prior perturbation. The researcher found that this normally happened in short rallies of up to four shots.

Perturbations were caused from all over the court, excluding the front four cells, although the majority of perturbations were played from the backhand side close to the sidewall in cells 9 and 16. This may be because players are more consistent on the backhand side and it is here they feel most comfortable playing a perturbation, although players may also be under pressure here, and not in control of the 'T'.

McGarry *et al.* (1999) found that strong and weak shots are the most common cause for perturbations. When a player is under pressure in the back corners, they will play a short defensive shot, in order to allow themselves time to recover to the 'T'; by creating a perturbation they are placing both their opponent and themselves under pressure as the stable rhythm of play has been disturbed. From the data gathered by England Squash it can be seen that overall winners and errors were played from the backhand side at the back of the court (Figure 14.12). These data are similar to those of profile by perturbations confirming that the backhand side is the more dominant side in a squash game. Winners were played from cell

1, 4, 9 and 12 and errors were played from 9, 12, 13 and 16, showing no similarities to the perturbation data gathered; after conducting a chi-square analysis it was found that the two profiles were significantly different ($\chi^2 = 41.2$; $p < 0.001$). Another difference between the two profiles was players played a considerable number of perturbations from the four cells around the 'T', in comparison to both the winner and error profiles, indicating that perturbations are more often than not caused by opponents' weak shots. This indicates that perturbation profiles may have more similarities with the England Squash winner profiles compared to the error profiles. A significant difference between the two profiles was expected as, when analysing disturbances in the system, the process is being investigated, whereas the data gathered by England Squash is considering the end result; therefore this paper is investigating the process that causes the outcome.

Comparing the perturbation profile with the winner profile shows that the front four cells (1–4) are used to a greater extent when playing winners than when playing perturbations. This may be because players are winning from weak defensive shots, such as the boast, which is played to the front of the court. This is an important

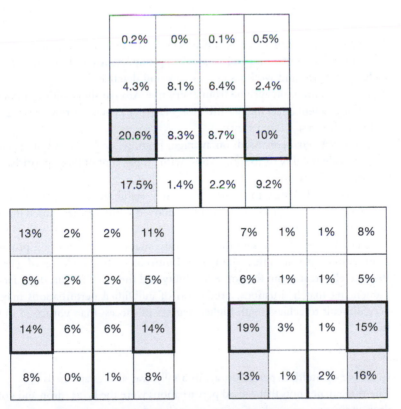

FIGURE 14.12 Performance profiles for male squash. Top is where players play perturbations from; bottom left is England Squash's winner distribution, and bottom right error distribution.

consideration as shots such as the boast were one of the main causes of perturbations, thus indicating players should be in an attacking position when attempting a perturbation. Cells 5–12 were used more often when creating perturbations, confirming the use of perturbations in an attacking situation, as this is the area closest to the 'T'. The back four cells (13–16) were used equally in both profiles apart from cell 13, which was used considerably more in the perturbation profile, probably due to the defensive style of play in the back corner. The fact that this row is used a similar amount in each profile is interesting as it shows that winners have been created from these cells too. Although there was a significant difference between the two profiles, when taking into consideration the fact that the perturbation profile is the process of getting to the winner profile, some similarities begin to emerge between them.

14.6 Conclusions

It was concluded that the identification and analysis of perturbations and their location was consistent and reliable.

Soccer

- Arsenal's characteristic patterns of play were identified enabling the prediction of future match outcomes and highlighting important coaching information such as strengths and weaknesses in attack and defence.
- A goal was scored, on average from every five Arsenal shots with lost control the most efficient attacking perturbation (42.9 per cent shots resulted in goals) and foul the least (10 per cent).
- In defence Arsenal conceded, on average, from every 7.5 shots but appeared to show vulnerability to attacking runs, with 75 per cent of those perturbations resulting in goals.
- It was concluded that total shot frequency stabilised after eight matches; however, the varying tactical strategies employed within games caused the data to show high variability.
- Further attempts to integrate these tactical variations into profiling provided more consistent results than the method introduced by Hughes et al. (1997).
- Because elite teams aim for unpredictability and there is a multitude of factors influencing match situations, prediction of individual perturbations may be very difficult to achieve with higher degrees of success than witnessed in this study.

Squash

- Evidence of multiple perturbations in a rally was also established.
- The three main shots that caused perturbations were the boast, drop and volley drop indicating going short causes most disturbances in the system.
- The backhand side at the back of the court was where most perturbations were played. After comparing the perturbation profile to the winner and error

profiles, significant differences were found between the two profiles, indicating perturbations provide further in-depth analysis of notational analysis of squash.

- After conducting a case study on two elite male players it was found that there were significant differences between the two players' profiles. Subject 1 used perturbations in a more attacking style whereas Subject 2 used perturbations in a defensive way, showing variations in the use of perturbations.

- McGarry and Franks (1994) found previous performance could be used to predict next matches' response; this should be investigated to see whether perturbations can be used to predict future performance.

Practical applications

There are a few practical messages to be taken from the data analyses; they are interesting but have limited practical value for the coach because of the general nature of these analyses. They confirm that perturbations are a reliable way of analysing key elements of performances. The work has demonstrated that this type of qualitative assessment of important events is reliable as long as there is plenty of training and the reliability of the systems and operators is assessed. Of course football scouts have been using similar, but subjective, systems for generations. The important message here is the capability of using this type of tested and tried system, perhaps in conjunction with a video tagging system such as Focus X2, SportsCode or Dartfish, to assess the relative abilities of your own players, units and team; and to do the same on your opponents to examine how they will be trying to put your defence under pressure.

15

MOMENTUM AND 'HOT HANDS'

*Mike Hughes, Nic James, Michael T. Hughes,
Stafford Murray, Ed Burt and Luke Heath*

15.1 Introduction

Research on the 'hot hand' myth tries to find evidence of support or refutation whether athletes elevate their performance following streaks of success (Gilovich *et al.*, 1985; Tversky and Gilovich, 1989a, 1989b; Ayton *et al.*, 1991; Berry *et al.*, 1999; Koehler and Conley, 2003). Mainly explored in professional basketball but also in other sports, the belief that a player is more likely to score next time when he just scored with his last two or three attempts is a controversially discussed topic. Gilovich *et al.* (1985) exposed the 'hot hand' as a fallacy. Results in this area led to considerations about the existence of streaks in other sports but results are various (Bürger, 2009).

Looking at a team's performance from a physical point of view their momentum might indicate unexpected turning points in defeat or success. Scientists describe this value as requiring some effort to start but also that it is relatively easy to keep going once a sufficient level is reached (Reed and Hughes, 2006). Unlike football, rugby, handball and many more sports, a regular volleyball match is not limited by time but by points that need to be gathered. Every minute more than one point is won by either one team or the other. That means a series of successive points enlarges the gap between the teams, making it more and more difficult to catch up with the leading one. This concept of gathering momentum, or the reverse in a performance, can give the coaches, athletes and sports scientists further insights into winning and losing performances.

15.2 The 'hot hand' myth

Numbers gained from analysing American and National Baseball League players in the seasons 1987, 1988 and 1989, using 501 Bernoulli trials, could not prove whether players have streaks of successful or unsuccessful hitting (Albright, 1993).

A Bernoulli trial is an experiment with only two possible outcomes. These are usually denoted success and failure and hold the properties that the probability of the occurrence of each outcome is the same in each trial and the occurrence of one excludes the occurrence of the other in any given trial. Although some players showed significantly streaky performance, the overall data were more consistent with a model of randomness.

Starting off with a quite supporting attitude towards the 'hot hand' and trying to keep points of criticism from prior research in mind, Koehler and Conley (2003) tried to offer new evidence for the 'hot hand' phenomenon. They suggested that the NBA Long Distance Shootout contest is a superior context in comparison to free throws (Gilovich *et al.*, 1985; Wardrop, 1995). Due to the difficulty of the shots, the short time span and the three-shot run they claimed the former as a more appropriate setting for perceived hotness. None but two of the 23 best 3-point shooters in professional basketball showed any sequential dependency in their performance. Moreover the comparison of expected and observed runs did not show any unusual streaks of success. A last attempt to reveal evidence of 'hot hands' by seeking for connections between spontaneous outbursts by the contest announcer and players' performance also failed. Despite the numerous publications reviewed and assessed by Bar-Eli and colleagues (2006), definite statistical evidence is still missing.

Analysing the sport of volleyball, Raab (2002) evaluated 37,000 rows of sequences of successful spikes and misses from more than 200 players of the German First National Volleyball League. It was found that half showed significant autocorrelation between successive shots. Moreover, these were also related to high base rates. In detail: the probability to hit a successful spike after a preceding winner was significantly higher than after a miss. Therefore, the sequences cannot be considered as random and the 'hot hand' myth is not a fallacy. Furthermore the 'hot hand' was approved to have a much greater influence on decision making (Who receives the next set?) than the base rate of a player. That means even a player with a lower base rate is still more likely to get the next chance to hit if he just scored one or more points in a row than his team mate with a higher base rate (Raab, 2002).

The implication of the 'hot hand' on the momentum of athletes' performance is a closely related area of research. Both deal with suspicions that effects of hotness or momentum might results from other influencing factors and are therefore masked. In rich contexts a Bernoulli model probably oversimplifies and may significantly distort streak probabilities (Kaplan, 1990). Dealing with these difficulties, investigations in hockey based on Bernoulli trials models stated the 'hot goalie hypothesis' in conjunction with the 'dominant team hypothesis'. Morrison and Schmittlein (1998) named these as the main influences for the increase of the probability p for the superior team to win. Despite similar team strengths in the National Hockey League playoffs, the probability for each superior team to win at a certain stage of a best-out-of-7 series did not equal 0.5. Instead the maximum likelihood method resulted in the $p = 0.73$ Bernoulli model. As coaches often use the goalie they consider being 'hot' during the playoffs the researchers assumed the 'hot goalie hypothesis' as one of the highly influencing factors but are well aware of other affects.

15.3 Momentum through notational analysis studies

Momentum investigations also contain dependencies between performances or questions if future performances are reliant upon past streaks. Squash and volleyball share the characteristic of being played up to a certain amount of points. Squash was examined according to the momentum of players by Hughes *et al.* (2007a). The initial aim was to expand normative profiles of elite squash players using momentum graphs of winners and errors to explore 'turning points' in a performance.

Together with the analysis of one's own performance it is essential to have an understanding of your opposition's tactical strengths and weaknesses. By modelling the opposition's performance it is possible to predict certain outcomes and patterns, and therefore intervene or change tactics before the critical incident occurs. The modelling of competitive sport is an informative analytic technique as it directs the attention of the modeller to the critical aspects of data that delineate successful performance (McGarry and Franks, 1996a, 1996b). Using tactical performance profiles to pull out and visualise these critical aspects of performance, players can build justified and sophisticated tactical plans.

Acknowledgment of the importance of notational analysis to improving performance was best demonstrated by the appointment of full-time analysts with the England and Scottish squash squads. Indeed, Murray and Hughes (2001) showed how modern technology and its application can provide tactical profiles of players and their opponents. These profiles are not dissimilar to those pioneered by Hughes (1985), and extended by Hughes and Robertson (1998), but are more soundly based in terms of reliability and have the requisite amounts of data to create stable profiles.

The research of Hughes *et al.* (2006a) aimed to extend these ideas and explore a new application of these analysis techniques to develop 'momentum profiles' through notational analysis. They defined positive momentum as a player hitting successive winners, negative momentum as a player hitting errors, and if the player is passive, not hitting winners or making errors, then the player's momentum will stay the same. This work was a first step in trying to apply these ideas of momentum within a game and correlate them with overall performance in the elite playing world.

The momentum curves all show interesting aspects of players' performances – in Figure 15.1, for example, Sarah Fitzgerald was playing 'steadily' for the first two games but, round about rally 10 of game 3, something happened and she suddenly started playing much more positively and sustained this to win the match. What happened at this point in the game? Examining more graphs like this one, it seemed that players had positive and negative swings in momentum. Do these cycles occur regularly and do they have repetitive properties?

15.3.1 Momentum graphs – the beginning in squash

The initial data collection used a real-time analysis system that is based on a programme designed by Hughes and Robertson (1998) and later computerised to speed up the process (Murray and Hughes, 2001). This system provides an analysis of winners and errors, gathering data such as the number of shots in a rally, the position from which the rally ending shot was hit, who hit it, and the type of rally ending shot. By writing another analysis program we calculated a running score (momentum) for a player during a game. We gave a winning shot by a player a '+1' score, an error a '−1' score, and if the opponent hit the rally end shot, or it was a let, the running score stayed the same (Figure 15.1). This could just as easily be done with scoring, or positive and negative phases of play, in any team game (Locke, 2005; Reed and Hughes, 2006).

With the data processed by the software it was possible to present the two sets of data for both players at the same time, see Figures 15.1 and 15.2. It is possible to examine these curves and see where the 'turning points' in the match occurred. For the coach and/or the team psychologist to discuss with the player what happened at these turning points would enhance insight into each respective performance.

Figure 15.3 shows another way that we could present these data; we termed this form of presentation a 'cumulative' momentum graph. In this graph the momentum of each player 'interacts' – so that a winner by a player will move the graph upwards, whereas an error by the player moves it downwards. The opposite applies

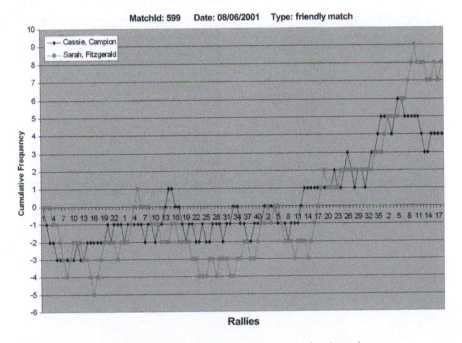

FIGURE 15.1 Example of 'momentum analysis' graph

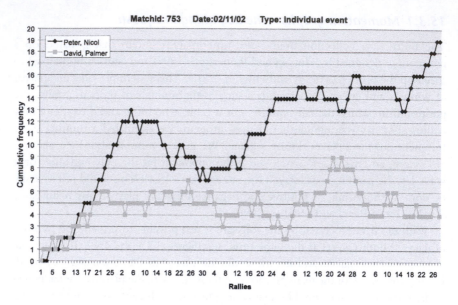

FIGURE 15.2 Example of 'momentum analysis' graph.

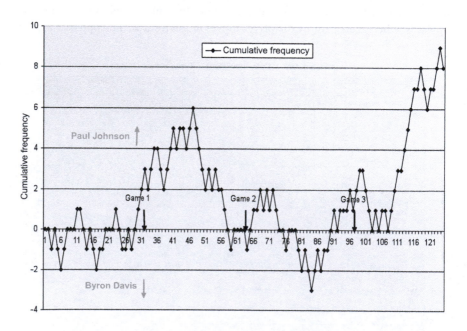

FIGURE 15.3 Example of a cumulative momentum analysis graph.

to the other player – a winner moving the graph downward and an error moving it upwards. In this way one curve represents the interactive momentum of the match, with each player having their positive areas on each side of the abscissa, and the turning points can be seen clearly.

Figures 15.4, 15.5 and 15.6 show a clear example of these different forms of presentation. Figure 15.4 is the impressive profile of PM, showing a positive increasing curve throughout the match. Figure 15.5 shows a similar profile for DE, apart from a big trough at the start of the match. Looking at these two profiles, it is difficult to see who won the match and where the turning points occurred. Although DE's curve does not reach as high as PM's at the end, this is not the important factor – it is the slope of the curves that is important, so perhaps we could divine from this that DE won the match. But if we examine the cumulative 'interactive' momentum graph of the two players (Figure 15.6), the patterns of momentum become much clearer. By marking where the end of each game occurs, it is easy to see that PM won the first game easily, just lost the second, won the third again very easily, but then lost momentum, losing the fourth and fifth games. A coach would be very interested in talking about concentration and application at some of these critical points in the match where the momentum shifted so starkly.

In Figure 15.7 the x-axis represents the number of rallies in the match. The y-axis on the right side represents momentum: +1, +2, –1, –2, etc. . . . The y-axis on the left side represents the number of shots in each rally. This corresponds with the dark red vertical bars. So the graph of momentum is now superimposed on to a graphical representation of the respective lengths of the rallies in the match. These data were requested by the physiologist working with the English squash players to see whether we could see any fatigue effects – losses of momentum, or otherwise, by players after long rallies in the latter stages of a match.

15.3.1.1 Momentum in volleyball

Using post-event analysis, Bürger (2009) examined 1066 rallies according to positive, negative or passive momentum. All available sets were either assigned to the successful or the unsuccessful side. The contribution of winners and errors from both sides was almost equal (succ: 534; unsucc: 532). From all tagged games momentum and cumulative frequency graphs were compiled. As visual apparentness cannot evaluate significant differences between winning and losing performance, all data were systematically analysed for successive winners and errors. Positions and lengths of strings of winners and errors were identified using algorithms performed in GNU Octave. Depending on their position these successive winners or errors were assigned to groups forming *start* (S), *middle* (M) and *end* (E) of each set. Therefore the absolute number of points played per set (e.g. 45 points) was divided by three and for example the first 15 points assigned to *start*, the next to *middle* and the last 15 points to *end*. This was to detect patterns induced by the different psychological stresses appearing within a set. The shortest streak would

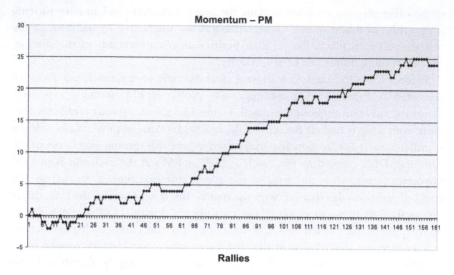

FIGURE 15.4 The momentum graph of PM in his match with DE.

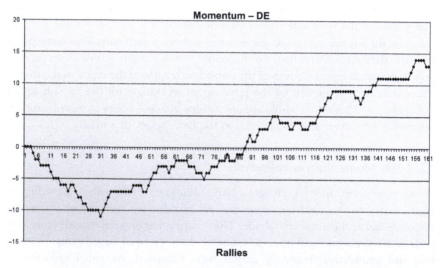

FIGURE 15.5 The momentum graph of DE in his match with PM.

be the successive occurrence of two positive or negative actions and the longest one had eight errors in a row. Effectively, there were nearly twice as many positive (21 > 12) and less negative (75 < 103) strings on the successful teams' side. Differing distributions of streaks, no matter whether positive or negative, could not be found related to the pace of the game. Successful teams' streaks at the beginning (S27), middle (M33) and end (E36) were not significantly different (χ^2 (2) = 4.26, $p \geq 0.05$) compared to unsuccessful teams' streaks (S38, M27, E50).

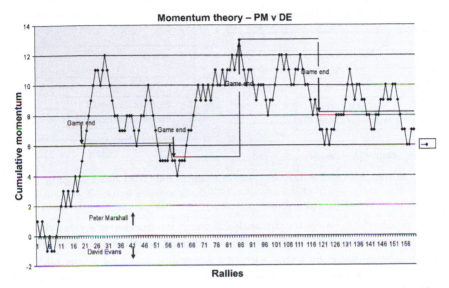

FIGURE 15.6 The cumulative momentum graph of PM and DE in their match, with game-by-game analysis.

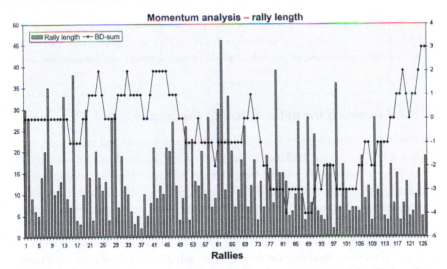

FIGURE 15.7 An example of an individual player's momentum with rally length.

It can be stated that there are obvious tendencies towards more and longer strings of positive momentum and shorter and fewer strings of negative momentum for successful teams at a non-elite level (Bürger, 2009). In relation to the pace of the game, winning and losing teams did not show different distributions of streaks no matter whether looking at positive or negative streaks. Furthermore, using Raab's measure of streakiness (2002) that explores whether a winner is more likely to occur after a winner or after an error, the rejection of the 'hot hand' hypothesis was the

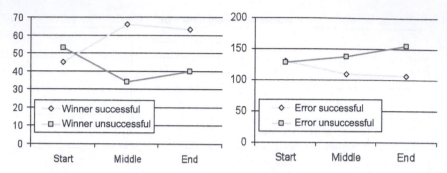

FIGURE 15.8A AND B Development of winners and errors along the game.

only possible conclusion for the analysed teams within Bürger's research. Still, the development and ratios of winners and errors are worth mentioning. Whereas the number of successful teams' winners increased up to a peak in the middle of a set, the unsuccessful teams' development of winners was contrary (Figure 15.8a). The number of errors made by both sides was evenly high during the first third of a set. However, the direction of development for teams showing an overall bad performance was straight upwards, whereas successful teams manage to avoid errors in the pace of a set and to level to the end (Figure 15.8b).

Probably the investigation at an elite level of play may give more significant answers if the maintaining of periods of positive momentum can define a successful team.

15.3.2 Examining the patterns within the graphs

Matches of elite squash players ($N = 8$ per player; six male and six female, all in the top 40 in the world rankings at the time) were analysed to test whether the better players had more positive momentum patterns. This was completed by examining the length of the 'peaks' of momentum in a match, and their corresponding amplitudes, and also comparisons of these 'positive' characteristics to those considered 'negative', that is the 'troughs' of momentum (see Figure 15.9). The peak lengths and heights were measured for each player and averaged; the same process was used for obtaining the averages for each player of their respective trough heights and lengths. Inevitably, large variations were found within each player's set of data, but all of these characteristics of the profiles stabilised to within 10 per cent of their respective means within six of the eight matches, for all the players (see Figure 15.10a and 15.10b for examples). A χ^2 analysis was used for comparison purposes and the patterns showed significant differences between players ($p < 0.05$).

The troughs in the data did not show any clear patterns with respect to world ranking, but the lengths of the peaks in momentum showed that, for both men and women, the world number ones, both men and women, had values well in excess of players below them. These lengths also had an almost perfect correlation

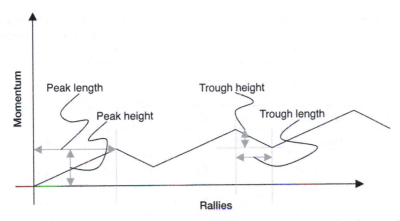

FIGURE 15.9 Example of aggregated patterns of peaks and troughs of application by the players during a match.

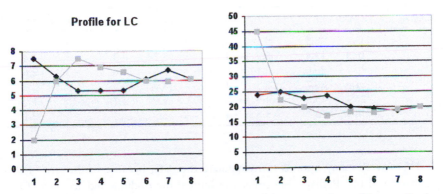

FIGURES 15.10A AND B Examples of stabilisation of the mean values of the amplitude of the peaks for two of the players (the cumulative means for the matches were calculated in both directions to give an estimate of the effect of outliers in the data).

($r = -0.83$) with the world ranking of the women; this was not so for the men. It was felt that the women's data were more homogeneous than those of the men, most of the women's matches were against each other, whereas those of the men had a number of matches against lower ranked players, thus skewing the data for this sort of comparison.

χ^2 analysis was used and showed significant differences between patterns (of peaks, peak lengths, troughs and trough lengths) of the players ($p < 0.05$). Interestingly, the data of the world men's number two reflect this particular player's reputation as being brilliant but mercurial, while that of the number one clearly demonstrate his application skills, his steadiness, and his desire to dominate his opponents. In the data of some matches of this player, it was observed that he did not make two consecutive errors in the whole match.

TABLE 15.1 The lengths and amplitudes of upswings (peaks, of ≥ 2) and downswings (troughs, of ≤ −2) in momentum for six elite female and six elite male players, averaged over eight matches for each player.

WOMEN

World	Peaks				Troughs			
Ranking	Length	SD	Height	SD	Length	SD	Depth	SD
1	33.4	22	6.8	3.5	11.7	13.7	−4.9	2.5
2	30.6	16.5	8.5	4.8	14.6	9	−5.2	1.7
3	20.2	10.6	5.9	3.4	17.6	15	−3.8	2.2
7	22.4	14.8	7.1	6	10.4	8.2	−2.6	0.6
8	14.3	12.4	4.3	2.9	11.5	9.2	−3.2	1.6
12	15.9	10	4.9	3.4	26.2	20	−3.2	1.8

MEN

World	Peaks				Troughs			
Ranking	Length	SD	Height	SD	Length	SD	Depth	SD
1	45.4	28.5	9	5.7	12.9	10.3	−3.6	0.9
2	16.3	12.4	5.2	4.1	9.7	8.3	−3.2	1.4
7	20.1	20.6	5.1	5	13.5	12.8	−3.9	2.6
8	21.8	20.7	5	4.6	14.5	10.3	−3.8	2
15	23.4	15.8	4.4	2.8	9.9	5.7	−3	1
33	18.9	13	5.8	4	15	16.4	−3.5	2.1

There were many options to manipulate the data, because of the size of the database available. Perhaps data collection limited the findings and accuracy. One suggestion was to collect data from matches where the players were both ranked in the top 20 at the time of the match. However, a player's ranking only tells part of the story. One player may be better than another but has just started playing on tour. Another player might be past his prime and ranked in the top twenty only because he has been playing on tour for such a long time. The male player, ranked 33, had been number two, is 32 years old and had been injured for some time; he is not playing much now, but when he does compete he is still a very good player. So, retrospectively, he was not a good choice.

This research is a beginning of a new way of extending notational analysis. Studying momentum and linking it to psychological factors could benefit a player's performance. Often players lose concentration or allow themselves to be disturbed by a refereeing decision or the behaviour of their opponent; these will be easily identified by momentum charts, pinpointing the moment. The players can then discuss the video of these critical incidents with the respective psychologists, hopefully training themselves to better levels of application, like the world number ones.

This study demonstrates a quantitative, yet qualitative, approach to psychological momentum. Both the world number one male and female players have averages of peak length significantly higher than their peers. Further research needs to be done to analyse why their peaks are longer and steeper. A questionnaire could be designed to ask players questions about individual matches or overall performance before or after a match. Clips of a previous match can be shown on video and then another questionnaire could be applied.

But in order to provide significant information, these studies need to maintain an interdisciplinary modus operandi. At the current time, few analysts, coaches and athletes are aware of momentum analysis, but this paper attempts to show that momentum can be helpful in performance development. We invite other researchers to explore these applications.

15.3.3 Perturbations in sports match play

The concept of open (complex) systems is a theory that seeks to explain how regularity emerges from within a system that consists of many degrees of freedom in constant flux. Theoretically, dynamic patterns are founded on, and greatly inspired by, the pioneering work of Hermann Haken, who introduced the concept of non-equilibrium phase transitions within natural patterns (Haken, 1983). At the heart of this theory is how patterns are formed in complex systems with small changes *to* the system prompting large (nonlinear) changes *in* the system. Kelso, Turvey and colleagues have been instrumental in applying these types of theory to the experimental analysis of perception and action (for a review, see Kelso, 1995). In these patterns, contents aren't contained but are revealed by the system's dynamics. Understanding of these theories within brain and behaviour sciences has opened up entirely new research avenues including synergies, cooperation, and control and order parameters.

In the first instance it was recognised that some characteristics of dynamic systems – namely transient periods of instability – were occurring naturally within observed sports performance. McGarry and Franks (1995) therefore reasoned, and later confirmed (McGarry et al., 1999) that a disrupting perturbation occurred when the usual stable rhythm of play was disturbed by extreme elements of high or low skill. Using the assertions of Haken (1983) it became clear to those researchers following McGarry, that the analysis of perturbations in sport offered a more critical and dynamic method of investigation and therefore a significant step towards effective support to coaches and performance.

During the last decade, studies using these and related theories have attempted to provide a theoretical basis to sports – and most relevantly, performance analysis – research. Understanding has been sought in terms of feature identification (Ferreira et al., 2003; Palut and Zanone, 2005) and essential variables which characterise pattern formation (Hughes and Reed, 2005; Palut and Zanone, 2005). However, our understanding of these and other critical behaviours of sports systems remains in its infancy.

Match play sports exhibit rhythms when competitors perform at equal levels. A perturbation exists where the usual stable rhythm of play is disturbed by extreme elements of high or low skill. In soccer, should the resulting instabilities in playing patterns lead to a shot on goal, then the outcome is termed a critical incident.

> If we study a system only in the linear range of its operation where change is smooth, it's difficult if not impossible to determine which variables are essential and which are not.
>
> Most scientists know about nonlinearity and usually try to avoid it.
>
> Here we exploit qualitative change, a nonlinear instability, to identify collective variables, the implication being that because these variables change abruptly, it is likely that they are also the key variables when the system operates in the linear range.
>
> (Kelso, 1995)

Research confirming the existence of perturbations by McGarry and Franks (1995) in squash identified particularly weak or strong shots that place one player at a recognised disadvantage to another.

Squash lends itself strongly to the dynamical system theory as the game is always played between two players; therefore the behaviour of one directly affects the behaviour of the other (Hughes *et al.*, 2006a). McGarry *et al.* (1999) began to analyse squash as a dynamical system, first by investigating whether the system can be detected as switching between periods of stability and instability from visual inspections. Independent observers were able to identify those behavioural transitions, or perturbations, that were held as switching the system from and to regions of stability and instability. The identification of perturbations from visual inspections of soccer behaviour was likewise reported by Hughes and Franks (1997). These ideas are explored in detail by Murray *et al.* (2008).

Many sports can therefore be seen as an open system that exists in a dynamic equilibrium or stable state (McGarry and Franks, 1995). An open system displays rhythmical patterns and often displays invariant behaviour. In order to control the rhythm of the game, it is essential to attempt to keep your opponent under pressure and not in control of the centre of the court, called the 'T' (Miles and Khan, 1988). When a disturbance in a dynamical system occurs, it is defined as a perturbation – in squash this is a very good shot that therefore upsets the rhythm of the rally and puts physical pressure on the opposing player. Hence perturbations exist in an open system where the normal constant rhythm of play is disturbed by excessive elements of high, or low, skills. This consequently results in a particular outcome (Hughes and Reed, 2005), which places one of the players, or a team, at a disadvantage, for example their displacement on court.

Match play in squash alternates intermittently between stable and unstable behaviour; it is at the boundaries or transition points of these behaviour states that 'critical incidents' are most likely to be detected (McGarry *et al.*, 2002). When perturbations arise they do not all lead to critical incidents, which place a player under severe pressure, though, these critical incidents can be overcome by a defensive shot or sharp movement that will re-establish the rally's stability.

Hughes *et al.* (2001, p. 23) had suggested that concentrating upon the critical aspects of soccer play 'could make the ensuing analyses not only easier but more relevant'. A perturbation in soccer is hence defined as an incident that changes the rhythmic flow of attacking and defending; for instance a penetrating pass, change of pace or any moment of skill that creates a disruption in the defence.

Hughes *et al.* (2000a) attempted to confirm and define the existence of perturbations in association football; 12 common attacking and defending variables were identified from English football that led to scoring opportunities. These 12 causes were shown to occur consistently, covering all possible eventualities and had high reliability. After further analyses of the 1996 European Championship matches (*N* = 31), Hughes *et al.* (2000a) attempted to create a profile for nations that had played more than five matches. Although the work supported English league traits for successful and unsuccessful teams, there was insufficient data for the development of a comprehensive normative profile. Consequently, although failing to accurately predict future performance, Hughes *et al.* (2000a) had introduced the method of using perturbations to construct a prediction model, and had identified six attacking skills and six defensive skills that contributed most to the creation of perturbations (Figure 15.11).

In match play, teams may alter tactics and style according to the game state/nature; for instance a team falling behind may revert to a certain style of play to create more goal-scoring chances and therefore skew any data away from an overall profile. Consequently, although Hughes *et al.* (2000a) had classified perturbations, the method had failed to distinguish between the game states, which prevented the generation of stable and accurate performance profiles.

In some instances, a disruption in the rhythm of play may not result in a shot, owing to high defensive or a lack of attacking skill. Developing earlier work on British league football, Hughes *et al.* (2000b) analysed how international teams

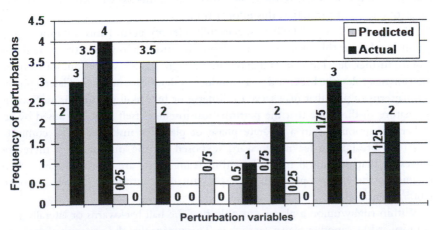

FIGURE 15.11 A comparison of predicted and actual frequencies of shots by Manchester United and Newcastle United for each of the perturbation variables by Newcastle in one match.

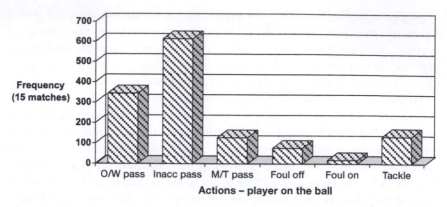

FIGURE 15.12 The frequency of actions by the player on the ball that led to perturbations.

stabilised or 'smoothed out' the perturbation. Hughes *et al.* (2000b) identified three categories of perturbation that did not lead to shots on goal; actions by the player in possession, actions by the receiver and interceptions. Although Hughes *et al.* (2000b) highlighted the requirement for improved technical skill, by combining the data of many teams the conclusions provided little benefit for coaches of specific teams and highlighted the need for analysis of individual 'team "signatures"' (Figure 15.12).

Rugby union, while posing many of the same structural characteristics as football, is arguably a more complex sport. This complexity of performance often leads to a huge amount of data being collected from a single performance, making its analysis and relevance often extremely confusing to both coach and performer. And with the advent of systems such as ProZone, we continue to expand the depth and range of data available to the professional coach; therefore relying upon largely subjective decisions to ration this information.

The work of Locke (2005) to successfully identify perturbations within rugby union has begun this process of data 'concentration'. However, these methods require further development and application; rugby, as a result of one of its most fundamental rules (the backward pass), produces a significant number of lateral phases and patterns of play that may serve to disperse or hide skill perturbations. Such is the nature of the game that the perturbation instance itself may be caused by an earlier disruption within a separate phase of play; for instance, backs committing to a breakdown leaving forwards exposed on the outside. It is therefore suggested that dynamical methods within team sports are more relevant when examining the *phase* of play rather than instant of occurrence – of which Locke (2005) identified 18.

Within rugby union a player can only pass the ball backwards or laterally (i.e. not forwards) to another player, or kick it. This means that the majority of progress made by an attacking team occurs through repetitive cycles of passing the ball, running to make ground and being tackled. Each of these cycles (greatly simplified) is called a phase of play. Teams within top-flight rugby union possess very well-organised defences that tend to produce stable phases of play that can continue for significant periods of time. Although, as Locke (2005) suggests, it can appear that neither team appears to be in definite control of a particular phase, the outcome of that phase is – more often than not – a positive or negative for the team in possession.

Supported by basic coaching knowledge, it is proposed that phases of play can be categorised into positive, negative or 'neutral' moments. It is a simple step to suggest therefore that teams who maintain consecutive, positive 'phases of play' (what will later be termed momentum), will be more likely to create significant disruptions in the defence (perturbations) that in turn lead to scoring opportunities. Reed and Hughes (2006) suggested the following arguments against skill/instant perturbations:

- Teams within top-flight sport possess very well organised defences which tend to produce stable phases of play which can continue for significant periods of time contests exhibiting a general tendency to stability.
- Such is the nature of many sports, that the perturbation instance itself may be caused by an earlier disruption within a separate phase of play. For instance:
  – Rugby Union backs committing to a breakdown leaving forwards exposed on the outside.
  – Soccer centre back losing his positioning which stretches the defence elsewhere.
- Perturbations become 'hidden' or confused by a multitude of connecting variables and factors.

Figures 15.13 and 15.14 show the analyses of two under-16 International Rugby Union matches (producing ~360 bits of data) notated using SportsCode Elite, post-event, and using this 'momentum of positive/negative phases of play' approach. Essentially phases of play were classified into three categories (positive, negative and neutral), but with subcategories to provide coaching feedback. Subsequent data analysis used basic algorithms to convert SportsCode edit list data into numerical vales for presentation and analysis purposes. In this instance a positive phase equated to +1, negative to −1 and neutral 0. Perturbations and scores (for and against) were notated, with corresponding times.

Figure 15.13 shows the interaction between the two teams, with positive momentum for Wales (negative for England) being indicated as the curve moves above the abscissa; positive momentum for England (negative for Wales) is shown as the curve plunges downwards – so it is the slope of the curve that shows the current state of momentum. In this example Wales started well (10 mins), had a fairly level patch for about 20 mins and then finished the half very strongly. The second half was not so good – in fact the metaphor 'all down hill' fits exactly.

In Figure 15.14 the scores have also been indicated. This match shows a similar falling away of momentum by the Welsh team. But if the team analyst had an in-event system of this nature, it would be clear that changes needed to be made,

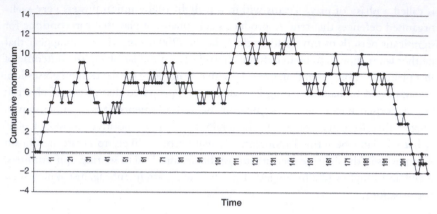

FIGURE 15.13 Cumulative momentum plot for match 1.

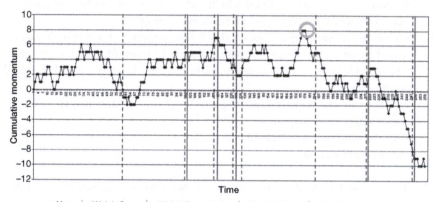

Key | = Welsh Score | = Welsh Perturbation | = English Score | = English Perturbation

Where a value of ±1 equates to 3 consecutive phases of identical classification
(i.e. 3 positive Welsh phases = +1, 3 negative = –1)

FIGURE 15.14 Match 2 – cumulative total phase scores with perturbation indicators.

in spite of the Welsh try 10 mins from the end. The subsequent substitutions might have prevented the final match-winning try by the English team 2 mins from the end. Any coaches in any team match play sports can probably translate these examples to their own sports.

- Reed and Hughes (2006) have considered momentum to be the cumulative effect of phases of play; simply, each phase contributes towards a team's momentum.
- While some evidence has been presented to substantiate these claims, these data serve only to introduce the subject, in a crude and simplistic fashion.
- However, the ability of these methods to portray a great deal of information simply and effectively, while retaining fundamental performance and dynamic information, provides significant advantages over traditional notation methods.

- As we have seen, these data can act as a powerful first point of reference — and with further development may enable:

  - immediate interventions based on momentum profile;
  - profiling.

- Although the published evidence in favour of momentum (psychological or otherwise) is ambiguous at best, coaching resources continue to refer to the subject extensively, thus suggesting that many of our existing notation methods based around scoring and performance indicators are inherently flawed.

- For example, momentum can be gained (and lost) without points or goals being scored, as demonstrated within this paper. This is precisely the reason that the score does not always reflect the state of play, and why the better or stronger team or player does not always win.

- The data presented within this paper serve to introduce the concept and illustrate the potential of dynamic momentum analyses. It is hoped therefore, that future research develops the points raised within this study, enhancing our understanding and procedures of analysis.

So far research on momentum has been mostly limited to individual performance either in basketball, baseball, billiards, squash, tennis and so forth. The question arises whether momentum is transferable to team games such as volleyball or not. Moreover, are sequences of winners and errors, represented as momentum graphs, able to detect differences within the pace of the game?

An outstanding performance from one player such as an ace or a point scoring attack may transfer positive momentum to the rest of the team. Herbert (1991) stated that the seconds before the serve in volleyball are a very critical moment. Uncertainty of one player can develop to a full blown anxiety attack influencing the whole team. He describes this phenomenon from his own point of view as a women's coach as follows:

> The dead-ball period leading up to the whistle that initiates the serve produces, in my opinion, more anxiety than any other time during competition. In all other phases of the game, players are moving, reading, and reacting to the multiple, changing cues that characterize the rapid flow of play during rallies. Their minds are occupied by with the second-by-second demands of keeping up with the pace of the game. But in this one instance before play begins, with players standing in place, waiting for the triggering effect of the serve, negative and unproductive thoughts can invade the receiving team's side of the net.
>
> (Herbert, 1991)

This shows that negative momentum is even more threatening and therefore needs to be avoided in individual sports and even more in team games. Bürger (2009) explored the idea of momentum in volleyball.

15.3.4 Momentum and perturbations in other team sports

Performance profiles are suggested to be a description of a pattern of performance from an analysed team or individual (Hughes *et al.*, 2001). The early work of Sanderson and Way (1979) and Hughes (1986) highlighted that the formation of a database of matches that provide information regarding patterns of play could be considered representative of the subject used to form the database. Through these databases, players and coaches may use the findings to prepare and analyse an individual's performance before playing the match. This is now a formidable tool in a player's or team's preparation and performances (Murray and Hughes, 2001).

Momentum is a physical term that refers to the quantity of motion that an object has and can be defined as 'mass in motion'. Murray and Hughes (2001) were the first to introduce the concept of momentum analysis in squash, and from this analysis, players were able to see their momentum through the match – these data curves were calculated using the rally's ending shot, positive changes for winners, negative changes for errors.

Hughes *et al.*'s (2006a) study of momentum in elite players shows there is conclusive evidence that management of this momentum by elite squash players correlated strongly with the world rankings of the players. Hughes *et al.* (2006a) examined the winners and errors of a number of players' matches from which they calculated each player's momentum profile. It is recognised by most coaches in squash that it is not the last shot in the rally that is the most important, hence the complex rally analyses of Sanderson and Way (1979) and most subsequent researchers (Hughes, 1986; Hughes and Robertson, 1998; Hughes *et al.*, 2006a). By recording the perturbations in rallies, the 'pressure shots' are being entered into the database; it seems logical then that profiles drawn up on these shot data will present more informed ways in which a player puts his or her opponents under pressure, and conversely, how they themselves react to these types of pressure situations.

The function of the investigation by Hughes *et al.* (2006a) was to assemble momentum profiles of elite male and female squash players by using perturbations in performance, and compare these with momentum profiles calculated from the same matches using winners and errors. Information from these profiles will then be compared to those profiles gathered by more traditional means (Murray and Hughes, 2001).

The way in which the players use perturbations within their match play can be identified from the momentum graphs. The more defensive usage of Ricketts and Lincou can be distinguished from their similar graph patterns; whereas the more attacking style of Palmer detects a different pattern that emerges within the momentum graphs. From the case studies, it is assumed that the momentum graphs using perturbations do not illustrate any representation of whether a player won the match, as is identified from the winner error momentum graphs produced from this study and Hughes *et al.*'s (2006a) work on momentum. The case study approach identified that the use of perturbations in calculating momentum, in conjunction with momentum graphs from winners and errors, produces another form of representation of how players perform. It is felt, however, that the sequential nature of the data and the interaction of the players inhibit the normalisation of these data – in so doing the unique 'signature' of each performance would be lost. But, from the perturbation momentum graphs, there is clear evidence that these patterns do complement the traditional methods of creating profiles which should enable coaches to analyse in more depth the performance of players, and their opponents, and to forge future game plans (Figures 15.15 and 15.16).

It was concluded that there was shown to be no comparison between the momentum using winner and errors, to the momentum using perturbations. Nevertheless, after conducting a case study on some of the subjects, indications of usage patterns of perturbations within matches started to emerge from the momentum graphs, which identified specific styles of play. Adding the data from

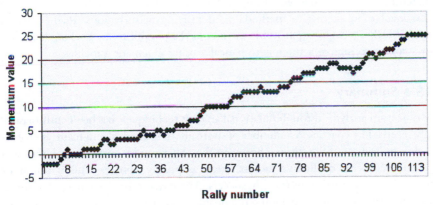

FIGURE 15.15 The winner and error momentum graph of TL in his match with DP.

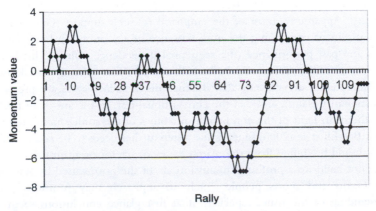

FIGURE 15.16 The perturbations momentum graph of TL in his match with DP.

different matches was deemed to be counterproductive to the true value of using these graphs and also the sequential nature of the data involved. There is evidence to indicate that momentum using perturbations can further the analysis in squash. This study also concluded that the physiological characteristics of physical conditioning has an effect upon the amount of perturbations caused. This could be attributed to a player becoming more urgent towards the end of a match and performing more high-risk shots, as evident through rally lengths imposed with the momentum graphs using perturbations.

Further research into the points of critical momentum shift could be investigated as to whether situations of the match, for example refereeing decisions, caused some critical swings in momentum within matches. This could be analysed qualitatively by interviewing the players and coaches after the match to see whether there were areas of the match where they thought that the momentum shifted and for what reasons. From the results, the interviews could be analysed correspondingly with the momentum graphs to identify and confirm the critical incidents within the match and what created momentum instabilities. An extension of this research could also involve an alternative method for identifying perturbations. Rather than a trained analyst recognising them by eye, it could be possible to use tracking hardware or software to highlight them automatically using kinematic variables.

15.4 Summary

Momentum analysis, through notational analysis techniques, has been enthusiastically received by coaches in a number of sports, both individual and team. It enables a clear indication of the turning points in the match, and is particularly interesting when used with qualitative factors, such as positive phases (rugby union or basketball) or perturbations (squash, soccer). These researches have been developed with the primary aim of expanding the profiling repertoire of performance analysts in their quest of supporting the coaches and their athletes.

The 'hot hands' research is aimed at establishing, or otherwise, that athletes who are in a winning streak are more likely to keep 'winning' – this is still an area of ambiguity. Apparently, most of the empirical research supports Gilovich *et al.*'s (1985) argument concerning the non-existence of a relationship between future success and past performance (the sequential dependence claim). This has been strongly evident in professional basketball and in a few other sports. However, simulation studies demonstrate that fluctuations in success rates are present (the non-stationarity claim), and that the conventional tests in use are often unable to detect them. In light of the conflicting outcomes of the studies presented in this review, Bar-Eli *et al.* (2006) suggest that a step further needs to be taken. First, the debate should be shifted from the search for evidence for or against the existence of the 'hot hand' to a profound discussion about the norms used by statisticians, psychologists and sports people. Such an approach may promote a better understanding of the issue, especially if at first glance conclusions seem to be contradictory. Second, further theoretical progress around the structure of the environment in which a 'hot hand' belief is likely to emerge or change is also needed, as has already been proposed by Burns (2004). An important step forward, then, would be to detect the situational factors that enable us to judge the value of the belief (a fallacy vs. an adaptive strategy) for decision making. Finally, a research strategy that validates the scientific debate's importance to real life decisions in sports (such as betting, allocation decisions, etc.) is required. Such a strategy would allow us to become prescriptive in this research field for many specific situations, sports, or decision-making problems. Koehler and Conley (2003) asserted that no single study could be the last word on this topic. It may well be that hot hands do exist, but their presence is affected by factors related to the nature of the task performed, the level of expertise, or some psychological (or emotional) variable. If streak hitters or shooters do exist, future research should identify the conditions in which they may emerge. On the other hand, if athletic performance is unconditionally not elevated due to past success, obviously the mental techniques (recommended by sport psychologists) commonly used in both training and competitions should be reconsidered.

It should be emphasised that the aims of the researchers in this area are very different to the aims of the researchers in momentum analysis, although involved in very similar concepts, and consequently their analytical procedures and statistical processes are therefore different. These differences in aims have not been understood by some researchers (O'Donoghue and Brown, 2009).

16

PERFORMANCE PROFILING

Mike Hughes, Michael T. Hughes, Nic James,
Julia Wells and Stafford Murray

16.1 Introduction

Recent research has reformed our ideas on reliability, performance indicators and performance profiling in notational analysis – also statistical processes have come under close scrutiny, and have generally been found wanting. These are areas that will continue to develop to the good of the discipline and the confidence of the sports scientist, coach and athlete. If we consider the role of a notational analyst (Figure 16.1, see Hughes, 2004a) in its general sense in relation to the data that the analyst is collecting, processing and analysing, then there are a number of steps that will be required to facilitate the production of a performance profile:

1 defining performance indicators;
2 determining which are important;
3 establishing the reliability of the data collected;
4 ensuring that enough data have been collected to define stable performance profiles;
5 comparing sets of data;
6 modelling performances.

The recent advances made into the research and application of the mathematical and statistical techniques commonly used and required for these processes will be discussed and evaluated in this chapter and examples of different ideas of how to present the performance profiles will be shown.

16.2 Processes in creating performance profiles

16.2.1 Performance indicators

A performance indicator is a selection, or combination, of action variables that aims to define some or all aspects of a performance. Analysts and coaches use performance indicators to assess the performance of an individual, a team, or elements of a team. They are sometimes used in a comparative way, with opponents, other athletes or peer groups of athletes or teams, but often they are used in isolation as a measure of the performance of a team or individual alone.

Through an analysis of game structures and the performance indicators used in recent research in performance analysis, Hughes and Bartlett (2002) defined basic rules in the application of performance indicators to any sports. In every case, success is relative, either to your opposition, or to previous performances of the team or individual.

To enable a full and objective interpretation of the data from the analysis of a performance, it is necessary to compare the collected data to aggregated data

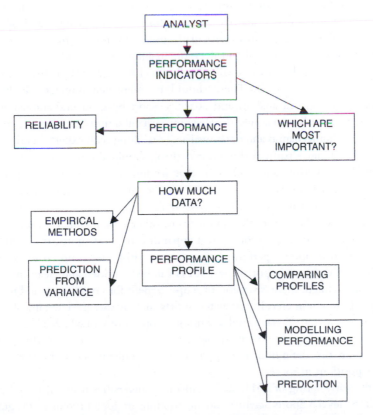

FIGURE 16.1 A schematic chart of the steps required in moving from data gathering to producing a performance profile.

of a peer group of teams, or individuals, that compete at an appropriate standard. In addition, any analysis of the distribution of actions across the playing surface must be normalised with respect to the total distribution of actions across the area.

Performance indicators, expressed as non-dimensional ratios, have the advantage of being independent of any units that are used; furthermore, they are implicitly independent of any one variable. They also allow, as in the example of bowling in cricket (see Hughes and Bartlett, 2002), an insight into differences between performers that can be obscure in the raw data. The use of non-dimensional analysis is common in fluid dynamics, which offers empirical clues to the solution of multivariate problems that cannot be solved mathematically. Sport is even more complex, the result of interacting human behaviours; to apply simplistic analyses of raw sports data can be highly misleading. Current research (Hughes *et al.*, 2001; James *et al.*, 2005; O'Donoghue, 2005) is examining how normative profiles are established – how much data are required to reliably define a profile and how this varies with the different types and natures of the data involved in any analysis profile. This area is discussed in detail later.

Many of the most important aspects of team performance cannot be 'teased out' by biomechanists or match analysts working alone – a combined research approach is needed (Figure 16.2). This is particularly important for information processing – both in movement control and decision making. We should move rapidly to incorporate into such analyses qualitative biomechanical indicators that contribute to a successful movement. These should be identified interactively by bio-mechanists, notational analysts and coaches, sport-by-sport and movement-by-movement, and validated against detailed biomechanical measurements in controlled conditions. Biomechanists and notational analysts, along with experts in other sports science disciplines – particularly motor control, should also seek to agree on, and measure, those performance indicators that are important from this perspective.

This could help to clarify, for example, whether the movement variability, which has been measured in such skills as basketball shooting and cricket batting, is a function of the behaviour of the opponents or other team members or due to noise in measurements or the motor control apparatus. In most sports, it is found that the perceived important performance indicators (PIs) vary from coach to coach. Therefore, if the most important sets of PIs can be identified and clear operational definitions defined, there is significant scope/benefit for consultancy and research, particularly in commercially orientated sports such as soccer. The aim of a study by Hughes *et al.* (2012) was to utilise a unique opportunity in which a large number of performance analysts were available, collectively, to discuss the problem surrounding the definition and application of performance indicators for the various positions in soccer.

In the early spring of 2011, staff from nine universities from all over Europe, brought 51 level 3 Sports Science students to Hungary for an Intensive Programme in Performance Analysis of Sport (IPPAS). The 12 staff, all experts in performance analysis (PA), were also supplemented by three more experts from different

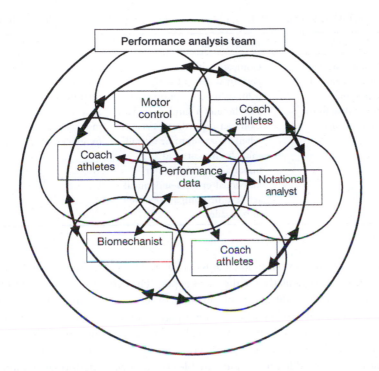

FIGURE 16.2 A digital systems approach to the data sharing that the interactive commercial systems have enabled for performance analysts working with coaches and athletes.

Source: Hughes, 2004a.

commercial PA software companies from Scotland, Europe and South Africa. The 'experts' had a total of over 200 years of experience of PA between them, ranging from 32 years to 3 years. The most experienced 'experts' ($N = 5$) acted as mentors, introducing the area, defining the aims and managing the groups. The remaining staff ($N = 10$) and the 51 students were distributed as evenly as possible across seven groups; the aim of each group was to define the key PIs for one of the positions in soccer. The positions used were: goalkeepers; full backs; centre backs; holding midfield; attacking midfield; wide midfield; and strikers.

In conclusion, seven general classifications of positions in a soccer team, and respective sets of key performance indicators (KPIs), were defined for each of these classifications within five category sets:

- physiological
- tactical
- technical – defending
- technical – attacking and
- psychological.

TABLE 16.1 Categorisation of the application of different performance indicators in games

Match classification	Biomechanical	Technical/Tactical
Always compare with opponents' data and, where possible, with aggregated data from peer performances.	Compare with previous performances and with team members, opponents and those of a similar standard. Consider normalising data when a maximum or overall value both exists and is important or when inter-individual or intra-individual across-time comparisons are to be made.	Always normalise the action variables with the total frequency of that action variable or, in some instances, the total frequency of all actions.

The cumulative discussions found that KPIs differed from position to position within the team, most particularly for the goalkeeper. The KPIs for the outfield players were similar in form, differing only in their order of importance. This enabled a 'generic' set of skills required for outfield players in soccer, bearing in mind that the importance of these specific skills will differ from position to position.

For the different types of games considered, it has become clear that the classification of the different action variables being used as performance indicators follow rules that transcend the different sports. These are summarised in Table 16.1. Most of the research community in performance analysis have not followed these simple rules to date. The utility of performance analysis could be considerably enhanced if its practitioners agreed and implemented such rules in the future.

16.2.2 Analysis of the relative importance of performance indicators

Defining performance indicators is based on prior knowledge and research of the effect of relevant factors on relevant dependent variables. However, in many areas, defining PIs remains difficult to do accurately. This is due to the complexity of the behaviour of interest as well as the large number of relevant factors. Many factors are often difficult to define and measurements used may be of limited reliability and validity. To be able to comment appropriately (accurately and relevantly) on a given sport, it is necessary to know exactly which PIs are relevant to the results. Coaches and, to some extent, notational analysts have traditionally relied upon experience and their own ideas about their sport. This has led to a huge spectrum of PIs being used in some sports, particularly soccer. But as databases of multiple sporting events, such as the rugby or the soccer world cups or repeated grand slam events in tennis, are compiled by comprehensive and sophisticated computerised analyses, then comparative evaluation of PIs should be possible – using the outcomes of the tournaments as a correlating factor. Two recent pieces of research have given a starting point in the methodology to assess the relative importance of PIs.

Luhtanen *et al.* (2002) analysed offensive and defensive variables of field players and goalkeepers in the EURO 2000 soccer tournament and related the results to the final team ranking in the tournament. All matches ($N = 31$) of the EURO 1996 and 2000 were recorded using video and analysed by three trained observers with a computerised match analysis system. The written definitions of each event (pass, receiving, run with the ball, shot, scoring trial, defending against scoring trial, interception and tackle) were applied in analysing the matches.

The quantitative (number of executions) and qualitative (percentage of success-ful executions) game performance variables were as follows: passes, receivings, runs with ball, scoring trials, interceptions, tackles, goals and goalkeeper's savings. The total playing times were recorded and the game performance results were standardised for 90 minutes' playing time. Team ranking in each variable (quantita-tive and qualitative) was used as a new variable. The final ranking orders in the EURO 1996 and EURO 2000 tournaments were explained by calculating the rank correlation coefficients between team ranking in the tournament and ranking in the following variables: ranking of ball possession in distance, passes, receiving, runs with the ball, shots, interceptions and tackles. Selected quantitative and qualitative sum variables were calculated using ranking order of all obtained variables, only defensive variables and only offensive variables. The means and standard devia-tions of the game performance variables were calculated. Ranking order in each variable was constructed. Spearman's correlation coefficients (95 per cent confidence interval (CI) were calculated between all ranking variables describing game per-formance. In this way the relative importance of the variables was assessed. Although this research was orientated towards explaining the success of the top teams, and did not explore different combinations of PIs, nor did they non-dimensionalise the variables, the methodology used would seem one way of ordering the huge spectrum of 'would-be' performance indicators that appear in the literature.

O'Donoghue *et al.* (2003) and O'Donoghue and Williams (2004) used a variety of statistical, predictive and modelling techniques in attempts to anticipate the results in the 2002 World Cup in soccer and the 2003 World Cup in rugby union. Some of their statistical techniques also point the way to future research being able to perhaps quantify objectively the relative importance of the PIs that determine success in a sport. Each factor as well as the match score was represented as a difference between the superior team and the inferior team. They used very simple per-formance variables, that were not measured in-match as in the Luhtanen *et al.* paper, just the world ranking, the distance travelled to the tournament and the amount of rest between matches. Among the many techniques used in these two papers, O'Donoghue *et al.* used multiple linear regression and binary linear regression. Using large databases to construct their predictive models, they created equations in which the relative size of the coefficients of the respective variables in these equations denote their relative importance. These methods have certain problems associated with them but, given the large databases of in-match analysis variables that are now available at many of the centres of research in performance analysis of sport throughout the world, this methodology would seem to point to an even better way to assess quantitatively the relative importance of PIs in any sport.

16.2.3 Reliability

It is vital that the reliability of a data gathering system is demonstrated clearly and in a way that is compatible with the intended analyses of the data. The data must be tested in the same way and to the same depth that they will be processed in the subsequent analyses. In general, the work of Bland and Altman (1986) has transformed the attitude of sport scientists to testing reliability; can similar techniques be applied to the non-parametric data that most notational analysis studies generate? There are also a number of questions that inherently re-occur in these forms of data-gathering.

Analysing 72 research papers recently published under the banner of notational analysis, Hughes *et al.* (2002a) found that 70 per cent did not report any reliability study and a large proportion of the remaining used questionable processes given the recent ideas in reliability testing in sports science (Atkinson and Nevill, 1998). In some cases the reliability studies were executed on summary data, and the system was then assumed to be reliable for all of the other types of more detailed data analyses that were produced. The most common form of data analysis in notation studies is to record frequencies of actions and their respective positions on the performance area; these are then presented as sums or totals in each respective area. What are the effects of cumulative errors nullifying each other, so that the overall totals appear less incorrect than they actually are?

Hughes *et al.* (2002a) suggested that the following conditions should be applied.

- The data should initially retain their sequentiality and be cross-checked item against item.
- Any data processing should be carefully examined as these processes mask original observation errors.
- The reliability test should be examined to the same depth of analysis as the subsequent data processing, rather than being performed on just some of the summary data.
- Careful definition of the variables involved in the percentage calculation is necessary to avoid confusion in the mind of the reader, and also to prevent any compromise of the reliability study.
- It is recommended that, as a measure of the differences between the medians or means, the calculation of % differences is based upon

$$\sum \frac{\text{mod}\left(V_1 - V_2\right)}{V_{mean}} \times 100\%$$

(where V_1 and V_2 are variables, V_{mean} their mean, mod is short for modulus and Σ means 'sum of').

- That non-parametric tests, such as Mann-Whitney, Kruskal Wallis and χ^2 be used to measure the respective variances of these data about their respective medians (or means).

16.2.4 Establishing the stability of performance profiles

16.2.4.1 Empirical methods

It is an implicit assumption in notational analysis that, in presenting a performance profile of a team or an individual, a 'normative profile' has been achieved. Inherently this implies that all the variables that are to be analysed and compared have all stabilised. Most researchers assume that this will have happened if they analyse enough performances. But how many is enough? In the literature there are large differences in sample sizes. Hughes, Evans and Wells (2001) trawled through some of the analyses in recent research to show the differences (Table 16.2). They suggested that there must be some way of assessing how the data (PIs) within a study are stabilising. Many research papers in match analysis present data taken from an arbitrarily selected number of performances.

The nature of the data themselves will also effect how many performances are required – five matches may be enough to analyse passing in field hockey; would you need ten to analyse crossing or perhaps 30 for shooting? *Not the size of the mean but the variance!*

The way in which the data are analysed also will effect the stabilisation of performance means – data that are analysed across a multi-cell representation of the playing area will require far more performances to stabilise than data that

TABLE 16.2 Some examples of sample sizes for profiling in sport

Research	Sport	N (matches for profile)
Reep and Benjamin (1969)	Soccer	3,216
Eniseler et al. (2000)	Soccer	4
Larsen et al. (2000)	Soccer	4
Hughes et al. (1988)	Soccer	8 (16 teams)
Tiryaky et al. (1997)	Soccer	4 and 3 (2 groups)
Hughes (1986)	Squash	12, 9 & 6 – 3 groups
Hughes and Knight (1995)	Squash	400 rallies
Hughes and Williams (1988)	Rugby Union	5
Smyth et al. (2001)	Rugby Union	5 and 5
Blomqvist et al. (1998b)	Badminton	5
O'Donoghue (2001)	Badminton	16, 17, 17, 16, 15
Hughes and Clarke (1995)	Tennis	400 rallies
O'Donoghue and Ingram (2001)	Tennis	1328<rallies<4300 (8 groups)

are analysed on overall performance descriptors (e.g. shots per match). It is misleading to test the latter and then go on to analyse the data divided into further positional detail.

Hughes *et al.* (2001) suggested a practical way of examining whether a true performance profile has reached stable means: calculations of percentage variance from the 'end mean' were determined and then plotted appropriately. From this study the following conclusions were made:

- This method clearly demonstrated that those studies assuming that 4, 6 or 8 matches or performances were enough for a normative profile, without resorting to this sort of test, are clearly subject to possible flaws. The number of matches required for a normal profile of a subject population to be reached is dependent upon the nature of the data and, in particular, the nature of the performers.
- The main problem associated with any primary study aiming at establishing previously unrecorded 'normal' performance profiles remains reliability and accuracy. Any future studies that proclaim data as a performance profile should provide supportive evidence that the variable means are stabilising. A percentage error plot showing the mean variation as each match/player is analysed is one such technique. This can be adapted to different sports when analysing profiles/templates of performance.

For the working performance analyst the results provide an estimate of the minimum number of matches to profile an opponent's rally-end play. While the results may be limited, the methodology of using graphical plots of cumulative means in attempting to establish templates of performance has been served.

16.2.4.2 Confidence intervals

The procedure outlined above is expensive in terms of time when collecting data for the first time and is limited in its applicability in many cases due to fluctuations in factors such as team changes, maturation and the fact that some performances never stabilise. James *et al.* (2005) suggested an alternative approach whereby the specific estimates of population means are calculated from the sample data through confidence limits (CLs). CLs represent upper and lower values between which the true (population) mean is likely to fall based on the observed values collected. Calculated CLs naturally change as more data are collected, typically resulting in the confidence interval (upper CL minus lower CL) decreasing. Confidence intervals (CIs) were therefore suggested to be more appropriate as performance guides compared to using mean values. Using a fixed value appears to be too constrained due to potential confounding variables that typically affect performance, making prescriptive targets untenable.

From a theoretical perspective, James *et al.* argued that the use of CIs can also add significance to the judgement of the predictive potential of a data set, i.e.

whether enough data have been collected to allow a reasonable estimation. For their investigation a criterion was formulated to test the rate of change of the CI for stability. Initially, 95 per cent CIs were calculated for each performance indicator as soon as enough match data had been collected ($N = 2$) and each time more data were added the new CI was calculated. This meant that CIs could be constructed for each performance indicator after 2, 3 and ... N matches respectively. Behavioural frequencies fell outside the 95 per cent CI more often for small data sets and less often as the data set increased. However, this was inevitable as any measure related to the mean of a data set becomes progressively more resistant to change as the data set increases.

The data in Table 16.3 are an example of this type of presentation; it is a very useful way of assessing the stability of an analyst's data. I feel that the more this method is used then the more easily will analysts be able to interpret the CIs in relation to the experimental goals of their research or consultancy work.

16.2.4.3 Normative profiles of sports performance (O'Donoghue, 2005)

Performance indicators in sport are not stable properties of individual competitors or teams and a single athlete's (or team's) performance will vary from match to match. For this reason, Hughes *et al.* (2001) developed a technique for determining 'normative profiles in performance analysis'. This paper proposes an alternative technique that represents not only the typical performance of a team or individual but also the spread of performances. The technique also relates the set of PIs for a team or individual to normative data for a relevant population of teams or individuals. This provides a useful means of interpreting sports performance data. Grand Slam singles tennis is used as an example of the application of the proposed technique for determining a normative profile of a team's or individual's performance. It is recognised that the mean value for each PI within the typical performance is critically important information that should be supported by rather than replaced by percentile bandings.

Figure 16.3 shows that Venus Williams's mean first service speed was consistently above the 95th percentile; her highest 75 per cent of performances for this PI are in the highest 5 per cent for the whole sample. Her mean second serve speed was not as high in relation to our sample of 143 elite female players. The percentage of points won when a second serve was required, the percentage of double faults played and the percentage points where she went to the net are PIs where her inter-quartile range was equivalent to the spread of values for 45 per cent of the sample of 143 female players (a difference of nine 5-percentile bands between the player's lower and upper quartile values). This indicates that performance with respect to these performance indicators was erratic, close to the inter-quartile range of the whole sample.

This paper introduced a new method of normative performance profiling for sport, which has been illustrated in Figure 16.3. O'Donoghue (2005) stated that

TABLE 16.3 Mean profiles and 95 per cent confidence limits for the positional clusters of prop, hooker and lock

	Prop (N = 3)★★★★			Hooker (N = 1)			Lock (N = 4)★★		
	Mean	+CL	−CL	Mean	+CL	−CL	Mean	+CL	−CL
Successful tackles	4.01	4.96	3.06	4.25	5.59	2.91	5.73	6.81	4.64
Unsuccessful tackles	0.73	1.12	0.33	0.51	1.01	0	0.76	1.15	0.37
Successful carries	4.25	5.32	3.18	3.51	5.37	1.66	2.20	2.81	1.60
Unsuccessful carries	0.23	0.44	0.01	0.40	0.80	0	0.03	0.08	0
Successful passes	1.76	2.46	1.06	0.87	1.68	0.06	1.23	1.76	0.69
Unsuccessful passes	0.47	0.98	0	0	0	0	0.20	0.33	0.07
Handling errors	0.33	0.56	0.09	0.27	0.69	0	0.68	0.94	0.41
Normal penalties	0.68	0.97	0.39	0.40	0.79	0	1.12	1.47	0.77
Yellow cards	0.05	0.11	0	0.08	0.24	0	0.09	0.20	0
Tries scored	0.02	0.07	0	0.10	0.31	00	0	0	0
Successful throw-ins	–	–	–	9.76	11.85	7.66	–	–	–
Unsuccessful throw-ins	–	–	–	2.94	4.09	1.79	–	–	–
Successful lineout takes	–	–	–	–	–	–	4.05	4.83	3.28
Unsuccessful lineout takes	–	–	–	–	–	–	0.43	0.71	0.15
Successful restart takes	–	–	–	–	–	–	0.65	0.91	0.39
Unsuccessful restart takes	–	–	–	–	–	–	0.59	0.90	0.27

Note: ★p <.05 ★★p <.01 ★★★ p <.001.

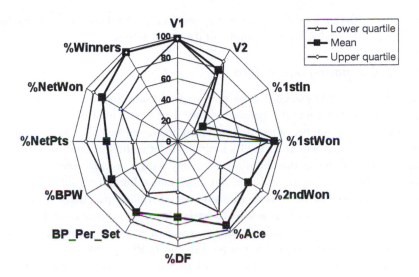

FIGURE 16.3 A normative performance profile for Venus Williams (26 matches).

the method has four key advantages over the technique proposed by Hughes *et al.* (2001). First, the technique is concise allowing all of the performance indicators to be displayed on a single radar chart. A disadvantage in how the technique of Hughes *et al.* (2001) has been used is that a chart is produced for each performance indicator showing how the evolving mean changes as matches are added. For example, Hughes *et al.* (2001) describe an example for women's rugby union where six such charts were used. While each graph relates the difference between the evolving and eventual (cumulative) mean to the stated limits of error, a single table could show how many matches were required for each performance indicator to stabilise. The second advantage is that the technique proposed here represents the mean as well as the variability for each performance indicator, whereas the technique of Hughes *et al.* (2001) focused exclusively on the mean. This is an important advantage as variability is a recognised part of sports performance, effecting work-rate of players in team games (O'Donoghue, 2004) as well as tactical aspects (Wells *et al.*, 2004). The third advantage is that the performance indicators are related to performance norms for the population of interest. The proposed method of producing a normative performance profile allows the relative level and consistency of each performance indicator to be interpreted. The technique of Hughes *et al.* (2001) does not relate performance indicators to population norms and one could argue that it should not include the word 'normative' in its name. A fourth advantage is that the technique can be tailored to compare the typical performances of different performers or to compare different types of performance by the same performer.

The method and output are excellent; the only drawback that O'Donoghue does not discuss is that you need a large database on which to perform these types of analyses, which is not always possible for the working analyst. But, we now have three different methods of enquiring empirically into the stability of the data in your profiles and different examples of data presentation.

16.2.5 Comparing sets of data

Hughes *et al.* (2001) extended their survey of reliability methods used in recent research to also examine the types of statistical processes used in the analyses of data in a selected number of research papers in notational analysis. The subsequent data analyses (see Table 16.4) used a multiplicity of techniques but there were a large number of studies that did not present any statistics to compare sets of data. Those labelled 'not specific' did cite probability values, but did not mention which statistical process had been used. In a number of studies, parametric techniques were used with data that were non-parametric; although, in some cases, the means of the data sets appeared ordinal, they were often means of nominal data and therefore the use of a parametric test put the conclusions at risk.

There are many similarities in the nature of the data generated by experiments in performance analysis of sport. Parametric statistical techniques are often applied to notational analysis data, either through ignorance, or lack of availability of the relevant software. Correlation was the most common technique used in confirming reliability, when a technique was used. Bland and Altmann (1986) demonstrate unequivocally what a waste of time it was using correlation to test for differences between sets of data that have similar distributions – for example, all reliability studies.

Hughes *et al.* (2002a) recommended the processes shown in Figure 16.4 for comparing sets of data, depending upon the nature of these data. Although Atkinson and Nevill (1998) have produced a definitive summary of reliability techniques in sports medicine, the only attempt to make recommendations in the use of techniques in performance analysis for solving some of the common

TABLE 16.4 An analysis of the different statistical processes used in subsequent data analyses in some randomly selected performance analysis research papers

Statistical processes for data analysis	No.	(%)
Chi-square	21	29
None	19	26
Not specific	12	17
t-test	8	11
ANOVA	5	7
Factor analysis	2	3
ANCOVA	1	1
Mann-Whitney	1	1
Hotelling T^2 test	1	1
Wilcoxon	1	1
Bivariate analysis	1	1
Total	72	100

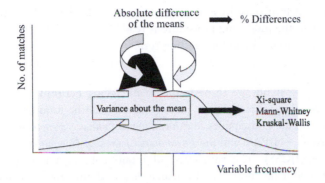

FIGURE 16.4 Processes for comparing sets of data.

problems associated with these types of data was that by Nevill *et al.* (2002). This is written very much from a statistician's point of view, particularly extolling the virtues of the high power software GLIM. They concluded that investigating categorical differences in discrete data using traditional parametric tests of significance (e.g. ANOVA, based on the continuous symmetric normal distribution) is inappropriate. More appropriate statistical methods were promoted based on two key discrete probability distributions, the Poisson and binomial distributions. In the opinion of Nevill *et al.* (2002), the first approach is based on the classic χ^2 test of significance (both the goodness-of-fit test and the test of independence). The second approach adopts a more contemporary method based on log-linear and logit models using the statistical software GLIM. Although investigating relatively simple one-way and two-way comparisons in categorical data, both approaches result in very similar conclusions, which is comforting to the 'old guard' notational analysts who have been using χ^2 for the last few decades. However, as soon as more complex models and higher-order comparisons are required, the approach based on log-linear models is shown to be more effective. Indeed, when investigating factors and categorical differences associated with binomial or binary response variables, such as the proportion of winners when attempting decisive shots in squash or the proportion of goals scored from all shots in association football, logit models become the only realistic methods available. Nevill *et al.* concluded that with the help of such log-linear and logit models, greater insight into the underlying differences or mechanisms in sport performance can be achieved.

16.2.6 *Presenting performance profiles*

The modelling of competitive sport is an informative analytic technique because it directs the attention of the modeller to the critical aspects of data which delineate successful performance. The modeller searches for an underlying signature of sport performance which is a reliable predictor of future sport behaviour. Stochastic models have not yet, to our knowledge, been used further to investigate sport at the behavioural level of analysis. However, the modelling procedure is readily applicable to other sports and could lead to useful and interesting results.

(Franks and McGarry, 1996, p. 363)

Some exciting trends are to be found in modelling performances and match play, using a variety of techniques; many examples can be found in the journals now available in these disciplines, the *International Journal of Performance Analysis of Sport* (electronic – eIJPAS) and the *International Journal of Computers in Sport Science* (electronic – eIJCSS). The simplest, and traditional, form is using empirical methods of producing enough performance data to define a performance profile at that particular level. Some researchers are extending the use of these forms of data bases to attempt to predict performances; stochastic probabilities, neural networks and fuzzy logic have been used, singly or in combinations, to produce the outputs. McGarry and Perl (2004) presented a good overview of models in sports contest that embraces most of these techniques. So far results have been disappointing in practical terms. Early research of modelling in sport includes Mosteller (1979), who set out guidelines when he developed a predictive model, and these ideas are eminently practical and many researchers in the area use these, or modifications of these to delimit their models.

Alexander *et al.* (1988) used the mathematical theory of probability in the game of squash. Mathematical modelling can describe the main features of the game of squash and can reveal strategic patterns to the player. Squash is an example of a Markov chain mathematical structure – a similar technique was used later by McGarry and Franks (1996c). Alexander *et al.* went on to recommend practical strategies at 8–8 in a game, in calling to finish on 9 or 10, the choice being that of the player receiving serve, based on these relative probabilities of winning rallies. This is one of the few practical outcomes from this form of modelling.

Other attempts to model team games (Ladany and Machol, 1977) theoretically have tended to founder upon the complexity of the numbers of variables involved and, at that time, did not base their predictions upon sound databases. The advent of computer notation systems has enabled the creation of large databases of sports performances in different sports; these in turn have helped the development of a number of different techniques in modelling performance in sport. These will be discussed under the following generic headings:

*   Empirical modelling
*   Stochastic modelling
*   Momentum
*   Perturbations – dynamic systems
*   Statistical techniques
*   Artificial intelligence

    –   Expert system
    –   Neural networks

16.2.6.1 Empirical models

Hughes (1985) established a considerable database on different standards of squash players. He examined and compared the differences in patterns of play between recreational players, country players and nationally ranked players, using the computerised notational analysis system he had developed. The method involved the digitisation of all the shots and court positions, and these were entered via the QWERTY keyboard. Hughes (1986) was able then to define models of tactical patterns of play, and inherently technical ability, at different playing levels in squash. Although racket developments have affected the lengths of the rallies, and there have been a number of rule changes in the scoring systems in squash, these tactical models still apply to the game today. This study was replicated, with a far more thorough methodology, for the women's game by Hughes *et al.* (2001).

Fuller (1990) developed and designed a Netball Analysis System and focused on game modelling from a database of 28 matches in the 1987 World Netball Championships. There were three main components to the research – to develop a notation and analysis system, to record performance, and to investigate the prescience of performance patterns that would distinguish winners from losers. The system could record how each tactical entry started; the player involved and the court area through which the ball travelled; the reason for each ending; and an optional comment. The software produced the data according to shooting analysis; centre pass analysis; loss of possession; player profiles; and circle feeding. Fuller's (1990) intention of modelling play was to determine the routes that winning, drawing and losing teams took and to identify significantly different patterns. From the results, Fuller was able to differentiate between the performances of winning and losing teams. The differences were both technical and tactical.

The research was an attempt to model winning performance in elite netball and more research is needed in terms of the qualitative aspects, i.e. how are more shooting opportunities created? The model should be used to monitor performance over a series of matches, not on one-off performances.

Treadwell, Lyons and Potter (1991) suggested that match analysis in rugby union and other field games has centred on game modelling and that their research was concerned with using the data to predict game contents of rugby union matches. They found that clear physiological rhythms and strategic patterns emerged. They also found that at elite level it was possible to identify key 'windows', i.e. vital 'moments of chronological expectancy where strategic expediency needs to be imposed'. It appears that international matches and successful teams generate distinctive rhythms of play that can exhibit a team fingerprint or 'heartbeat'. Lyons (1988) had previously analysed 10 years of Home Nations Championship matches to build up a database, and from this was able to predict actions for a match to limits of within three passes and two kicks.

16.2.6.2 Examples

One of the best ways of learning about presentation of the data that make up a performance profile is to read the ideas that other researchers and analysts have used before – stealing these ideas is fine if you reference them (sound research), but not so good if you omit from where you got your ideas (plagiarism).

Soccer

Example 1

The principle of performance feedback can be at either team level (as below), or positional level, e.g. all midfield players, or at the individual level. The main issue, however, irrespective of who the feedback is aimed at, is recognising that performance naturally varies between matches and so an unusual value obtained from one match does not necessarily indicate a poor or exceptionally good performance. It is far better, and more convincing, if trends are recorded over time. Figure 16.5 indicates that player D has not been very successful in his aerial challenges compared to the other centre backs (data taken from Taylor *et al.*, 2004).

This performance is over six matches, which is thought to be a reasonable number of matches for a performance to be considered representative of typical performance, although this number is dependent upon the typical variability of the performance between matches (Hughes *et al.*, 2001). Indeed every match is a unique event and therefore any collection of matches is deemed to be a random (stochastic) sample of a population of matches (all matches pertaining to the team or teams being analysed). Thus, any small sample has the potential of not accurately reflecting the variability inherent in all of the performances of a team or teams.

Presenting a team's match performance relative to previous performances allows the coach to see which aspects of the games were unusual very easily. To illustrate this procedure, ten matches for a British professional soccer team were analysed

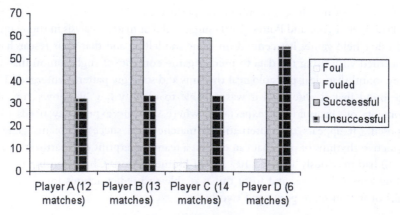

FIGURE 16.5 A comparison of aerial challenge outcomes for four centre backs playing for a professional British soccer team.

(post-event) using the Noldus 'Observer Video Pro' behavioural measurement software package (Noldus Information Technology, 1995). Thirteen performance indicators were arbitrarily selected from a study by Taylor *et al.* (2005) and the data for the tenth game transformed relative to the previous nine matches (see Jones *et al.*, 2004b for comprehensive details of this). The formula for this transformation is shown in equation 1 (taken from Jones *et al.*, 2004b):

$$\text{Transformed score} = 15 * \left(\frac{x - \text{Mdn}}{\text{IQR}} \right) + 50 \tag{16.1}$$

Where x = the PI value for the tenth match, *Mdn* = the median and IQR = the inter-quartile range for the previous nine matches.

While the calculations are relatively simple, the theory behind the above transformation is a little more complex (see Jones *et al.*, 2004b and James *et al.*, 2005 for full details). The resultant form chart (Figure 16.6) is quite simple to interpret with a standardised PI value of 50, indicating performance at the same level as previous matches. Standardised values greater than 65 indicate performance was above the seventy-fifth percentile and less than 35 is below the twenty-fifth percentile.

Example 2

In this respect, the study of Hughes and Probert (2006) was innovative in two ways:

i)   by analysing the exact technical requirements of each position;
ii) by using qualitative data within a quantitative system.

The aim of this study was to analyse every individual's technical ability that competed in the European Football Championships of 2004. This measure was based on a subjectively drawn continuum that analyses a player's technical movement throughout the game. It was investigated whether technical differences occur between player positions and between successful and unsuccessful teams.

Data were gathered from matches within the European Championships of 2004, which were held in Portugal. This tournament was chosen as it provided an ideal environment for a comparison to be made between elite-level players competing in an elite sporting environment. Data were collected using a hand notation system, in the form of a table. The table consisted of six columns: player number; technique performed; technique rating; pitch position; time of action; and any outcome (if applicable).

Figures 16.7 to 16.10 respectively show the frequency distribution of players' actions across the seven games, according to their positional role.

Figure 16.11 shows a frequency distribution for the total number of actions performed across each position. It shows how midfielders consistently have the highest frequency count, except for heading, tackling and throw-ins, all of which are displayed most frequently by the defenders.

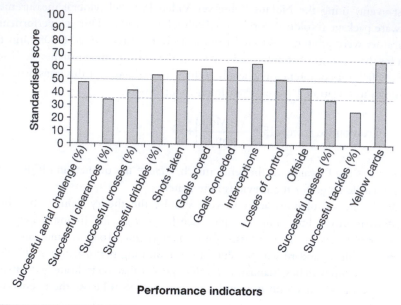

Performance indicator	Actual match value	Median (9 matches)
Successful aerial challenges (%)	50%	52%
Successful clearances (%)	85%	93%
Successful crosses (%)	25%	29%
Successful dribbles (%)	76%	73%
Shots taken	18	13
Goals scored	4	2
Goals conceded	3	2
Interceptions	23	15
Losses of control	10	10
Offside	0	2
Successful passes (%)	70%	75%
Successful tackles (%)	58%	75%
Yellow cards	3	1

FIGURE 16.6 Form chart of the tenth match compared against performances from the previous nine matches for a professional British soccer team.

The Chi-squared test of independence indicates that significant differences occur between the frequency distributions of defenders and midfielders ($p < 0.05$), defenders and strikers ($p < 0.05$) and between midfielders and strikers ($p < 0.05$).

This trend could perhaps be explained due to the varying number of subjects analysed and the varying patterns of play used. In order to get a more accurate representation, a mean distribution of the quality of techniques performed per position will be more accurate.

Displaying a mean technique rating per position (Figure 16.12) shows a distinct deviation from the overall frequency distribution. From not being the highest ranked in any variable in Figure 16.11, strikers are now found to be the highest ranked in receiving the ball (0.95), running with the ball (1.29), dribbling (1.3) and in the execution of free kicks (1.0). Defenders, however, still rank highest for heading the ball (1.10), tackling (1.28) and now also shooting (0.71). Midfielders have, however, retained their high rank for both passing (0.95) and crossing (0.90).

The reported p values from the Chi-squared test of independence report that no differences between the average quality of ratings across playing positions are significant ($p > 0.05$).

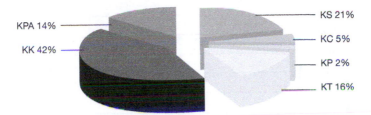

FIGURE 16.7 Distribution of goalkeepers' on the ball actions.

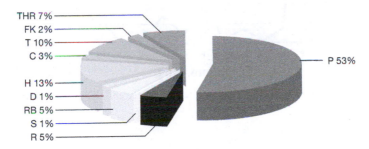

FIGURE 16.8 Distribution of defenders' on the ball actions.

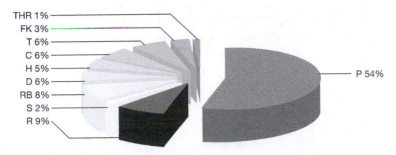

FIGURE 16.9 Distribution of midfielders' on the ball actions.

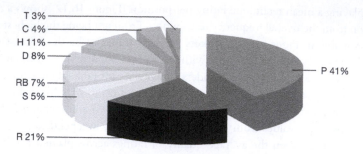

FIGURE 16.10 Distribution of strikers' on the ball actions.

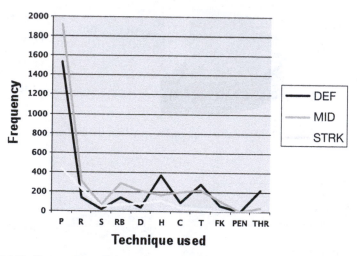

FIGURE 16.11 Comparison of the techniques used between defenders, midfielders and strikers.

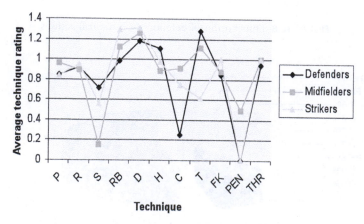

FIGURE 16.12 Average quality rating of techniques used across playing positions.

Distribution of technique ratings across player position for selected performance variables

Passing

All positions show a trend of +1 and 0 rated passes being the most frequent. Apart from +2 rated passes, all other ratings show a low frequency of occurrence.

A significant difference was found between the passing distribution of defenders and midfielders ($p < 0.05$) and defenders and strikers ($p < 0.05$). No significant difference was found between midfielders and strikers ($p > 0.05$).

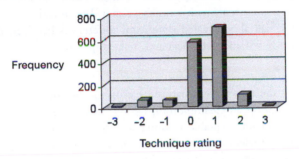

FIGURE 16.13 Distribution of defenders' passing technique ratings.

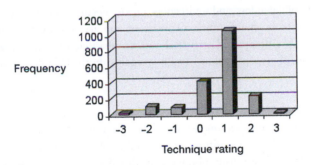

FIGURE 16.14 Distribution of midfielders' passing technique ratings.

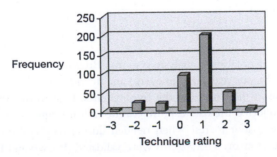

FIGURE 16.15 Distribution of strikers' passing technique ratings.

Shooting

The frequency distributions for shooting were far more diverse than for passing. More data can be seen at the two extreme ends of the continuum, especially for midfielders and strikers. A Chi-squared test revealed that significant differences do occur between defenders and midfielders ($p < 0.05$) and defenders and strikers ($p < 0.05$).

Heading

Although defenders have the highest frequency of headers, they also are the most consistent with very few headers possessing a minus rating. Strikers' headers appear to be far more inconsistent, with a much greater data spread.

Heading the ball also revealed significant differences between defenders and midfielders ($p < 0.05$) and defenders and strikers ($p < 0.05$).

Crossing

The data show the inconsistent nature of crossing the ball across for all playing positions at the European Championships 2004. All positions show occurrences of both excellent and unacceptable crossing technique on a number of occasions. Defenders and midfielders ($p < 0.05$) and defenders and strikers ($p < 0.05$) again showed significant differences between the sets of data.

Tackling

The majority of defenders' and midfielders' tackles occur at either +1 or +2. Strikers' tackles appear to be much more inconsistent and are positioned right across the ratings scale. A Chi-squared statistical test emphasised this by revealing significant differences between strikers' tackling against both defenders and midfielders ($p < 0.05$).

Receiving the ball

Receiving the ball shows a much greater distribution of the data across technique ratings between all player positions, compared to other performance variables. No significant difference was found between midfielders and strikers running with the ball ratings ($p > 0.05$). Significant differences were, however, found between defenders and midfielders ($p < 0.05$) and defenders and strikers ($p < 0.05$).

Example 3

Squash

Two computerised notational analysis systems (Brown and Hughes, 1995, and Murray *et al.*, 1998), one real-time (in event) and the other lapsed time (post event) were used to collect the data from the five matches. Due to the amount of data that was being collected the data capture was done from digital video recordings. This allowed the analyst to rest when needed during data collection, therefore minimising any user error. The systems were validated (Brown and Hughes, 1995 and Murray *et al.*, 1998) and an inter-operator test used to confirm reliability (Murray

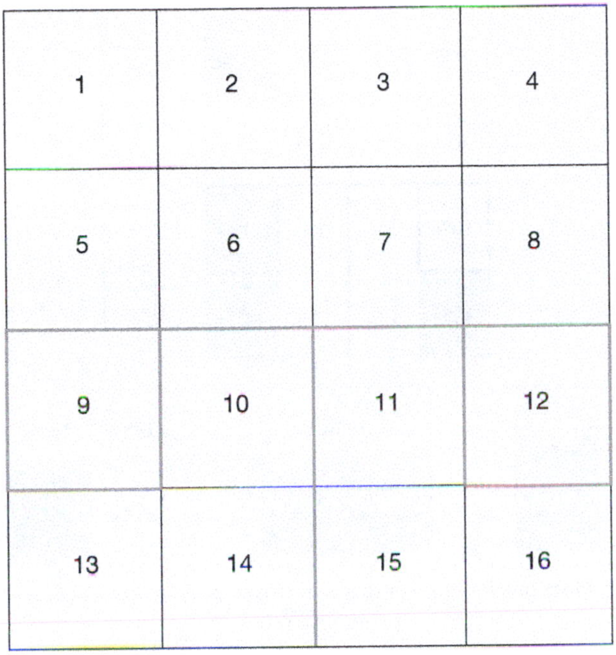

1	2	3	4
5	6	7	8
9	10	11	12
13	14	15	16

FIGURE 16.16 Example of 16 cell division of squash court.

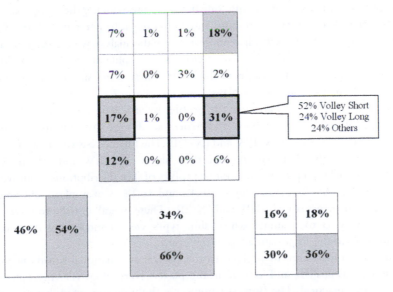

FIGURE 16.17 An example of normalised distribution data.

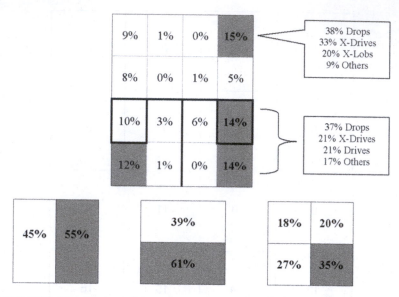

FIGURE 16.18 Distribution of shots that were two shots before a winner by Player A ((*N*–2)W).

et al., 1998 and Hughes *et al.*, 2000d). The court was divided into 16 cells (Figure 16.6) for the purpose of data collection.

As a result of some more feedback from the players, it was decided to combine the data from the five matches into one figure, again reducing the complexity level of the data. Also the data were normalised, and put into percentage form (Figure 16.17). Areas of the court that had unusual data in the analysis were further examined with respect to the shot types. The court was also split into forehand/backhand, front/back and the four quarters of the court. These more simple sets of data can more easily be put into tactical plans.

Additional depth was given to the profiles by analysing the distribution across the court of not only the winners and errors, but also the distribution of shots that preceded the end shot – (*N*–1)W and (*N*–1)E. The full analysis system also enabled the analyses of the shot that preceded these shots – (*N*–2)W and (*N*–2)E. Using these we could then present the positive profiles of shot distributions, from winners (W), (*N*–1)E, (*N*–2)W (see Figures 16.17 and 16.18 as examples); and negative profiles from errors (E), (*N*–1)W and (*N*–2)E. These overall distributions were also further analysed to examine which shot types were contributing most to the frequencies in the important areas of the court.

These profiles were then given to the players at a national squad; again, the feedback was positive and ideas from the players were often very perceptive and always very practical. The British champion at the time suggested that we go one layer deeper in the analysis and analyse the shot selection of the top players from the four corners of the court (Figure 16.19). This form of analysis assists the players in building a constructive rally and anticipating the opposition's next shot.

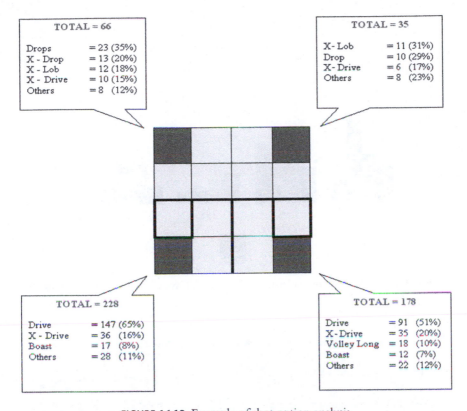

TOTAL = 66

Drops	= 23 (35%)
X - Drop	= 13 (20%)
X - Lob	= 12 (18%)
X - Drive	= 10 (15%)
Others	= 8 (12%)

TOTAL = 35

X - Lob	= 11 (31%)
Drop	= 10 (29%)
X - Drive	= 6 (17%)
Others	= 8 (23%)

TOTAL = 228

Drive	= 147 (65%)
X - Drive	= 36 (16%)
Boast	= 17 (8%)
Others	= 28 (11%)

TOTAL = 178

Drive	= 91 (51%)
X - Drive	= 35 (20%)
Volley Long	= 18 (10%)
Boast	= 12 (7%)
Others	= 22 (12%)

FIGURE 16.19 Example of shot option analysis.

A further analysis produced by the real-time system is the rally length analysis (Figure 16.20). This provides information on varying winner : error ratios over varying rally lengths. Players were especially receptive to this data as it often provided a focus for the mental approach to the tactics; for example, a major very highly ranked opposition player showed a 1:3 W:E ratio in rallies over 15 shots. The next English player to play this opponent counted to 16 shots in his head before playing the ball to the front of the court. He won 3–1, beating this player for the first time in his career.

A discussion with the SRA psychologist highlighted her interest in extremes of body language and the resultant outcomes of the next three or four rallies. We realised that we had the outcome data in the computer from the SWEAT analyses. By writing another analysis program we calculated a running score (momentum) for a player during a game. We gave a winning shot by a player a '+1' score, an error a '−1' score, and if the opponent hit the rally end shot, or it was a let, the score stayed the same (Figure 16.21). This would also show any swings in momentum during the match, then the video could be used to analyse the body language and try to understand the reason for these swings.

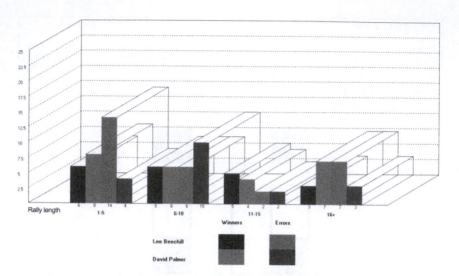

FIGURE 16.20 W : E frequencies from the SWEAT system with respect to length of rally.

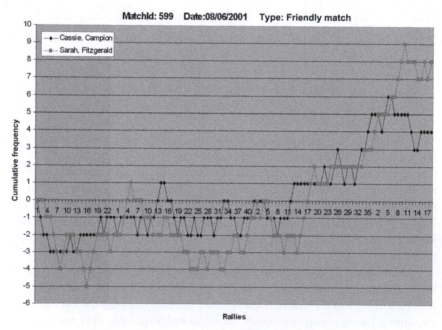

FIGURE 16.21 Example of 'momentum analysis' graph.

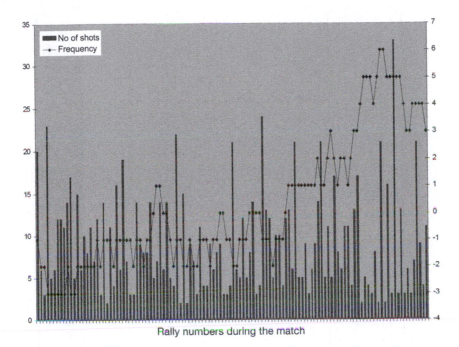

FIGURE 16.22 Example of momentum analysis with rally length included.

When the physiologist saw these graphs he asked whether we could incorporate the rally length into the graphs. He was interested to see whether these swings may be related to fitness aspects. By analysing the rally in relation to the momentum this could be observed (Figure 16.22).

We are still discovering the potential of the 'momentum graphs' as they have only recently been developed. But they do seem such a strong indicator of the mental strength of a player during the different stages of a match and it is felt that there could be more that can be explored with these analyses. The exciting part is how the analyses are pulling together all the different parts of the sports science support team.

Empirical models enable both the academic and consultant sports scientist to make conclusions about patterns of play of sample populations of athletes within their sport. This, in turn, gives the academic the potential to examine the development and structures of different sports with respect to different levels of play, rule changes, introduction of professionalism, etc. The consultant analyst can utilise these models to compare performances of peer athletes or teams with whom the analyst is working.

16.2.6.3 Stochastic models

Historically, the prediction of sports performance has been a concept usually reserved for those associated with the betting culture. However, in reality, each and every

TABLE 16.5 Marks awarded for each prediction

Method	Marks Awarded					
	Group Matches (40)	Quarter-finals (4)	Semi-finals (2)	3rd Place Play Off (1)	Final (1)	Total (48)
Human-based methods						
Best Individual Human	39.00	4.00	2.00	1.00	0.00	46.00
Mean Human Prediction	35.63	3.45	1.17	0.26	0.31	40.66
Expert Focus Group	37.00	4.00	1.00	0.00	1.00	43.00
Computer-based methods						
Multiple linear regression (satisfies assumptions)	38.00	4.00	1.00	0.00	0.00	43.00
Multiple linear regression (violates assumptions)	38.00	4.00	1.00	0.00	1.00	44.00
Binary logistic regression	37.00	4.00	1.00	0.00	1.00	43.00
Neural networks with numeric input	37.00	4.00	1.00	0.00	1.00	43.00
Neural network with binary input – 4 middle layer nodes	34.00	3.00	1.00	0.00	1.00	39.00
Neural network with binary input – 8 middle layer nodes	34.00	4.00	1.00	0.00	1.00	40.00
Neural network with binary input – 16 middle layer nodes	36.00	4.00	1.00	0.00	1.00	42.00
Neural network with binary input – 32 middle layer nodes	37.00	4.00	1.00	0.00	1.00	43.00
Simulation Program	38.50	4.00	1.00	0.00	1.00	44.50

person involved within sport will subconsciously process information to predict sports performance. Performance prediction could be described as the ability to draw conclusions upon the outcome of future performance, based upon the combined interaction of previously gathered information, knowledge or data. For players and coaches, predictions are often made about forthcoming opponents, based upon previous encounters and known traits. Therefore, is it not reasonable to assume that with valid and reliable information, using the correct techniques, the accurate prediction of performance should be possible? From a sports science perspective, the most common approaches to performance prediction use large amounts of data and apply statistical techniques (Büchner *et al.*, 1997). Human predictions, however, are entirely derived from one's underpinning knowledge and subjective bias, although the 'experts' are able to accommodate a greater understanding and opportunity for the element of chance and uncertainty, unlike computerised models of performance prediction that are entirely statistically driven, such as multiple linear regression.

In an evaluation of human and computer-based prediction models for the 2003 Rugby World Cup (Table 16.5), O'Donoghue and Williams (2004) identified that the best human predictor performed better than any computer-based model, although the mean score of all the human predictions fell below each of the computer-based models that were used, unquestionably a result of the subjectivity within human prediction. Interestingly, in a similar study during the 2002 Soccer World Cup (O'Donoghue *et al.*, 2003), although the best computer-based models outperformed the human predictors once again, their overall effectiveness in predicting results was far inferior compared to the 2003 Rugby World Cup. Ironically, only the human-based focus group was able to predict four of the eight quarter-finalists and no method predicted more than one of the semi-finalists, whereas *all* of the computer-based models for the 2003 Rugby World Cup predicted seven of the eight quarter-finalists and three of the four semi-finalists. However, this is understandable, considering the inherent differences between soccer and rugby union. Very few upsets occur within rugby union and with only one drawn match during World Cup rugby from 1987 (O'Donoghue *et al.*, 2004), results generally go to form. Research by Garganta and Gonçalves (1997) led to the notion that among team sports, soccer presents one of the lowest success rates in the ratio of goals scored to the number of attacking actions performed, subsequently increasing the likelihood of drawn matches and upsets. This considered, unlike rugby union in which the number of points scored is far greater, the accurate prediction of soccer matches is far more difficult, a notion shared by O'Donoghue and Williams (2004) and demonstrated by O'Donoghue *et al.* (2003).

Making suggestions upon the types of data that should be used is difficult and ultimately reliant upon what is actually available. Historically, research in soccer, and similar team sports, that has attempted to identify the characteristics of a successful team has used game-related performance indicators rather than factors such as distance travelled (Hughes *et al.*, 1988, Yamanaka *et al.*, 1993). By using process-orientated data, such as pass completion, shots on target and entries into the attacking third for example, a more accurate picture of a team's abilities would be created that directly relates to the dynamic processes involved in soccer. Although large databases of such information are available, the validity of the data in terms of defining successful performance is questionable and unsubstantiated. In order for performance prediction to move forward, not only within soccer, it is imperative that issues such as this are addressed, along with the continued development of valid and reliable methods of performance prediction.

By using MLR, a number of conditions must be accepted in considering its use as a prediction tool. The method is not based upon any 'artificial learning' process in order to generate predictions and predicts each game on its own merit without consideration for other factors. The simulation package used by O'Donoghue (2004) favoured Brazil to win the 2002 World Cup, rather than France who were the strongest team in the tournament. The model took into consideration the probabilities of qualifying from the group stages and then progressing through the knock-outs against different ranked opposition and predicted that Brazil had a greater chance of winning the fixture against France, should they have actually qualified from the group stages, because of the events preceding the potential tie. However, MLR would simply identify that France had both a superior rank and far less travelling distance than Brazil and would predict France to win the tie. This simplistic approach of MLR and indeed other algorithmic methods such as binary logistic regression is their fundamental drawback, although the results of these research papers quoted proved that even the most simplistic approach can be relatively effective.

16.2.6.4 Perturbations – dynamic systems

Modelling human behaviour is implicitly a very complex mathematical exercise that is multidimensional, and these dimensions will depend upon two or three spatial dimensions together with time. But the outcomes of successful analyses offer huge rewards, as Kelso (1995) pointed out:

- If we study a system only in the linear range of its operation where change is smooth, it's difficult if not impossible to determine which variables are essential and which are not.
- Most scientists know about nonlinearity and usually try to avoid it.
- Here we exploit qualitative change, a nonlinear instability, to identify collective variables, the implication being that because these variables change abruptly, it is likely that they are also the key variables when the system operates in the linear range.

See Chapter 14 for a full explanation and examples of perturbation analyses.

16.2.6.5 Momentum

See Chapter 15 for a full explanation and examples of momentum analyses.

16.2.6.6 Artificial intelligence

Bartlett (2004) presented a broad overview of artificial intelligence (AI) encompassing speech recognition, natural language processing, computer vision (which would include online motion analysis systems that automatically track and assign markers, e.g. EVA real time, Vicon), and decision making. He suggested that the intelligent core of AI included:

- expert systems:
  - rule-based;
  - fuzzy;
  - frame-based; and
  - their uses.
- artificial neural networks (ANNs):
  - biological and artificial neural networks,
  - the Perceptron,
  - multi-layer neural networks,
  - recurrent neural networks (we won't consider these),
  - self-organising neural networks, and
  - their uses.

Expert systems

Rule-based expert systems
These are, effectively, a database combined with a knowledge base, 'reasoning' and a user interface (Negnevitsky, 2002). They can encompass a knowledge base that contains specific knowledge for 'domain', e.g. diagnosis of sports technique 'errors'. The 'reasoning' comes from rules that can be relations, recommendations, directives, strategies or heuristics. They can include logic operations, just as a computer program will contain conditional operators. The inference engine 'reasons' by linking the rules with the facts, and finally, the explanation facilities explain how a conclusion was reached and why a specific fact is needed.

Uncertainty in expert systems
In most applications, knowledge rules based on simple logic, as in the mixed technique example, do not apply. This 'uncertainty' can be managed by (Bayesian) probability theory, e.g.:

- IF 'counter-rotation' is high;
- THEN 'technique' is mixed ($p = 0.8$).

This example was chosen to illustrate that much information is vague – 'high' in the above example has in recent research varied from 10 to 20 to as much as 30 to 40 degrees. This type of information is classed as 'fuzzy'.

Fuzzy expert systems
The difference between 'crisp' and 'fuzzy' knowledge is shown for fast bowling in Figure 16.23. This type of representation deals with fuzzy knowledge, which may be shown by linear or non-linear (e.g. sigmoidal) functions. Qualitative statements ('Hedges'), such as 'a little' or 'very' can be used to modify the fuzzy shapes. Domain knowledge can be interpreted by fuzzy rules, similar to those for rule-based systems but using fuzzy logic not simple logic. They offer great potential in quantifying the vagueness of much knowledge.

Frame-based expert systems
In these expert systems, knowledge is represented as 'frames', with 'attributes', rather as in many conventional databases. They 'structure' knowledge; for example, a frame-based system might contain a player's name, weight, height, age, position in last game, goals scored, passes made, tackles made, infringements and so on. By using 'object-oriented programming' frames communicate with each other by rules. Frames can belong to 'classes', e.g. forwards, midfielders, defenders, keepers.

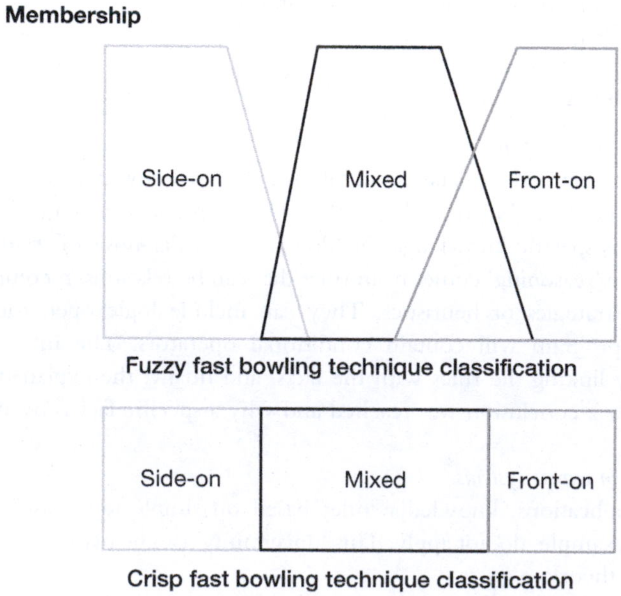

Membership

Fuzzy fast bowling technique classification

Crisp fast bowling technique classification

FIGURE 16.23 A comparison of 'crisp' and 'fuzzy' knowledge for fast bowling.
Source: Bartlett, 2004.

Expert systems – advantages

- separate knowledge from processing, unlike conventional programs;
- provide an explanation facility;
- can deal with incomplete and vague data;
- can model fuzzy human decision-making;
- are good for diagnosis;
- 'shells' for development of expert systems are widely available (e.g. add-ons to MATLAB).

Expert systems – disadvantages

- need to acquire knowledge from experts; this is a major problem;
- very domain-specific; the fast bowling system could not be used for javelin throwing;
- opaque relationships between rules;
- in general, do not have an ability to 'learn';
- have to manage conflicts between rules;
- ineffective rules searching – trawl through all rules in each cycle;
- relatively complex programs.

Expert systems in performance analysis
Bartlett (2004) reported that a search of Medline with 'expert systems' yielded 480 references, but when these were redefined toward 'sport' or 'exercise' the results were reduced to nine strikes, and none of these was on sport. Expert systems in gait analysis (Shortcliff, 1976; Dziezanowski et al., 1985; Tracy et al., 1979; Hirsch et al., 1989; Weintraub et al., 1990; Bekey et al., 1992) offer a great deal more than any other areas of performance analysis. They have been shown to be relatively successful and can identify abnormalities that human observations missed.

The development and application in gait analysis of such advanced systems can be explained by a number of contributory factors (Bartlett, 2004). Gait analysis is complex but there has been a strong developmental motivation – patient health. Clinicians are expensive and invariably very well paid. There are very confined expert domains and the analyses are laboratory-based so automatic systems are commonplace. There are vast amounts of data and there are many experts in this field.

The lack of applications in performance analysis of sport can be attributed to the fact that in sport the analyses are even more complex than gait analysis. There has been weak 'developmental motivation', as coaches and sport scientists are not highly paid – they are poorly paid generally in comparison to the health profession. There are further difficulties because the analyses are often field-based, prohibiting, to date, automatic tracking. The great number and variety of sports create a large amount of various specialists – technique analysts, notational analysts – thus in turn making a broad expert domain. There are not a lot of data for technique analysis expert systems and comparatively fewer experts in each specific field than gait analysis.

It is still surprising that these types of expert systems have not been taken up and applied in the area of coaching. The type of diagnostic logic needed in the coaching of technique lends itself perfectly to the structure of rule-based expert systems. Perhaps this is an area that we can see developing hand in hand with coach development and education. In terms of modelling sports performance and for research purposes, other AI tools appear more promising.

Neural networks

The future of research within performance prediction undoubtedly lies in the development of AI systems such as neural networking. In simplistic terms, an artificial neural network is a computer simulated mathematical model of the neurons within the human brain that is able to learn from experience (Negnevitsky, 2002). It was suggested by O'Donoghue and Williams (2004) that neural networks are commonly used to analyse complex information and could ultimately be used as a tool for predicting soccer matches using the complex game related data identified previously. However, it must be accepted that predicting the outcome of sports performance consistently and accurately is unlikely to be made possible; even with the most sophisticated of computerised systems, after all, it is the unpredictability of sport that continues to capture the imagination of millions of people across the world.

16.2.6.7 Summary of modelling and prediction

In an evaluation of human and computer-based prediction models, including neural networks, for the 2003 Rugby World Cup, O'Donoghue and Williams (2004) identified that the best human predictor performed better than any computer-based model, although the mean score of all the human predictions fell below each of the computer-based models that were used, unquestionably a result of the subjectivity within human prediction. Interestingly, in a similar study during the 2002 Soccer World Cup (O'Donoghue *et al.*, 2003), although the best computer-based models outperformed the human predictors once again, their overall effectiveness in predicting results was far inferior compared to the 2003 Rugby World Cup. Ironically, only the human-based focus group was able to predict four of the eight quarter-finalists and no method predicted more than one of the semi-finalists, whereas *all* of the computer-based models for the 2003 Rugby World Cup predicted seven of the eight quarter-finalists and three of the four semi-finalists. However, this is understandable, considering the inherent differences between soccer and rugby union. Very few upsets occur within rugby union and with only one drawn match during World Cup rugby from 1987 (O'Donoghue *et al.*, 2004), results generally go to form. Research by Garganta and Gonçalves (1997) led to the notion that among team sports, soccer presents one of the lowest success rates in the ratio of goals scored to the number of attacking actions performed, subsequently increasing the likelihood of drawn matches and upsets. This considered, unlike rugby union in which the number of points scored is far greater, the accurate prediction of soccer matches is far more difficult, a notion shared by O'Donoghue and Williams (2004) and demonstrated by O'Donoghue *et al.* (2003).

There is a range of statistical methods that can be used to predict performance, such as multiple linear regression, discriminant function analysis, binary logistic regression, forms of artificial intelligence such as artificial neural networks, or indeed any combination of these. The analysis of sports behaviours using stochastic processes would seem to represent the most complete type of model for sports contests to date. This observation is unsurprising given the widespread uses of statistics based on probabilities in many different fields (e.g. actuarial tables, insurance statistics, stock market forecasts, sports betting, etc.). Indeed, the behaviours in sports contests would seem to be good candidates for this type of analysis, not least since the strategies for sports contests are often designed on the basis of future expectations (e.g. the use of strategies based on 'percentage play'). This said, some limitations of this type of analysis (for squash contests) were reported, indicating that any such type of system description on the basis of probability is not as straightforward as might otherwise be imagined. These results led in time to the consideration of a new type of description for sports contests. However, the data required to pursue the description of sports contests as a dynamical system remains sparse at the time of writing.

Finally, we briefly considered the use of neural networks for recognising structures, or processes, within sports contests. Each of these system descriptions, while incomplete, may assist in our understanding of the behaviours that form sports contests. Furthermore, these descriptions for sports contests need not be exclusive of each other, and a hybrid type of description (or model) may be appropriate in the future, a suggestion that remains only a point of conjecture at this time. For these reasons, further research on sports contests using various types of system descriptions is warranted. The use of simulation procedures in the modelling of sports contests will continue to be a useful technique in the pursuit of these objectives.

16.3 Profiling in canoeing – a practical example

Canoe and kayak slalom analysis typically involves identifying time losses/gains by an athlete in comparison to their competitors to identify moves that are quicker and to provide objective feedback to their athlete on how good their performance was. O'Donoghue and Longville (2004) documented a step-by-step procedure of how they developed their notation system for netball. This needs analysis, evolutionary approach was adapted for the current study with the outcome of an analysis template that could be used real–time (limited data input) and lapsed–time (additional data input for more complex analysis). As O'Donoghue (2008) stated, it was necessary to have an optimal set of performance indicators to provide sufficient information but small enough to be collected reliably in real–time. Meetings with the coaches and athletes identified the benefits that performance analysis could provide and the performance indicators thought to be beneficial (Table 16.6). These measures were not simple in many cases; for example, split times can be used at different parts of the course and be determined by upstream and downstream gates.

TABLE 16.6 Performance indicators used in the analysis of canoe/kayak slalom

Performance classification	Technical	Tactical
Run time (inc. pens)	Penalties	Penalties
Run time (exc. pens)	Moves	Moves
Penalties	Type of gates	Type of gates
Split times	Time loss/gains	Time loss/gains
	Technique	Techniques used
	Water features	Water features
	Stroke count	Strokes used

Ultimately, the utility of these times lay in the ability of the analyst to identify performance standards (peer-related) and quantify differences in times (course-specific) with identifiable reasons for the time differentials. The next stage of development aims to identify season trends, e.g. an athlete may lose the majority of time in the upstream gates, with a view to incorporating this information in a coherent performance enhancement strategy.

16.3.1 Data reliability

In the area of applied performance analysis it is vital to ensure that data obtained are accurate and reliable. The importance of this is paramount as the data are used to impact on the coaches' feedback to the athletes performing. The aim of this study was to examine intra-observer and inter-observer reliability of data from a real-time and lapsed-time analysis of canoe and kayak slalom competition and training. Slalom runs from five international standard paddlers (canoe and kayak) in various competitions and training scenarios were analysed using a combination of four observers (two analysts and two elite coaches). The real-time data were based on split times only (stopwatch), a time analysis instrument that is used by coaches on a daily basis in many sports. The lapsed-time data were analysed using a tagging panel developed in a video analysis software package (www.dartfish.com), and developed with the expertise of experienced analysts and elite canoe/kayak slalom coaches. The events identified for lapsed-time analysis included split times, gate penalties, gate type, techniques used in specific moves, water features and the event information (athlete, date, event etc.). The accuracy of measurement was explored for each of these variables. For real-time versus lapsed-time analysis of split times the accuracy was within ≤ 0.21 s (inter-observer only). For lapsed-time analysis of split times the error was ≤ 0.18 s for intra-observer and ≤ 0.2 s for inter-observer analysis. Hunter *et al.* (2007) carried out similar time splits analysis focusing on stroke analysis of canoe slalom. Their error of measurement for time taken between gates and turns was ≤ 0.21 s and ≤ 0.39 s for intra-observer and inter-observer analysis, respectively. The percentage accuracy for gate penalties, gate type, water features and event information was 100 per cent for both intra- and inter-observer reliability. The analysis of techniques used for intra-observer comparisons revealed that 95 per cent of the time identical technique classification occurred. Inter-observer analysis revealed identical technique identification was achieved 90 per cent of the time. Due to the variety of techniques used at a given time by kayak slalom paddlers, further investigation is required into identifying clearer definition of terms. This is evident in a number of studies when analysing technique/movement classifications; for example, Hunter *et al.* (2007) produced 81 per cent for identical stroke identification.

16.3.2 Examining performance indicators

16.3.2.1 Broad PIs

Race percentages

Unlike many individual sports (e.g. running and jumping events in athletics), canoe slalom does not have world records because every course is different, and even the same course will change from day to day. It then becomes very difficult for coaches and analysts to enable comparisons in order to contextualise individual performances. This brings challenges to training sessions when determining what a relatively good performance was, and how this could be compared with the world's best. In canoe slalom the men's single kayak class (k1men) produces the fastest performance in a competition. Traditionally, coaches and athletes have compared their times in training to those of the k1men (mixed standards), but basing performance in training on inconsistent measures could be misleading. It is desirable to be able to identify better defined PIs for athletes' performances in training.

This study explored the performances of canoe slalom athletes in training and their comparison to international standards so that the following performance question could be answered: how does an analyst contextualise an athlete's performance in training? Competition results from International Canoe Slalom races (Senior Europeans, World Cups and World Championships 2009–2012) were collated. The k1men's class winners were determined as the 100 per cent benchmark. All other times in the same races were calculated from this winning time to give each athlete and/or position (third, fifth, tenth, twentieth places) a percentage from the benchmark. The k1men athletes in training were monitored throughout the season to examine how their times compared to the k1men winner's benchmark, and their virtual best score (VB) as a group was calculated on these comparisons. This VB percentage was then used within the training results in order to determine a performance benchmark in line with international standards.

16.3.2.2 Results

International standards were produced to establish benchmarks (PIs) for first, third, fifth, tenth and twentieth placings respectively (Table 16.7 – example percentages from 2011 season).

TABLE 16.7 Race percentages for 2011 (calculated from winning k1men's time)

2011	1st (%)	3rd (%)	5th (%)	10th (%)	20th (%)
K1M average	100	102.4	103.8	103.9	104.9
C1M average	105.3	106.9	108.3	110.6	112.9
C2 average	112.0	115.1	117.5	119.6	125.9
K1W average	114.0	116.5	117.7	120.3	123.3
C1W average	135.3	143.3	156.3	191.6	
		Finals		SF	Qs

The k1men training group's VB produced percentages of a top three standard and above. This equated to an average score of 1 per cent off the winner's time. This showed that our k1men training group were producing performances in line with top three international standard competitions. With this evidence we were able to confidently produce performance percentages for all classes and compare training to international standards. This method was continuously reviewed during following seasons in relation to the changing k1men training group and current international competition standards. These findings can give confidence to the athletes and their coaching/support team by clearly comparing performance standards in training to international standards. It can be used to determine performance improvement and the potential standards for an individual. It also points to a new way for defining PIs in sports where there are continuously changing environments and conditions and hence performances, such as golf, skiing, surfing, sailing, for example.

16.3.2.3 Specific PIs

Upstream (round pole) analysis

Within a slalom course design there are always either six or seven upstream gates (new rule 2013: six upstream gates only) that the athlete has to negotiate with the rest of the gates being downstream gates. The coaches identified time around the upstream as an important indicator of a successful performance. In Hunter *et al.* (2008), elite canoe slalom coaches also worked with the researchers to develop their performance variables which were obtainable from video footage of canoe slalom competition. The upstream gate was identified as a 'turn' and was divided into four sections. There was no clear reason for why the 'turn' in the upstream gate was separated into the respective sections. The challenge for this method is that each upstream gate is fairly unique with different approaches (first quarter) and exits away (fourth quarter) from the gate determined by the position of previous gates and the next gate required to negotiate the course. The only variables that are potentially repeatable are the second and third quarter respectively. This is what the coaches and analyst in the current study identified in the 2005/2006 season as the 'round the pole' time.

Potentially there are two methods that can be used in order to break down the upstream move, the 'whole' upstream time (similar to Hunter *et al*.'s 2008 work) and the 'round the pole' time, which is evaluated in this study. The main difference between the two is that the 'whole' upstream time is based on the entry time into the upstream gate, the time to turn around the upstream gate, and the time away from the upstream gate. The 'round the pole' time is based only on the time to turn around the upstream gate. Both of these techniques were evaluated in their application to competition and training situations in canoe and kayak slalom.

The start position for timing 'round the pole' motion is when the front of the athlete's body (lowest point closest to spray-deck) crosses the imaginary line. This imaginary line is perpendicular to the gate line position. The lowest point of the athlete's body was selected as this undergoes the least body movement during this activity. In contrast, the upper torso was observed to produce more variability of movement and was therefore considered to produce less accurate results.

16.3.2.4 Implications for coaching

For the first time in slalom coaching there was a variable that could be measured on any upstream on any course. The ability to analyse upstream moves in training without having to compare them to another athlete's time was an important step for coaching support. This was a breakthrough for performance analysis and coaching in the sport of canoe slalom. How exactly the coaches are benefitting from this analysis method is currently being explored. One expert coach in particular was keen to explore 'round the pole' time splits only, as a performance indicator, allowing the entry and exit to be excluded from the overall upstream time and adjusting the protocol appropriately so that it was more consistent and suitable for cross comparison. It also made the analyses quicker to produce, which is vital in applied performance analysis support. However, even though this method was quick it was felt important to explore the difference between the data gathered from the 'whole upstream time' with the method of 'round the pole' time. Are we getting the same/similar results or are the messages completely different? How does this affect the way we use the analysis?

There were positive relationships between round the pole time and the whole upstream time. The relationships do vary in strength; however, at this level of athlete (elite) those small relationships could still be viewed as significant. Elite athletes' margins are extremely small and as shown already in the results they are very consistent on certain moves (very small differences in time). In c1 and k1 men's class events it was clear to see that any upstream gate, with a round the pole time of 2.5 seconds and above, have all produced slower whole upstream times. There are clear positives and limitations that have been highlighted to ensure the user of this method fully understands the process and its level of application. Methods to move the upstream analysis forward would involve breaking upstream gates into levels of technical difficulty and types of techniques used. This would develop the analysis further by providing more detail and strengthening the interpretation of the analysis by directing the coach/analyst/athlete quicker towards the indicator of performance. Also, having this data linked straight to the video will enhance the analysis even further. Another area to investigate is course-specific analysis. This would involve analysing a variety of international courses around the world to see whether they have their own 'gold' standard upstream template. There have been a number of World Cup and World Championship races at courses such as Augsburg (Germany), La Seu D'Urgell (Spain), Prague (Czech Republic) and Tacen (Slovenia). This information could assist in coaching sessions/training camps at these courses leading into the competition. For example, where are the slowest upstreams and what techniques can an athlete use to overcome this? These are marginal gains that every elite athlete is looking for to win the race.

16.4 Conclusions

It has been suggested that the processes necessary for an analyst working either as a consultant or an academic researcher are as follows:

1   defining performance indicators;
2   determining which are important;
3   establishing the reliability of the data collected;
4   ensuring that enough data have been collected to define stable performance profiles (performance profiling);
5   comparing sets of data;
6   modelling performances.

It was concluded that recent research has demonstrated:

- clear methods for determining which performance indicators are relevant and which are more important;
- simple absolute measures of reliability need to be used together with accepted non-parametric measures of variance;
- that if performance profiles of teams or individual athletes are being applied, then some measures of confidence in the stability of these profiles need to expressed;
- the comparison of sets of data in notational analysis needs to be considered carefully, as the data are usually non-parametric and conform most likely to Poisson and Binomial distributions. The use of χ^2 seems to be a simple answer; however, as soon as more complex models and higher-order comparisons are required, the approach based on log-linear models is shown to be more effective;
- the sensitivity of these χ^2 and log-linear models to the small differences in performance, that differentiate between winning and losing at the elite level, is open to question;
- that there are many techniques used to model sport; some of these are providing the greatest challenges to notational analysts and mathematicians alike.

It is clear that the working notational analyst must have a broad set of technological, mathematical and statistical skills and be prepared to maintain and extend those skills just as the research in this area develops the knowledge base. Further research is urgently needed in some of these areas:

- How do we define performance indicators in a general and generic sense? At the moment they are arbitrarily defined for each sport depending upon the subjective opinions of the analyst and/or coach.
- The statistical methods that we use are improving, but more work needs to be done on making the more sophisticated systems more transparent, in terms of how they relate to the experimental aims of the comparisons, and also the basic practical demand of them being easier to apply.
- The sensitivity of the tests needs to be examined – how can we determine the significant differences in performance when the increments of comparison are very small?
- More research in modelling in performance analysis is vital as we extend our knowledge and databases into those exciting areas of prediction.

Using the word prediction in the same phrase as sport almost certainly creates a form of an oxymoron, because of the inherent nature of sport. Nevertheless, working towards the extended aims of modelling, and therefore forecasting, must be the most exciting of the ways to further develop performance analysis.

17

RULE CHANGES IN SPORT AND THE ROLE OF NOTATION

Jason Williams

17.1 Introduction

Any sporting event is defined and played within a predetermined framework of rules and the number and complexity of these rules may differ significantly. The process for changing them occurs within the environment of a governing body or administrators, but little is known about why they occur. Traditional sport that is played today is the product of many years of evolution and development, but little is known about why these rules change. This chapter will review literature regarding rule changes in sport and will identify and categorise why rules change in sport and investigate the use of notation in tracking the changes.

Cooper (1994) found that over a period of years, rules for various games evolved following certain guidelines, just as rules of conduct evolved in society. The reasons for rule change presented by Cooper were specific to American football and were based on his analysis of the history of rule changes. His work did not take into consideration the different types of sports and the types of stresses that those sports are placed under. However, his work did present some clear indications as to why rules change within sport. Research conducted by Kew (1986) highlighted the way that rules change within game playing in invasive games. He defined three 'Moments' within the development of a sport. The first he defined as the 'Basic challenge', whereby the basic theory or aim of the game was introduced. The second moment or 'Establishment' was deciding on rules to prescribe actions and make the challenge difficult and interesting. Finally, the third moment, the 'Consolidation' phase corresponded to preserving or enabling rules that were designed to ensure the continuous possibility for the realisation of 'Depth' features, and therefore sustain credibility.

Kew (1987) continued his research on rule changes within sport using basketball, hockey and different codes of football. He found that sports change their rules frequently, but little is known of the processes through which such changes are impelled. In his paper he categorised two types of rule change; the first was the definitive rule – a concern to re-establish and re-emphasise the key characteristics of that specific sport. An example of this may be illustrated with basketball as a variety of ball-handling skills should be displayed in this game. In order to ensure the continuity of the variety of ball-handling skills, changes in the rules need to be made to neutralise the advantage of the taller player and ensure that ball handling skills remain an important aspect of the game. The second category he defined as a shared concern about what must be preserved, enhanced or enabled in order to sustain the viability of the sport.

Gardiner *et al.* (1998) had a more controversial viewpoint with regard to rule changes. They stated rule changes are merely tinkered with and are often carried out with the aim of short-term expediency, often to placate external pressures such as sponsors and television. They also put forward the argument that rule changes are needed to secure the integrity of modern sport in the context of making it a commodity. The argument was made that sport was becoming more like a product that can be bought or sold in order to generate income in order to ensure the survival of that particular sport. Their work further stated that rule changes are required to try and re-establish the vitality and balance in a particular sport, introduce new skills and strategies to confront these new rules, creating the continual need for change. They continued by stating that changes to the rules of a sport commonly emerge from a desire to increase the appeal of the sport for players and spectators and to ensure its survival.

Hammond *et al.* (1999) stated that the rules of a game commonly emerge from a desire to increase the appeal of a sport for players and spectators and to ensure its survival. Their work on netball attributed rule changes to three main factors. The first of these was defined as 'Player performance', which meant that players become bigger, faster and stronger with time. Second, 'Technological advancement' was defined as the development of sporting accessories, scientific tools and aids. They also noted that 'Commercial pressures' played a role in the development of rules. The results of their study showed the importance of systematically analysing the effect of rule changes, and also highlighted that even relatively minor changes to rules have an effect on play.

17.1.1 Safety

The safety and well-being of participants in any given sport may be considered as an important factor in the formation of a new rule, whether the changes have a direct or indirect effect on players' safety. In order to investigate the importance of safety and rule changes, the discussion will be categorised into two parts. The first part is defined as contextual, a direct intervention to the rules that is introduced to combat technical offences, such as foul or dangerous play, and safety equipment. The second is defined as environmental, a set of rules that address less specific issues such as participation level, environment and fluid intake.

Contextual rule changes or rule changes that are specific to player safety are documented in a few publications. The NCAA magazine (1982) identified the extent of rule changes with regard to safety in American football. They stated that between 1969 and 1982, the NCAA Football Rules Committee made a total of 64 injury prevention rule changes involving personal fouls, penalty enforcement, un-sportsmanlike conduct, equipment, the field and signals. Green (1985) also documented rule changes that were introduced specifically for safety. He examined Canadian amateur gridiron football and noted why the rule was introduced alongside the rule itself. This work illustrated how much sport has developed over the last 40 years and that basic safety issues, such as the high tackle, although seeming very obvious now, had to go through the process of being introduced. Their work recognised that as the chronological order of the introduction of rule changes was documented, the changes became less radical and more specific. Their work recognised that rule changes with regard to safety are not as radical as when the sport was first introduced, as the majority of 'serious' injuries have been reduced.

Sports such as American football, lacrosse and cricket have undergone changes regarding safety equipment. When safety equipment was introduced, great stress was placed on reducing the number of injuries that occurred within the game, but at the same time ensuring that the changes did not have a detrimental effect. Rugby union has recently seen much discussion with regard to safety equipment in the form of padded protection. Gerrard (1998) has showed that some items of padding can be of some benefit to the individual, depending on where the padding is. In addition, Wilson (1998) discussed protection with regard to protective headgear in rugby union and compared it with other sports. Their work recognised that the introduction any item of padding needs careful consideration by the administrators as there is always a chance of the individual relying on padding or testing rules through this new protection. This in turn may then create problems within the game by introducing new types of injuries or introducing new problems to a sport.

Hackney (1994) highlighted issues relating to player safety and discussed how to prevent and manage injuries in sport through adhering to the rules. The compliance of a rule in a sport was also stressed in the study made by Kujala *et al.* (1995) on acute injuries in soccer, ice hockey, volleyball, basketball, judo and karate. Their research found that each sport had a specific injury profile and that the best way to deal with this was to introduce preventative measures such as improving the rules, supported by careful refereeing. Kirkendall *et al.* (1995) documented the types of injury in American football and found that changes in rules led to reductions in one type of injury and increases in others. One example he gave was that neck injuries decreased dramatically since spearing (using the head as a battering ram when tackling) was outlawed, but shoulder tears increased when the blocking rules were changed. His work recognised that sometimes rules introduced to ensure safety create other problems.

Many problems associated with injuries are connected to the lack of rules or poor implementation of rules. Parkkari *et al.* (2001) undertook an extensive literature review of a range of sports and their associated injuries to try and find out whether sports injuries could be prevented. They stated that in every sport they examined, rule changes were imperative to player safety and should be continually examined to ensure their safety. The theory of testing a new rule on a group of players was also advised by Burry and Calcinai (1988), with their research on spinal injuries in rugby union. Their work stressed the effect of rule changes in reducing injuries, highlighting the dramatic drop in cervical injuries after changes to the scrum and 'tackled ball' rules in New Zealand rugby union.

The above discussion recognised the importance of rule changes that directly influence safety in sport. In addition to rules that are implemented to counter specific areas of dangerous areas of play, rule makers must also consider participatory and environmental factors of a sport. There are also issues with the level at which the sport is played, such as at the professional and amateur level, for men and women, and problems with the differences in the game for children and adults.

The weather conditions in which a sport is played are difficult to control, which causes a number of problems with regard to safety. In sports such as basketball or ice hockey, these problems are of less significance because the conditions are generally always the same, as they are played indoors. A controlled environment such as this rarely occurs in outdoor sports, which may have a major impact on the way the sport is played and the safety of the players. The environmental effect on the athlete competing in sport is discussed in detail by Thein (1995), who stated that the environment can facilitate or inhibit performance, or it can cause serious illness or death. Research conducted in rugby league (Hodgson Phillips *et al.*, 1998; Gissane *et al.*, 1998) found a direct correlation between conditions and injury and argued that when the rules of a sport are changed administrators must be aware that the sport, if played on a global scale, can be played in different conditions.

Sport administrators continually work to ensure that players' safety is guaranteed on the sporting arena. Specific problems with regard to foul play or injuries can be dealt with directly through implementing changes within the game using rule changes. However, there are also many safety issues that are not as obvious, but should also be considered. These changes may be more difficult to standardise because of the indirect nature of the safety concerns. The direct or indirect safety implications of changes within the game may also conflict with the spectacle, speed or enjoyment of the game both by participant and spectator. The issue of ensuring the safety and at the same time ensuring that participants enjoy the sport is a problem that the administrators of the game constantly need to address.

17.1.2 Natural development and progression

The issue of safety is only one of the influences that change the rules of a sport. Another reason that may be considered is that of natural development and progression. Over time, areas of a sport change due to physical changes of the participants or the pushing and testing of the rules by the coaches or the individuals who take part. Training regimes have improved, scientific analysis has grown and there has been a general increase in support for sportsmen and women. Other changes involve areas such as cheating, player size and speed of the sport or improvements in equipment. The stress placed on the rules by such changes may mean that certain rules need updating or rewriting in order to keep the game competitive and fair. This section will discuss these areas of change and will investigate the effect that each has on changing the rules of a game.

It may be considered that rules are introduced to a sport to maintain some form of order and ensure that it is played in a fair manner. It is argued that cheating or testing the boundaries of a rule is an action that takes place in a majority of sporting activities. When a rule is broken, then some form of penalty is awarded against the offending person, such as a free kick in football or a false throw in the javelin event in athletics. There are different ways in which cheating occurs and different reasons as to why rules are broken. The constant pushing and testing of a set of rules creates pressures to create new rules to combat them thorough examinations by players and coaches. Thus a continual cycle is created where established and new rules are constantly being tested (Leaman, 2001).

Prior to any further discussion it is important at this stage to distinguish between the intentional and the unintentional breaking of rules in sport. Loland (1998) defined intentional cheating as breaking the rules to get an unfair advantage and trying to get away with the offence without getting penalised. Unintentional cheating is defined by rule violations where the offender breaks the rules by accident. For example, in football this may be an accidental 'handball' or late tackle. This theory can be developed further with respect to the pressure that is placed on the rules. If a rule is consistently broken, whether the break is intended or not, stress is still being placed on that specific rule. The effect that this has on the sport is the same and there is no distinction between the devious cheat and the accidental cheat. For the purpose of this study, both types of rule breaking shall be referred to as cheating.

Leaman (2001) discussed cheating in more detail and questioned what is morally wrong with it. He argued that cheating may add a new dimension to the sport and that the sport may become more interesting if the rules are stretched in some way. He suggested that cheating in sport is part of its structure and is taken into consideration in its rules. He further argued that if cheating is recognised as an option that both sides may morally take up, then, in general, the principles of equality and justice are not affected. This argument leads on to a set of rules that exist below the surface of the intended rules, thus creating a subset that players adhere to. Leaman also suggested that athletes in certain sports simply come to expect and engage in a certain amount of on-field rule violations. The basis for his argument was that cheating should be accepted as a part of the sport and therefore should be accepted as part of the sports progression and change.

Lumpkin et al. (1999) argued that there has been an increase in rule breaking at the elite level because of the pressures placed on athletes to win for financial gain. Emphasis has been placed on winning rather than developing skill and having fun. Athletes realise early in their sporting experiences that only winners receive multi-million pound contracts, endorsements and clothing. When such importance is placed on winning, athletes may turn to drugs to enhance their performance to gain an advantage over the opposition. Drugs in sport are a problem that undermines the very ethos of competing on a level playing field. When such pressure is placed on a sportsperson to win they may try any means possible in order to do so, which then moves cheating from on the field to off it. It may be said that the guile and deviancy that some sports people introduce on the field through pushing the rules to their full extent is far removed from the clinical cheating that may happen off the field (Coakley, 2001).

The act of breaking a rule of any sport, whether the action is intended or not has an effect on the way a sport is played and commentators may argue whether its effect is of benefit or detriment to the sport. However, it is difficult to ignore its effect on the way a sport changes over time. As with any set of rules, some will be strained or broken to try and gain some form of advantage over the opposition, such as binding in the scrum in rugby union or the offside law in football, but these are part of the make-up of the game. The motivation for breaking a rule may vary from simple bad sportsmanship to the need to win for financial gain. With such a driving force behind the need to cheat it may be considered difficult to accept the argument that breaking the rules of a sport is good for the sport's development.

Another area that places stress on the rules of a sport in a less confrontational manner is the size and the speed of the sports men and women that take part. A common contention is that a sport played 30 or 40 years ago is considerably different to the level it is practised at today because of the size and the speed of the participants. Norton et al. (1999) conducted work into the changes that have occurred within Australian rules football investigating the changes in game speed and player size over a 30-year period. They used height and mass data on players that were obtained from official records of registered players. These data showed a significant increase in both areas and in combination with this they found that the speed of the game had approximately doubled over the same time period.

Alongside bigger players, there are also pressures on the rules from the speed of the sport. This may encompass areas such as the speed of athletes' running, techniques employed with individual actions and increased endurance. Potter and Carter (1995) noted that the ball in play time in rugby union had increased between world cups. In parallel to the increase in the ball-in-play time they also noted that there had been an increase in the number of actions that occurred within a game. The same was also found with the women's world cup with an increase in ball-in-play time (Thomas et al., 2003). Giatsis (2003) and his work on volleyball has also recognised the game becoming faster and more intense. His research recognised that match duration increased and that new rule changes introduced a more exciting game. Norton et al. (2001) investigated Australian football and again found that the game was getting faster, which they attributed to improved ground conditions. They concluded that the game speed at the top level of Australian football had approximately doubled over the last 40 years. From these studies, it would be possible to argue that sport has become faster, which would suggest that the same sport, with the same rules, is being played at a quicker pace.

Pressures such as these may be more prevalent in some sports than others. Sports such as rugby union have seen problems due to an increase of player speed and size. In comparison, sports such as football have seen fewer changes to the rules. It is unclear whether this applies to the non-elite participants of the sport, as there is very little research in this area. However, it should be recognised that in many sports, players are getting faster, fitter and bigger and they must play within rules that were written for a sport that was played with a different type of player. Therefore, rules need to change to ensure that it is kept exciting and challenging and caters for the modern athlete.

Technology has also had its part in the development of sport with the equipment used (Krauss, 2004). Perhaps this can be best illustrated with the comparison of the association football ball that was used at the turn of the last century and today's ball. The ball used then was untreated leather, which meant that when it got wet, it would double or triple in weight. This differs greatly from the scientific design of the football that is kicked on today's modern football pitches. Haake *et al.* (2000) explored changing the size of a ball in tennis by 6 per cent in order to reduce its speed. They found that the introduction of a larger ball slowed down the game of tennis for all strokes and increased the time available for the receiver to return the ball. Baseball bat manufacturers, through modern technology, have been able to create aluminium bats that are lighter in weight than wooden bats, but still meet the required standards (Kelly and Pedersen, 2001). This meant that the batsman could hit the ball much further and harder than usual. Other consequences of this are that scoring increased and the sport became more dangerous. Examples such as these illustrate the effect of changing the equipment used by the participants of the sport. It is argued that these changes are made to improve the game in order to increase speed, power or simply to make the game more competitive, but attention should also be paid to how much the game changes.

In summary, a sport may change over time within its own boundaries without external pressures. Athletes may get bigger, stronger, and fitter and faster, which in turn may mean that the sport may have to change the rules to accommodate such developments. At the same time, participants will always want to stretch the rules in some way by intentionally or unintentionally cheating. The development and improvements in equipment have also meant that changes are introduced into the way a game is played. Changes such as these illustrate the constant testing of rules and exemplify that the rules of a game, when pressured, need to be changed in order to keep the game competitive and enjoyable to play and watch.

17.1.3 Entertainment, commercialisation and media

Professional sports have emerged as global businesses and have become a lucrative product that can be bought and sold. There has also been much discussion as to the ethical issues involved in the use of money within the sport. Many commentators have argued that the commercialisation of a sport may be of equal benefit and detriment to the sport. It is suggested that most changes within sport are introduced through changes to its rules, which are often made to try and make the sport more entertaining and exciting for its participants and spectators. However, it may be argued that the growing influence of commercialisation and the media may be having more of an effect on the sport than people realise. Indeed, it is only in the last 20 or 30 years that sports have seen the majority of changes to their rules (Coakley, 2001), which may well have occurred because of pressures from the media to make the sport more exciting.

Mason (1999) examined sport as a product and stated that sport, while initially produced to provide entertainment for spectators, is also produced for four distinct groups. He categorised these groups into: first, fans who support teams and buy the associated merchandise; second, television and media companies who purchase rights to show sports as television programmes; third, the clubs that build facilities and support lower clubs; and finally, corporations that purchase teams outright and provide sponsorship. Many changes within the sport have been to make the sport more entertaining, but the question then needs to be asked, for whom is the sport being made entertaining.

Many commentators fear that sport is being alienated from spectators and is developing more into a media product. Cousens (1997) documented the explosion in revenue gained from television contracts with American sports. She gave the example of American football and the escalation of the revenue gained from television rights. From 1961, when individual NFL teams sold their rights for an average of $332,000 the revenue, by 1994, had grown to $1.6 billion. Fennell et al., (1990) stated, 'contracts have been so lucrative that they have changed the very nature of professional sports'. For the sports purist, the power given to the media has become a worrying development, with the sport alienating them and moving more towards corporate organisations and private ownership. Hope (2002) discussed this in his work on the New Zealand All Blacks rugby team. He argued that global media and corporate sponsorship were threatening the nationally constituted heritage of All Black rugby. Research such as this suggests that many professional sports are developing into a product that may be bought or sold as a commodity.

The research undertaken by Tyrrell (1980) developed this argument and he documented the changes that occurred within baseball with its transition from the amateur to professional code. He argued that once large sums of money had been invested, the demands for a quicker and a more exciting game intensified, with significant changes in the techniques of play facilitated by changes in equipment, in the rules of pitching and in the increased competition brought about by professionalism itself. There was a need to make the game more exciting, and one of the methods of doing this was to change the rules of that game. The question then arises as to whether these improvements are for the participants of the sport, or the people watching it. Davies (1999) discussed this problem with rugby union and the problems with the changes to its rules. He argued that the changes to the game used to occur for reasons of simplicity and of clarity, or to remove dangerous play. He stated that television was now the primary motivating force in changing rules. Boyle and Haynes (2000) also discussed this point with their work on the power of the media within sport. They noted that sport had to adapt to the needs of television, and not necessarily the other way round. They listed sports that had developed into a more television friendly format, such as rugby league, rugby union and cricket.

Sport in America generates a huge amount of revenue through television and advertising. American football is one of the most popular sports there and thus generates a huge amount of income. In 1970, when the game was being reformed, teams and leagues were not decided by stadium capacities, attendance records or by the calibre of quarterbacks, but by market research men. The standard by which professional football's new leagues were formed was based on the comparative quality of their respective television markets (Johnson, 1971). Chandler (1988) argued that sport has been developed through a series of rule changes to ensure that it generated as much interest and excitement as possible for the spectator, as well as generating money for the media and advertisers. From 1970 to 1980 the rules in American football were changed to increase unpredictability and tension, which led to high-scoring games, which the American audiences preferred. Rule changes with regard to making the game more exciting for television have continued over the years in order to make the sport more entertaining for the television viewer. Many American sports have been especially tailored to appeal to millions of potential viewers who were not devoted followers of the games themselves. Sport was transformed to compete more successfully with other forms of entertainment. Football and baseball, through introducing new rules, cheerleaders, men dressed in chicken uniforms dancing on dugouts, exploding scoreboards, artificial grass and tight-fitting uniforms, tinkered with the fundamental nature of their sports (Rader, 1984). A look at the rule books of sporting organisations clearly shows that there are literally thousands of rules today that did not exist 20 years ago in sport (Coakley, 2001).

Coakley stated that rule development and rule change associated with commercialisation are usually intended to do a combination of five things: 1) speed up the action, so that fans won't get bored; 2) increase scoring to generate excitement; 3) balance competition, so that events will have uncertain outcomes; 4) maximise the dramatic moments in the competition; and 5) provide commercial breaks in the action, so that sponsors can advertise products. Arguably, these changes are improving sport, making it more exciting and enjoyable. Some commentators consider these points as a worrying development within sport and that the changes are being forced on sport, undermining the natural progression that sports undergo and introducing artificial changes that may be causing irreversible damage to its very ethos.

Table 17.1 shows the increasing need to promote sport to a larger audience that has seen many rule changes in recent years. A quest has been undertaken to develop sport into an exciting and marketable product that will generate revenue for itself, which in theory will improve it with better facilities and support for both

TABLE 17.1 Milestone deals between TV companies and English football bodies 1983–1997

	1983	1985	1986	1988	1992	1997
Length of contract (yrs)	2	0.5	2	4	5	4
Broadcaster	BBC/ITV	BBC	BBC/ITV	ITV	BSkyB	BSkyB
Rights fee (£m)	5.2	1.3	6.3	44	191.5	670
Annual rights fee (£m)	2.6	2.6	3.1	11	38.3	167.5
Number of live matches per season	10	6	14	18	60	60
Fees per live match (£m)	0.26	0.43	0.22	0.61	0.64	2.79

(Booth and Doyle, 1997)

players and spectators. It may also be argued that this cycle may appear to be one that will be impossible to break out of. A particular sport requires money to compete with other sports, so it must be more exciting to play and watch. There are many sports with little spectator interest, very exciting to play, but are struggling to survive as they have very little revenue. This then creates the cycle of the rich sports getting richer and the smaller, poorer sports decreasing in popularity and losing revenue. It may also be considered that poorer sports are under constant pressure to change their sport to try and compete with their richer counterparts. Of course, this also applies to richer sports, which are under pressure to maintain the interest in their sport. It is impossible to ignore these issues, so developments within a sport must be carefully audited, to ensure that it does not become too product focused, alienating itself from the people who follow it.

17.2 The role of notational analysis in tracking the effect of rules changes

It may be considered that the effect of rule changes on traditional sports cannot be objectively determined unless there is some form of measure associated with it. Notational analysis may be used to objectively gauge the effect of any rule change within any particular sport, but very little formal use is made of it. However, there have been some academic studies using notation to examine the effect of changes on game play. Examples of this work have measured explicit changes such as rules that were introduced to increase ball in play time, or to increase the amount of action in a game through measuring the number of passes. Research also indicates that there are many other areas of a sport that may be unintentionally affected by a new rule. Rule changes may introduce both positive and negative aspects to a game and many problems associated with rules that aren't properly analysed and discussed can result in turning a sport into chaos (Longmore, 1994). The following section will detail the role of notation in tracking the effect of rule changes in a sport through examining research that has been undertaken in the area.

The importance of making the sport more entertaining was the driving force behind changes introduced within Gaelic football in 1990. They were introduced to increase the game's ball-in-play time in order to make the game more attractive. The changes related to sideline kicks such as free kicks and goal kicks, which under the new rules were to be taken from the hand, as opposed to the ball being placed on the floor. Doggart *et al.* (1993) used a hand notation system to notate and analyse the time saved by the rule changes and the specific aspects of play that contributed to the changes in playing time. Their work discovered that the time of the ball-in-play time increased by 2 per cent. Other findings showed that there was a noticeable increase in the number of possessions gained and tackles made. The intended increase in the ball-in-play time also introduced other changes within the game that the authorities may or may not have perceived would happen. Their work highlighted some important issues that authorities need to be aware of when changing the rules of their sport.

The desired and actual outcome of new rules on a sport was highlighted with analysis by Hughes and Sykes (1994) of the back pass rule to the goalkeeper in soccer. Their analysis found that there were significantly fewer back passes to the goalkeeper as a form of time-wasting and thus the goalkeeper had less possession of the ball. Their work also found that the game was made more frantic due to less time and space in the middle of the pitch. The research concluded that although there was an increase in defensive errors, there was no increase in either the number of shots or goals as expected. It was also concluded that time-wasting due to back passes to the goalkeeper was significantly reduced but at the cost of a more congested midfield playing area. The intended outcome of less time-wasting due to back passes was reduced, but at the same time other unforeseen areas of the game were being affected.

Watts (2005) investigated a new scoring system in professional men's squash, which was introduced in order to make the game more appealing to television audiences. The aim of the study was to analyse any changes in the game structure or differences in the patterns of play occurring among men's elite squash while playing in competition under the old (point per rally to 15) and new (point per rally to 11) scoring systems. He concluded that the results showed that the new scoring system produced a significant increase in number of winners, and the number of unforced errors per match decreased. It was also concluded that the new method of scoring had no significant change in patterns of play, but produced shorter games and increased the number of critical points compared to the old method.

Football was again the subject of analysis with an experimental rule change introduced by FIFA in 1994 within semi-professional football in order to make the game more attractive to spectators and to improve specific aspects of play. The aim of this rule change was to provide more continuous entertaining football, more play in the attacking third and more goals through attacking opportunities. Odetoyinbo *et al.* (1997) analysed a selection of games to test these objectives. The work showed that the ball spent more time in play and significantly less throw-ins and kick-ins were conceded in the defending third. When interviewed, the managers felt that fragmentation of play had resulted because players paused over their choice of a throw-in or kick-in. In addition, they believed that the need for attacking creativity when gaining entry into the scoring area was lessened, to the detriment of the game. They also felt that the ball-in-play time was less than before the new rules were introduced, where in fact the opposite of this was true.

The idea of making a sport more marketable was one of the reasons for changes to clothing and ball colour in the one-day game in cricket. Scott *et al.* (1999), in their work on the effect of the change in ball colour, found that there was no significant difference with regard to catching and concluded that the change had no detrimental effect on the game. Scott noted that this was considered as a positive move by the authorities, but it must be noted that the work was carried out after the change had been implemented. The results may have been more controversial if there had been significant differences in changing the colour of the ball. A good idea to promote the game and increase the marketing potential of the game may have been an embarrassing introduction. Rule changes were introduced in cricket in an attempt to make the game more popular and to attract more sponsorship and media coverage. Howells (2000) investigated the one-day game and the effect of introducing a 30-yard circle in which all except two fielders were positioned. This new rule was enforced for the first 15 overs of each innings for each team. The research concluded that this led to the tactics in this period of play becoming more important and varied. New strokes previously redundant were once more introduced to the game with the result of a more exciting opening to the innings.

Pritchard *et al.* (2001) assessed the impact of an experimental scoring system upon elite men's badminton. The changes were introduced in order to make the game more exciting to watch, raising its appeal to the mass media and increasing interest from television companies. Previous changes to the game included modernisation of the presentation at the Sydney Olympics, changes in setting procedure and now saw the introduction of a new scoring format. Their work concluded that the changes were a positive step for elite men's badminton and the new structure was better suited to television. Games were shorter and there were more breaks during which commercials and analysis could occur.

In 1997, the International Rugby Board (IRB, 1997) devised a charter that documented the principles on which the game of rugby union is based. It was suggested that the charter should act as a checklist for judging the mode of play and that the game would maintain its unique character. The IRB believed that this charter would benefit the game because a standard would exist against which the game could be judged. It was believed that it would help prevent anecdotal changes and that any changes would be within the game's unique character. In addition, the IRB set up a game analysis centre to determine the effect of any rule change and highlight any areas of concern within the game (Thomas and Williams, 2001). This work involved the general notation of the game in different areas, such as the scrum, lineout and penalties. This enabled the IRB to analyse in detail the state of the game in any one area over any time period. Objective and impartial information such as this permitted a clearer snapshot of the game to be taken, removing subjective analysis from the argument for rule changes.

The strength of documenting changes that occur within a sport enables administrators to recognise whether a rule has had a positive, negative or unforeseen effect, or whether areas of the sport need changing. It enables the administrators to measure the effect that the new rule has had on any problem areas and empowers them to objectively view perceived problems in a game. It has been recognised that unforeseen areas of the game may change by altering their rules, and a change in one area of a sport may lead to other changes that were not perceived. It was also noted that the objective qualities of notational analysis permitted the administrators of a sport to observe any changes, enabling them to objectively view the effect that changes may or may not have.

17.3 Rules and cheating

Acts of rule breaking or cheating can create a huge amount of discussion in the media, where a famous player may turn the outcome of the game with a single illegal action, such as Thierry Henri's handball in a World Cup qualifier (Kempson, 2009) or 'the hand of God' incident with Diego Maradona (Burns, 1987).

The definition of cheating has undergone philosophical discussion, with researchers having slightly different theories on what constitutes cheating. The distinction between breaking a rule and cheating is a delicate one, where the intention of breaking the rule distinguishes one from the other. Leaman (2001) and Feezell (1988) recognised intentional cheating as where there is some predetermined methodical reason for breaking the rules of the game, which would be in the form of a predetermined action that would result in a positive outcome for the instigator of the illegal action. As a performance analyst, it would be difficult to distinguish between intentional or unintentional cheating; for example, in football, players may be in an offside position without realising or a place kicker in rugby union may unintentionally place the kicking tee closer to the posts. Whether the act of cheating was intentional or unintentional is contentious, therefore the definition of an intentional and unintentional cheating action would have to be subjective, which would rely on the analyst's knowledge of the sport and input from people involved in the sport.

Wertz (1981) and McDonald (1996) described sporting competition as being defined and controlled by constitutive and regulative rules. Constitutive rules are those that are defined in the rule book and make up the fundamental aspects of the game that players and officials adhere to. Further to these rules, regulative rules were defined as those rules that players adhered to that do not exist in the rule book; such rules are not written down, but exist as 'agreements' between players. For example, when a player has been seriously injured on a football field, the team in possession sometimes kicks the ball into touch so that the player can be treated, which usually results in the injured player's team returning the ball to the opposition in the next play. The result of breaking either type of rule differs as, if one of the

TABLE 17.2 Examples of the types of cheating using Fraleigh's (2003) definition within different sports

	Injury	Technical	Movement/ Competition	Not interfering	Time/Position
Football	Maliciously tackling a player	Holding the shirt of another player after they have passed them with the ball	Tripping up a player who is not in possession of the ball	Standing in an offside position to receive the ball	Taking time to substitute players to reduce the amount of playing time
Rugby	Stamping on a player's head	Collapsing the scrum after the ball has been put in	Obstructing an opponent player who wishes to tackle the player in possession of the ball	Handling the ball in the scrum	Positioning the ball closer to the posts when taking a penalty goal
Squash	Hitting a player with a racket	Pushing a player as they are playing a stroke	Blocking a player when they are trying to play a shot	Handling the ball before a stroke	Taking too much time to serve the ball

constitutive rules is broken, if observed by the official, the offending team or player is penalised; however, if a regulative rule has been broken, then there is no official penalty. It is suggested that the two categories of rule breaking could both be termed as cheating, as the rules of the sport that control game play are broken, be it a constitutive or regulative rule. Prior work in performance analysis has included the analysis of penalties and free kicks in sport, with focus on the constitutive rules of the game (Whitaker and Hill, 2005; van Rooyen *et al.*, 2006; Eaves *et al.*, 2008). Undertaking research on regulative rules would be more difficult as these rules are not written in any book; therefore, any analysis would require research into defining the regulative rules used within a game.

Table 17.2 summarises the work conducted by Fraleigh (2003) which defined the following categories of cheating, and although he stated that he didn't believe that these categories encapsulated all possible forms of cheating, in terms of developing a generic model for cheating, his definitions could be used within performance analysis.

- *injury* – acts that intend to injure an opponent in order to reduce their effectiveness;
- *technical* – acts that intend to negate the earned advantage of an opponent when the opponent is in possession;
- *movement/competition* – acts that prevent or restrict the movements of an opponent who is not in a position of earned advantage;
- *not interfering* – acts that intend to gain an illicit advantage for the violator without interfering with an opponent;
- *time/position* – acts that are intended to reduce a negative impact of time or position of the violator's effectiveness.

In summary, of the definitions presented by the researchers, there are some distinct categorisations that could be used in performance analysis to develop a generic model to analyse cheating in sport; these are illustrated in Figure 17.1. First, it is recognised that cheating occurs with or without intention and this aspect could be used within an analysis of cheating, but the analyst must be able to subjectively decide whether a cheating action was intended. There are constitutive and regulative rules that control game play; however, regulative rules would be difficult to identify without good knowledge of the sport as they are not formally recognised within sports. Creating indicators on cheating around constitutive rules would be relatively uncomplicated as they would be developed within the rules of the game. Finally, it is suggested that cheating can be defined within generic categories that could be applied to all sport for analysis within and between sports.

The development of this research aimed to define cheating in terms of developing a practical conceptual model for the performance analyst to use within their sport or for the comparison of sports. Previous analysis on cheating in sport has focused on the breaking of constitutive rules, analysing penalties and free kicks, with no reference to any regulative rules, intention or the generic nature of cheating.

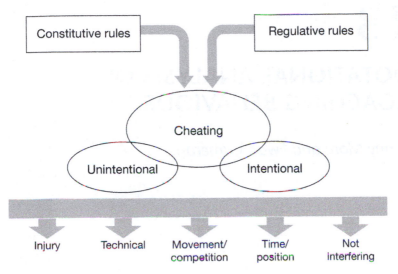

FIGURE 17.1 A model for the analysis of cheating.

The research undertaken has drawn from the philosophical nature of cheating and the categories of cheating that have been put forward, and turned this into a practical method of further analysis into cheating. Possible ways to progress the research have been suggested so that the impact and effect of cheating in sport can be fully explored by the performance analyst using the model presented in this research.

17.4 Conclusion

It is suggested that rules change within a sport for either safety, the natural development of the sport, or finally, from external pressures such as the media and commercial organisations. The use of performance analysis within a sport to evaluate rule changes enables administrators to recognise whether a rule has had a positive, negative or unforeseen effect, or whether areas of the sport need changing. It enables the administrators to measure the effect that the new rule had on any problem areas and empowers them to objectively view perceived problems in a game. Further to this, another aspect of analysis of how rules are tested and stretched would be to analyse the different forms of cheating within the model suggested within this chapter.

18

NOTATIONAL ANALYSIS OF COACHING BEHAVIOUR

Kenny More and Ewan Cameron

18.1 Introduction: notational analysis and the coaching process

A primary function of coaching is to provide athletes with the opportunity to acquire, refine and learn skills that will produce a successful performance in competition. A significant part of this requires the design of training opportunities. To this end, there is a proliferation of materials to support the coach in content selection and, as previous chapters have evidenced, considerable guidance on methods to identify, then systematically observe and analyse, aspects of individual and team performance for subsequent training.

However, less well established is the role of notational analysis in monitoring the instruction and feedback the coach delivers in the training and competition environments. If we consider the significant time devoted to the formal analysis of performance, followed by the careful and informed selection of training content, it would seem appropriate to further the rationale and means of monitoring effectiveness of coach behaviour within the coaching process.

Effective coaching is crucial to the pursuit of optimal sporting performance, and the more effective the coaching, the more fully the coach's role will benefit athlete performance. Current literature suggests that coaching behaviour continues to be guided by the traditions of the sport, the coaches' intuition, and the emulation of other coaches (Partington and Cushion, 2013), though this emulation can be helpful to developing coaches in their evaluation of behaviour. However, research into coaching effectiveness must continue with attempts to analyse, describe and modify a variety of coaching behaviours, building on its initial teacher effectiveness framework, where teaching skills were viewed as a science and, therefore, amenable to systematic observation and analysis. It is also acknowledged that aspects of coaching behaviour can also be examined by interpretive and semi-structured interviews (O'Donoghue and Mayes, 2013).

Notational analysis of the coaching process promotes the objective assessment of behaviour and can, therefore, provide insight into variables deemed important in determining effectiveness. This systematic process can provide valid and reliable information that can accurately describe coaching behaviour, and advances in computer/device and audio–visual technology have enhanced the efficiencies of data acquisition, analysis and feedback. It is now possible, for example, to analyse verbal coaching behaviour using an interactive audio–visual software tool on an iPad, to provide meaningful and timely output on the coach's performance. The utility of such methods as part of an intervention strategy has real application for those in coach mentoring capacities, and examples prevail at the Scottish Football Association, the International Rugby Board, and within the National Soccer Coaches Association of America (NSCAA) of the USA.

18.2 Evolution of the analysis of coaching behaviour

18.2.1 A historical perspective

In the 1950s, the American Educational Research Association stated that after 40 years of research into teaching effectiveness, during which a vast number of studies was carried out, few outcomes had advanced the assessment and modification of teaching behaviour. It was ultimately criticized as being a blind search for the qualities of good teaching. However, by the end of the 1970s teacher process variables, the variables concerned with the actual activities of classroom teaching, became the focus. Researchers began to study skills and strategies for organization, instruction, and feedback provision, as these were shown to relate to teacher performance, as measured by student achievement. It became clear that teachers should have their teaching observed, receive regular feedback on these observations, and be provided with the necessary support to effect improvement.

A substantial body of evidence suggested that this feedback should be based on information gathered through systematic observation (the adoption of notational analysis techniques), because intuitive observation and analysis was unlikely to be a powerful enough tool to create lasting improvement. Creating a systematic and objective process would help ensure a more complete description and understanding of performance was gained, and more quantifiable evidence to present to the teacher. This would allow greater precision of information, allowing goals to be set and subsequently monitored.

Systematic observation permits a trained observer to use the observational instrument to observe, record and analyse events and behaviours, with the assumption that the other observers, using the same observational instrument, and viewing the same sequence of events, would agree with the recorded data. Only through such methods could the observation and data acquisition process provide reliable, accurate and consistent information for the assessment of effectiveness. Each instrument would be designed to produce information on specific variables, and be tailored to the goals of a particular observation. They would reflect the scope and complexity of the behaviour under observation, as well as consider the means of input/output (hand notation or computer-assisted) and the timescale for data (real–time or post-event). Over the last 40 years these instruments have advanced significantly, and been adapted for sports coaching.

18.2.2 Systematic observation instruments

One of the first instruments used to observe instructional behaviour was the Flanders Interaction Analysis System (FIAS). It was designed to analyse verbal teaching behaviour under the headings of teacher talk, student talk and silence. The strengths of FIAS were compelling, and the first attempts to analyse teaching in physical education were modifications of that system. Computer-aided tools for the physical education environment then emerged with ALT-PE (Metzler, 1981) and PETEACH (Hawkins et al., 1994).

During the late 1980s and early 1990s the Centre for Sports Analysis at the University of British Columbia undertook the task of extending and improving upon existing techniques and instruments. Specific attention was directed towards the recording of coaching and athlete behaviours during team sport practices. Of specific relevance here was the Coach Analysis Instrument (CAI), which was designed to analyse the verbal behaviours of the coach when organizing and instructing within a defined segment of practice. Although previous instruments had identified the nature of verbal coaching behaviours, More and Franks (1996) believed these early instruments did not fully describe the instructional style in use. Any strategy to modify coaching behaviour, based on selected and independent findings, failed to recognize the complexity of effective instruction and would be limited to the scope of the original instrument. After refinements were made to its original structure, the CAI produced a quantitative analysis profile reflective of every comment made during observed practice. It was used in conjunction with an audio/video-taped recording of the session, allowing the user to recall that representation of the previously recorded behaviour.

While this structure was originally mapped onto the keyboard of a computer, its most recent application has been through performance analysis software FocusX2 (www.performanceinnovation.net). This software has maintained the integrity of the data being logged on each comment, but permits instant compilation and display of summary data, and instant interactive access to the video associated with the data. This has very recently been updated with the launch of Focus X2i, a fully interactive video analysis and visual feedback app for the iPad. Figure 18.1 shows the screen architecture for the creation and review of data on the verbal behaviour of coaches.

This most recent advancement provides great flexibility and, as many people have identified, live coding can be an advantage and, perhaps more importantly, be essential if the purpose is to provide immediate feedback for a supportive intervention. As tablet-based technology continues to improve, solutions such as that provided by Performance Innovation Ltd. can enable different approaches to

FIGURE 18.1 Display screen of Focus X2i

be taken in analysing coach behaviour. This is particularly relevant when on the training field where the coaches enable recording, measurement and provision of real-time feedback as part of their development.

In 2008, Brown and O'Donoghue used the Dartfish package (www.dartfish. com) to develop a split screen solution for analysing coaching behaviour. When filming a 60-minute netball coaching session two cameras were used, with one focusing on the coach and the other looking at the wider view of coach and athlete behaviour. The coach also wore a microphone in order to make a clear recording of the coach's verbal behaviour, without requiring that they compromise the two filming points in order to capture this. This scenario gave them a synchronized multi-screen and clear audio record, which they could then 'tag' using a coaching behaviour system developed within Dartfish.

Examining other examples of systematic observation instruments enables a better understanding of the motivations and needs behind their development. In 2012, Cushion *et al.* outlined the evolution of the Coach Analysis and Intervention System (CAIS). The development of CAIS was based on the belief that systematic observation provides descriptive baseline data of actual coaching behaviours, and that this area of study, and coaching in general, remains under-researched. While a number of tools in existence had been explored, such as the Arizona State University Observation Instrument (ASUOI), the view of Cushion *et al.* was that none of these tools was sufficiently sensitive to the coaching context when looking at coaching behaviours and practice. Existing tools simply reflected the areas of behaviour being researched by the authors at that time. They noted that the accuracy of any behavioural records, emergent from observational research, rely upon the ability of the instrument to distinguish and measure crucial coaching behaviours (Brewer and Jones, 2002; Horn 2002), and that the existing tools had not been designed with sufficient recognition of context alongside behaviours. They shared the view that this would lead to overly simplistic description and therefore discrepancies between the situational behaviours and those actually recorded (Brewer and Jones, 2002).

Context was key for Cushion *et al.*, who identified that even within a particular sport at a specific competitive level, coach behaviour could be examined in both competition and training environments (which also have different states such as 'training form' and 'playing form'), and at different times of the season. Their determination was to further develop the CAIS that had been built using SportsCode analysis software (www.sportstec.com).

There are clearly a range of sports, environments, levels of coach and athlete ability to consider when analysing sports coaching. Cushion *et al.* (2012) took the view that existing systems are not grasping this subtlety because the behaviours defined within the instruments simply do not allow for these differences. The emphasis here is not to settle for using tools because they happen to be available, but to identify what it is the coach wants to observe and measure and importantly the related contextual information in which the behaviour is observed. Having identified these, it is then possible to determine whether existing tools are satisfactory, or whether an enhanced or even bespoke solution will satisfy the requirement. Because these solutions are based on digital audio/video recordings of coaching practice, the system's outputs can provide powerful video clips of any selected behaviour, combinations of behaviours, or coaching moments (Cushion *et al.*, 2012). It has been our experience that good audio recordings are similarly important when observing and providing feedback on those behaviours and moments within a coaching environment.

18.3 Purpose and examples of published work

From these foundations of analysing different aspects of teaching and coaching behaviours, the volume of work now in existence through observational analysis is significant. In addition, the validity of using performance analysis for understanding and developing coaches is well established.

We recognize at least three main application areas for existing and future work.

18.3.1 Building a knowledge base of coaching behaviour

Building a knowledge base will enable a better understanding of coaching behaviour for use in education, review and on-going learning about sports coaching practices. A wide range of literature exists describing coach behaviour across a number of different sports, environments and age groups. Changing coaches' practice and behaviour requires that coaches can recognize what they do, and what the assumptions are underlying their performance (Harvey *et al.*, 2010).

There are in fact many aspects of coaching that can be targeted as the focus for such study, and many that remain under-researched. The tools and approaches used in these areas of study continue to evolve, as good questions and areas requiring further research are identified. For example, in 2006 Smith and Cushion published a study to investigate the working behaviours of six top-level professional soccer coaches, having identified one such area of neglect as being that of the professional youth coach, and more specifically the working behaviours of English youth coaches. This piece of work used a combination of a modified version of the ASUOI and semi-structured interviews. Of interest was their speculation that 'silence' is in fact a deliberate coaching strategy, and in the course of their study recognized that it emerged in fact as the most common behaviour employed by the coaches within their sample. Silence had previously been categorized as 'off task' (Claxton, 1988). The work is an interesting example in many ways, not least that it provides good examples of how many good questions regarding understanding coach behaviour remain unanswered.

In 2013, Partington and Cushion conducted a study to investigate the coaching behaviours of elite English youth soccer coaches in different practice settings to gain insight into the coaches' cognitive processes underpinning these behaviours. This study takes account of the different contexts of coaching behaviours. In order to complete their work, Partington and Cushion used a modified version of the CAIS. Their study identified a relationship between practice type and coach behaviour, and in doing so underlined the need to be better aware of context when looking at coaching behaviours.

A review of the existing literature relating to scientific knowledge of coaching behaviour serves not only to provide valuable insight, but also to assist greatly in identifying areas requiring further study and in posing additional questions.

18.3.2 Building a knowledge base related to the impact of coaching behaviours

This area of study has less published work than that described above, and yet is as important. It sets out to understand how different coaching behaviours impact upon the teams and athletes being coached. In 1979, Curtis *et al.* published 'Scrutinising the skipper: A study of leadership behaviours in the dugout'. This paper emphasized the reaction to and perception of coaching behaviours, as well as the behaviours themselves. Again identifying another area of under-researched work, they developed and utilized the 'Coaching Behaviour Assessment System' (CBAS) to look at 12 categories of behaviour. A previous study by these authors had proposed that the effect of coaching behaviours on team attitudes is determined by how players perceive these behaviours, and also, that players' attitudes should be more closely related to their perceptions of a coach's behaviour than to his/her actual behaviour. The broadening of context is an interesting aspect of this study where the authors identify that the events immediately preceding the behaviour set the stage for the psychological effect of the behaviour itself. This area merits significant further work, and would have significance in sports psychology as well as coaching and leadership.

18.3.3 Developing effective coaching behaviours

It is natural that, along with learning about coaching behaviour and its impact, one would want to provide the opportunity to utilize that knowledge to develop and educate coaches. This area allows coaches to be measured during their development, and to support interventions along the way.

In 1996, More and Franks set out to ensure that the opportunity to practice coaching skills with the provision of systematic feedback would be widely recognized as beneficial to the coaching skills. They followed guidance from educational research where change could be expedited if attention is on one process variable and only a few coaching behaviours are selected for change at any one time. By using the CAI, and focusing on the process variable of verbal behaviour, attempts were made to use a data-driven intervention strategy to improve the verbal behaviour of coaches. More and Franks viewed a typical training session as having distinct segments, each segment being composed of a number of drills that are devoted to coaching the skills and concepts of that particular segment (see Figure 18.2).

The CAI was designed to allow an observer to collect and subsequently analyse data pertaining to the organization and instruction components of these

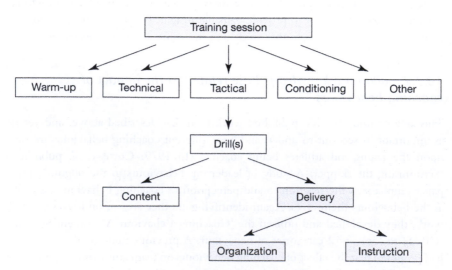

FIGURE 18.2 A training session can be represented as a hierarchical model with a continuous timeline of activity segments.

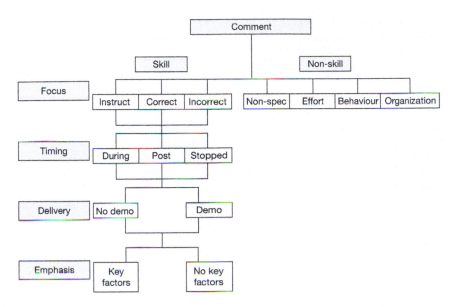

FIGURE 18.3 The structure of the instructional component, representing four levels of data entry for each verbal comment.

drills. The organizational component consists of the verbal behaviour displayed while explaining the organizational goals of the drill. As such, all comments were grouped and separated from the instructional component. The instructional component consisted of all other coaching information, with clear operational criteria for each separate and definable comment (See Figure 18.3).

This CAI was presented to a panel of observational analyst experts, members of the Coaching Association of Canada and other members of the coaching fraternity. There was a clear consensus as to its completeness and validity as a measuring tool, and as a mechanism of professional development. Appropriate intra- and inter-observer reliability measures were conducted to ensure that recorded behaviours were attributable to the coach and not the observer.

18.3.3.1 Understanding the data

In the example of the CAI, the major source of information is the quantitative comment summary data. As a result, the researchers at UBC decided to create quantitative targets for the different dimensions of verbal behaviour. However, while the precise value of any specific target was not considered critical, it was anticipated that these targets would benefit the coaches when interpreting their data, generate motivation to change a particular behaviour, and provide a reference whereby they could evaluate the magnitude of the resulting change. These targets were estimates of effective coaching behaviour based upon an understanding of relevant research literature, and dialogue with coach educators.

TABLE 18.1 Example data from one coach using coaching behaviour analysis

	Analysis of coaching behaviour: Coach 1					
Skill comments	83 (%)	(> 80) (%)	Non-skill comments	17 (%)	(< 20) (%)
Focus:			Focus:		
Instruction	56	(40)	Organizational		
Feedback on correct performance	32	(40)	Social (behaviour/effort)		
Feedback on incorrect performance	12	(20)	Non-specific		
Timing:					
During performance	45	(30)			
Post performance	43	(60)			
Stopped (freeze)	12	(10)			
Delivery:					
Demonstration	N = 4				
Emphasis:					
Key factors	81	(80)			
Non key factors	19	(20)			

The results table (Table 18.1) provides a typical display of summary data on the instructional component of the CAI. Target behaviours (discussed in the next section) are provided in brackets for comparative purposes only and may be changed as needed.

18.3.3.2 Skill or non-skill-related comments

Skill-related comments are interactions directed at the athletic performance of the learners, while non skill-related comments are interactions directed at the organization and social behaviour of the learners. More effective coaches spend more time instructing the proposed content of the session and providing skill-related feedback than do those who are less effective. Intuitively, this suggests that more effective coaches spend less time organizing the athletes and providing behavioural feedback. It is believed that a necessity for increased amounts of behavioural feedback may reflect a lack of effective planning or organization. Improving those coaching qualities would allow them to spend a greater proportion of time giving skill-related instruction and feedback or allow more time for physical practice of the skill.

18.3.3.3 The focus of skill-related comments

The need for coaching comments to include information is compelling. When given in the form of instructions, the comments will relate to how the skill should be performed, and should pertain specifically to the skills and concepts that the drill is designed to improve. For example, in a soccer drill designed to improve the skill of crossing, verbal instruction should concentrate on the player's ability to gain the required pace, direction and flight of the ball. Once the skill has been executed, the coach can make comment on the quality of the performance in relation to its goal. Motor learning research promotes feedback as the single most important variable (except for practice itself, see Chapter 1) in learning a motor task. Because coaches are responsible for much of the augmented feedback received by athletes, it is crucial that the feedback given reflects effective strategies. Augmented feedback produces learning, not by reward or punishment, but by the provision of information on the action and, where necessary, on how to change and improve subsequent actions. Coaches, therefore, should ensure their information reinforces the specific aspects that are 'correct', or identify the 'incorrect' aspects to be modified. Thus, regardless of the success of the action, the inclusion of information ensures comments are neither general nor 'non-specific'. In terms of seeking a balance to feedback on 'correct' and 'incorrect' performance, research suggests a differential use of strategy based on the age and ability of the athletes involved.

18.3.3.4 The timing of skill-related comments

In developing a strategy for their verbal behaviour, the coach should be aware of the attentional capacity of athletes as they learn. If the skill is low in complexity, or familiar to the athlete, the athlete's information-processing system can effectively handle other stimuli at the same time. This is not true if the task requires full allocation of their attention. Consideration must be given to the amount and timing of instruction and feedback. Successful coaches have been shown to deliver a significant amount of information as soon as their athletes are free from the immediate demands of performance. This temporal location allows a strong association between the athlete's perception of the action and the augmented feedback delivered by the coach. A related issue to the timing of instruction and feedback is the frequency with which it is given. Practice with the athletes receiving feedback after every performance has been shown to be beneficial for the (temporary) performance of skill, but detrimental to the (relatively permanent) learning of skill. This principle, known as the guidance hypothesis, suggests that immediate performance is facilitated because the athlete is guided towards the target performance, but that learning is degraded as the athlete is not forced to attend to sensory feedback or detect errors. In practice (and depending on the specific activity), feedback should be frequent in initial practice to guide the athlete towards the goal of the action, then systematically less frequent as practice continues to force the athlete's self-detection processes.

18.3.3.5 The delivery of skill-related comments

A very effective way of delivering information is to support it with a visual demonstration. Also known as modelling, demonstrations can aid learning by accurately and skilfully portraying the critical features of performance. This creates an internal model that guides the athlete's response and provides a standard against which feedback is compared. The demonstration should be accompanied by succinct verbal instructions that ensure the athlete's attention is directed to the key aspects of performance.

Demonstrations can occur before the skill is attempted, to give the learners the idea of the movement, or during practice to confirm and extend the athlete's understanding of the performance; they can be performed by the coach or one of the athletes, provided the person is skilled in the act of demonstration; and can be delivered in slow motion to give a clear representation of physical relationships of body parts, or at normal speed to give a clear representation of the timing necessary for optimum performance (see earlier Chapters 1 and 2 for more details on modelling and demonstration).

18.3.3.6 The emphasis of skill-related comments

The need for coaching comments to include information seems conclusive. However, it would seem vital that the information given should pertain to the skills and concepts that the drill is designed to improve. For example, in a football drill designed to improve crossing ability, information based on the required pace, direction and flight of the crossed ball should prevail, and not issues such as ball reception or dribbling prior to the delivery of the cross. While these may, instinctively, be commented upon, it is clearly desirable that the majority of information be focused on the 'key factors'; these are factors that the coach has deemed beforehand to be critical to successful performance of the skill (in this example 'crossing').

18.3.3.7 The case for non-skill related comments

Those comments considered to be non–skill-related, i.e. organization, effort, behaviour and non–specific, also contribute to the quality of the learning environment. For example, occasional use of an enthusiastic or forcefully delivered comment to motivate or bring back on–task behaviour will have a positive effect on the concentration and application of the athletes. However, should these types of comments become commonplace, the coaching practice will not engage the athletes, and issues such as the original organization or content selection may be in need of revision.

18.3.3.8 The modification of coaching behaviour

The opportunity to practise relevant skills, with the provision of systematic feedback, has long been shown to improve sporting skills. However, it is now widely recognized that this process will also benefit teaching and coaching skills. For example, educational research has shown that change can be expedited if attention is on one process variable, and only a few teaching behaviours are selected for change at any one time. In the example given of the CAI above, the process variable is verbal coaching behaviour, and behaviours for change may be limited to only the 'timing' and 'emphasis' of comments.

More and Franks (1996) tested the usefulness of the CAI as a means of generating data to drive an intervention strategy. Four coaches were observed and analysed across 12 soccer practice sessions. This constituted four sessions during 'baseline', four sessions during 'intervention' and four sessions during 'follow-up'. Coaches A, B and C received intervention feedback through the CAI data, where selected behaviours were highlighted for discussion, and videotaped evidence was used to illustrate discussion points. Coach D was provided with video tapes of his own performance, and told to formulate and implement any of his own recommendations. Written journals and audio-tape recordings were also utilized to promote insight into the complexity of verbal behaviour and the 'human factors' that affect behaviour modification.

Change was quantified according to the 'organizational' and 'instructional' components of the CAI. Interpretation of cumulative values for organizational effectiveness revealed marked improvement in Coaches A and B's behaviour following intervention, and marginal improvement in the clarity and conciseness of Coach C. Marginal change was also reported in the organizational behaviour of Coach D, although this was not maintained. Instructional effectiveness was assessed by Time-Series Analysis, according to recognized criteria. There was evidence from each behaviour dimension that change can occur and be maintained as a result of exposure to the CAI intervention strategy. However, this was clearly contingent on the coaches' understanding of what was asked of them, and remaining focused and committed to changing these particular behaviours. The analysis of Coach D's behavioural change suggested that there were limitations to the sensitivity of discretionary viewing, as only two dimensions of behaviour resulted in positive change.

This research provided support that the modification of behaviour can occur through the systematic collection of valid and reliable information. Such intervention can oversee the fine-tuning of existing skills and/or the identification and acquisition of new skills, the information generated being used as direct feedback to reinforce appropriate performance, or to identify weakness and recommend change. However, it is difficult to ascertain why consistent, desirable change did not occur in all dimensions of analysed behaviour, or as readily for one coach as for another. Three reasons were proposed for this differential success in modifying behaviour, and these resonate with findings from contemporary studies.

First, the information that is delivered should be linked to the overall goal of more effective coaching performance. The coaches need to understand the consequences of more effective verbal behaviour, i.e. the link to the learning properties of feedback, and the resultant effect on athlete performance and improvement. Second, the coach should feel supported by the 'supervisor's' attention. While the intervention sessions of this study tried to address areas for change in a supportive and collaborative manner, it is likely that not all information was accepted by the different individuals. Such perceptions were evident in the reactions of the coaches and their journal entries. It has since proved beneficial for the 'supervisor' to use instances of positive behaviour even when addressing areas of weakness. Third, the context in which the intervention strategy occurs has an impact on likely success. If not enough importance is attached to the results of the intervention, there may be little incentive for the coach to accept prescriptive comment and strive for improvement. Where, for example, certification is not the end result, significant intrinsic motivation is required to commit to the need for change, and remain focused on any targets set.

While the CAI and other intervention strategies have provided evidence that modification can occur across a range of coaching behaviours, including those that require the balancing and orchestration of behaviour, further research could investigate the optimal dissemination of any intervention strategy. In recent years the delivery of the CAI to both soccer and rugby coaches has 'packaged' information into two stages: first, by educating coaches on the nature and complexity of their verbal behaviour in advance of them becoming the focus of analysis and modification; second, by increasing sensitivity to their baseline behaviours, thus providing a much better platform for subsequent prescription.

18.4 Summary

While coaching behaviour remains the most studied aspect of sports coaching, with over 50 per cent of the published work in coaching between 1970 and 2001 falling into the focus category of 'behaviour' (Gilbert and Trudel, 2004), there exists a great deal of scope for further work in this area. Almost all of the published literature reviewed by the authors for this chapter either explicitly state this as an area of need, or pose good questions meriting further research and analysis. Theme fields such as coaching science continue to develop, and by nature, require descriptive studies for basic understanding and accumulation of knowledge (Gilbert and Trudel, 2004). Because of the breadth of variation that exists in terms of sports, age groups, culture and geography, etc. there are many areas of sports coaching that remain under-researched in terms of understanding coaching behaviours.

19

PERFORMANCE ANALYSIS IN THE MEDIA

Nic James

19.1 Introduction

Performance analysis is usually thought of in terms of providing feedback for players and coaches to enable improvement in sports performance. This is not necessarily so, as media coverage of sport often adds statistical detail to their reporting of events for the purpose of informing the sports fan. Consequently, two separate explanations for carrying out performance analysis can be seen to exist, i.e. by those involved in a sport for performance improvement and by media groups for the enlightenment of sports fans. Identifying this distinction also raises the interesting question as to what extent these two performance analysis tasks differ or indeed are similar. This chapter will focus on presenting performance analysis as commonly depicted in the media. Some reference will be made to academic and professional sports teams' use of similar information, although this will not be exhaustive since other publications offer more of this type of information. For example, students of sport have been well served by previous books edited by Hughes and Franks (1997, 2004) as well as original research published in scientific journals, e.g. *electronic International Journal of Performance Analysis in Sport*. Soccer players and coaches have also had a book written for them (Carling *et al.*, 2005) detailing the types of analysis performed at elite clubs. There have also been books aimed at the general public; one that achieved bestseller status in the USA (Lewis, 2003) told the account of how Billy Beane, a highly talented but low achieving baseball player, became general manager of the Oakland Athletics and transformed the team's fortunes by picking new players solely on the analysis of their playing statistics rather than trusting his scouts' reports and recommendations.

Newspaper, television and internet coverage of sporting events usually presents performance analysis in the form of summary statistics or 'performance indicators' to use the terminology of Hughes and Bartlett (2002). These statistical insights are often debated over in the television studio by the assembled pundits or form the basis of in-depth analysis in the newspapers. However, they may also be used as the basis of the topic of conversation in school playgrounds, university cafeterias and business meeting rooms all over the world. Indeed, these statistics are now so common that it would be surprising if anyone with an interest in sport was not familiar with this form of performance analysis, although they might not recognise it as such.

This chapter will review the type of information portrayed in the various forms of media and discuss the extent to which they achieve their aim of describing the events of the sport in question. Potential limitations of these methods are also discussed with suggestions given for how performance analysts working for sports teams or undertaking research might amend or apply these methods.

19.2 Classifying games

The characteristics of a sport determine how the media present both the play itself and the performance analysis results, mainly in an attempt to maximise the enjoyment and interest of the readers/viewers. The sports selected in this chapter are the most watched and read about, at least in relation to the media coverage afforded them. However, while the techniques for performance analysis illustrated here are related to the sports that receive more media coverage than others, they are often transferable to other related sports. For example calculating the ratio of forced compared to unforced errors in tennis is applicable to squash, badminton, table tennis etc. Indeed, the extent to which the statistics portrayed for one sport are applicable to another is largely determined by the degree of similarity between sports. Consequently, this chapter will present the media's portrayal of performance analysis in three different sections: invasion; net and wall; and striking and fielding sports. This classification scheme for sports is based on the objectives and structure of the games (Read and Edwards, 1992) and relates well to the different perform-ance analysis techniques portrayed in the media.

19.3 Invasion games

Invasion games are characterised by playing areas that can be split into two halves, where the objective is for one team to defend its half and attack the opponent's half. Invasion games tend to be among the most popular spectator sports, although different ones are popular depending on the part of the world. The common characteristics of these sports include passing, shooting and tackling, and performance analysis interest tends to centre on aspects of play such as set pieces, field position, time in possession and scoring. The examples given here are taken from soccer, rugby union and basketball, although the techniques could just as easily apply to American football, netball, hockey etc.

19.3.1 Soccer

The 'beautiful game' attracts massive media interest in much of the world and currently seems to be increasing its worldwide audience. The rules of the game are simple, although the offside laws may stretch this contention somewhat, but performance analysis of 22 players interacting intermittently is somewhat more complex. Newspapers in the UK devote more column inches to soccer than any other sport but the extent to which they portray performance analysis statistics is relatively limited (see Figure 19.1).

The chart presented in Figure 19.1 was replicated in virtually every British newspaper at the time of writing using the same performance indicators, although some chose not to include all of them. This suggests that one or two independent companies collect these statistics and sell them to the newspapers, e.g. Opta Sportsdata (www.sportingstatz.com) provide statistics for a number of media companies. However, if this was the case you would expect the same values in each newspaper. To test this hypothesis O'Donoghue (2007) compared seven Sunday newspaper reports on three FA Premier League soccer matches, using the same indicators as Figure 19.1, and found limited agreement between them. This would suggest that the reliability of this information is questionable, which is surprising given that in many instances a lot of time, effort and money has been invested in their collection. The extent to which this potential lack of precision is important, however, is determined by what the statistics are to be used for. In the main, of course, they are simply to provide additional information for the reader, and in this instance, it may be argued that precision is not essential. However, if the statistics and the way in which they are presented are also utilised by sports teams, then incorrect statistics could well be problematical. My experience of sports coaches and players involved in high-level sport, suggests that they tend to prefer to use the statistics provided by their own performance analysts. This is because

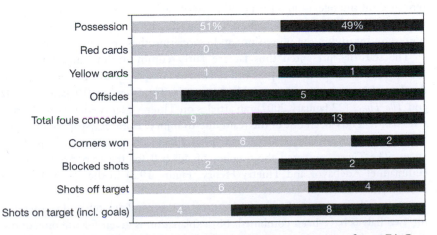

FIGURE 19.1 Match stats as presented in *The Sunday Times* newspaper for an FA Cup match won 3–0 by the League One side.

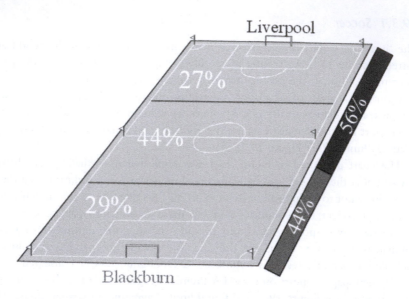

FIGURE 19.2 Possession percentages for a FA Premier League soccer match.

the collection of performance information is then under the control of the coaches who can determine what and how this information is collected.

Television coverage of soccer presents similar information although in a far more visual manner, e.g. shots are often presented as arrows starting from the point of the kick and finishing where the ball crossed the goal line. Recently Sky television introduced an interactive service that can present the match statistics as they change throughout the match. For example, ball possession is presented as a percentage (in the style of Figure 19.2) which is continuously updated by Sky's analyst and refreshed on the television screen at the end of each possession. For the interested future performance analyst therefore, it is possible to work out how Sky defines possession by timing the possessions and comparing these results with Sky's.

The statistics presented thus far are fairly common and utilised regularly. However, individual newspapers and television companies also provide more in-depth analyses from time to time. For example *The Guardian* (19 January 2007) and *The Times* (22 January 2007) ran articles on Thierry Henry, the Arsenal striker who had recently been out of the team due to injury. Both newspapers attempted to show, via performance analysis, how Henry had influenced Arsenal's perform-ances. *The Times* compared the touches of the ball for the two Arsenal strikers (Emmanuel Adebayor and Thierry Henry, Figure 19.3) in the 2–1 win against Manchester United (21 January 2007).

The touch graphics in Figure 19.3 represent the whole match and so therefore the two halves have been combined. No explanation is given for the direction of attack although in this instance it is fairly self-explanatory, given the attacking roles of both players. *The Guardian* chose to depict the passing endpoints for two of

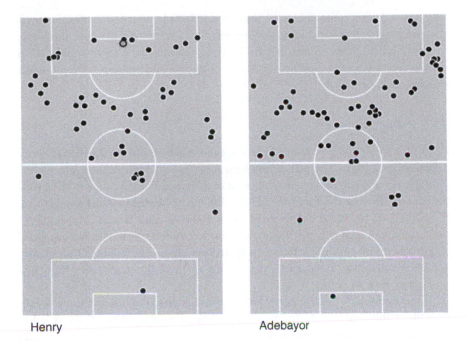

Henry   Adebayor

FIGURE 19.3 Touch graphics for Thierry Henry and Emmanuel Adebayor (grey dot represents Henry's headed goal).

Without Henry: Wigan 0 Arsenal 1 (13/12/06)				With Henry: Arsenal 4 Charlton 0 (02/01/07)			
40	45	33	30	27	44	61	63
37	20	21	13	44	64	59	46
24	24	40	25	24	52	47	32
→ Direction of play				→ Direction of play			

FIGURE 19.4 Passing end points for Arsenal with and without Thierry Henry.

Arsenal's previous matches to show how Arsenal play with more varied passing when Henry is present in the side (Figure 19.4).

As Figure 19.4 shows, the match depicting Arsenal without Henry is characterised by fewer passing end points in comparison to the match with Henry. Also when Henry was playing there was a greater tendency to use the left side of the pitch, which is where he tends to operate. However, this type of analysis risks erroneous conclusions. Why? Well, the selection of just one match to represent typical play is dangerous. How do we know that the matches selected were not very unusual ones, quite unlike the normal matches played by Arsenal? Of course, it is also possible that they are very representative. The point is that it is impossible to know on the basis of one match. Thus a performance analyst would collect passing end points for a number of matches both with and without Henry to make conclusions more reliable.

19.3.2 Rugby union

Rugby union involves teams of 15 players, each of whom can be classified as either a forward or a back. The play of the forwards tends to involve the eight players working as a single unit, often in small areas of the pitch. For the majority of viewers the complexities of the forwards' play is difficult to understand. In comparison, the backs tend to spread out over the pitch and their play is relatively simple to understand. Consequently, television pundits often try to explain what has happened and provide replays of the action to help analyse the events. Statistical summaries are often provided (Table 19.1) as a means of showing where one team had superiority over the other.

When comparing performances such as those depicted in Table 19.1, it is easy to look at the values in isolation, without regard to the other values or other potentially important information. For example, the tackles made and tackles missed should be considered together. In the example in Table 19.1, Wales missed what appears to be a very high percentage of tackles, 25.0 per cent (8 out of 32, 8 + 24) compared to 10.0 per cent by Ireland (4 out of 40). The fact that Ireland attempted more tackles suggests that Wales had more possession of the ball, confirmed by the possession percentage, but also that Wales used their possession to run at the Irish defence more so than Ireland did against Wales. This factor also needs to be considered when looking at the errors made by Wales, who, although they made more than Ireland (10 against 9), would not consider this an inferior performance as the handling errors should be considered with respect to the total number of times the ball was handled (Hughes and Bartlett, 2002); in this case the evidence suggests that Wales handled the ball more than Ireland.

TABLE 19.1 Summary statistics for the first half of the Six Nations match between Wales and Ireland played on the 4 February 2007

Wales		Ireland
51%	Total possession	49%
56%	Total territory	44%
24	Tackles made	36
8	Tackles missed	4
9	Ball won in opposition 22	3
52	Passes completed	40
22	Possession kicked	18
10	Errors made	9

It is usually the case that an individual's or a team's statistics need to be considered in light of other information. For example, Hughes and Bartlett (2002) suggest that performances may be considered relative to typical performance standards by similar teams or previously accomplished standards by the same team. Thus, the values in Table 19.1 do not provide evidence of a particularly good or poor performance by either team as, for example, in isolation, we do not know whether winning the ball nine times in the opposition's 22 is a particularly good or bad performance. We do know that Wales won the ball three times as often in the opponent's 22 as Ireland did, which indicates superiority, but is this a typical value for a team of this standard? Also, what the statistics do not reveal is that Ireland scored a try from one of these three turnovers in the opposition's 22, something that Wales were unable to do from their nine. Hence, while the total territory values give an indication of how the match had been played, the score at half-time, Wales 9 Ireland 12, indicates a marked difference in success rate.

The statistics presented in Table 19.1 reflected overall team performance. However, the media often provide statistics in relation to individuals, usually to highlight outstanding performances or those of the supposed key players, be it during or after the match. For example Sky television showed Opta Index statistics for Lawrence Dallaglio's performance in a match between Wasps and Perpignan (13 January, 2007) to indicate that he had made ten tackles and carried the ball seven times. Without knowledge of what a player in his position usually does in matches of this sort it is impossible to know whether his performance is out of the ordinary or not. Performance analysts working for rugby teams will collect this sort of information for all of their players on a match–by–match basis (e.g. James et al., 2005). This will enable them to assess whether players had good or bad games, and coaches can utilise summary information gained from a number of matches to determine where players' strengths and weaknesses lie, which in turn can suggest training drills to improve performance or form the basis of selection decisions.

19.3.3 Basketball

Basketball involves teams of five players trying to score baskets which are usually worth two points but if the shot is from outside the three point line then an extra point is awarded. Fouls can result in free throws which are worth one point each, although usually two free throws are awarded. Once a basket is scored, possession passes to the team scored against, which results in rapid turnovers of possession. Since elite teams (this refers to National Basketball Association (NBA) data) have relatively high successful shooting percentages (approximately 45 per cent field goal, 35 per cent three point and 80 per cent free throw), basketball is characterised by high scores (about 100 pts per team). The nature of the game also means that each player's contribution to the team's performance can be broken down into scoring indices (assists, field goals, three point shots, free throws) and attempts to win possession (rebounds, steals, blocks and turnovers). A typical team's performance over a season is given in Table 19.2 (data from www.nba.com/bulls/stats).

TABLE 19.2 Player averages for the Chicago Bulls 2005/2006 regular season

Player	G	GS	MPG	FG (%)	3p (%)	FT (%)	OFF	DEF	TOT	APG	SPG	BPG	TO	PF	PPG
							Player averages 2005/2006 regular season								
Ben Gordon	80	47	31.0	.422	.435	.787	.50	2.20	2.70	3.0	.94	.06	2.25	3.00	16.9
Kirk Hinrich	81	81	36.5	.418	.370	.815	.40	3.20	3.60	6.3	1.16	.26	2.32	3.10	15.9
Luol Deng	78	56	33.4	.463	.269	.750	1.60	5.00	6.60	1.9	.92	.64	1.35	1.60	14.3

Key: G – Games played; GS – Games started; MPG – minutes per game; FG% – field goal percentage; 3p% – 3pt percentage; FT% – field throw percentage; OFF – offensive rebounds; DEF – defensive rebounds; TOT – total rebounds per game; APG – assists per game; SPG – steals per game; BPG – blocks per game; TO – turnovers per game; PF – personal fouls; PPG – points per game.

The NBA website provides up-to-date statistics throughout the season and includes archive information from previous seasons. This information is used by the media to identify individual players' histories and to compare current form with previous accomplishments. This use of previous accomplishments is a good method of putting statistics into perspective. Hughes and Bartlett (2002) recommend presenting statistical information with respect to previous performance standards, both of the same team or player and other teams. For example Ben Gordon's shooting performance (0.422 FG per cent, 0.435 3p per cent, 0.787 FT per cent; Table 19.2) could be put into perspective by comparing these statistics with his career statistics (0.428 FG per cent, 0.414 3p per cent, 0.841 FT per cent; www.nba.com/playerfile/ben_gordon/inde14.html?nav=page, accessed on 31/01/07). The two sets of statistics are relatively similar although these are based on 80 games for the 2005/6 season and 207 for his career. From this comparison we can only say that he appears pretty consistent but we do not know how good this performance is. If we also compare his shooting performance with the best performer during the 2005/6 season, Kobe Bryant (0.45 FG per cent, 0.347 3p per cent, 0.85 FT per cent; www.nba.com/playerfile/ben_gordon/index.html?nav=page, accessed on 31/01/07), we can see that his percentages are slightly better for three pointers but lower for free throws. Interestingly, Gordon was only ranked 47 in shooting (although this is out of 434 players). This is because the shooting ranking is based on points per game (Kobe Bryant scored 35.4 points per game) and not the success rate of shots. Clearly, Gordon did not take as many shots per game as Bryant. In order to put Gordon's shooting prowess into perspective it might be advisable to compare his performance with say the top 50 in the shooting rankings. Figure 19.5 shows that Gordon's field goal and free throw success rates are pretty typical of the performances of the top 50 rated scoring players that season. His three point shooting is one standard deviation better than the top 50 average

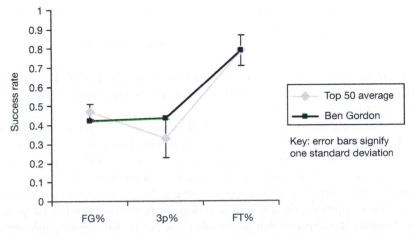

FIGURE 19.5 Ben Gordon's shooting success rate compared with the top 50 rated shooters during the 2005/6 season.

which equates to one more basket every ten attempts. It may be the case therefore, that Gordon, who has fewer than three full seasons of NBA experience, may in future be given the opportunity to shoot more often, by his team mates and coaches, in recognition of his excellent shooting success rate.

19.4 Net and wall games

Net and wall games are characterised by opponents sequentially trading shots until a shot is not returned or is played out of the boundaries of the playing area. In this manner points are won or lost until a winner is declared. Net and wall games tend to be played by individuals, pairs and teams with different games often played in small isolated parts of the world; e.g. squash and racketball are very similar but different games popular in different parts of the world. The common characteristics of these sports include serving, court coverage, shot selection and shot execution. General interest tends to centre on certain aspects of play such as the influence of serving, winners, errors and points won, although the media coverage of these statistics is sporadic. This section will focus on tennis as it has the most media coverage in this sports category.

The 2007 Australian Open tennis championships, like the other tennis grand slam events, produce all of the statistics typically used in the media for tennis (www.australianopen.com). The statistics for the first round of the men's event are presented in Table 19.3. This format has limited potential for trying to determine how individual matches progressed but does offer some insights into men's tennis in general, albeit on this type of playing surface, as court surface has been shown to affect the way in which rallies are played (O'Donoghue and Ingram, 2001). For example, there was an unforced error every three rallies (unforced errors/number of points). This seems quite high but would need to be checked against values achieved in previous tournaments to see whether this is normal or not. It may be indicative of the way men's tennis is played currently, i.e. players go for their shots, since there was also a winner played every 2.85 rallies. However, these values can only be interpreted sensibly by comparing the values with previous match values.

Event statistics are also available on an individual basis for a number of statistics. For example, the effectiveness of the women's first serve can be assessed via Table 19.4.

Comparison data are only effective if all factors are considered, however. In Table 19.4 the first serve points won are based on only two matches. If a particular player had been unlucky enough to play two very difficult matches, in comparison to another who had two easy wins, then the percentages would likely reflect this disparity rather than indicate a superior serving ability. In this instance a check of the number of points played would help distinguish whether this had happened. On doing so, it is apparent that the number one player, Kuznetsova, only served 52 service points, less than any of the other players in the top eight, suggesting she may well have had an easier draw than the others.

TABLE 19.3 Summary statistics of the men's event of the 2007 Australian Open tennis championships

	1st round
Matches played	64
5 Set matches	15
4 Set matches	18
3 Set matches	28
Sets played	235
Tie breaks played	42
Total games	2,269
Winners	4,980
Return games won	532
Server points won	8,858
Unforced errors	4,728
Total points	14,197
First serves in	8,485
% 1st serves in	57
Total aces	1,232
Total double faults	553
1st Serve pts won	6,066
% 1st Serve pts won	71
% 2nd Serve pts won	44

TABLE 19.4 Individual first serve statistics from the women's event of the 2007 Australian Open tennis championships

Rank	Player	Country	Matches	First serve points won
1	S. Kuznetsova	RUS	2	43 of 52 = 83 %
2	S. Williams	USA	2	55 of 68 = 81 %
3	A. Molik	AUS	2	65 of 83 = 78 %
4	A. Ivanovic	SRB	2	49 of 63 = 78 %
5	V. Zvonareva	RUS	2	51 of 66 = 77 %
6	A. Chakvetadze	RUS	2	59 of 77 = 77 %
7	P. Schnyder	SUI	2	62 of 81 = 77 %
8	L. Safarova	CZE	2	52 of 68 = 76 %
9	M. Sharapova	RUS	2	63 of 83 = 76 %
10	D. Safina	RUS	2	53 of 70 = 76 %

Technology was highly visible at the 2007 Australian Open, such that performance analysis was available live on the internet site as well as being available for players to utilise to check line calls (a maximum of two per set). IBM's 'Pointtracker' system (Figure 19.6) was available on the Australian Open website to view ongoing matches and replay previous ones. The viewpoint could be altered as well as other factors such as the number of visible shots, the display of serve and return of serve speeds as well as the speed of a winner. A further interesting feature was the ability

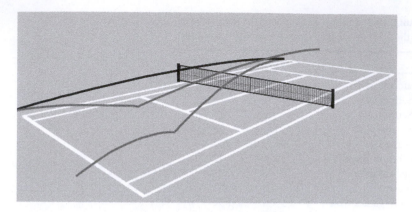

FIGURE 19.6 Visual representation of the 'IBM Pointtracker' system used at the 2007 Australian Open tennis championships.

to select a single category of shot, e.g. backhand unforced errors. This type of analysis can be useful for individual player feedback to highlight strengths and weaknesses.

The collection of live performance data has great potential but is also liable to error. Depending on the technology used, the chance of making mistakes is related to the time in which the data needs to be captured. In tennis the ball is hit between the players in a relatively small period of time, meaning that there is a limited time frame in which to record the necessary details. If you consider Table 19.3 it can be appreciated that some of the statistics can be derived from the match score, e.g. number of sets. More detail is required to determine the number of points and further information is required to determine the number of net points, winners etc. If these details are recorded by hand then as the number of things that are needed to be recorded per point increases so too does the likely error rate. If an automated system is possible, of course, then the error rate can theoretically be reduced to zero.

It is not uncommon for performance analysis researchers to utilise statistics gained from websites for their publications. Clearly, some account needs to be taken as to the accuracy of these match statistics. O'Donoghue (2007) compared the number of points he deemed to be net points in US Open tennis matches with the values reported on the US Open internet site (www.usopen.org). He found a systematic bias with 1.95 more net points being reported on average for each player in each set on the internet site than he recorded. O'Donoghue suggested that this difference was likely to have been due to how one defines a net point. However, while he could detail his definition it was impossible to determine the definition used by the US Open since this detail is not reported.

19.5 Striking and fielding games

Striking and fielding games tend to lend themselves well to the collection of performance statistics. This is because the different skills required can be broken down into many parts, each of which can be represented statistically. However, the two exemplar sports illustrated here show how the media's portrayal of the different sports can be dramatically different. Golf coverage on television tends to minimise the role of statistics while cricket has invested in the latest technology to produce visually stunning and informative performance analysis.

19.5.1 Golf

Golf has a long tradition (complete records go back to 1980 on the Professional Golfers' Association of America (PGA) website, www.pgatour.com) of collecting performance statistics; presumably, as just stated, there are many easily distinguishable skills involved in the game, e.g. driving distance, greens in regulation (GIR) and number of putts. The PGA website lists and continuously updates 30 different performance statistics although 17 of these relate directly to scoring outcomes, e.g. number of birdies.

Surprisingly, television companies do not avail themselves of these statistics very much. It is usual for them to select just a few statistics for one player, e.g. fairways hit, GIR and number of putts, to illustrate their performance on a particular round. This is useful if the viewer is knowledgeable about these statistics and, more importantly, the range in values that correspond to good and poor performances. In contrast to this limited presentation, the PGA website provides comprehensive statistics as well as visual and statistical information for each player on each hole of all PGA events. For example, using 'TourCast', powered by IBM's ShotLink system, each shot played in the FBR Open (1–4 February 2007) at TPC Scottsdale can be viewed with detailed information regarding shot distances also given. Figure 19.7 shows the outcome of the eventual winner Aaron Baddeley's first two shots on the par 4 11th hole (rated the hardest hole on the day averaging 4.18 shots) during his first round, with details regarding the distance of each shot and the resulting distance to the flag. The accuracy of this information appears to be considerable, given that distances are measured to inches. However, the measurement devices used (laser rangefinders and GPS systems) are typically accurate to about 1 yard at best, although this is still pretty impressive.

A recent innovation on the PGA web site is an attempt to simplify the various performance statistics into four values, power, accuracy, short game and putting, called the PGA Tour Skill Rating. Power relates to the power off the tee (average driving distance) but also factors in the percentage of drives that go over 300 and 320 yards. Accuracy combines driving accuracy with GIR and proximity to the hole for approach shots over 100 yards only. Short game uses all statistics for shots to the green from less than 100 yards, i.e. rough, sand, and utilises scrambling and GIR percentages from this distance. Putting uses all putting performances split into distances from the hole. This is an interesting attempt to answer one of the criticisms of performance statistics in golf, namely that they are not distinct variables. For example, GIR is widely regarded as a good indication of approach shot accuracy. However, if one player drives on average 300 yards compared to another player

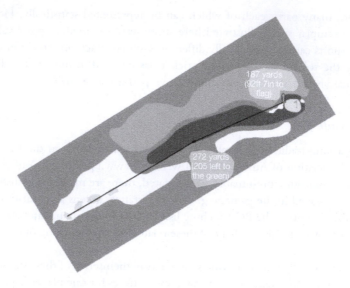

FIGURE 19.7 Visual representation of the 'IBM TourCast' system used on the PGA website.

only 250 yards then, if everything else was equal, the longer driver would typically have much easier approach shots and consequently the GIR would not be a fair comparison. In practice, the longer drivers tend to be less accurate and therefore play more approach shots from the rough. However the GIR statistic is bound to be a composite measure of both approach shot accuracy and driving performance. Hence the new accuracy measure explicitly combines elements of both driving and approach shots. It is too early to say how well these new measures will be received by players, scientists and sports fans but this does appear to have some merit.

19.5.2 Cricket

Fielding games are characterised by playing areas into which one team hits a ball and the other tries to retrieve it. While the rules for the different sports in this category differ, the objective is for the fielding side to minimise the opponent's score by catching, throwing and bowling successfully. General interest in games such as cricket and baseball tends to centre on aspects of play such as scoring rates, types of bowling delivery and shot selection. Fielding games are extremely popular, although not all over the world, and the media tends to produce very impressive performance analysis statistics.

Cricket has a long record of collecting statistics, recorded each year in the book 'Wisden'. Records are accessible online (http://content-usa.cricinfo.com/wisdenalmanack) and date back to 1864. These records are comprehensive and easily available to the media and public alike. The following example is primarily

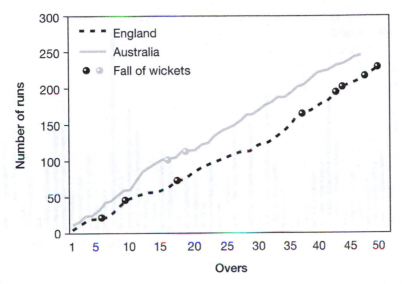

FIGURE 19.8 Cumulative runs scored in the one day international between Australia and England.

taken from Sky Sports live coverage of the Commonwealth Bank One Day International (ODI) Series between Australia and England at the MCG, Melbourne on 12 January 2007. Figure 19.8 shows how the runs were accumulated by both teams as they progressed through the allotted 50 overs. The chart also indicates where wickets fell and shows how Australia was always ahead of England's scoring rate. However, what is not so clear from this chart is how dramatically Australia outscored England in the early overs (see Figure 19.9).

Hughes and Bartlett (2002) suggest that performance indicators such as scoring rate should not be viewed in isolation of the opponent's performance. This does not mean a comparison, as in Figures 19.8 and 19.9, is sufficient. Rather they mean that a team's scoring is not only a reflection of their batting performance but also is dependant on the opposition's bowling performance. The television coverage gave the bowling statistics for both the current match (Table 19.5) as well as ODI career averages (Table 19.6).

Although the commentators did not explicitly link the England batting to the Australian bowling the two sets of statistics were regularly displayed. From a performance analyst's point of view, the Econ statistics (Tables 19.5 and 19.6) are most informative as they show that only two of the Australian bowlers (M. G. Johnson and M. J. Clarke) had better Econ rates during this match than their ODI averages. This would suggest that the Australian bowlers as a team performed at around their average, suggesting that the English batsmen did not have a particularly bad day, rather they were only allowed to score at the typical rate allowed by the Australian bowlers. Of course, other factors come into play in a single match such as conditions that favour the batsmen rather than the bowlers. Performance analysts

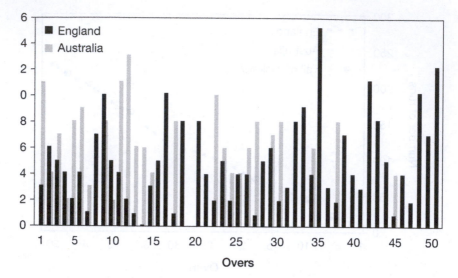

FIGURE 19.9 Runs scored each over in the one day international between Australia and England on 12 January 2007.

TABLE 19.5 Australian bowling statistics for the one day international between Australia and England on 12 January 2007

Bowler	Overs	Maidens	Runs	Wickets	Strike rate	Econ
G. D. McGrath	10	0	40	2	20.00	4.00
N. W. Bracken	9	0	46	3	33.33	5.11
S. R. Clark	10	0	58	1	10.00	5.80
M. G. Johnson	10	2	34	2	20.00	3.40
M. J. Clarke	8	0	35	0	0.00	4.38
C. L. White	3	0	27	0	0.00	9.00

Key: Strike rate is the number of wickets taken per 100 overs bowled. Econ is the number of runs conceded per over bowled.

TABLE 19.6 Australian bowling one day international career statistics

Bowler	Strike rate	Econ
G. D. McGrath	35.00	3.82
N. W. Bracken	28.20	4.36
S. R. Clark	36.00	5.50
M. G. Johnson	30.00	5.15
M. J. Clarke	41.30	5.24
C. L. White	48.00	7.50

working with a team are thus cautious about reading too much into the statistics from one match and prefer to look at trends over a series of matches.

The Hawkeye system (www.hawkeyeinnovations.co.uk), owned by The Television Corporation and introduced by Channel 4 in the UK in 2001, enables broadcasters to calculate the speed of each bowl as well as a range of visual information. This system has also reportedly been used by the England cricket team for post-match analysis. Figure 19.10 shows how the batsman (Cook) responded to balls delivered by McGrath. This type of analysis can be useful for both bowlers and batsmen to identify strengths and weakness in technique.

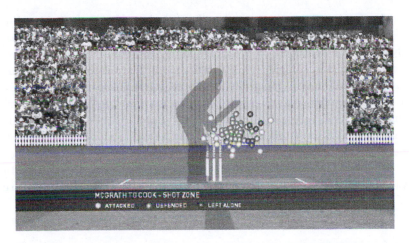

FIGURE 19.10 Bowling deliveries by McGrath to Cook in the Fourth Day of the Third Test between England and Australia in Perth, 14–18 December 2006.

Source: reproduced with permission from Hawk-Eye Innovations.

FIGURE 19.11 Bowling delivery by Panesar to Hayden in the Third Day of the Third Test between England and Australia in Perth, 14–18 December 2006.

Source: reproduced with permission from Hawk-Eye Innovations.

Other facets of performance can be visually represented such as where a bowler's deliveries land for each batsman, or for all right-handed batsmen. This is the strength of the Hawkeye system, particularly for media presentations, as this flexibility is immediately available and allows presenters to select the aspect of play they wish to display. This visual information also provides some objective information to the long enduring debate regarding leg before wicket (lbw) decisions (Figure 19.11) which must be a good thing!

19.6 Summary

It would seem that the media currently utilises a wide range of techniques to display the outputs of performance analysis. However, the extent to which performance analysis is used is dependent on the sport and the medium in which the results are presented. The most comprehensive statistics are, not surprisingly, available on the internet while the most sophisticated technology is primarily used on television. Television companies and newspapers tend to use statistics to illustrate a point they wish to make and consequently do not overly concern themselves with scientific rigour. For this reason sports teams prefer to utilise their own performance analysts rather than rely on statistics published in the media. In conclusion, it is suggested that the media provides variable quality performance analysis, which should not always be relied upon, but adds significantly to the enjoyment of the sports fans.

REFERENCES AND BIBLIOGRAPHY

Agresti, A. (1990). *Categorical Data Analysis*. New York: Wiley.

Agresti, A. (1996). *An Introduction to Categorical Data Analysis*. New York: Wiley.

Al-Abood, S. A., Davids, K. and Bennett, S. J. (2001). Specificity of task constraints and effects of visual demonstrations and verbal instructions in directing learner's search during skill acquisition. *Journal of Motor Behavior, 33*, 295–305.

Albright, S. C. (1993). A statistical analysis of hitting streaks in baseball. *Journal of the American Statistical Association, 88*, 1175–1183.

Alexander, D., McClements, K. and Simmons, J. (1988). Calculating to win. *New Scientist*, 10 December, 30–33.

Altman, D. G. and Gardner, M. J. (2002). Regression and correlation. In D. G. Altman, D. Machin, T. N. Bryant and M. J. Gardner (eds) *Statistics with Confidence*, pp. 86–88. Bristol: BMJ.

Aminian, K., Robert, P., Jéquier, E. and Schutz, Y. (1995). Incline, speed, and distance assessment during unconstrained walking. *Medicine and Science in Sports and Exercise, 27*, 226–234.

Annett, J. (1993). The learning of motor skills: Sports science and ergonomics perspectives. *Ergonomics, 37*, 5–16.

Ashford, D., Bennett, S. J. and Davids, K. (2006). Observational modeling effects for movement dynamics and movement outcome measures across differing task constraints: A meta-analysis. *Journal of Motor Behavior, 38*, 185–205.

Atkin, M., Anderson, D., Francis, B. and Hinde, J. (1989). *Statistical Modelling in GLIM*. Oxford: Clarendon Press.

Atkinson, G. and Nevill, A. (1998). Statistical methods for assessing measurement error (reliability) in variables relevant to sports medicine. *Sports Medicine, 26*, 217–238.

Atkinson, G. and Nevill, A. M. (2001). Selected issues in the design and analysis of sport performance research. *Journal of Sports Sciences, 19*, 811–827.

Aughey, R. J. (2011). Applications of GPS technologies to field sports. *International Journal of Sports Physiology Performance, 6*, 295–310.

Aughey, R. J. and Falloon, C. (2010). Real-time versus post-game GPS data in team sports. *Journal of Science and Medicine in Sport, 13*(3), 348–349.

Ayton, P., Hunt, A. J. and Wright, G. (1991). Randomness and reality. *Journal of Behavioral Decision Making, 4*, 222–226.

Badets, A., Blandin, Y. and Shea, C. H. (2006). Intention in motor learning through observation. *The Quarterly Journal of Experimental Psychology, 59*, 377–386.

Bahamonde, R. E. (2000). Changes in angular momentum during the tennis serve. *Journal of Sports Sciences, 18*, 579–592.

Bandura, A. (1986). *Social Foundations of Thought and Action: A Social Cognitive Theory.* Englewood Cliffs, NJ: Prentice-Hall.

Bangsbo, J., Norregaard, L. and Thorso, F. (1991). Activity profile of professional soccer. *Canadian Journal of Sports Science, 16*, 110–116.

Bardens, R. (1965). Critical incidents in the instruction of beginning swimming. Dissertation, Columbia University.

Bardy, B. G., Oullier, O., Bootsma, R. J. and Stoffregen, T. A. (2002). Dynamics of human postural transitions. *Journal of Experimental Psychology: Human Perception and Performance, 28*(3), 499–514.

Bar-Eli, M., Avugos, S. and Raab, M. (2006). Twenty years of 'hot hand' research: Review and critique. *Psychology of Sport and Exercise, 7*(6), 525–553.

Barris, S. and Button, C. (2008). A review of vision-based motion analysis in sport. *Sports Medicine, 38*(12), 1025–104.

Bartlett, R. M. (1999). *Sports Biomechanics: Reducing Injury and Improving Performance.* London: E & FN Spon.

Bartlett, R. M. (2000). Performance analysis: Is it the bringing together of biomechanics and notational analysis or an illusion? In J. R. Blackwell (ed.) *Proceedings of Oral Sessions, XIX International Symposium on Biomechanics in Sports.* San Francisco, CA: University of San Francisco, pp. 328–331.

Bartlett, R. M. (2001). Performance analysis: Can bringing together biomechanics and notational analysis benefit coaches? *The International Journal of Performance Analysis in Sport* at www.catchword.com.titles/14748185, *1*, 122–126.

Bartlett, R. M. (2003). The science and medicine of cricket: An overview and update. *Journal of Sports Sciences, 21*, 733–752.

Bartlett, R. M. (2004). Artificial intelligence in performance analysis. In P. O'Donoghue and M. Hughes (eds) *Notational Analysis of Sport VI*, pp. 213–219. Cardiff: UWIC.

Bartlett, R. (2007). *Introduction to Sports Biomechanics*, 2nd edn. London; Routledge.

Bartlett, R. M. and Bussey, M. (2011). *Sports Biomechanics: Reducing Injury and Improving Performance*, 2nd edn, pp. 178–200. London: E & FN Spon.

Bartlett, R. M., Pillar, J. and Miller, S. A. (1995). A three-dimensional analysis of the tennis serves of National (British) and County standard male players. In T. Reilly, M. D. Hughes and A. Lees (eds) *Science and Racket Sports*, pp. 99–102. London: E & FN Spon.

Bartlett, R. M., Stockill, N. P., Elliott, B. C. and Burnett, A. F. (1996). The biomechanics of fast bowling in men's cricket: A review. *Journal of Sports Sciences, 14*, 403–424.

Bartlett, R., Button, C., Robins, M., Dutt-Mazumber, A. and Kennedy, G. (2012). Analysing team coordination patterns from player movement trajectories in soccer: Methodological considerations. *International Journal of Performance Analysis in Sport, 12*, 398–424.

Barton, G., Lisboa, P. and Lees, A. (2000). Topological clustering of patients using a self-organizing neural map. *Gait and Posture, 11*, 57.

Bate, R. (1988). Football chance: Tactics and strategy. In T. Reilly, A. Lees, K. Davids and W. Murphy (eds), *Science and Football*. London: E & FN Spon.

Bauer, H. U. and Schöllhorn, W. I. (1997). Self-organizing maps for the analysis of complex movement patterns. *Neural Processing Letters, 5*, 193–199.

Beccarini, C., Madella, A. and Carbonaro, G. (1993). Training and competition databases for coaches. In *International Association for Sports Information 9th Scientific Congress Papers*, pp. 1–7. Rome: IASI.

Beek, P. J. and Beek, W. J. (1989). Stability and flexibility in the temporal organisation of movements: Reaction to G. J. van Ingen Schenau *Human Movement Science, 8*, 347–356.

Beek, P. J., Peper, C. E. and Stegeman, D. (1995). Dynamical models of movement co-ordination. *Human Movement Science, 14*, 573–608.

Behan, H. (2006). Personal Communication. August.

Beilock, S. L. and Carr, T. H. (2001). On the fragility of skilled performance: What governs choking under pressure? *Journal of Experimental Psychology: General, 130*, 701–725.

Beilock, S. L. and Gray, R. (2012). From attentional control to attentional spillover: A skill-level investigation of attention movement, and performance outcomes. *Human Movement Science, 31*, 1473–1499.

Beilock, S. L., Carr, T. H., MacMahon, C. and Starkes, J. L. (2002). When paying attention becomes counterproductive: Impact of divided versus skill-focused attention on novice and experienced performance of sensorimotor skills. *Journal of Experimental Psychology: Applied, 8*, 6–16.

Bekey, G. A., Kim, J. J., Gronley, J. K., Bontrager, E. L. and Perry, J. (1992). GAIT-ER-AID: An expert system for diagnosis of human gait. *Artificial Intelligence in Medicine, 4*, 293–308.

Bekkering, H., Wohlschläger, A. and Gattis, M. (1996). Motor imitation: What is imitated? *Corpus, Psyche et Societas, 3*, 68–74.

Berry, S. M., Reese, C. S. and Larkey, P. D. (1999). Bridging different eras in sports. *Journal of the American Statistical Association, 94*(447), 661–676.

Best, R. J., Bartlett, R. M. and Sawyer, R. A. (1995). Optimal javelin release. *Journal of Applied Biomechanics, 11*, 371–394.

Black, C. B., Wright, D. L., Magnuson, C. E. and Brueckner, S. (2005). Learning to detect error in movement timing using physical and observational practice. *Research Quarterly in Exercise and Sport, 76*, 28–41.

Bland, J. M. (2000). *An Introduction to Medical Statistics*, 2nd edn. Oxford: Oxford University Press.

Bland, J. M. and Altman, D. G. (1986). Statistical methods for assessing agreement between two methods of clinical measurement. *The Lancet, 1*, 307–310.

Blandin, Y., Proteau, L. and Alain, C. (1994). On the cognitive processes underlying contextual interference and observational learning. *Journal of Motor Behavior, 26*, 18–26.

Blomqvist, M., Luhtanen, P. and Laakso, L. (1998a). Validation of a notational analysis system in badminton. *Journal of Human Movement Studies, 35*, 137–150.

Blomqvist, M., Luhtanen, P. and Laakso, L. (1998b). Game performance and game understanding in badminton of Finnish primary school children. In A. Lees, I. Maynard, M. Hughes and T. Reilly (eds) *Science and Racket Sports II*, pp. 269–275. London: E & FN Spon.

Boddington, M. K., Lambert, M. I., St Clair Gibson, A. and Noakes, T. D. (2001). Reliability of a 5-m multiple shuttle test. *Journal of Sports Sciences, 19*, 3, 223–228.

Booth, D. and Doyle, G. (1997). UK television warms up for the biggest game yet: Pay-per-view. *Media, Culture and Society, 19*, 277–284.

Bourbousson, J., Seve, C. and McGarry, T. (2010). Space–time coordination dynamics in basketball: part 1. Intra- and inter-couplings among player dyads. *Journal of Sports Sciences, 28*(3), 339–347.

Boyle, R. and Haynes, R. (2000). *Power Play: Sport, the Media and Popular Culture*. London: Longman.

Bradley, P., O'Donoghue, P., Wooster, B. and Tordoff, P. (2007). The reliability of ProZone MatchViewer: A video-based technical performance analysis system. *International Journal of Performance Analysis in Sport*, 7(3), 117–129.

Brewer, C. J. and Jones, R. L. (2002). A five-stage process for establishing contextually valid systematic observation instruments: The case of rugby union. *The Sport Psychologist*, 16, 139–161.

Brown, D. and Hughes, M. D. (1995). The effectiveness of quantitative and qualitative feedback on performance in squash. In T. Reilly, M. D. Hughes and A. Lees (eds) *Science and Racket Sports*, pp. 232–237. London: E & FN Spon.

Brown, E. and O'Donoghue, P. G. (2008). A split screen system to analyse coach behaviour: A case report of coaching practice. *International Journal of Computer Science in Sport*, 7(1), 4–17.

Brown, L. (1993). *The New Shorter Oxford English Dictionary*. Oxford: Clarendon Press.

Brown, S. (2012). Everton at forefront of performance analytics usage in Premier League. Retrieved 1 December 2013, from www.si.com/more-sports/2012/05/01/performance-analytics.

Buchanan, J. J., Ryu, Y. U., Zihlman, K. and Wright, D. L. (2008). Observational practice of relative but not absolute motion features in a single-limb multi-joint coordination task. *Experimental Brain Research*, 191, 157–169.

Buchheit, M., Al Haddad, H., Simpson, B. M., Palazzi, D., Bourdon, P. C., Di Salvo, V. and Mendez-Villanueva, A. (2013). Monitoring accelerations with GPS in football: Time to slow down? *International Journal of Sports Physiology and Performance*, 9, 442–445.

Büchner, A. G., Dubitzky, W., Schuster, A., Lopes, P., O'Donoghue, P. G., Hughes, J. G., Bell, D. A., Adamson, K., White, J. A., Anderson, J. M. C. C. and Mulvenna, M. D. (1997). Corporate evidential decision making in performance prediction domains. *13th Conference of Uncertainty in Artifical Intelligence (UAI '97)*. Providence, Rhode Island.

Buckhout, R. (1982). Eyewitness testimony. In U. Neisser (ed.) *Memory Observed: Remembering in Natural Contexts*, pp. 116–129. San Francisco, CA: Freeman & Co.

Bueckers, M. J. A., Magill, R. A. and Hall, K. G. (1992). The effect of erroneous knowledge of results on skill acquisition when augmented information is redundant. *Quarterly Journal of Experimental Psychology*, 44, 105–117.

Bullock, D., Grossberg, S. and Guenther, F. (1996). Neural network modeling of sensory-motor control in animals. In H. N. Zelaznik (ed.) *Advances in Motor Learning and Control*, pp. 263–292. Champaign, IL: Human Kinetics.

Bürger, P. (2009). Exploring performance indicators through winners and errors in non-elite female volleyball. Unpublished Master's Thesis, University of Wales Institute, Cardiff.

Burns, B. D. (2004). Heuristics as beliefs and as behaviors: The adaptiveness of the 'hot hand'. *Cognitive Psychology*, 48, 295–331.

Burns, J. (1987). *Hand of God: The Life of Diego Maradona*. London: Bloomsbury.

Burry, H. C. and Calcinai, C. J. (1988). The need to make rugby safer. *British Medical Journal*, 6616(296), 149–150.

Bylander, T., Weintraub, M. A. and Simon, S. R. (1993). QWADS: Diagnosis using different models for different subtasks. In J.-M. David, J.-P. Krivine and R. Simmons (eds) *Second Generation Expert Systems*, pp. 110–130. Berlin: Springer Verlag.

Cadopi, M., Chatillon, J.F. and Baldy, R. (1995). Representation and performance: Reproduction of form and quality of movement in dance by eight- and eleven-year-old novices. *British Journal of Psychology*, 86, 217–225.

Cahill, N., Lamb, K., Worsfold, P., Headey, R. and Murray, S. (2013). The movement characteristics of English Premiership rugby union players. *Journal of Sports Sciences*, 31(3), 229–237.

Calvo-Merino, B., Glaser, D. E., Grèzes, J., Passingham, R. E. and Haggard, P. (2005). Action observation and acquired motor skills: An fMRI study with expert dancers. *Cerebral Cortex*, *15*, 1243–1249.

Calvo-Merino, B., Grèzes, J., Glaser, D. E., Passingham, R. E. and Haggard, P. (2006). Seeing or doing? Influence of visual and motor familiarity in action observation. *Current Biology*, *16*, 1905–1910.

Cardinale, M. (2011). Science in Sport. Quo Vadis. Retrieved 1 December 2013, from www.leadersinsport.com/the-leader/marco-cardinale-science-in-sport-quo-vadis/.

Carling, C., Williams, A. M. and Reilly, T. (2005). *Handbook of Soccer Match Analysis: A Systematic Approach to Improving Performance*. Abingdon, Oxon: Routledge.

Carling, C., Reilly, T. and Williams, A. M. (2009). *Performance Assessment for Field Sports*. London: Routledge.

Carling, C., Bloomfield, J., Nelsen, L. and Reilly, T. (2008). The role of motion analysis in elite soccer. *Sports Medicine, 38*(10), 839–862.

Carroll, W. R. and Bandura, A. (1982). The role of visual monitoring in observational learning of action patterns: Making the unobservable observable. *Journal of Motor Behavior, 14*, 153–167.

Carroll, W. R. and Bandura, A. (1985). Role of timing of visual monitoring and motor rehearsal in observational learning of action patterns. *Journal of Motor Behavior, 17*, 269–281.

Carroll, W. R. and Bandura, A. (1990). Representational guidance of action production in observational learning: A causal analysis. *Journal of Motor Behavior, 22*, 85–97.

Carrozza, S., Baldassarre, G., Vastola, R. and Gomez Paloma, F. (2011). Performance analysis and its didactic applicability in the motor-sports and educational field. *Journal of Physical Education and Sports Science, 13*(2), 182–186.

Carter, A. (1996). Time and motion analysis and heart rate monitoring of a back-row forward in first class rugby union football. In M. Hughes (ed.) *Notational Analysis of Sport – I and II*, pp. 145–160. Cardiff: UWIC.

Cashman and M. McKernan (eds) (1981). *Sport: Money, Morality and the Media*. Sydney: New South Wales University Press.

Castagna, C., Abt, G. and D'Ottavio, S. (2004). Activity profile of international-level soccer referees during competitive matches. *The Journal of Strength Conditioning Research, 18*(3), 486–490.

Castellano, J., Blanco-Villasenor, A. and Alvarez, D. (2011). Contextual variables and time–motion analysis in soccer. *International Journal of Sports Medicine, 32*, 415–421.

Chandler, J. M. (1988). *Television and National Sport: The United States and Britain*. Chicago, IL: University of Illinois Press.

Chapman, A. E. and Sanderson, D. J. (1990). Muscular coordination in sporting skills. In by J. M. Winters and S.L-Y. Woo (eds) *Multiple Muscle Systems: Biomechanics and Movement Organization*, pp. 608–620. New York: Springer-Verlag.

Chinchilla Mira, J. J., Pérez Turpin, J. A., Martínez Carbonell, J. A. and Jove Tossi, M. (2012). Offensive zones in beach volleyball: Differences by gender. *Journal of Human Sport and Exercise*, 3(7), 727–732.

Chiviacowsky, S. and Wulf, G. (2005). Self-controlled feedback is effective if it is based on the learner's performance. *Research Quarterly for Exercise and Sport, 76*, 42–48.

Chow, J. W. and Knudson, D. V. (2011). Use of deterministic models and exercise biomechanics research. *Sports Biomechanics, 10*, 1219–233.

Church, S. and Hughes, M. D. (1986). Patterns of play in Association Football. A computerised analysis. Communication to First World Congress of Science and Football, Liverpool, 13–17 April.

Clark, J. E. (1995). On becoming skillful: Patterns and Constraints. *Research Quarterly for Exercise and Sport*, *66*, 173–183.

Claxton, B. (1988). A systematic observation of more and less successful high school tennis coaches. *Journal of Teaching in Physical Education*, *7*, 302–331.

Clemente, F. M., Couceiro, M. S., Martins, F. M. L., Mendes, R. and Figueiredo, A. J. (2013). Measuring collective behaviour in football teams: Inspecting the impact of each half of the match on ball possession. *International Journal of Performance Analysis in Sport*, *13*, 678–689.

Clifford, B. and Hollin, C. (1980). Effects of type of incident and the number of perpetrators on eyewitness memory. *Journal of Applied Psychology*, *65*, 364–370.

Coakley, J. (2001). *Sport in Society: Issues and Controversies*. New York: McGraw-Hill.

Cohen, J. (1988). *Statistical Power Analysis for the BehavioralSciences*, 2nd edn. Hillsdale, NJ: Lawrence Erlbaum Associates.

Collet, C. (2013). The possession game? A comparative analysis of ball retention and team success in European and international football, 2007–2010. *Journal of Sports Sciences*, *31*(2), 123–136.

Collier, G. L. and Wright, C. E. (1995). Temporal rescaling of simple and complex ratios in rhythmic tapping. *Journal of Experimental Psychology: Human Perception and Performance*, *21*, 602–627.

Cook, D. P. and Strike, S. C. (2000). Throwing in cricket. *Journal of Sports Sciences*, *18*, 965–973.

Cooper, D. L. (1994), Sports rule changes over the years. *Strength and Conditioning*. *16*(4), 70–73.

Cooper L. A. and Shepard R. N. (1973). Chronometric studies of the rotation of mental images. In W. G. Chase (ed.) *Visual information processing*, pp. 75–176. New York: Academic Press.

Correia, V., Araújo, D., Davids, K., Fernandes, O. and Fonseca, S. (2011). Territorial gain dynamics regulates success in attacking sub-phases of team sports. *Psychology of Sport and Exercise*, *12*, 662–669.

Court, M. (2007). Voice recognition software for soccer analysis. In H. Dancs, M. Hughes and P. O'Donoghue (eds) *Notational Analysis of Sport – VII*, p. 87. Cardiff: UWIC.

Cousens, L. (1997). From diamonds to dollars: The dynamics of change in AAA baseball franchises. *Journal of Sports Management*, *11*, 316–334.

Coutts, A. J. and Duffield, R. (2010). Validity and reliability of GPS devices for measuring movement demands of team sports. *Journal of Science and Medicine in Sport*, *13*(1), 133–135.

Coynel, D., Marrelec, G., Perlbag, V., Pélégrini-Isaac, M., Van de Moortele, P-F., Ugurbilm K., Doyon, J., Benali, H. and Lehéricy, S. (2010). Dynamics of motor-related functional integration during motor sequence learning. *Neuroimage*, *49*, 759–766.

Craik, F. I. M. and Lockhart, R. S. (1972). Levels of processing: A framework for memory research. *Journal of Verbal Learning and Verbal Behavior*, *11*, 671–684.

Crilly, A. J. (1991). *Fractals and Chaos*. London: Springer-Verlaag.

Cross, E. S., Hamilton, A. F. de C. and Grafton, S. T. (2006). Building a motor simulation de novo: Observation of dance by dancers. *NeuroImage*, *31*, 1257–1267.

Crossman, E. R. F. W. (1959). A theory of acquisition of speed skill. *Ergonomics*, *2*, 153–166.

Croucher, J. S. (1996). The use of notational analysis in determining optimal strategies in sports. In M. Hughes (ed.) *Notational Analysis of Sport – I & II*, pp. 3–20. Cardiff: UWIC.

Cummins, C., Orr, R. and O'Connor, H. (2013). Global positioning systems (GPS) and microtechnology sensors in team sports: A systematic review. *Sports Medicine*, *43*, 1025–1042.

Curtis, B., Smith, R. E. and Smoll, F. L. (1979). Scrutinizing the skipper: A study of leadership behaviours in the dugout. *Journal of Applied Psychology*, *64*(4), 391–400.

Cushion, C., Harvey, S., Muir, B. and Nelson, L. (2012). Developing the Coach Analysis and Intervention System (CAIS): Establishing validity and reliability of a computerised systematic observation instrument. *Journal of Sport Sciences*, *30*(2), 201–216.

Dancs, H. Hughes, M. and O'Donoghue, P. (eds) (2006). *Notation of Sport VII*. Cardiff: CPA, UWIC.

Davids, K., Button, C. and Bennett, S. (2008). *Dynamics of Skill Acquisition: A Constraints-led Approach*. Champaign, IL: Human Kinetics.

Davids, K., Glazier, P., Araújo, D. and Bartlett, R.M. (2003a). Movement systems as dynamical systems: The role of functional variability and its implications for sports medicine. *Sports Medicine*, *33*, 245–260.

Davids, K., Shuttleworth, R., Araújo, D. and Renshaw, I. (2003b). Understanding constraints on physical activity: implications for motor learning theory. In R. Arellano and A Oña (eds) *Proceedings of Second World Congress on Science of Physical Activity and Sports*. Granada, Spain: University of Granada Press.

Davies, G. (1999). Screen tests could turn off rugby's faithful supporters. *The Times*, 3 December, p. 60.

Deeny, S. P., Hillman, C. H., Janelle, C. M. and Hatfield, B. D. (2003). Cortico-cortical communication and superior performance in skilled marksmen: An EEG coherence analysis. *Journal of Sport & Exercise Psychology*, *25*, 188–204.

Deeny, S. P., Haufler, A. J., Saffer, M. and Hatfield, B. D. (2009). Electroencephalographic coherence during visuomotor performance: A comparison of cortico-cortical communication in experts and novices. *Journal of Motor Behavior*, *41*, 106–116.

Del Rey, P. (1972). Appropriate feedback for open and closed skill acquisition. *Quest*, *17*, 42–45.

Dellaserra, C. L., Gao, Y. and Ransdell, L. (2014). Use of integrated technology in team sports: A review of opportunities, challenges, and future directions for athletes. *Journal of Strength and Conditioning Research*, *28*, 556–573.

Di Salvo, V., Collins, A., McNeill, B. and Cardinale, M. (2006). Validation of Prozone®: A new video-based performance analysis system. *International Journal of Performance Analysis of Sport*, *6*(1), 108–119.

Di Salvo, V., Gregson, W., Atkinson, G., Tordoff, P. and Drust, B. (2009). Analysis of high intensity activity in Premier League soccer. *International Journal of Sports Medicine*, *30*, 205–212.

Doggart, L., Keane, S., Reilly, T. and Stanhope, J. (1993). A task analysis of Gaelic football. In T. Reilly, J. Clarys and A. Stibbe (eds) *Science and Football II*, pp. 186–189. London: E & FN Spon.

Downey, J. C. (1973). *The Singles Game*. London: E. P. Publications.

Downey, J. C. (1992). Analysing racket sports. Presentation at the First World Congress of Performance Analysis, Burton, Merseyside.

Dowrick, P. W. (1999). A review of self-modeling and related interventions. *Applied and Preventative Psychology*, *8*, 23–29.

Draper, N. R. and Smith, H. (1981). *Applied Regression Analysis*, 2nd edn. New York: Wiley.

Drust, B., Atkinson, G. and Reilly, T. (2007). Future perspectives in the evaluation of the physiological demands of soccer. *Sports Medicine*, *37*(9), 783–805.

Duarte, R., Araujo, D., Correia, V. and Davids, K. (2012). Sports teams as superorganisms. Implications of sociobiological models of behaviour for research and practice in team sports performance analysis. *Sports Medicine*, *42*(8), 633–642.

Duthie, G., Pyne, D. and Hooper, S. (2003). Applied physiology and game analysis of rugby union. *Sports Medicine*, *33*(13), 973–991.

Duthie, G., Pyne, D. and Gabbett, T. (2008). Skill and physiological demands of open and closed training drills in Austrilian Football. *Journal of Strength and Conditioning Research, 20*, 208–214.

Dziezanowski, J. M., Bourne, J. R., Shiavi, R., Sandall, H. S. H. and Guy, D. (1985). GAITSPERT: An expert system for the evaluation of abnormal human locomotion arising from stroke, *IEEE Transactions on Biomedical Engineering, 32*, 935–942.

Eaves, S. J., Hughes, M. D. and Lamb, K. L. (2008). Assessing the impact of the season and rule changes on specific match and tactical variables in professional rugby league football in the United Kingdom. *International Journal of Performance Analysis in Sport, 8*(3), 104–118.

Edelmann-Nusser, J., Hohmann, A. and Henneberg, B. (2002). Modelling and prediction of competitive swimming performance in swimming upon neural networks. *European Journal of Sport Science, 2*(2), 1–10.

Edgecomb, S. J. and Norton, K. I. (2006). Comparison of global positioning and computer-based tracking systems for measuring player movement distance during Australian football. *Journal of Science and Medicine in Sport, 9*(1), 25–32.

Ehrlenspiel, F. (2001). Paralysis by analysis? A functional framework for the effects of attentional focus on the control of motor skills. *European Journal of Sport Science, 1*, 1–11.

Elliott, B. C. (2000). Back injuries and the fast bowler in cricket. *Journal of Sports Sciences, 18*, 983–991.

Elliott, B. C., Burnett, A., Stockill, N. P. and Bartlett, R. M. (1996). The fast bowler in cricket: A sports medicine perspective. *Sports Exercise and Injury, 1*, 201–206.

Eniseler, N., Dogan, B., Aydin, S., Üstün, S.V. and Tabkiran, Y. (2000). Area and time analysis of duels in matches of the Turkish football team in elimination stages of the European Cup. In M. Hughes (ed.) *Notational Analysis of Sport III*, pp. 67–71. Cardiff: CPA, UWIC.

Eom, H. J. (1988). A mathematical analysis of team performance in volleyball. *Canadian Journal of Sports Science, 13*, 55–56.

Feezell, R. M. (1988). On the wrongness of cheating and why cheaters can't play the game. *Journal of the Philosophy of Sport, 15*, 57–68.

Feiner, S. K. (2002). Augmented reality: A new way of seeing. *Scientific American*, April, 50–55.

Fennell, T., Jenish, D., Cazzin, J., Todd, D., Daly, J., Harrison, M. and Gregor, A. (1990). The riches of sport. *Macleans*, April, 42–45.

Ferreira, P. F., Volossovitch, A. and Gonçalves, I. (2003). Methodological and dynamic perspective to determine critical moments on sport game. *International Journal of Computer Science in Sport, 2*(2), 119–122.

Flanagan, J. C. (1954). The critical incident technique. *Psychological Bulletin, 51*(4), 327–358.

Fleissig, G. (2001). The biomechanics of throwing. In J.R. Blackwell (ed.) *Proceedings of Oral Sessions, XIX International Symposium on Biomechanics in Sports*, pp. 61–64. San Francisco: University of San Francisco.

Fraleigh, W. P. (2003). Intentional rules violations: One more time. *Journal of the Philosophy of Sport, 30*, 166–176.

Franks, I. M. (1988). Analysis of Association Football. *Soccer Journal*, September/October, 35–43.

Franks, I. M. (1993). The effects of experience on the detection and location of performance differences in a gymnastic technique. *Research Quarterly for Exercise and Sport, 64*(2), 227–231.

Franks, I. M. (1996). Use of feedback by coaches and players. In T. Reilly, J. Bangsbo and M. Hughes (eds) *Science and Football III*, pp. 267–278. London: E & FN Spon.

Franks, I. M. (2000). The structure of sport and the collection of relevant data. In A. Baca (ed.) *Computer Science in Sport*, pp. 226–240. Vienna: OBV and HPT.

Franks, I. M. and Goodman, D. (1984). A hierarchical approach to performance analysis. *SPORTS*, June, 1–12.

Franks, I. M. and Goodman, D. (1986a). A systematic approach to analyzing sports performance. *Journal of Sports Sciences*, *4*, 49–59.

Franks, I. M. and Goodman, D. (1986b). Computer-assisted technical analysis of sport. *Coaching Review*, May/June, 58–64.

Franks, I. M. and Miller, G. (1986). Eyewitness testimony in sport. *Journal of Sport Behavior*, *9*, 39–45.

Franks, I. M. and Nagelkerke, P. (1988). The use of computer interactive video technology in sport analysis. *Ergonomics*, *31*(99), 1593–1603.

Franks, I. M. and Maile, L. J. (1991). The use of video in sport skill acquisition. In P. W. Dowrick (ed.) *Practical Guide to Using Video in the Behavioral Sciences*, pp. 231–243. New York: Wiley.

Franks, I. M. and Miller, G. (1991). Training coaches to observe and remember. *Journal of Sports Sciences*, *9*, 285–297.

Franks, I. M. and McGarry, T. (1996). The science of match analysis. In T. Reilly (ed.) *Science and Soccer*, pp. 363–375. London: E & FN Spon.

Franks, I. M., Wilberg, R. B. and Fishburne, G. J. (1982–1983 edn) The process of decision making: An application to team games. *Coaching Science Update*, 12–16.

Franks, I. M., Goodman, D. and Miller, G. (1983a). Analysis of performance: Qualitative or quantitative. *SPORTS*, March, 1–8.

Franks, I. M., Goodman, D. and Miller, G. (1983b). Human factors in sport systems: An empirical investigation of events in team games. *Proceedings of the Human Factors Society 27th Annual meeting*, pp. 383–386.

Franks, I. M., Goodman, D. and Paterson, D. (1986). The real time analysis of sport: an overview. *Canadian Journal of Sports Sciences*, *11*, 55–57.

Franks, I. M., Nagelkerke, P. and Goodman, D. (1989). Computer controlled video: An inexpensive IBM based system. *Computers in Education*, *13*(1), 33–44.

Frencken, W. G., Lemmink, K. A. and Delleman, N. J. (2010). Soccer-specific accuracy and validity of the local position measurement (LPM) system. *Journal of Science and Medicine in Sport*, *13*(6), 641–645.

Frencken, W., Lemmink, K., Delleman, N. and Visscher, C. (2011). Oscillations of centroid position and surface area of soccer teams in small-sided games. *European Journal of Sport Science*, *11*(4), 215–223.

Fuller, N. (1990). Computerised performance analysis in netball. In J. Alderson, N. Fuller and P. Treadwell (eds) *Match Analysis in Sport: A 'State of Art' Review*, pp. 15–18. Leeds: National Coaching Foundation.

Fuller, N. (1994). Game modelling in netball through computerised performance analysis. Master's Dissertation, Sheffield University.

Fullerton, H. S. (1912). The inside game: The science of baseball. *The American Magazine*, *LXX*, 2–13.

Furlong, J. D. G. (1995). The service in lawn tennis: How important is it? In T. Reilly, M. D. Hughes and A. Lees (eds) *Science and Racket Sports*, pp. 266–271. London: E & FN Spon.

Gabbett, T. J. (2010). GPS analysis of elite women's field hockey training and competition. *The Journal of Strength and Conditioning Research*, *24*(5), 1321–1324.

Gamble D., O'Donoghue, P. G. and Young, E. (2007). Activity profile and heart rate response of referees in Gaelic football. *World Congress of Science and Football 6*. Antalya, Turkey: January 2007.

Gardiner, S., Felix, A., James, M., Welch, R. and O'Leary, J. (1998). *Sports Law*. London: Cavendish.

Garganta, J. and Gonçalves, G. (1996). Comparison of successful attacking play in male and female Portuguese national soccer teams. In M. D. Hughes (ed.) *Notational Analysis of Sport – I & II*, pp. 79–85. Cardiff: UWIC.

Garganta, J., Maia, J. and Basto, F. (1997). Analysis of goal scoring patterns of European top level soccer teams. In T. Reilly, J. Bangsbo and M. D. Hughes (eds) *Science and Football III*, pp. 246–250. London: E & FN Spon.

Garis, R. A. (1966). Critical incidents in the instruction of gymnastic activities for girls. Dissertation, Columbia University.

Gerrard, D. F. (1998). The use of padding in Rugby Union. *Sports Medicine*, 25(5), 329–332.

Gerisch, G. and Reichelt, M. (1993). Computer- and video-aided analysis of football games. In T. Reilly, J. Clarys and A. Stibbe (eds) *Science and Football II*, pp. 167–173. London: E & FN Spon.

Giatsis, G. (2003). The effect of changing the rules on score fluctuation and match duration in the FIVB women's beach volleyball. *International Journal of Performance Analysis in Sport*, 3(1), 57–64.

Gilbert, W. D. and Trudel, P. (2004). Analysis of coaching science research published from 1970–2001. *Research Quarterly for Exercise and Sport*, 75(4), 388–399.

Gilovich, T., Vallone, R. and Tversky, A. (1985). The hot hand in basketball: On the misperception of random sequences. *Cognitive Psychology*, 17, 295–314.

Gissane, C., Jennings, D., White, J. and Cumine, A. (1998). Injury in summer rugby league football: The experience of one club. *British Journal of Sports Medicine*, 32, 149–152.

Glass, L. and Mackey, M. C. (1988). *From Clocks to Chaos: The Rhythms of Life*. Alexandra, NJ: Princeton University Press.

Glazier, P. S. (2010). Game, set, match? Substantive issues and future directions in performance analysis. *Sports Medicine*, 40(8), 65–634.

Glazier, P. S. and Davids, K. (2009). Constraints on the complete optimisation of human motion. *Sports Medicine*, 39(1), 15–28.

Glazier, P. S. and Robins, M. T. (2013). Self-organisation and constraints in sports performance. In T. McGarry, P. O'Donoghue and J. Sampaio (eds) *Routledge Handbook of Sports Performance Analysis*, pp. 42–51. London: Routledge.

Glazier, P. S., Davids, K. and Bartlett, R. M. (2003). Dynamical systems theory: A relevant framework for performance-oriented sports biomechanics research. *Sportscience*, 7, 85–92.

Gleick, J. (1988). *Chaos: Making a New Science*. London: Penguin Books.

Goncalves, B. V., Figueira, B. E., Macas, V. and Sampaio, J. (2014). Effect of player position on movement behaviour, physical and physiological performances during an 11–a-side football game. *Journal of Sports Sciences*, 32(2), 191–199.

Goodwin, J. E. and Meeuwsen, H. J. (1995). Using bandwidth knowledge of results to alter relative frequencies during motor skill acquisition. *Research Quarterly for Exercise and Sport*, 66, 99–104.

Grant, A., Reilly, T., Williams, M. and Borrie, A. (1998). Analysis of the goals scored in the 1998 World Cup. *Insight – The FA Coaches Association Journal*, 2(1), 18–22.

Gray, A. and Drewett, J. (1999). *Flat Back Four: The Tactical Game*. London: Boxtree.

Gray, A. J., Henkins, D., Andrews, M. H., Taaffe, D. R. and Glover, M. L. (2010). Validity and reliability of GPS for measuring distance travelled in field-based team sports. *Journal of Sports Sciences*, 28, 1319–1325.

Gray, R. (2004). Attending to the execution of a complex sensorimotor skill: Expertise differences, choking, and slumps. *Journal of Experimental Psychology: Applied*, 10, 42–54.

Green, T. (1985). Rule changes for safety in Canadian amateur football. *Audible*, Spring, 26–30.

Gregson, W., Drust, B., Atkinson, G. and Salvo, V.D. (2010). Match-to-match variability of high-speed activities in Premier League soccer. *International Journal of Sports Medicine*, *31*, 237–242.

Grehaigne, J-F., Bouthier, D. and David, B. (1996). Soccer: the players' action zone in a team. In M. D. Hughes (ed.) *Notational Analysis of Sport – I & II*, pp. 27–38. Cardiff: CPA, UWIC.

Grehaigne, J. F., Bouthier, D. and David, B. (1997). Dynamic-system analysis of opponent relationships in collective actions in soccer. *Journal of Sports Sciences*, 15, 137–149.

Griffin, K. and Meaney, K. S. (2000). Modeling and motor performance: An examination of model similarity and model type on children's motor performance. *Research Quarterly for Exercise and Sport*, *71*, A-56, 67.

Gronlund, S. D., Carlson, C. A. and Tower, D. (2007). Episodic Memory. In F. T. Durso (ed.) *Handbook of Applied Cognition*, 2nd edn, pp. 111–136. Chichester: Wiley.

Guadagnoli, M. A. and Lee, T. D. (2004). Challenge point: A framework for conceptualizing the effects of various practice conditions in motor learning. *Journal of Motor Behavior*, *36*, 212–224.

Haake, S. J., Chadwick, S. G., Dignall, R. J., Goodwill, S. and Rose, P. (2000). Engineering Tennis – Slowing the game down. *Sports Engineering*, *3*(2), 131–143.

Hackney, R. G. (1994). ABC of sports medicine nature, prevention and management of injury in sport. *British Medical Journal*, *308*, 1356–1359.

Haken, H. (1983). *Synergetics, an Introduction: Non-equilibrium Phase Transitions and Self-Organisation in Physics, Chemistry and Biology*. Berlin: Springer.

Hall, C., Moore, J., Annett, J. and Rodgers, W. (1997). Recalling demonstrated and guided movements using imaginary and verbal rehearsal strategies. *Research Quarterly for Exercise and Sport*, *68*, 136–144.

Hammond, J., Hosking, D. and Hole, C. (1999). An exploratory study of the effectiveness of rule changes in netball: Communications to the Fourth International Conference on Sport. *Journal of Sport Sciences*, *17*, 916–917.

Harbourne, R. T. and Stergiou, N. (2009). Movement variability and the use of nonlinear tools: principles to guide physical therapist practice. *Physical Therapy*, *89*(3), 267–282.

Harley, J. A., Lovell, R. J., Barnes, C. A., Portas, M. D. and Weston, M. (2011). The interchangeability of GPS and semiautomated video-based performance data during elite soccer match play. *Journal of Strength and Conditioning Research*, *25*(8): 2334–2336.

Harris, S. and Reilly, T. (1988). Space, teamwork and attacking success in soccer. In T. Reilly, A. Lees, K. Davids and W. Murphy (eds) *Science and Football*, pp. 322–328. London: E & FN Spon.

Harvey, S., Cushion, C. and Massa-Gonzalez, A. (2010). Learning a new method: Teaching games for understanding in the coaches' eyes. *Physical Education Sport Pedagogy*, *15*(4), 361–382.

Hawkins, A., Sharpe, T. L. and Ray, R. (1994). Toward instructional process measurability: An interbehavioural field systems perspective. In R. Gardener, D. M. Saintano, J. O. Cooper, T. E. Heron, W. L. Heward, J. Eshleman and T. A. Grossi (eds) *Behaviour Analysis in Education: Focus on Measurably Superior Instruction*, pp. 241–255. Pacific Grove, CA: Brooks/Cole.

Hay, J. G. and Reid, G. (1982). *Anatomy, Mechanics and Human Motion*. Englewood Cliffs, NJ: Prentice-Hall.

Hay, J. G. and Reid, J. G. (1988). *Anatomy, Mechanics and Human Motion*, 2nd edn. Englewood Cliffs, NJ: Prentice-Hall.

Hay, J. G. and Yu, B. (1993). Analysis of the approach run: Mike Powell USAT&F Championships, 1993. Report, Biomechanics Laboratory, University of Iowa.

Held, R. (1965). Plasticity in the sensory-motor system. *Scientific American, 213*, 84–94.

Held, R. and Hein, A. (1958). Adaptation of disarranged hand-eye coordination contingent upon re-afferent stimulation. *Perceptual and Motor Skills, 8*, 87–90.

Held, R. and Hein, A. (1963). Movement-produced stimulation in the development of visually guided behavior. *Journal of Comparative and Physiological Psychology, 56*, 872–876.

Heller, B. W., Veltnik, P. H., Pijkhoff, N. J. M., Rutten, W. L. C. and Andrews, B. J. (1993). Reconstructing muscle activation during normal walking: A comparison of symbolic and connectionist machine learning techniques. *Biological Cybernetics, 69*, 327–335.

Herbert, M. (1991). *Insights and Strategies of Winning Volleyball.* University of Illinois, Champaign, IL: Leisure Press.

Herbert, P. and Tong, R. (1996). A comparison of the positional demands of wingers and back row forwards using movement analysis and heart rate telemetry. In M. D. Hughes (ed.) *Notational Analysis of Sport – I and II*, pp. 177–182, Cardiff: UWIC.

Higuchi, T., Imanaka, K. and Hatayama, T. (2002). Freezing degrees of freedom under stress: Kinematic evidence of constrained movement strategies. *Human Movement Science, 21*, 831–846.

Higuchi, K., Katayama, T., Iwai, S., Hidaka, M., Horiuchi, T. and Maki, H. (2003). Fate of DNA replication fork encountering a single DNA lesion during oriC plasmid DNA replication *in vitro*. *Genes to Cells, 8*, 437–449.

Hirotsu, N. and Wright, M. (2002). Using a Markov process model of an association football match to determine the optimal timing of substitution and tactical decisions. *Journal of the Operational Research Society, 53*(1), 88–96.

Hirsch, D. E., Simon, S. R., Bylander, T., Weintraub, M. A. and Szolovits, P. (1989). Using causal reasoning in gait analysis, *Applied Artificial Intelligence, 3*, 253–272.

Hodges, N. J. and Coppola, T. (in press). Probing how we learn and what we think we learn from observational practice of a novel action. *Psychological Research* (e-print available, doi: 10.1007/s00426-014-0588-y).

Hodges, N. J. and Lee, T. D. (1999). The role of augmented information prior to learning a bimanual visual-motor coordination task: Do instructions of the movement pattern facilitate learning relative to discovery learning? *British Journal of Psychology, 90*, 389–403.

Hodges, N. J. and Franks, I. M. (2000). Focus of attention and coordination bias: Implications for learning a novel bimanual task. *Human Movement Science, 19*, 843–867.

Hodges, N. J. and Franks, I. M. (2001). Learning a coordination skill: Interactive effects of instruction and feedback. *Research Quarterly for Exercise and Sport, 72*, 132–142.

Hodges, N. J. and Franks, I. M. (2002). Modelling coaching practice: The role of instruction and coaching. *Journal of Sports Sciences, 21*, 793–811.

Hodges, N. J. and Franks, I. M. (2004). Instructions, demonstrations and the learning process: Creating and constraining movement options. In A. M. Williams and N. J. Hodges (eds), *Skill Acquisition in Sport: Research, Theory and Practice*, pp. 145–174. London: Routledge.

Hodges, N. J., McGarry, T. and Franks, I. M. (1998). A dynamical system's approach to the examination of sport behaviour: Implications for tactical observation and technical instruction. *Avante, 4*, 16–38.

Hodges, N. J., Chua, R. and Franks, I. M. (2003). The role of video in facilitating perception and action of a novel coordination movement. *Journal of Motor Behavior, 35*, 247–260.

Hodges, N. J., Hayes, S., Breslin, G. and Williams, A. M. (2005). An evaluation of the minimal constraining information during movement observation and reproduction. *Acta Psychologica, 119*, 264–282.

Hodges, N. J., Williams, A. M., Hayes, S. J. and Breslin, G. (2006). End-point and endeffector information in modeling. *Journal of Sports Sciences, 20*, 253–269.

Hodges, N. J., Hayes, S. J., Eaves, D., Horn, R. and Williams, A. M. (2006). End-point trajectory matching as a method for teaching kicking skills. *International Journal of Sport Psychology*, *37*, 230–247.

Hodgson Phillips, L., Standen, P. J. and Batt M. E. (1998). Effects of seasonal change in rugby league on the incidence of injury. *British Journal of Sports Medicine*, *32*, 144–148.

Hogan, J. C. and Yanowitz, B. A. (1978). The role of verbal estimates of movement error in ballistic skill acquisition. *Journal of Motor Behavior*, *10*, 133–138.

Holmes, P. and Calmels, C. (2008). A neuroscientific review of imagery and observation use in sport. *Journal of Motor Behavior*, *40*, 433–445.

Holzreiter, S. H. and Köhle, M. E. (1993). Assessment of gait patterns using neural networks. *Journal of Biomechanics*, *26*, 645–651.

Höner, O., Hunt, A., Pauletto, S., Röber, N., Hermann, T. and Effenberg, A. O. (2011). Aiding movement with sonification in 'Exercise, Play and Sport'. In T. Hermann, A. Hunt and J. G. Neuhoff (eds) *The Sonification Handbook*, pp. 525–553. Berlin: Logos Publishing House.

Hong, S. L. and Newell, K. M. (2006). Change in the organisation of degrees of freedom with learning. *Journal of Motor Behavior*, *38*(2), 88–100.

Hope, W. (2002). Whose All Blacks? *Media, Culture and Society*, *24*(2), 235–253.

Horn, R., Williams, A. M. and Scott, M. A. (2002). Learning from demonstration: The role of visual search from video and point-light displays. *Journal of Sport Sciences*, *20*, 253–269.

Horn, T. S. (2002). Coaching effectiveness in the sport domain. In T. S. Horn (ed.), *Advances in Sport Psychology*, pp. 309–354. Champaign, IL: Human Kinetics.

Howells, C. (2000). A comparison of the tactics used by three groups of teams in the first 15 overs of the 1999 cricket World Cup. Unpublished dissertation, BSc Sport and Exercise Science, Cardiff.

Hristovski, R., Davids, K. Araújo, D. and Passos, P. (2011). Constraints-induced emergence of functional novelty in complex neurobiological systems: Basis for creativity in sport. *Nonlinear Dynamics, Psychology, and Life Sciences*, *15*(2), 175–206.

Hubbard, M. and Alaways, L. W. (1989). Rapid and accurate estimation of release conditions in the javelin throw. *Journal of Biomechanics*, *22*, 583–595.

Hughes, C. (1973). *Football Tactics and Teamwork*. Wakefield: E. P. Publishing.

Hughes, C. (1980). *Soccer: Tactics and Skills (The Football Association)*. London: British Broadcasting Co. and Queen Anne Press.

Hughes, M. D. (1985). A comparison of the patterns of play of squash. In I. D. Brown, R. Goldsmith, K. Coombes and M. A. Sinclair (eds) *International Ergonomics '85*, pp. 139–141. London: Taylor & Francis.

Hughes, M. D. (1986). A review of patterns of play in squash. In J. Watkins, T. Reilly and L. Burwitz (eds) *Sports Science*, pp. 363–368. London: E & FN Spon.

Hughes, M. (1988). Computerised notation analysis in field games. *Ergonomics*, *31*, 1585–1592.

Hughes, M. (1993). Notational analysis of football. In T. Reilly, J. Clarys and A. Stibbe (eds) *Science and Football*, pp. 151–159. London: E & FN Spon.

Hughes, M. (1995a). Using notational analysis to greate a more exciting scoring system for squash. In G. Atkinson and T. Reilly (eds) *Sport, Leisure and Ergonomics*, pp. 243–247. London: E & FN Spon.

Hughes, M. D. (1995b). Computerised notation of racket sports. In T. Reilly, M. Hughes and A. Lees (eds) *Science and Racket Sports*, pp. 249–256. London: E & FN Spon.

Hughes, M. (1996). Perturbation effect in soccer. *Third World Congress of Notational Analysis of Sport*. Antalya, Turkey, September.

Hughes, M. (ed.) (1998a). *Notational Analysis of Sport – I & II*. Cardiff: UWIC.

Hughes, M. D. (1998b). The application of notational analysis to racket sports. In A. Lees, I. Maynard, M. D. Hughes and T. Reilly (eds) *Science and Racket Sports II*, pp. 211–220. London: E & FN Spon.

Hughes, M. D. (ed.) (2000a). *Notational Analysis of Sport – III*. Cardiff: UWIC.

Hughes, M. (2000b). Do perturbations exist in soccer? In M. Hughes (ed.) *Notational Analysis of Sport – III*, pp. 16–24. Cardiff: UWIC.

Hughes, M. (2001). Perturbations and critical incidents in soccer. In M. Hughes and F. Tavares (eds) *Notational Analysis of Sport – IV*, pp. 23–33. Porto: Faculty of Sports Sciences and Education, University of Porto.

Hughes, M. D. (2002). From analysis to coaching. In D. Milanovic and F. Prot (eds) *Kinesiology: New Perspectives*, pp. 30–53. Zagreb: Faculty of Kinesiology, University of Zagreb.

Hughes, M. D. (2004a). Performance analysis: A 2004 perspective. *International Journal of Performance Analysis Sport* (electronic), 4(1), 103–109.

Hughes, M. D. (2004b). Performance analysis: A mathematical perspective. *International Journal of Performance Analysis Sport* (electronic), 4(2), 97–139.

Hughes, M. D. (2005). Notational analysis. In R. Bartlett, C. Gratton and C. G. Rolf (eds) *Encyclopaedia of International Sports Studies*, pp. 1–7. London: Routledge.

Hughes, M. and Cunliffe, S. (1986). Notational analysis of field hockey. *Proceedings of the BASS Conference*, September, Birmingham University, pp. 161–187.

Hughes, M. and McGarry, T. (1989). Computerised notational analysis of squash. In M. Hughes (ed.) *Science in Squash*, pp. 156–168. Liverpool: Liverpool Polytechnic.

Hughes, M. and Franks, I. M. (1991). A time–motion analysis of squash players using a mixed-image video tracking system. *Ergonomics*, 37, 23–29.

Hughes, M. and Sykes, I. (1994). Computerised notational analysis of the effects of the law changes in soccer upon patterns of play. *Journal of Sport Sciences*, 12(1), 180.

Hughes, M. and Clarke, S. (1995). Surface effect on patterns of play of elite tennis players. In T. Reilly, M. Hughes and A. Lees (eds) *Science and Racket Sports*, pp. 272–278. London: E & FN Spon.

Hughes, M. and Knight, P. (1995). Playing patterns of elite squash players, using English and point-per-rally scoring. In T. Reilly, M. Hughes and A. Lees (eds) *Science and Racket Sports*, pp. 257–259. London: E & FN Spon.

Hughes, M. and Franks, I. M. (1997). *Notational Analysis of Sport*. London: E & FN Spon.

Hughes, M. and Moore, P. (1998). Movement analysis of elite level male serve and volley tennis players. In A. Lees, I. Maynard, M. Hughes and T. Reilly (eds) *Science and Racket Sports II*, pp. 254–259. London: E & FN Spon.

Hughes, M. and Robertson, C. (1998). Using computerised notational analyisis to create a template for elite squash and its subsequent use in designing hand notation systems for player development. In A. Lees, I. Maynard, M. Hughes and T. Reilly (eds) *Science and Racket Sports II*, pp. 227–234. London: E & FN Spon.

Hughes, M. and Williams, D. (1998). Examination of playing patterns in Rugby Union using a computerised data gathering and analysis system. Presentation at the Science of Rugby Conference, Glasgow, June.

Hughes, M. D. and Bell, K. (1999). Performance profiling in cricket. In M. D. Hughes, F. Tavares and C. Moya (eds) *Notational Analysis of Sport – IV*, pp. 201–208. Porto: Facultat do Physica.

Hughes, M. D. and Franks, I. M. (2001). *pass.com*. Cardiff: UWIC.

Hughes, M. and Tavares, F. (eds) (2001). *Notational Analysis of Sport – IV*. Porto: Faculty of Sports Sciences and Education.

Hughes, M. and Bartlett, R.(2002). The use of performance indicators in performance analysis. *Journal of Sports Science, 20,* 739–754.

Hughes, M. and Murray, S. (2002). Performance profiling in squash and other individual sports. UKSI Website: www.uksi.com, March.

Hughes, M. and Wells, J. (2002). Analysis of penalties taken in shoot-outs. *eIJPAS International Journal of Performance Analysis Sport* (electronic), *2,* 55–72.

Hughes, M. and Franks, I. M. (2004). *Notational Analysis of Sport II – Improving Coaching and Performance in Sport.* London: E & FN Spon.

Hughes M. and Franks, I. M. (2005). Analysis of passing sequences, shots and goals in soccer. *Journal of Sports Sciences, 23,* 509–514.

Hughes, M. T. and Hughes, M. D. (2005). The evolution of computerised notational analysis through the example of squash. *International Journal of Computers in Sport Science, 4,* 5–20.

Hughes, M. and Reed, D. (2005). Creating a performance profile using perturbations in soccer. In D. Milanovic and F. Prot (eds) *Proceedings of 4th International Scientific Conference on Kinesiology, Opatija,* pp. 34–53. University of Zagreb, Croatia, September.

Hughes, M. and Probert, G. (2006). A technical analysis of elite male soccer players by position and success. In H. Dancs, M. Hughes and P. O'Donoghue (eds) *Notational Analysis of Sport – VII,* pp. 76 – 91. Cardiff: UWIC.

Hughes, M. D. and Franks, I. M. (2008). *Essentials of Performance Analysis.* London: E & FN Spon.

Hughes, M., Robertson, K. and Nicholson, A. (1988). An analysis of 1984 World Cup Association Football. In T. Reilly, A. Lees, K. Davids and W. Murphy (eds) *Science and Football,* pp. 363–367. London: E & FN Spon.

Hughes, M., Franks, I. M. and Nagelkerke, P. (1989). A video-system for the quantitative motion analysis of athletes in competitive sport. *Journal of Human Movement Studies, 17,* 212–227.

Hughes, M., Dawkins, N. and David, R. (2000a). Perturbation effect in soccer. In M. Hughes (ed.) *Notational Analysis of Sport – III,* pp. 1–14. Cardiff: CPA, UWIC.

Hughes, M., Dawkins, N. and Langridge, C. (2000b). Perturbations not leading to shots in soccer. In M. Hughes (ed.) *Notational Analysis of Sport – III,* pp. 108–116. Cardiff: CPA, UWIC.

Hughes, M. D., Wells, J. and Matthews, C. (2000d). Performance profiles at recreational, county and elite levels of women's squash. *Journal of Human Movement Studies, 39,* 85–104.

Hughes, M., Evans, S. and Wells, J. (2001). Establishing normative profiles in performance analysis. *International Journal of Performance Analysis Sport* (electronic), *1,* 4–27.

Hughes, M., Cooper, S-M. and Nevill, A. (2002a). Analysis procedures for non-parametric data from performance analysis. *International Journal of Performance Analysis Sport* (electronic), *2,* 6–20.

Hughes, M., Fenwick, B. and Murray, S. (2006a). Expanding normative profiles of elite squash players using momentum of winners and errors. *EIJPAS International Journal of Performance Analysis in Sport* (electronic), *6,* 1, 145–154.

Hughes, M., Hughes, M. T. and Behan, H. (2007b). The evolution of computerised notational analysis through the example of racket sports. *International Journal of Sports Science and Engineering, 1,* 3–28.

Hughes, M., Dawkins, N., David, R. and Mills, J. (2000c). The perturbation effect and goal opportunities in soccer. *Journal of Sports Sciences, 16,* 20.

Hughes, M., Ponting, R., Murray, S. and James, N. (2002b). Some example of computerised systems for feedback in performance analysis. UKSI Website: www.uksi.com, October.

Hughes, M. D., Howells, M., Hughes, M. and Murray, S. (2007a). Using perturbations in elite men's squash to generate performance profiles. In A. Lees, J.-F. Kahn and I. Maynard (eds) *Science and Racket Sports IV*, pp. 222–227. London: E & FN Spon.

Hughes, M., Watts, A., White, C. and Hughes, M. T. (2009). Game structures of elite male squash under different rules. In A. Lees, J.-F. Kahn and I. Maynard (eds) *Science and Racket Sports IV*, pp. 227–231. London: E & FN Spon.

Hughes, M., Appleton, R., Brooks, C., Hall, M. and Wyatt, C. (2006b). Notational analysis of elite men's water-polo. In H. Dancs, M. Hughes and P. O'Donoghue (eds) *Notational Analysis of Sport – VII*, pp. 275–298. Cardiff: UWIC.

Hughes, M., Archer, B., James, N., Dancs, H., Caudrelier, T. and Vuckovic, G. (2010). Behaviour patterns of elite coaches working with elite student athletes. In M. D. Hughes, H. Dancs, K. Nagyvaradi, T. Polgar, N. James, G. Sporis and G. Vuckovic (eds) *Research Methods and Performance Analysis*, pp. 162–171. Szombathely: WHU.

Hughes, M., Fuller, O., Hughes, M., Murray, S., James, N., & Vuskovic, G. (2011). The efficiency and ergonomics of different data entry systems in real-time and lapsed-time computer notation systems. *Proceedings from: The 6th INSHS International Christmas Sport Scientific Conference.* Retrieved from http://bib.irb.hr/datoteka/513213.Xmass-conference-BOOK.pdf#page=249.

Hughes, M., Caudrelier, T., James, N., Redwood-Brown, A., Donnelly, I., Kirkbride, A. and Duschesne, C. (2012). Moneyball and soccer: An analysis of the key performance indicators of elite male soccer players by position. *Journal of Human Sport and Exercise*, 7, 402–412.

Hunter, A. (2009). Canoe slalom boat trajectory while negotiating an upstream gate. *Sports Biomechanics*, 8(2), 105–113.

Hunter, A., Cochrane, J. and Sachlikidis, A. (2007). Canoe slalom: Competition analysis reliability. *Sports Biomechanics*, 6(2), 155–170.

Hunter, A., Cochrane, J. and Sachlikidis, A. (2008). Canoe slalom competition analysis. *Sports Biomechanics*, 7(1), 24–37.

Iberall, A. S. and Soodak, H. (1987). Physics for Complex Systems. In F. Eugene Yates, Alan Garfinkel, Donald O. Walter and G. B. Yates (eds) *Self-Organizing Systems, Life Science Monographs*, pp. 499–520.

Indonesia (2003). Retrieved 1 August 2003, from www.indo.com/distance.

International Rugby Board (1997). *Charter on the Game.* Dublin: International Rugby Board.

James, N. (2006). Notational analysis in soccer: Past, present and future. In H. Dancs, M. Hughes and P. O'Donoghue (eds) *Notational Analysis of Sport – VII*, pp. 35–53. Cardiff: CPA, UWIC.

James, N., Mellalieu, S. D. and Jones, N. M. P. (2005). The development of position-specific performance indicators in professional rugby union. *Journal of Sports Sciences*, 23(1), 63–72.

Janelle, C. M. and Hatfield, B. D. (2008). Visual attention and brain processes that underlie expert performance: Implications for sport and military psychology. *Military Psychology*, 20, S39–S69.

Jennings, D., Cormack, S., Coutts, A. J., Boyd, L. J. and Aughey, R. J. (2010). The validity and reliability of GPS units for measuring distance in team sport specific running patterns. *International Journal of Sports Physiology and Performance*, 5, 328–341.

Johansson, G. (1975). Visual motion perception. *Scientific American*, 232, 76–89.

Johnson, W. O. (1971). *Super Spectator and the Electric Lilliputians.* Boston, MA: Little, Brown & Co.

Johnston, R. J., Watsford, M. L., Pine, M. J., Spurrs, R. W., Murphy, A. J. and Pruyn, E. C. (2012). The validity and reliability of 5-Hz global positioning system units to measure team sport movement demands. *Journal of Strength and Conditioning Research*, 26(3), 758–765.

Jones, P. D., James, N. and Mellalieu, S. D. (2004a). Possession as a performance indicator in soccer. *International Journal of Performance Analysis of Sport*, 4(1), 98–102.

Jones, N. M. P., Mellalieu, S. D. and James, N. (2004b). Team performance indicators as a function of winning and losing in rugby union. *International Journal of Performance Analysis in Sport*, 4, 1, 61–71.

Jovanovic, M., Sporis, G., Omrcen, D. and Fiorentini, F. (2011). Effects of speed, agility, quickness training method on power performance in elite soccer players. *The Journal of Strength and Conditioning Research*, 25(5), 1285–1292.

Kal, E. C., van der Kamp, J. and Houdijk, H., (2013). External attentional focus enhances movement automatization: A comprehensive test of the constrained action hypothesis. *Human Movement Science*, 32, 527–539.

Kalveram, K. T. (1999). A modified model of the Hebbian synapse and its role in motor learning. *Human Movement Science*, 18, 185–199.

Kantak, S. S. and Winstein, C. J. (2012). Learning-performance distinction and memory processes for motor skills: A focused review and perspective. *Behavioural Brain Research*, 228, 219–231.

Kaplan, J. (1990). Letter to the editor: More on the 'hot hand', *Chance*, 3, 6.

Kasai, J. and Mori, T. (1998). A qualitative 3D analysis of forehand strokes in table tennis. In A. Lees, I. Maynard, M. D. Hughes and T. Reilly (eds) *Science and Racket Sports II*, pp. 201–205. London: E & FN Spon.

Kay, B. A. (1988). The dimensionality of movement trajectories and the degrees of freedom problem: A tutorial. *Human Movement Science*, 7, 343–364.

Keating, J. G., Owens, F., Adamson, K. and McTear, S. (1995). Extracting articulatory data from speech using artificial neural networks, *Proceedings of the 13th IASTED International Conference on Applied Informatics*, Innsbruck, Austria, 21–22 February, pp. 91–93.

Kelly, M. and Pedersen, P. (2001). Hardball–hardbat: A call for change from aluminium to wooden baseball bats in the NCAA. *The Sport Journal*, 4(3),1–5.

Kelso, J. A. S. (1991). Anticipatory dynamical systems, intrinsic pattern dynamics and skill learning. *Human Movement Science*, 10, 93–111.

Kelso, J. A. S. (1995). *Dynamic Patterns: The Self Organization of Brains and Behaviour*. Cambridge: Bradford Books.

Kelso, J. A. S. and Schöner, G. (1988). Self-organization of coordinative movement patterns. *Human Movement Science*, 7, 27–48.

Kelso, J. A. S., Holt, K. G., Rubin, P. and Kugler, P. N. (1981). Patterns of human interlimb coordination emerge from the properties of nonlinear limit cycle oscillatory processes: Theory and data. *Journal of Motor Behavior*, 13, 226–261.

Kempson, R. (2009). Hand of Henry shatters Ireland – France striker's 'Maradona moment' sends Trapattoni's men out of World Cup. *The Times*, p. 108.

Kernodle, M. W. and Carlton, L. G. (1992). Information feedback and the learning of multiple-degree-of-freedom activities. *Journal of Motor Behaviour*, 24, 187–196.

Kernodle, M. W., Johnson, R. and Arnold, D. R. (2001). Verbal instruction for correcting errors versus such instructions plus videotape replay on learning the overhand throw. *Perceptual Motor Skills*, 92, 1039–1051.

Kew, F. (1986). Playing the game: An ethnomethodological perspective. *International Review for the Sociology of Sport*, 21(4), 305–321.

Kew, F. (1987). Contested rules: An explanation of how games change. *International Review for the Sociology of Sport*, 22(2), 125–135.

Kirkcaldy, B. D. (1983). Catastrophic performances. *Sportwissencraft*, 13(1), 46–53.

Kirkendall, D. T., Speer, K. P. and Garrett, J. R. (1995). Injuries in American football. In T. Reilly, J. Bangsbo and M. Hughes (eds) *Science and Football – III*, pp. 132–138. London: E & FN Spon.

Kirkendall, D. T., Leonard, K. and Garrett, Jr, W. E. (2004). On the relationship of fitness to running volume and intensity in female soccer players. *Journal of Sports Science, 22,* 549–550.

Knudson, D. V. (2007). Qualitative biomechanical principles for application to coaching. *Sports Biomechanics, 6,* 109–118.

Knudsen, D. V. and Morrison, C. S. (1997). *Qualitative Analysis of Human Movement.* Champaign, IL: Human Kinetics.

Knudson, D. V. and Morrison, C. S. (2002). *Qualitative Analysis of Human Movement,* 2nd edn. Champaign, IL: Human Kinetics.

Koehler, J. J. and Conley, C. A. (2003). The 'Hot Hand' myth in professional basketball. *Journal of Sport and Exercise Psychology, 25,* 253–259.

Krakauer, J. W. (2009). Motor learning and consolidation: The case of visuomotor rotation. *Advances in Experimental Medicine and Biology, 629,* 405–421.

Krane, V. (1992). Conceptual and methodological considerations in sport anxiety research: From the inverted-U hypothesis to catastrophe theory. *Quest, 44*(1), 72–87.

Krauss, M. (2004). Equipment innovations and rules changes in sports. *Current Sports Medicine Reports, 3,* 272–276.

Kreighbaum, E. and Barthels, K. M. (1990). *Biomechanics: A qualitative approach for studying human movement.* New York: Macmillan.

Krustrup, P., Mohr, M., Amstrup, T., Rysgaard, T., Johansen, J., Steensberg, A., Pedersen, P. K. and Bangsbo, J. (2003). The yo-yo intermittent recovery test: Physiological response, reliability, and validity. *Medicine and Science in Sports and Exercise, 35*(4), 697–705.

Kujala, U. M., Taimela, S., Antti-Poika, I., Orava, S., Tuominen, R. and Myllynen, P. (1995). Acute injuries in soccer, ice hockey, volleyball, basketball, judo and karate: Analysis of national registry data. *British Medical Journal, 311,* 1465–1468.

Lacome, M., Piscione, J., Hager, J-P. and Bourdin, M. (2014). A new approach to quantifying physical demand in rugby union. *Journal of Sports Sciences, 32*(3), 1–11.

Ladany, S. P. and Machol, R. E. (eds) (1977). *Optimal Strategies in Sports.* Amsterdam: North Holland.

Lago, C. (2007). Are winners different from losers? Performance and chance in the FIFA World Cup 592 Germany 2006. *International Journal of Performance Analysis in Sport, 7,* 36–47.

Lago, C. (2009). The influence of match location, quality of opposition, and match status on possession strategies in professional association football. *Journal of Sports Sciences, 27*(13), 1463–1469.

Lago-Ballesteros, J., Lago-Peñas, C. and Rey, E. (2012). The effect of playing tactics and situational variables on achieving score-box possessions in a professional soccer team. *Journal of Sports Sciences, 30*(14), 1455–1461.

Lago-Peñas, C., Rey, E. and Lago-Ballesteros, J. (2012). The influence of effective playing time on physical demands of elite soccer players. *The Open Sports Science Journal, 5,* 188–92.

Lago-Peñas, C., Rey, E., Lago-Ballesteros, J., Casáis, L. and Domínguez, E. (2011). The influence of a congested calendar on physical performance in elite soccer. *The Journal of Strength and Conditioning Research, 25*(8), 2111–2117.

Lai, Q. and Shea, C. H. (1998). Generalized motor program (GMP) learning: Effects of reduced frequency of knowledge of results and practice variability. *Journal of Motor Behavior, 30,* 51–59.

Laird, P. and Waters, L. (2008). Eyewitness recollection of sport coaches. *International Journal of Performance Analysis in Sport, 8,* 76–84.

Lapham, A. C. and Bartlett, R. M. (1995). The use of artificial intelligence in the analysis of sports performance: A review of applications in human gait analysis and future directions for sports biomechanics. *Journal of Sports Sciences, 13,* 229–237.

Larsen, O., Zoglowek, H. and Rafoss, K. (2000). An analysis of team performance for the Norwegian women soccer team in the Olympics in Atlanta 1996. In M. Hughes (ed.) *Notational Analysis of Sport – III*, pp. 112–117. Cardiff: CPA, UWIC.

Larson, K. M., Bodin, P. and Gomberg, J. (2003). Using 1–Hz GPS data to measure deformations caused by the Denali fault earthquake. *Science, 300*(5624), 1421–1424.

Larssen, B. C., Ong, N. T. and Hodges, N. J. (2012). Watch and learn: Seeing is better than doing when acquiring consecutive motor tasks. *PLOS ONE, 7* (doi:10.1371/journal.pone.38938).

Latash, M. L., Scholz, J. P. and Schöner, G. (2002). Motor control strategies revealed in the structure of motor variability. *Exercise and Sport Science Reviews, 30,* 26–31.

Leaman, O. (2001). Cheating and fair play in sport. In W. J. Morgan, K. V. Meier and A. J. Schneider (eds) *Ethics in Sport*, pp. 91–99. East Peoria, IL: Versa Press.

Lee, A. J. and Garraway, M. W. (2000). The influence of environmental factors on rugby football injuries. *Journal of Sport Sciences, 18,* 91–95.

Lee, T. D. (2012). Contextual interference: Generalizability and limitations. In N. J. Hodges and A. M. Williams (eds) *Skill Acquisition in Sport*, 2nd edn, pp. 79–93. New York: Routledge.

Lee, T. D. and Carnahan, H. (1990). Bandwidth knowledge of results and motor learning. *The Quarterly Journal of Experimental Psychology, 42,* 777–789.

Lee, T. D., Swinnen, S. P. and Verschueren, S. (1995). Relative phase alterations during bimanual skill acquisition. *Journal of Motor Behavior, 27,* 263–274.

Lee, W. A. (1984). Neuromotor synergies as a basis for coordinated intentional action. *Journal of Motor Behavior, 16,* 136–170.

Lees, A. (2002). Technique analysis in sports: A critical review. *Journal of Sports Sciences, 20,* 813–828.

Lees, A. and Nolan, L. (1998). The biomechanics of soccer: A review. *Journal of Sports Sciences, 16,* 211–234.

Lees, A. and Barton, G. (2004). A characterisation of technique in the soccer kick using a Kohonen neural network analysis. In J. Cabrys and T. Reilly (eds) *Proceedings of the 5th World Congress of Science and Football*, London: E & FN Spon, pp. 112–119.

Lees, A., Barton, G. and Kershaw, L. (2003). The use of Kohonen neural network analysis to qualitatively characterize technique in soccer kicking. *Journal of Sports Sciences, 21,* 243–244.

Lees, A., Maynard, I., Hughes, M. and Reilly, T. (eds) (1998). *Science and Racket Sports II.* London: E & FN Spon.

Lewis, M. D. (2000). The promise of dynamic systems approaches for an integrated account of human development. *Child Development, 71*(1), 36–43.

Lewis, M. (2003). *Moneyball: The Art of Winning an Unfair Game.* London: W. W. Norton.

Lewis, M. and Hughes, M. D. (1988). Attacking play in the 1986 World Cup of Association Football. *Journal of Sport Science, 6,* 169.

Lewthwaite, R. and Wulf, G. (2012). Motor learning through a motivational lens. In N. J. Hodges and A. M. Williams (eds) *Skill Acquisition in Sport*, 2nd edn, pp. 3–21. New York: Routledge.

Liao, C. and Masters, R. S. W. (2001). Analogy learning: A means to implicit motor learning. *Journal of Sports Sciences, 19,* 307–319.

Liebermann, D. G. (1997). Temporal structure as a primitive of movement for skill acquisition. In M. Bar-Eli and R. Lidor (eds) *Proceedings of the World Conference of Sport Psychology*, Wingate Institute, Israel, pp. 496–499.

Liebermann, D. G., Raz, T. and Dickinson, J. (1988). On intentional and incidental learning and estimation of temporal and spatial information. *Journal of Human Movement Studies, 15,* 191–204.

Liebermann, D. G., Katz, L., Hughes, M. D., Bartlett, R. M., McClements, J. and Franks, I. M. (2002). Advances in the application of information technology to sport performance. *Journal of Sports Sciences, 20,* 755–769.

Liu, H., Hopkins, W., Gómez, M. A. and Molinuevo, J. S. (2013). Inter-operator reliability of live football match statistics from OPTA Sportsdata. *International Journal of Performance Analysis in Sport, 13* (3), 803–821.

Locke, D. (2005). Profiling RU teams through perturbation analysis. Unpublished Master's Thesis, University of Wales Institute, Cardiff.

Lohse, K. R., Jones, M. C., Healy, A. F. and Sherwood, D. E. (2014a). The role of attention in motor control. *Journal of Experimental Psychology: General, 143,* 930–948.

Lohse, K. R., Wadden, K., Boyd, L. A. and Hodges, N. J. (2014b). Motor skill acquisition across short and long time scales: A meta-analysis of neuroimaging data. *Neuropsychologia, 59,* 130–141.

Loland, S. (1998). Fair play: Historical anachronism or topical ideal? In M. J. McNamee and S. J. Parry (eds), *Ethics and Sport,* pp. 57–64. London: E & FN Spon.

Longmore, A. (1994). Absurd cup rule obscures football's final goal. *The Times,* 1 February, p. 51.

Lothian, F. and Farrally, M. (1994). A time–motion analysis of women's hockey. *Journal of HumanMovement Studies, 26,* 255–265.

Luhtanen, P., Belinskij, A., Häyrinen, M. and Vänttinen, T. (2002). A computer aided team analysis of the Euro 2000 in soccer. *International Journal of Performance Analysis in Sport, 1,* 74–83.

Lumpkin, A., Stoll, S. K. and Beller, J. M. (1999). *Sport Ethics: Applications for Fair Play.* London: McGraw-Hill.

Luxbacher, J. and Klein, G. (1993). *The Soccer Goalkeeper.* Champaign, IL: Human Kinetics.

Lyle, J. (2002). *Sports coaching concepts.* London: Routledge.

Lyons, K. (1988). *Using Video in Sport.* Huddersfield: Springfield Books.

Lyons, K. (1996). Lloyd Messersmith. In M. Hughes (ed.) *Notational Analysis of Sport – I & II,* pp. 49–59. Cardiff: UWIC.

McCullagh, P. and Caird, J. K. (1990). Correct and learning models and the use of model knowledge of results in the acquisition and retention of a motor skill. *Journal of Human Movement Sciences, 18,* 107–116.

McCullagh, P. and Weiss, M. R. (2001). Modeling: Considerations for motor skill performance and psychological responses. In R. N. Singer, H. A. Hausenblas and C. M. Janelle (eds) *Handbook of Sport Psychology,* 2nd edn, pp. 205–238. New York: Wiley.

McDonald, C. (1996). Toward the essential meaning of fair play as an aspiration of Olympism. Retrieved 12 November 2010, from www.la84foundation.org/SportsLibrary/ISOR/ISOR1996q.pdf.

McGarry, T. (2006). Identifying patterns in squash contests using dynamical analysis and human perception. *International Journal of Performance Analysis in Sport, 6*(2), 134–147.

McGarry, T. (2008). Probability analysis of notated event in sport contests: Skill and chance. In M. Hughes and I. M. Franks (eds) *The Essentials of Performance Analysis: An Introduction,* pp. 206–225. London: Routledge.

McGarry, T. (2009). Applied and theoretical perspectives of performance analysis in sport: scientific issues and challenges. *International Journal of Performance Analysis in Sport, 9,* 128–140.

McGarry, T. and Franks, I. M. (1994). A stochastic approach to predicting competition squash match-play. *Journal of Sports Sciences, 12,* 573–584.

McGarry, T. and Franks, I. M. (1995). Modeling competitive squash performance from quantitative analysis. *Human Performance, 8,* 113–129.

McGarry, T. and Franks, I. M. (1996a). Analysing championship squash match play: In search of a system description. In S. Haake (ed.) *The Engineering of Sport*, pp. 263–269. Rotterdam: Balkema.

McGarry, T. and Franks, I. M. (1996b). In search of invariance in championship squash. In M. D. Hughes (ed.) *Notational Analysis of Sport – I & II*, pp. 281 – 288. Cardiff: UWIC.

McGarry, T. and Franks, I. M. (1996c). Development, application and limitation of a stochastic Markov model in explaining championship squash performance. *Research Quarterly for Exercise and Sport*, *67*, 406–415.

McGarry, T. and Franks, I. M. (1996d). In search of invariant athletic behaviour in competitive sport systems: An example from championship squash match-play. *Journal of Sports Sciences*, *14*, 445–456.

McGarry, T. and Franks, I. M. (2000). On winning the penalty shoot-out in soccer. *Journal of Sports Sciences*, *18*, 401–409.

McGarry, T. and Franks, I. M. (2003). The science of match analysis. In T. Reilly and A. M. Williams (eds) *Science and Soccer*, 2nd edn, pp. 265–275. London: Routledge.

McGarry, T. and Perl, J. (2004). Models of sports contests: Markov processes, dynamical systems and neural networks. In M. D. Hughes and I. M. Franks (ed.) *Notational Analysis of Sport: Systems for Better Coaching and Performance in Sport*, pp. 227–242. London: Routledge.

McGarry, T. and Walter, F. (2007). On the detection of space–time patterns in squash using dynamical analysis. *International Journal of Computer Science in Sport*, *6*, 42–49.

McGarry, T., Khan, M. A. and Franks, I. M. (1999). On the presence and absence of behavioural traits in sport: An example from championship squash match-play. *Journal of Sports Sciences*, *17*, 297–311.

McGarry, T., Anderson, D. I., Wallace, S. A., Hughes, M. and Franks, I. M. (2002). Sport competition as a dynamical self-organizing system. *Journal of Sports Sciences*, *20*, 771–781.

McGinnis, P. M. and Newell, K. M. (1982). Topological dynamics: A framework for describing movement and its constraints. *Human Movement Science*, *1*, 289–305.

McLaughlin, E. and O'Donoghue, P. G. (2004). Analysis of primary school children's physical activity in the playground: A complementary approach, in P. G. O'Donoghue and M. D. Hughes (eds) *Performance Analysis of Sport*, pp. 233–240. Cardiff: CPA Press, UWIC.

MacLeod, H., Bussell, C. and Sunderland, C. (2007). Time–motion analysis of elite women's field hockey, with particular reference to maximum intensity movement patterns. *International Journal of Performance Analysis in Sport*, *7*(2), 1–12.

MacLeod, H., Morris, J., Nevill, A. and Sunderland, C. (2009). The validity of a non-differential global positioning system for assessing player movement patterns in field hockey. *Journal of Sports Sciences*, *27*(2), 121–128.

McPherson, D. A. (1991). *Order out of Chaos: The Autobiographical Works of Maya Angelou.* London: Virago Press.

Macutkiewicz, D. and Sunderland, C. (2011). The use of GPS to evaluate activity profiles of elite women hockey players during match-play. *Journal of Sports Sciences*, *29*(9), 967–973.

Magill, R. A. (2001a). Augmented feedback in motor skill acquisition. In R. N. Singer, H. A. Hausenblas and C. M. Janelle (eds) *Handbook of Sport Psychology*, 2nd edn, pp. 86–114. Wiley: New York.

Magill, R. A. (2001b). *Motor Learning: Concepts and Applications* (6th international edn). Singapore: McGraw-Hill International Editions.

Magill, R. A. and Wood, C. A. (1986). Knowledge of results precision as a learning variable in motor skill acquisition. *Research Quarterly for Exercise and Sport*, *57*, 170–173.

Magill, R. A. and Schoenfelder-Zohdi, B. (1996). A visual model and knowledge of performance as sources of information for learning a rhythmic gymnastics skill. *International Journal of Sport Psychology*, *24*, 358–369.

Magill, R. A. and Anderson, D. I. (2012). The roles and uses of augmented feedback in motor skill. In N. J. Hodges and A. M. Williams (eds) *Skill Acquisition in Sport*, 2nd edn, pp. 3–21. New York: Routledge.

Malolepszy, A. and Kacki, E. (2003). Genetic programming in medical diagnosis. *Studies in Health Technology and Informatics*, *95*, 44–49.

Malpass, R. and Devine, P. (1981). Guided memory in eyewitness identification. *Journal of Applied Psychology*, *66*, 343–350.

Marqués-Bruna, P., Lees A. and Grimshaw, P. (2007). Development of technique in soccer. *International Journal of Coaching Science*, *1*(2), 51–62.

Marshall, R. N. and Elliott, B. C. (2000). Long axis rotation: The missing link in proximal-to-distal sequencing. *Journal of Sports Sciences*, *18*, 247–254.

Martens, R., Burwitz, L. and Zuckerman, J. (1976). Modeling effects on motor performance. *Research Quarterly*, *47*, 277–291.

Maslovat, D., Brunke, K. M., Chua, R. and Franks, I. M. (2009). Feedback effects on learning a novel bimanual coordination pattern: Support for the guidance hypothesis. *Journal of Motor Behavior*, *41*, 45–54.

Maslovat, D., Hayes, S., Horn, R., & Hodges, N (2010a). Motor learning through observation, in D. Elliot and M. Khan (eds) *Vision and Goal-Directed Movement: Neurobehavioral Perspectives*, pp. 315–339. Champaign, IL: Human Kinetics.

Maslovat, D., Hodges, N. J., Krigolson, O. E. and Handy, T. C. (2010b). Observational practice benefits are limited to perceptual improvements in the acquisition of a novel coordination skill. *Experimental Brain Research*, *204*, 119–130.

Mason, D. S. (1999). What is the sports product and who buys it? The marketing of sports leagues. *European Journal of Marketing*, *33*(3), 402–418.

Masters, R. S. W. (1992). Knowledge, knerves and know-how: The role of explicit versus implicit knowledge in the breakdown of a complex motor skill under pressure. *British Journal of Psychology*, *83*, 343–358.

Masters, R. S. W. (2000). Theoretical aspects of implicit learning in sport. *International Journal of Sport Psychology*, *31*, 530–541.

Masters, R. S. W. and Maxwell, J. P. (2004). Implicit motor learning, reinvestment and movement disruption: What you don't know won't hurt you? In A. M. Williams and N. J. Hodges (eds) *Skill Acquisition in Sport: Research, Theory and Practice*, pp. 207–228. London: Routledge.

Masters, R. S. W. and Maxwell, J. (2008). The theory of reinvestment. *International Review of Sport and Exercise Psychology*, *1*, 160–183.

Messersmith, L. L. and Corey, S. M. (1931). Distance traversed by a basketball player. *Research Quarterly*, *2*(2), 57–60.

Metzler, M. (1981). A multi-observational system for supervising student teachers in physical education. *The Physical Educator*, *49*, 136–143.

Miall, R. C., Weir, D. J., Wolpert, D. M. and Stein, J. F. (1993). Is the cerebellum a Smith predictor? *Journal of Motor Behavior*, *25*, 203–216.

Miles, K. and Khan, R. (1988). *Jahangir and the Khan Dynasty*. London: Pelham Books.

Miller, S. A. and Bartlett, R. M. (1993).The effects of increased shooting distance in the basketball jump shot. *Journal of Sports Sciences*, *11*, 285–293.

Miller, S. A. and Bartlett, R. M. (1996). The relationship between basketball shooting kinematics, distance and playing position. *Journal of Sports Sciences*, *14*, 245–253.

Mohr, M., Krustrup, P. and Bangsbo, J. (2003). Match performance of high-standard soccer players with special reference to development of fatigue. *Journal of Sports Sciences*, *21*(7), 519.

More, K. G. and Franks, I. M. (1996). Analysis and modification of verbal coaching behaviour: The usefulness of a data driven intervention strategy. *Journal of Sports Sciences*, *14*, 523–543.

More, K. G. and Franks, I. M. (2004). Measuring coaching effectiveness. In M. Hughes and I. M. Franks (eds) *Notational Analysis in Sport: Systems for Better Coaching and Performance*, 2nd edn, pp. 242–256. London: E & FN Spon.

Morris, C. (1977). The most important points in tennis. In S. P. Ladany and R. E. Machol (eds) *Optimal Strategies in Sport*, pp. 131–140. Amsterdam: North Holland.

Morris, D. (1981). *The Soccer Tribe*. London: Jonathan Cape.

Morrison, D. G. and Schmittlein, D. C. (1998). It takes a hot goalie to raise the Stanley Cup. *Chance*, *11*(1), 3–7.

Mosteller, F. (1979). A resistant analysis of 1971 and 1972 professional football. In J. H. Goldstein (ed.) *Sports, Games & Play*, pp. 371–401. Mahwah, NJ: Lawrence Erlbaum Associates.

Moura, F. A., Martins, L. E. B., Anido, R. O., Ruffino, P. G. C., Barros, R. M. L. and Cunha, S. A. (2013). A spectral analysis of team dynamics and tactics in Brazilian football. *Journal of Sports Sciences*, *31*(14), 1568–1577.

Mukamel, R., Ekstrom, A., Kaplan, J., Iacoboni, M. and Fried, I. (2010). Single-neuron responses in humans during execution and observation of actions. *Current Biology*, *20*, 1–7.

Munro, B. H. (1997). *Statistical Methods for Health CareResearch*, 3rd edn. Philadelphia, PA: Lippincott-Raven.

Murray, S. and Hughes, M. (2001). Tactical performance profiling in elite level senior squash. In M. Hughes and I. M. Franks (eds) *pass.com*, pp. 185–194. Cardiff: CPA, UWIC.

Murray, S., Maylor, D. and Hughes, M. (1998). The effect of computerised analysis as feedback on performance of elite squash players. In A. Lees, I. Maynard, M. Hughes and T. Reilly (eds) *Science and Racket Sports II*, pp. 235–240. London: E & FN Spon.

Murray, S., Howells, M., Hurst, L., Hughes, M. T., Hughes M. D. and James, N. (2008). Using perturbations in elite men's squash to generate performance profiles. In A. Hoekelmann and M. Brummond (eds) *Performance Analysis of Sport VIII*, pp. 98–115. Magdeburg: School of Sport, Otto von Guericke Universitat.

Mylvaganam, R., Ramsay, N. and De Graca, F. (2002). *Sports Analysis System and Method*. International application published under the Patent Cooperation Treaty. International Publication Number WO 02/071334 A2. Retrieved from http://l2.espacenet.com/espacenet/bnsviewer?CY=ep&LG=en&DB=EPD&PN=WO02071334&ID=WO++02 071334A2+I+.

National Collegiate Athletic Association News. (1982). Football changes continue to improve safety, *9*(5), 3.

Negnevitsky, M. (2002). *Artificial Intelligence: A Guide to Intelligent Systems*. Harlow: Addison-Wesley.

Nevill, A. M., Atkinson, G. and Hughes, M. (2008). Twenty five years of sports performance research in the Journal of Sport Science. *Journal of Sports Sciences*, *26*, 413–426.

Nevill, A. M., Atkinson, G., Hughes, M. D. and Cooper, S.-M. (2002). Statistical methods for analysing sport performance and notational analysis data. *Journal of Sports Sciences*, *20*, 829–844.

Newell, K. M. (1986). Constraints on the development of coordination. In M. G. Wade and H. T. A. Whiting (eds) *Motor Development in Children: Aspects of Coordination and Control*, pp. 341–360. Dordrecht: Martinus Nijhoff.

Newell, K. M. (1991). Motor skill acquisition. *Annual Review of Psychology, 42*, 213–237.

Newell, K. M. (2003). Schema theory (1975): Retrospectives and prospectives. *Research Quarterly for Exercise and Sport, 74*(4), 383–388.

Newell, K. M. and Corcos, D. M. (1993). *Issues in Variability and Motor Control*. Champaign, IL: Human Kinetics.

Newell, K. M. and Jordan, K. (2007). Task constraints and movement organization: A common language. In W. Davis and G. Broadhead (eds) *Ecological Task Analysis and Movement*, pp. 5–23. Champaign, IL: Human Kinetics.

Newell, K. M., Morris, L. R. and Scully, D. M. (1985). Augmented information and the acquisition of skill in physical activity. In R. J. Terjung (ed.) *Exercise and Sport Science Reviews, 13*, 235–261.

Newell, K. M., Broderick, M. P., Deutsch, K. M. and Slifkin, A. B. (2003). Task goals and change in dynamical degrees of freedom with motor learning. *Journal of Experimental Psychology: Human Perception and Performance, 29*(2), 379–387.

Norton, K. I., Craig, N. P. and Olds, T. (1999). The evolution of Australian football. *Journal of Science and Medicine in Sport, 2*(4), 389–404.

Norton, K. I., Schwerdt, S. and Lange, K. (2001). Evidence for the aetiology of injuries in Australian football. *British Journal of Sport Medicine, 35*, 418–423.

Nussbaum, M. A., Chaffin, D. B. and Martin, B. J. (1997). A neural network model for simulation of torso muscle coordination. *Journal of Biomechanics, 30*, 251–258.

Oberstone, J. (2009). Differentiating the top English Premier League football clubs from the rest of the pack: Identifying the keys to success. *Journal of Quantitative Analysis in Sports, 5*(3), 1183–1200.

Odetoyinbo, K., Sapsford, P. and Thomas, S. (1997). Analysis of the effects for the 1994 FIFA experiment on semi-professional soccer. *Journal of Sport Sciences, 5*(1), 20.

O'Donoghue, P. (2001). Notational analysis of rallies in European club championship badminton. In M. Hughes and F. Tavares (eds) *Notational Analysis of Sport IV*, pp. 225–228. Porto: Faculty of Sports Sciences and Education, University of Porto, Portugal.

O'Donoghue, P. G. (2004). Match analysis in racket sports. In A. Lees, J. F., Khan and I. W. Maynard (eds) *Science and Racket Sports III*, pp. 155–162. London: Routledge.

O'Donoghue, P. (2005). Normative profiles of sports performance. *International Journal of Performance Analysis in Sport, 4*(1), 67–76.

O'Donoghue, P. (2007). Reliability issues in performance analysis. *International Journal of Performance Analysis in Sport, 7*(1), 35–48.

O'Donoghue, P. (2008). Principal components analysis in the selection of key performance indicators in sport. *International Journal of Performance Analysis in Sport, 8*(3), 145–155.

O'Donoghue, P. and Liddle, D. (1998). A notational analysis of time factors of elite men's and ladies' singles tennis on clay and grass surfaces. In A. Lees, I. W. Maynard, M. D. Hughes and T. Reilly (eds) *Science and Racket Sports II*, pp. 241–246. London: E & FN Spon.

O'Donoghue, P. and Ingram, B. (2001). A notational analysis of elite tennis strategy. *Journal of Sports Sciences, 19*, 107–115.

O'Donoghue, P. and Parker, D. (2001), Time–motion analysis of FA Premier League soccer competition. In M. Hughes and I. Franks (eds) *Performance Analysis, Sports Science and Computers*, pp. 263–266, Cardiff: UWIC Press.

O'Donoghue, P. and Tenga, A. (2001). The effect of score-line on work rate in elite soccer. *Journal of Sports Sciences, 19*(1), 25–26.

O'Donoghue, P. and Hughes, M. (eds) (2004). *Notational Analysis of Sport – VI*, Cardiff: UWIC (266 pages).

O'Donoghue, P. G. and Longville, J. (2004). Reliability testing and the use of statistics in performance analysis support: A case study from an international netball tournament. In P. G. O'Donoghue and M. D. Hughes (eds) *Performance Analysis of Sport 6*, pp. 1–7. Cardiff: CPA Press, UWIC.

O'Donoghue, P. G. and Williams, J. (2004). An evaluation of human and computer-based predictions of the 2003 Rugby Union World Cup. *International Journal of Computer Science in Sport (e)*, 3(1), 5–22.

O'Donoghue, P. G. and Brown, E. J. (2009). Sequences of service points and the misperception of momentum in elite tennis. *International Journal of Performance Analysis in Sport*, 9(1), 113–127.

O'Donoghue, P. G. and Robinson, G. (2009). Validation of the Prozone3® player tracking system: A preliminary report. *International Journal of Computer Science in Sport*, 8(1), 38–53.

O'Donoghue, P. G. and Mayes, A. (2013). Coach behaviour. In T. McGarry, P. D. O'Donoghue and J. Sampaio (eds) *Routledge Handbook of Sports Performance Analysis*, pp. 127–139. London: Routledge.

O'Donoghue, P.G, Dubitzky, W., Lopes, P., Berrar, D., Lagan, K., Hassan, D., Bairner, A. and Darby, P. (2003). An evaluation of quantitative and qualitative methods of predicting the 2002 FIFA World Cup, *Proceedings of the World Congress of Science and Football V*, Lisbon, Portugal, pp. 44–45.

O'Donoghue, P. G., Dubitzky, W., Lopes, P., Berrar, D., Lagan, K., Hassan, D., Bairner, A. and Darby, P. (2004). An Evaluation of quantitative and qualitative methods of predicting the 2002 FIFA World Cup, *Journal of Sports Sciences*, 22, 513–514.

Olds, T. (2001). The evolution of physique in male rugby union players in the twentieth century. *Journal of Sports Sciences*, 19, 253–262.

Olivia, T. A. (1987). Gemcat: A general multi-variate methodology for estimating catastrophe models. *Behavioural Science*, 32, 121–137.

Olsen, E. (1988). An analysis of scoring strategies in the World Championship in Mexico. In T. Reilly, A. Lees, K. Davids and W. Murphy (eds) *Science and Football*, pp. 373–376. London: E & FN Spon.

Olsen, E. and Larsen, O. (1997). Use of match analysis by coaches. In T. Reilly, J. Bangsbo and M. D. Hughes (eds) *Science and Football III*, pp. 209–220. London: E & FN Spon.

Ong, N. T. and Hodges, N. J. (2012). Mixing it up a little: How to schedule observational practice. In N. J. Hodges and A. M. Williams (eds) *Skill Acquisition in Sport*, 2nd edn, pp. 22–39. New York: Routledge.

Ong, N. T., Larssen, B. C. and Hodges, N. J. (2012). In the absence of physical practice, observation and imagery do not result in updating of internal models for aiming. *Experimental Brain Research*, 218, 9–19.

OPTA. (2012). Definiciones OPTA and Pack Trainning 2012/13. *OPTA Sportsdata*. Optasports. 2013. Retrieved from www.optasports.com.

Padulo, J., D'Ottavio, S., Pizzolato, F., Smith, L. and Annino, G. (2012). Kinematic analysis of soccer players in shuttle running. *International Journal of Sports Medicine*, 33(6), 459.

Palut, Y. and Zanone, P. G. (2005). A dynamical analysis of tennis: Concepts and data. *Journal of Sports Sciences*, 23, 1021–1032.

Parkkari, J., Kujala, U. M. and Kannus, P. (2001). Is it possible to prevent sports injuries? *Sports Medicine*, 31(14), 985–995.

Partington, M. and Cushion, C. (2013). An investigation of the practice activities and coaching behaviours of professional top-level youth soccer coaches, *Scandinavian Journal of Medicine and Science in Sports*, 23, 374–382.

Partridge, D. and Franks, I. M. (1989a). A detailed analysis of crossing opportunities from the 1986 World Cup (Part I). *Soccer Journal*, May–June, 47–50.

Partridge, D. and Franks, I. M. (1989b). A detailed analysis of crossing opportunities from the 1986 World Cup (Part II). *Soccer Journal*, June–July, 45–48.

Partridge, D. and Franks, I. M. (1993). Computer-aided analysis of sport performance: An example from soccer. *The Physical Educator, 50*, 208–215.

Partridge, D. and Franks, I. M. (1996). Analyzing and modifying coaching behaviours by means of computer aided observation. *The Physical Educator, 53*, 8–23.

Passos, P., Araujo, D., Davids, K., Gouveia, L., Milho, J. and Serpa, S. (2008). Information-governing dynamics of attacker–defender interactions in youth rugby union. *Journal of Sports Sciences, 26*(13), 1421–1429.

Passos, P., Milho, J., Fonseca, S., Borges, J., Araújo, D. and Davids, K. (2011). Interpersonal distance regulates functional grouping tendencies of agents in team sports. *Journal of Motor Behavior, 43*(2), 155–163.

Patterson, J. T. and Lee, T. D. (2013). Organizing practice: Effective practice is more than just reps. In D. Farrow, J. Baker and C. MacMahon (eds) *Developing Sport Expertise: Researchers and Coaches Put Theory into Practice*, 2nd edn, pp. 132–153. London: Routledge.

Patton, J. L., Wei, Y. J., Bajaj, P. and Scheidt, R. A. (2013). Visuomotor learning enhanced by augmenting instantaneous trajectory error feedback during reaching. *PLoS ONE, 8*: e46466.

Peakman, T. (2001). Perturbations in squash. Undergraduate dissertation. BSC Sports Coaching, UWIC, Cardiff.

Perl, J. (2001). Artificial neural networks in sports: New concepts and approaches. *International Journal of Performance Analysis in Sport, 1*, 106–121.

Perl, J. (2002a). Game analysis and control by means of continuously learning networks. *International Journal of Performance Analysis in Sport, 2*, 21–35.

Perl, J. (2002b). Adaptation, antagonism and system dynamics. In G. Ghent, D. Kluka and D. Jones (eds) *Perspectives: The Multidisciplinary Series of Physical Education and Sport Science, 4*, pp. 105–125. Oxford: Meyer & Meyer Sport.

Perš, J., Bon, M., Kovačič, S., Šibila, M. and Dežman, B. (2002). Observation and analysis of large-scale human motion. *Human Movement Science, 21*(2), 295–311.

Pettit, A. and Hughes, M. D. (2001). Crossing and shooting patterns in the 1986 and 1998 World Cups for soccer. In M. Hughes and I. M. Franks (eds) *pass.com*, pp. 267–276. Cardiff: CPA, UWIC.

Pingali, G., Opalach, A. and Jean, Y. (2000). Ball tracking and virtual replays for innovative tennis broadcasts. *15th International Conference on Pattern Recognition*. Barcelona, September 2000.

Pino Díaz-Pereira, M., Gómez-Conde, I., Escalona, M. and Olivieri, D. N. (2014). Automatic recognition and scoring of Olympic rhythmic gymnastic movements. *Human Movement Science, 34*, 63–80.

Pizzinato, A. (1997). Description of an approach to assest [sic] the technical and tactical training of novice tennis players. *STAPS: Revue des Sciences et Techniques des Activités Physiques et Sportive, 18*(43), 83–94.

Pollard, R. and Reep, C. (1997). Measuring effectiveness of playing strategies at soccer. *The Statistician, 46*, 541–550.

Pollard, R., Benjamin, B. and Reep, C. (1977). Sport and the negative binomial distribution. In S. P. Ladany and R. E. Machol (eds) *Optimal Strategies in Sport*, pp. 185–195. Amsterdam: North-Holland.

Portas, M. D., Harley, J. A., Barnes, C. A. and Rush, C. J. (2010). The validity and reliability of 1–Hz and 5–Hz global positioning systems for linear, multidirectional, and soccer-specific activities. *International Journal of Sports Physiology Performance, 5*(4), 448–458.

Porter, J., Wu, W. and Partridge, J. (2010). Focus of attention and verbal instructions: Strategies of elite track and field coaches and athletes. *Sport Science Review, 19*, 77–89.

Potter, G. and Carter, A. (1995). The four year cycle: A comparison of the 1991 and 1995 Rugby World Cup finals. In M. Hughes (ed.) *Notational Analysis of Sport III*, pp. 216–219. UWIC, Cardiff.

Priesmeyer, H. R. and Baik, K. (1989). Discovering the patterns of chaos. *Planning Review, 17*(6), 14–21.

Pritchard, S., Hughes, M. and Evans, S. (2001). Rule changes in elite badminton. In M. Hughes and I. Franks (eds) *Proceedings of the 5th World Congress of Performance Analysis, Sports Science and Computers (pass.com)*. UWIC, Cardiff, pp. 213–222.

Putnam, C. A. (1993). Sequential motions of body segments in striking and throwing skills: Descriptions and explanations. *Journal of Biomechanics, 26*, 125–135.

Quarrie, K. L. and Hopkins, W. G. (2007). Changes in player characteristics and match activities in Bledisloe Cup rugby union from 1972 to 2004. *Journal of Sports Sciences, 25*(8), 895–903.

Raab, M. (2002). Hot hand in sports: The belief in hot hand of spectators in volleyball. In M. Koskolou, N. Geladas and V. Klissouras (eds), *ECSS proceedings: Vol. 2. Seventh Congress of the European Congress of Sport Sciences*, p. 971. Athens: Trepoleos.

Rader, B. G. (1984). *In Its Own Image: How Television Has Transformed Sports*. London: Free Press.

Rahnama, N., Reilly, T. and Lees, A. (2002). Injury risk associated with playing actions during competitive soccer. *British Journal of Sports Medicine, 36*(5), 354–359.

Rampinini, E., Impellizzeri, F. M., Castagna, C., Coutts, A. J. and Wisloff, U. (2009). Technical performance during soccer matches of the Italian Series A League: Effect of fatigue and competitive level. *Journal of Science and Medicine in Sport, 112*, 227–233.

Rampinini, E., Bishop, D., Marcora, S., Ferrari Bravo, D., Sassi, R. and Impellizzeri, F. (2007). Validity of simple field tests as indicators of match-related physical performance in top-level professional soccer players. *International Journal of Sports Medicine, 28*(3), 228–235.

Ramsden, P. (1993). *Learning to Teach in Higher Education*. London: Routledge.

Randers, M. B., Mujika, I., Hewitt, A., Santisteban, J., Bischoff, R., Solano, R., Zubillaga, A., Peltola, E., Krustrup, P. and Mohr, M. (2010). Application of four different football match analysis systems: A comparative study. *Journal of Sports Sciences, 28*(2), 171–182.

Rask, J. M., Gonzalez, R. V. and Barr, R. E. (2004). Genetically-designed neural networks for error reduction in an optimized biomechanical model of the human elbow joint complex. *Computer Methods in Biomechanics and Biomedical Engineering, 7*, 43–50.

Read, B. and Edwards, P. (1992). *Teaching Children to Play Games*. Leeds: White Line Publishing.

Rebelo, A. N. and Soares, J. M. C. (1996a). A comparative study of time–motion analysis during the two halves of a soccer game. In M. Hughes (ed.) *Notational Analysis of Sport – I and II*, pp. 69–72, Cardiff: UWIC.

Rebelo, A. N. and Soares, J. M. C. (1996b). Endurance capacity of soccer players during pre-season and during playing season. In M. Hughes (ed.) *Notational Analysis of Sport – I and II*, pp. 73–78, Cardiff: UWIC.

Redwood-Brown, A., Bussell, C. and Bharaj, H. S. (2012a). The impact of different standards of opponents on observed player performance in the English Premier League. *Journal of Human Sport and Exercise, 7*(2), 341–355.

Redwood-Brown, A., Cranton, W. and Sunderland, C. (2012b). Validation of a real-time video analysis system for soccer. *International Journal of Sports Medicine, 33*(8), 635–640.

Reed, D. and Hughes, M. (2006). An exploration of team sports as a dynamical system. *International Journal of Performance Analysis in Sport, 6*(2), 114–125.

Reep, C. (1989). *Charles Reep: The Punter* (The Scottish Football Association). September, pp. 31–37.

Reep, C. and Benjamin, B. (1968). Skill and chance in association football. *Journal of the Royal Statistical Society*, Series A, *131*, 581–585.

Reep, C., Pollard, R. and Benjamin, B. (1971). Skill and chance in ball games. *Journal of the Royal Statistical Society*, *134*, 623–629.

Reilly, T. (ed.) (2003). *Science and Soccer*. London: E & FN Spon.

Reilly, T. and Thomas, V. (1976). A motion analysis of work-rate in different positional roles in professional football match-play. *Journal of Human Movement Studies*, *2*, 87– 97.

Reilly, T. and Williams, A. M. (eds). (2003). *Science and Soccer*. London: Routledge.

Reilly, T., Clarys, J. and Stibbe, A. (1991). *Science and Football II*. London: E & FN Spon.

Reilly, T., Hughes, M. and Lees, A. (eds) (1995). *Science and Racket Sports*. London: E & FN Spon.

Reilly, T., Bangsbo, J. and Hughes, M. (eds) (1997). *Science and Football III*. London: E & FN Spon.

Reilly, T., Lees, A., Davids, K. and Murphy, W. (eds) (1988). *Science and Football*. London: E & FN Spon.

Renshaw, I., Davids, K. and Savelsbergh, G. J. P. (2011). *Motor Learning in Practice: A Constraints-led Approach*. London: Routledge.

Renshaw, I., Chow, J. Y., Davids, K. and Hammond, J. (2010). A constraints-led perspective to understanding skill acquisition and game play: a basis for integration of motor learning theory and physical education praxis? *Physical Education and Sport Pedagogy*, *15*(2), 117–137.

Richardson, J. R. and Lee, T. D. (1999). The effects of proactive and retroactive demonstrations on learning signed letters. *Acta Psychologica*, *101*, 79–90.

Ridgewell, A. (2011). Passing patterns before and after scoring in the 2010 FIFA World Cup. *International Journal of Performance Analysis in Sport*, *11*(3), 562–574.

Rizzolatti, G. and Craighero, L. (2004). The mirror-neuron system. *Annual Review of Neuroscience*, *27*, 169–192.

Rizzolatti, G. and Sinigaglia, C. (2010). The functional role of the parieto-frontal mirror circuit: Interpretations and misinterpretations. *Nature Reviews Neuroscience*, *11*, 264–274.

Robins, M. T., Wheat, J., Irwin, G. and Bartlett, R. (2006). The effect of shooting distance on movement variability in basketball. *Journal of Human Movement Studies*, *50*, 217–238.

Ross, D., Bird, A. M., Doody, S. G. and Zoeller, M. (1985). Effects of modeling and video-tape feedback with knowledge results on motor performance. *Human Movement Science*, *4*, 149–157.

Rothstein, A. L. and Arnold, R. K. (1976). Bridging the gap: Application of research on videotape feedback and bowling. *Motor skills: Theory Into Practice*, *1*, 35–62.

Russell, M., Rees, G., Benton, D. and Kingsley, M. (2011). An exercise protocol that replicates soccer match-play. *International Journal of Sports Medicine*, *32*(7), 511–518.

Salmoni, A. W., Schmidt, R. A. and Walter, C. B. (1984). Knowledge of results and motor learning: A review and critical reappraisal. *Psychological Bulletin*, *95*, 355–386.

Sanderson, F. H. (1983). A notation system for analysing squash. *Physical Education Review*, *6*, 19–23.

Sanderson, F. H. and Way, K. I. M. (1979). The development of objective methods of game analysis in squash rackets. *British Journal of Sports Medicine*, *11*(4), 188.

Sanli, E. A., Patterson, J. T., Bray, S. R. and Lee, T. D. (2012). Understanding self-controlled motor learning protocols through the self-determination theory. *Frontiers in Psychology: Movement Science and Sport Psychology*, *3*, 611.

Sathyan, T., Shuttleworth, R., Hedley, M. and Davids, K. (2012). Validity and reliability of a radio positioning system for tracking athletes in indoor and outdoor team sports. *Behavioural Research, 44*, 1108–1114.

Savelberg, H. H. C. M. (1999). Assessment of the horizontal, fore-aft component of the ground reaction force from insole pressure patterns by using artificial neural nets. *Clinical Biomechanics, 14*, 585–592.

Savelberg, H. H. C. M. and Herzog, W. (1997). Prediction of dynamic tendon forces from electromyographic signals: An artificial neural network approach. *Journal of Neuroscience Methods, 78*, 65–74.

Schmidt, R. A. and Lee, T. D. (1999). *Motor control and Learning: A Behavioral Emphasis*, 3rd edn. Champaign, IL: Human Kinetics.

Schmidt, R. A. and Lee, T. D. (2005). *Motor Control and Learning*, 4th edn. Champaign, IL: Human Kinetics.

Schmidt, R. A. and Lee, T. D. (2011). *Motor Control and Learning: A behavioural emphasis*, 5th edn. Champaign, IL: Human Kinetics.

Schmidt, R. A. and Lee, T. D. (2014). *Motor learning and Performance: From Principles to Application*. Champaign, IL: Human Kinetics.

Schmidt, R. A., Lange, C. and Young, D. E. (1990). Optimizing summary knowledge of results for skill learning. *Human Movement Science, 9*, 325–348.

Schmidt, R. A., Young, D. E., Swinnen, S. and Shapiro, D. E. (1989). Summary knowledge of results for skill acquisition: Support for the guidance hypothesis. *Journal of Experimental Psychology: Learning, Memory, and Cognition, 15*, 352–359.

Schmidt-Nielsen, K. (1984). *Scaling: Why is Animal Size so Important?* Cambridge: Cambridge University Press.

Schöllhorn, W. I. and Bauer, H. U. (1998). Identifying individual movement styles in high performance sports by means of self-organizing Kohonen maps. In H. J. Riehle and M. Vieten (eds) *Proceedings of the XVI ISBS 98*, pp. 574–577. Konstanz Konstanz: ISBS.

Scholz, J. P. and Kelso, J. A. S. (1989). A quantitative approach to understanding the formation and change of coordinated movement patterns. *Journal of Motor Behavior, 21*(2), 122–144.

Scholz, J. P. and Kelso, J. A. S. (1990). Intentional switching between patterns of bimanual coordination depends on the intrinsic dynamics of the patterns. *Journal of Motor Behavior, 22*(1), 98–124.

Schöner, G., Zanone, P. G. and Kelso, J. A. S. (1992). Learning as change of coordination dynamics: Theory and experiment. *Journal of Motor Behavior, 24* (1), 29–48.

Schutz, R. W. (1970). A mathematical model for evaluating scoring systems with reference to tennis, *Research Quarterly for Exercise and Sport, 41*, 552–561.

Schutz, Y. and Chambaz, A. (1997). Could a satellite-based navigation system (GPS) be used to assess the physical activity of individuals on earth? *European Journal of Clinical Nutrition, 51*(5), 338–339.

Scott, S., Kingsbury, D., Bennett, S., Davids, K. and Langley, M. (1999). Effects of cricket ball colour and illuminance levels on catching behaviour in professional cricketers. *Ergonomics, 43*(10), 1681–1688.

Scoulding, A., James, N. and Taylor, J. (2004). Passing in the Soccer World Cup 2002. *International Journal of Performance Analysis in Sport, 4*(2), 36–41.

Scully, D. M. and Newell, K. M. (1985). Observational learning and the acquisition of motor skills: Toward a visual perception perspective. *Journal of Human Movement Studies, 11*, 169–186.

Sepulveda, F., Wells, D. M. and Vaughan, C. L. (1993). A neural network representation of electromyography and joint dynamics in human gait. *Journal of Biomechanics, 26*, 101–109.

Setterwall, D. (2003). Computerised video analysis of football – technical and commercial possibilities for football coaching. Unpublished Master's Thesis. Stockholms Universitet.

Shea, C. H. and Wulf, G. (1999). Enhancing motor learning through external-focus instructions and feedback. *Human Movement Science, 18*, 553–571.

Shephard, R. J. (1999). Biology and medicine of soccer: An update. *Journal of Sports Sciences, 17*, 757–786.

Shepard, R. N. and Metzler, J. (1971). Mental rotation of three-dimensional objects. *Science, 171*, 701–703.

Sherwood, D. E. (1988). Effect of bandwidth knowledge of results on movement consistency. *Perceptual and Motor Skills, 66*, 535–542.

Sherwood, D. E. and Rios, V. (2001). Divided attention in bimanual aiming movements: Effects on movement accuracy. *Research Quarterly for Exercise and Sport, 72*, 210–218.

Sherwood, D. E., Lohse, K. R. and Healy, A. F. (2014). Judging joint angles and movement outcome: Shifting the focus of attention in dart-throwing. *Journal of Experimental Psychology: Human Perception and Performance, 40*, 1903–1914.

Shmuelof, L., Krakauer, J. W. and Mazzoni, P. (2012). How is a motor skill learned? Change and invariance at the levels of task success and trajectory control. *Journal of Neurophysiology, 108*, 578–594.

Shortcliff, E. H. (1976). *Computer-Based Medical Consultation: MYCIN.* New York: Elsevier.

Sigrist, R., Rauter G., Riener R. and Wolf, P. (2013a). Augmented visual, auditory, haptic, and multimodal feedback in motor learning: A review. *Psychological Bulletin Review, 20*, 21–53.

Sigrist, R., Rauter, G., Riener, R. and Wolf, P. (2013b). Terminal feedback outperforms concurrent visual, auditory and haptic feedback in learning a complex rowing-type task. *Journal of Motor Behavior, 45*, 455–472.

Simpson, K. J., Shewokis, P. A., Alduwaisan, S. A. U. D. and Reeves, K. T. (1992). Factors influencing rearfoot kinematics during a rapid lateral braking movement. *Medicine and Science in Sports and Exercise, 24*(5), 586–594.

Smith, M. and Cushion, C. J. (2006). An investigation of the in-game behaviours of professional, top-level youth soccer coaches. *Journal of Sports Sciences, 24*(4), 355–366.

Smith, R. and Loschner, C. (2002). Biomechanics feedback for rowing. *Journal of Sports Sciences, 20*, 783–791.

Smyth, G., O'Donoghue, P. G. and Wallace, E. S. (2001). Notational analysis of contact situations in rugby union. In M. Hughes and F. Tavares (eds) *World Congress of Notational Analysis of Sport IV*, pp. 156–164. Portugal: FSEP, University of Porto.

Snedecor, G.W. and Cochran, W.G. (1989). *Statistical Methods*, 8th edn. Ames, IA: Iowa State University Press.

Snyder, K. M. and Logan, G. D. (2012). Monitoring-induced disruption in skilled typewriting. *Journal of Experimental Psychology: Human Perception and Performance, 39*, 1409–1420.

Soodak, H. and Iberall, A. (1978). Osmosis, diffusion, convection. *American Journal of Physiology: Regulatory, Integrative and Comparative Physiology, 235*(1), 3–17.

Sörös, G., Daiber, F. and Weller, T. (2013). Cyclo – A personal bike coach through the glass. Symposium on mobile graphics and interactive applications. *Proceedings of SIGGRAPH Asia 2013 Conference* held in Hong Kong, November 19–22, ACM, New York: article 99.

Sparrow, W. A. and Newell, K. M. (1998). Metabolic energy expenditure and the regulation of movement economy. *Psychonomic Bulletin and Review, 5*, 173–196.

Spencer, M., Lawrence, S., Rechichi, C., Bishop, D., Dawson, B. and Goodman, C. (2004). Time–motion anlaysis of elite field hockey with special reference to repeated-sprint activity. *Journal of Sports Science, 22*, 843–850.

Spinks, W., Reilly, T. and Murphy, A. (2002). *Science and Football IV*. London: Psychology Press.

Stacey, R. D. (1993). Strategy as order emerging from chaos. *Long Range Planning, 26*(1), 10–17.

Stefani, R. (1998). Predicting outcomes. In J. Bennett (ed.) *Statistics in Sport*, pp. 249–275. London: Arnold.

Ste-Marie, D. M., Rymal, A., Vertes, K. and Martini, R. (2011a). Self-modeling and competitive beam performance enhancement examined within a self-regulation perspective. *Journal of Applied Sport Psychology, 23*, 292–307.

Ste-Marie, D. M., Vertes, K., Rymal, A. and Martini, R. (2011b). Feedforward self-modeling enhances skill acquisition in children learning trampoline skills. *Frontiers in Psychology, 2*, 155.

Stockill, N. P. (1994). A three-dimensional cinematographic analysis of cricket fast bowling: A study of junior and senior fast bowling techniques. Unpublished Master's Thesis, the Manchester Metropolitan University.

Stretch, R. A., Bartlett, R. M. and Davids, K. (2000). A review of batting in men's cricket. *Journal of Sports Sciences, 18*, 931–949.

Stretch, R. A., Buys, F., Du Toit, D.E. and Viljoen, G. (1998). Kinematics and kinetics of the drive off the front foot in cricket batting. *Journal of Sports Sciences, 16*, 711–720.

Sunderland, C., Bussell, C., Atkinson, G., Alltree, R. and Kates, M. (2006). Patterns of play and goals scored in international standard women's field-hockey. *International Journal of Performance Analysis in Sport, 6*(1), 13–29.

Sussman, H. J. and Zahler, R. S. (1978). A critique of applied catastrophe theory in the behavioural sciences. *Behavioural Science, 23*, 28–39.

Swinnen, S. P. (1996). Information feedback for motor skill learning: A review. In H. N. Zelaznik (ed.) *Advances in Motor Learning and Control*, pp. 37–66. Champaign, IL: Human Kinetics.

Swinnen, S., Schmidt, R. A., Nicholson, D. E. and Shapiro, D. C. (1990). Information feedback for skill acquisition: Instantaneous knowledge of results degrades learning. *Journal of Experimental Psychology: Learning, Memory, and Cognition, 16*, 706–716.

Swinnen, S. P., Walter, C. B., Lee, T. D. and Serrien, D. J. (1993). Acquiring bimanual skills: Contrasting forms of information feedback for interlimb decoupling. *Journal of Experimental Psychology: Learning, Memory and Cognition, 19*, 1328–1344.

Swinnen, S. P., Lee, T. D., Verschueren, S., Serrien, D. J. and Bogaerds, H. (1997). Interlimb coordination: Learning and transfer under different feedback conditions. *Human Movement Science, 16*, 749–785.

Tan, K. C., Yu, Q., Heng, C. M. and Lee, T. H. (2003). Evolutionary computing for knowledge discovery in medical diagnosis. *Artificial Intelligence in Medicine, 27*, 129–154.

Tang, H. P., Abe, K., Katoh, K. and Ae, M. (1995). Three-dimensional cinematographical analysis of the badminton forearm smash: Movements of the forearm and hand. In T. Reilly, M. D. Hughes and A. Lees (eds) *Science and Racket Sports*, pp. 113–118. London: E & FN Spon.

Taub, E., Uswatte G. and Elbert T. (2002). New treatments in neurorehabilitation founded on basic research. *Nature Reviews Neuroscience, 3*, 228–236.

Tavares, F. and Gomes, N. (2003). The offensive process in basketball: A study in high performance junior teams. *International Journal of Performance Analysis in Sport, 3*(1), 34–39.

Taylor, J. B., Mellalieu, S. D. and James, N. (2004). Behavioural comparisons of positional demands in professional soccer. *International Journal of Performance Analysis in Sport, 4*, 1, 81–97.

Taylor, J. B., Mellalieu, S. D. and James, N. (2005). A comparison of individual and unit tactical behaviour and team strategy in professional soccer. *International Journal of Performance Analysis in Sport*, *5*, 2, 87–101.

Taylor, J. B., Mellalieu, S. D., James, N. and Shearer, D. A. (2008). The influence of match location, quality of opposition, and match status on technical performance in professional association football. *Journal of Sports Sciences*, *26*(9), 885–895.

Taylor, J. B., Mellalieu, S. D., James, N. and Barter, P. (2010). Situation variable effects and tactical performance in professional association football. *International Journal of Performance Analysis in Sport*, *10*, 3, 255–269.

Taylor, M. and Hughes, M. (1998). Analysis of elite under-19 tennis players. In A. Lees, I. Maynard, M. D. Hughes and T. Reilly (eds) *Science and Racket Sports II*, pp. 211–220. London: E & FN Spon.

Taylor, S. and Hughes, M. D. (1988). Computerised notational analysis: A voice interactive system. *Journal of Sports Sciences*, *6*, 255.

Thein, L.A. (1995). Environmental conditions affecting the athlete. *Journal of Orthopedic and Sports Physical Therapy*, *21*(3), 158–171.

Thelen, E. (1985). Developmental origins of motor coordination: Leg movements in human infants. *Developmental Psychobiology*, *18*(1), 1–22.

Thom, A. S. (1975). Momentum, mass and heat exchange of plant communities. In J. L. Monteith (ed.), *Vegetation and the Atmosphere*, Vol. 1, pp. 57–109. London: Academic Press.

Thomas, C. and Williams, J. (1999). The shape of the game. In C. Thomas (ed.) *Proceedings of the International Rugby Board World Conference*. NSW University, Sydney, pp. 4–36.

Thomas, C. and Williams, J. (2001). Mapping the world game. *Proceedings of the 5th World Congress of Performance Analaysis of Sport*, University of Wales Institute, Cardiff, July.

Thomas, C., Williams, J., Bown, R. and Jones, N. (2003). Patterns of Play in Elite Women's Rugby. In J. Cabrys and T. Reilly (eds) *Proceedings of the Fifth World Congress on Science and Football*. London: E & FN Spon, pp. 258–266.

Thomas, J. R. and Nelson, J. K. (1999). *Research Methods in Physical Activity*. Champaign, IL: Human Kinetics.

Tiryaki, G., Cicek, S., Erdogan, A. T., Kalay, F., Atalay, A. T. and Tuncel, F. (1997). The analysis of the offensive patterns of the Switzerland soccer team in the World Cup, 1994. In M. Hughes (ed.) *Notational Analysis of Sport – I & II*, pp. 91–98. Cardiff: UWIC.

Todorov, E., Shadmehr, R. and Bizzi, E. (1997). Augmented feedback presented in a virtual environment accelerates learning of a difficult motor task. *Journal of Motor Behavior*, *29*, 147–158.

Todorov, E., Shadmehr, R., Bizzi, E. (1997). Augmented feedback presented in a virtual environment accelerates learning of a difficult motor task. *Journal of Motor Behavior*, *29*, 147–158.

Townshend, A. D., Worringham, C. J. and Stewart, I. B. (2008). Assessment of speed and position during human locomotion using nondifferential GPS. *Medicine and Science in Sports and Exercise*, *40*(1), 124–132.

Tracy, K., Montague, E., Gabriel, R. and Kent, B. (1979). Computer-assisted diagnosis of orthopedic gait disorders. *Physical Therapy*, *59*, 268–277.

Travassos, B., Araujo, D., Vilar, L. and McGarry, T. (2011). Inter-personal coordination and ball dynamics in futsal (indoor football). *Human Movement Science*, *30*, 1245–1259.

Treadwell, P., Lyons, K. and Potter, G. (1991). The predictive potential of match analysis systems for rugby union football. In T. Reilly, J. Clarys and A. Stibbe (eds) *Science and Football II*, pp. 134–142. London: E & FN Spon.

Trevarthen, C. (1990). *Brain Circuits and Functions of the Mind: Essays in Honor of Roger W. Sperry*. New York: Cambridge University Press.

Tucker, W., Mellalieu, S. D., James, N. and Taylor, J. B. (2005). Game location effects in professional soccer: A case study. *International Journal of Performance Analysis in Sport*, 5(2), 23–35.

Tunaru, R. S. and Viney, H. P. (2010). Valuations of soccer players from statistical performance data. *Journal of Quantitative Analysis in Sports*, 6(2), Article 10.

Turvey, M. T. (2007). Action and perception at the level of synergies. *Human Movement Science*, 26, 657–697.

Tversky, A. and Gilovich, T. (1989a). The cold facts about the 'hot hand' in basketball. *Chance: New Directions for Statistics and Computing*, 2, 16–21.

Tversky, A. and Gilovich, T. (1989b). The 'hot hand': Statistical reality or cognitive illusion? *Chance: New Directions for Statistics and Computing*, 2, 31–34.

Tyrrell, I. (1980). Money and morality: The professionalism of American baseball. In R. Cashman and M. McKernan (eds) *Sport: Money, Morality and the Media*, pp. 67–74. Sydney: New South Wales University Press.

Ungerleider, L. G., Doyon, J. and Karni, A. (2002). Imaging brain plasticity during motor skill learning. *Neurobiology of Learning and Memory*, 78, 553–564.

Van der Linden, D. W., Cauraugh, J. H. and Greene, T. A. (1993). The effect of frequency of kinetic feedback on learning an isometric force production task in non-disabled subjects. *Physical Therapy*, 73, 79–87.

van Rooyen, M. K., Lambert, M. I. and Noakes, T. D. (2006). A retrospective analysis of the IRB statistics and video analysis of match play to explain the performance of four teams in the 2003 Rugby World Cup. *International Journal of Performance Analysis in Sport*, 6(1), 57–72.

van Rossum, J. H. A. (1997). *Motor Development and Practice: The Variability of Practice Hypothesis in Perspective*. Amsterdam: Free University Press.

Varley, M. C., Fairweather, I. H. and Aughey. (2012). Validity and reliability of GPS for measuring instantaneous velocity during accerleration deceleration and constant motion. *Journal of Sports Sciences*, 30, 121–127.

Vaz, L., Carreras, D. and Kraak, W. (2012). Analysis of the effect of alternating home and away field advantage during the Six Nations Rugby Championship. *International Journal of Performance Analysis in Sport*, 12(3), 593–607.

Vereijken, B. (1991). *The Dynamics of Skill Acquisition*. Meppel: Krips Repro.

Vereijken, B., van Emmerick, R. E. A., Whiting, H. T. A. and Newell, K. M. (1992). Freezing degrees of freedom in skill acquisition. *Journal of Motor Behavior*, 24, 133–142.

Vilar, L., Araújo, D., Davids, K. and Button, C. (2012). The role of ecological dynamics in analysing performance in team sports. *Sports Medicine*, 42(1), 1–10.

Vilar, L., Araújo, D., Davids, K. and Bar-Yam, Y. (2013). Science of winning soccer: Emergent pattern forming dynamics in association football. *Journal of Systems Science and Complexity*, 26(1), 73–84.

Vincent, W. (1995). *Statistics in Kinesiology*. Champaign, IL: Human Kinetics.

Vogt, S. (1996). The concept of event generation in movement imitation: Neural and behavioral aspects. *Corpus, Psyche et Societas*, 3, 119–132.

Von Holst, E. and Mittlestaedt, H. (1950). Das Reafferenzprinzip. *Naturwissenschaften*, 37, 464–467.

Waddell, D. B. and Gowitzke, B. A. (1977). An analysis of overhead badminton power strokes using high speed bi-plane photography. Communication to the International Coaching Conference, Malmö, Sweden, 3–7 May.

Waldron, M., Worsfold, P., Twist, C. and Lamb, K. (2011). Concurrent validity and test–retest reliability of a global positioning system (GPS) and timing gates to assess sprint performance variables. *Journal of Sports Sciences, 29*, 1613–1619.

Walter, F., Lames, M. and McGarry, T. (2007). Analysis of sports performance as a dynamical system by means of the relative phase. *International Journal of Computer Science in Sport, 6*(2), 35–41.

Wardrop, R. (1995). Simpson's paradox and the hot hand in basketball. *The American Statistician, 49*, 24–28.

Watts, A. (2005). Rule changes in elite men's squash. Unpublished dissertation, BSc Sport and Exercise Science, UWIC, Cardiff.

Weintraub, M. A., Bylander, T. and Simon, S. R. (1990). QUAWDS: A composite diagnostic system for gait analysis. *Computers Methods and Programs in Biomedicine, 32*, 91–106.

Weiss, M. R. and Kimberley, A. K. (1987). 'Show and tell' in the gymnasium: An investigation of developmental differences in modeling and verbal rehearsal of motor skills. *Research Quarterly for Exercise and Sport, 58*, 234–241.

Wells, G. L. and Leippe, M. (1981). How do triers of fact infer the accuracy of eyewitness identifications? Using memory for peripheral detail can be misleading. *Journal of Applied Psychology, 66*, 682–687.

Wells, J., O'Donoghue, P. and Hughes, M. (2004). The need to use representative player data from multiple matches in performance analysis. In P. O'Donoghue and M. Hughes (eds), *Performance Analysis of Sport VI*, pp. 241–244. Cardiff: UWIC.

Wertz, S. K. (1981). The varieties of cheating. *Journal of the Philosophy of Sport, 8*, 19–40.

Whitaker, T. C. and Hill, J. (2005). Problems associated with the analysis of the pattern of total cross-country eventing penalty scores at advanced level of competition in the United Kingdom. *International Journal of Performance Analysis in Sport, 5*(1), 51–60.

Williams, A. M., Ford, P., Causer, J., Logan, O. and Murray, S. (2012). Translating theory into practice: Working at the 'coal face' in the UK. In N. J. Hodges and A. M. Williams (eds), *Skill Acquisition in Sport*, 2nd edn, pp. 3–21. New York: Routledge.

Willingham, D. B. (1998). A neuropsychological theory of motor skill learning. *Psychological Review, 105*(3), 558–584.

Williams, J. J. (2007). The use of technology for analysis in rugby union television match coverage. *Proceedings of the Sixth International Symposium on Computer Science in Sport, Calgary, Canada, June 3–6*.

Williams, M. and Morgan, S. (2009). Horizontal positioning error derived from stationary GPS units: A function of time and proximity to building infrastructure. *International Journal of Performance Analysis in Sport, 9*(2), 275–280.

Wilson, A. M. and Watson, J. C. (2003). A catapult action for rapid limb protraction. *Nature, 421*, 35–36.

Wilson, B. D. (1998). Protective headgear in rugby union. *Sports Medicine, 25*(5), 333–337.

Wilson, B. D., Quarrie, K. L., Milburn, P. D. and Chalmers, D. J. (1999). The nature and circumstances of tackle injuries in rugby union. *Journal of Science and Medicine in Sport, 2*(2), 153–162.

Wilson, C., Simpson, S. E., van Emmerick, R. E. A. and Hamill, J. (2008). Coordination variability and skill development in elite triple jumpers. *Sports Biomechanics, 7*, 2–9.

Wilson, K. and Barnes, C. A. (1998). Reliability and validity of a computer based notational analysis system for competitive table tennis. In A. Lees, I. Maynard, M. Hughes and T. Reilly (eds) *Science and Racket Sports II*, pp. 265–268. London: E & FN Spon.

Winkler, W. (1996). Computer/video analysis in German soccer. In M. Hughes (ed.) *Notational Analysis of Sport – I & II*, pp. 19–31. Cardiff: UWIC.

Winstein, C. J. and Schmidt, R. A. (1989). Sensorimotor feedback. In D. H. Holding (ed.) *Human Skills*, pp. 17–47. New York: Wiley.

Winstein, C. J. and Schmidt, R. A. (1990). Reduced frequency of knowledge of results enhances motor skill learning. *Journal of Experimental Psychology: Learning, Memory, and Cognition*, *16*, 677–691.

Wisbey, B., Montgomery, P. G., Pyne, D. B. and Rattray, B. (2009). Quantifying movement demands of AFL football using GPS tracking. *Journal of Science and Medicine in Sport*, *13*, 531–536.

Witte, T. H. and Wilson, A. M. (2004). Accuracy of non-differential GPS for the determination of speed over ground. *Journal of Biomechanics*, *37*(12), 1891–1898.

Wolpert, D. M., Ghahramani, Z. and Jordan M. I. (1995). Are arm trajectories planned in kinematic or dynamic coordinates? An adaptation study. *Experimental Brain Research*, *103*, 460–470.

Wright, C., Atkins, S., Polman, R., Jones, B. and Sargeson, L. (2011). Factors associated with goals and goal scoring opportunities in professional soccer. *International Journal of Performance Analysis in Sport*, *11*(3), 438–449.

Wright, D. B. and Davies, G. M. (2007). Eyewitness testimony. In F. T. Durso (ed.) *Handbook of Applied Cognition*, 2nd edn, pp. 736–788. Chichester: Wiley.

Wulf, G. (2013). Attentional focus and motor learning: A review of 15 years. *International Review of Sport and Exercise Psychology*, *6*, 77–104.

Wulf, G. and Schmidt, R. A. (1996). Average KR degrades parameter learning. *Journal of Motor Behavior*, *28*, 371–381.

Wulf, G. and Weigelt, C. (1997). Instructions about physical principles in learning a complex motor skill: To tell or not to tell. *Research Quarterly for Exercise and Sport*, *68*, 362–367.

Wulf, G. and Prinz, W. (2001). Directing attention to movement effects enhances learning: A review. *Psychonomic Bulletin and Review*, *8*, 648–660.

Wulf, G. and Shea, C. H. (2004). Understanding the role of augmented feedback: The good, the bad, and the ugly. In N. J. Hodges and A. M. Williams (eds) *Skill Acquisition in Sport*, 1st edn, pp. 121–144. New York: Routledge.

Wulf, G., Lee, T. D. and Schmidt, R. A. (1994). Reducing knowledge of results about relative versus absolute timing: Differential effects on learning. *Journal of Motor Behavior*, *26*, 362–369.

Wulf, G., Shea, C. H. and Matschiner, S. (1998). Frequent feedback enhances complex motor skill learning. *Journal of Motor Behavior*, *30*, 180–192.

Wulf, G., McConnel, N., Gärtner, M. and Schwarz, A. (2002). Feedback and attentional focus: Enhancing the learning of sport skills through external-focus feedback. *Journal of Motor Behavior*, *34*, 171–182.

Yamanaka, K., Hughes, M. and Lott, M. (1993). An analysis of playing patterns in the 1990 World Cup for association football. In T. Reilly, J. Clarys and A. Stibbe (eds) *Science and Football II*, pp. 206–214. London: E & FN Spon.

Yan, B. and Li, M. (2000). Shot put technique using an ANN AMT model. In Y. Hong and D. P. Johns (eds) *Proceedings of the XVIII International Symposium on Biomechanics in Sports, Volume 2*, pp. 580–584. Hong Kong: The Chinese University.

Yan, B. and Wu, Y. (2000). The ANN-based analysis model of the sports techniques. In Y. Hong and D. P. Johns (eds) *Proceedings of the XVIII International Symposium on Biomechanics in Sports, Volume 2*. Hong Kong: The Chinese University, pp. 585–589.

Yeadon, M. R. (1997). Twisting double somersault high bar dismounts. *Journal of Applied Biomechanics*, *13*, 76–87.

Yeadon, M. R. and Challis, J. H. (1992). *Future Directions for Performance Related Research in Sports Biomechanics*. London: The Sports Council.

Yeadon, M. R. and Knight, J. P. (2012). A virtual environment for learning to view during aerial movements. *Computer Methods in Biomechanics and Biomedical Engineering, 15,* 919–924.

Young, W., Gulli, R., Rath, D., Russell, A., O'Brien, B. and Harvey, J. (2010). Acute effect of exercise on kicking accuracy in elite Australian football players. *Journal of Science and Medicine in Sport, 13*(1), 85–89.

Zanone, P. G. and Kelso, J. A. S. (1997). Coordination dynamics of learning and transfer: collective and component levels. *Journal of Experimental Psychology: Human Perception and Performance, 23*(5), 1454–1480.

Zatsiorsky, V. M. (2002). Multi-finger prehension. In K. E. Gianikellis (ed.) *Proceedings of the XXth International Symposium on Biomechanics in Sports,* pp. 491–498. Cáceres: University of Estremadura.

Zhang, N., Duan, L.Y., Li, L., Huang, Q., Du, J., Gao, W. and Guan, L. (2012). A generic approach for systematic analysis of sports videos. *ACM Transactions Intelligence Systems Technology, 3*(3), article 46.

Zheng, J-H. and Zu, X. F. (2009). The application analysis and investigation of multimedia technique in tennis teaching. In *IEEE Proceedings of the Second International Conference on Education Technology and Training, ETT '09,* Sanya, China, December 13–14, pp. 351–354.

INDEX